# EVOLUTIONARY WORLD GOVERNMENT

---

## *A Pragmatic Approach to Global Federation*

---

James A. Yunker

**Hamilton Books**

*Lanham • Boulder • New York • Toronto • Plymouth, UK*

Copyright © 2018 by
Hamilton Books
4501 Forbes Boulevard
Suite 200
Lanham, Maryland 20706
Hamilton Books Acquisitions Department (301) 459-3366

Unit A, Whitacre Mews, 26-34 Stannary Street,
London SE11 4AB, United Kingdom

Library of Congress Control Number: 2017956704
ISBN: 978-0-7618-6991-7 (cloth : alk. paper)
eISBN: 978-0-7618-6992-4

# Contents

# List of Figures

# 1

# Salvation or Damnation?

## Neither Utopia nor Dystopia

Apart from a tiny minority of world federalists, most people today hold decidedly negative opinions about world government. While it is widely agreed that the putative objectives of such a government—worldwide peace, security, prosperity, freedom and justice—are highly commendable in and of themselves, it is almost universally feared that what is very appealing in theory would turn out to be an unmitigated disaster in practice. According to conventional wisdom, any serious effort to establish a world government could easily ignite a global nuclear holocaust, and even if that threat were evaded and the government established, it would almost certainly degenerate, quickly or gradually as the case may be, into some nightmarish combination of totalitarian tyranny, bureaucratic strangulation, and cultural homogenization. What was intended to be a utopia would, by the inexorable law of unintended consequences, morph into a horrific dystopia. Instead of achieving salvation, we would incur damnation.

This book argues that this conventional viewpoint is not only very much mistaken, it constitutes a serious hazard to the future of global human civilization. Unthinking prejudice against any and all concepts of world government is impeding efforts to develop a sensible, workable plan for meaningful global political unity. A properly designed world government would provide firmer institutional support for humanity's ongoing efforts to avoid potentially deadly threats ranging from instantaneous nuclear holocaust to gradual environmental collapse.

It has to be strongly emphasized from the outset, however, that the specific form of world government advocated here is very much distinct from the form which is commonly envisioned among both the huge majority opposed to world government, and the small minority favorably disposed toward it. This commonly envisioned form is designated here the "omnipotent world state." The omnipotent world state would encompass all the nations in the world without exception, and it would monopolize all heavy armaments, including (especially) nuclear weapons. Although it would be a tricky matter (not to say impossible) getting all the nations of the world, especially the nuclear superpowers, to surrender their military forces to the authority of a world government, assuming that such a thing could be done, it seems that the possibility of nuclear world war would be virtually eliminated. The problem with this scenario, of course, is that such an all-powerful world state could very easily morph into a tyrannical monster. As Kenneth Waltz once put it: "And were world government attempted, we might find ourselves dying in the attempt, or uniting and living a life worse than death."[1]

Traditional world federalists have responded to Waltz's warning by arguing that if humanity continues indefinitely with the anarchic international system of today, sooner or later a nuclear war will erupt, and following that catastrophe the survivors would most definitely find themselves "living a life worse than death." Not only would the world economy have been shattered so that most of the survivors would be reduced to a subsistence standard of life, but more than likely the global political system would also have fragmented into a host of independent ministates, each one ruled over by a brutal warlord. Not only would prosperity have vanished, but so also freedom, democracy, humanitarianism, and respect for the rights of others. Humanity will have been reduced to the Hobbesian state of nature: "the war of all against all, where life is brutal, nasty and short."[2]

Traditional world federalists would probably add to these assertions that there is no good reason to expect a world state whose authority could not be militarily challenged to degenerate into tyranny. After all, history has demonstrated that the development of tyrannical conditions within nations (as, for example, with Hitler's Germany, Stalin's Soviet Union, and Mao's China) is usually associated with war or the fear of war with other nations. A militarily unchallengeable world state would not be subject to such fears. Therefore it is unlikely that people could be persuaded or coerced into doing things—or allowing things—that they would not do or allow if they were not living in fear of harsh impositions or actual invasions by malevolent outsiders.

While a plausible response to Waltz's "worse than death" warning could indeed be made, it is not my intention to provide such a response in this book. As a matter of fact, I myself fully subscribe to the belief that an omnipotent world state, of the sort normally envisioned by traditional world federalists, would represent an unacceptable threat to the legitimate national interests of its member nations, both at the present time and into the foreseeable future. But what I do not accept is that this is the end of the story as far as world government is concerned.

The fact is that there exist plausible institutional forms for a global political entity whose authority would lie somewhere between that of the relatively impotent United Nations of today, and the omnipotent world state generally envisioned by most people, whether they be advocates for or opponents of world government. The fact that the omnipotent world state would have too much authority, while the existent United Nations has too little, suggests that there might be a "happy medium" somewhere between these two extremes. Such a happy medium might provide a promising avenue toward the future development and improvement of international relations.

My own candidate for a properly designed global government is the "Federal Union of Democratic Nations." Membership in the Federal Union would be open to all nations of the world, but it is not anticipated that membership would be universal from the outset. Neither is it anticipated that the internal political system of every member nation would be fully democratic from the outset. The salient requirement would be that if the candidate member nation does not currently possess internal political institutions compatible with conventional definitions of democracy, it undertake a commitment to establish fully democratic internal political institutions at some unspecified time in the future. This provision is necessary to accommodate certain essential nations, most notably the People's Republic of China.

The Federal Union would be a *limited* federal world government, and the first critical element of its being limited is that membership would be *voluntary*: no nation would be required to become a member of the federation, and similarly, no member nation would be prevented from departing the federation at its own unilateral discretion, if it so desires. The second critical element of limitation is that no member nation would be required either to disarm or to surrender effective control over its military to the world federation. A Federal Union member nation would be permitted to retain independent control over as much military power, including strategic nuclear weapons, as it feels necessary to maintain its own security. There are additional elements of "limitation," but these two are the most critical.

The typical reaction of an unimaginative world federalist to this proposal would be contemptuous dismissal. Such a "world government," it would be asserted, would be absolutely no better than the United Nations of today. In fact, questions might be raised whether such a political entity could even be categorized as a legitimate "state." Certainly no national government of today would be comfortable allowing subsidiary units (states, provinces, districts, and so on) to retain independent control over weapons of mass destruction, and to depart from the nation at their own discretion.

While I readily concede that the establishment of the Federal Union of Democratic Nations along the envisioned lines would not necessarily have a dramatically improving effect on the condition of the world *in the short run*, I do not agree that this is the end of the story as far as this world government proposal is concerned. The Federal Union would possess the outward characteristics of a state: it would have legislative, executive, and judicial branches, significant armed forces under its direct control, powers of direct taxation, a capital city, a flag, an anthem, and so on. Key governmental officials would be popularly elected. As the tangible embodiment of mankind's aspirations toward a better world, it would possess moral authority as well as practical authority. It would therefore provide firmer institutional support than does today's United Nations, for ongoing efforts toward realization of the various worthwhile cosmopolitan goals that have been long embraced by most rational, informed, progressively minded people around the world.

The obvious hope is that in due course, after decades of successful operation, the member nations of the Federal Union would gradually grow more confident and would voluntarily reduce their independent military capabilities. Similarly, the hope is that eventually the reserved national right to departure from the federation would become a dead letter, a virtually forgotten holdover from the distant past. This is not to imply that these national rights would ever be formally abrogated, no matter how outdated and irrelevant they might eventually be perceived. Even if the Federal Union of Democratic Nations were to persist for an extremely lengthy period of historical time, these reserved national rights would remain perpetual components of its constitutional foundation.

In today's world, of course, the principle of national sovereignty is the foundation-stone of the international regime. This principle is so solidly entrenched that it is a veritable pipedream to imagine that nations will voluntarily surrender their military forces to the authority of an omnipotent world state. It is another pipedream that they will voluntarily adhere to a federation from which they would never be allowed to leave peacefully, no matter how oppressive that federation became. Given the self-evident realities of the contemporary world, either we will have a limited world government such as proposed herein, or we will have no world government at all. No world government at all is what we have now, and what we will continue to have into the foreseeable future—unless enough people discover that there does exist, despite much opinion to the contrary, a plausible path leading safely forward out of the dangerously unstable international situation of today, toward a better world.

In short, what is being proposed herein is *evolutionary* world government. An understandable initial reaction to the term "evolutionary world government" is that it means that the ongoing processes of global governance, with which we are familiar, will continue gradually and imperceptibly until one fine morning—perhaps 50 years from now, perhaps 100 years from now—people will wake up to discover that the condition of the world is exactly what it would be if there existed a formally established world government in operation. In other words, we should just go on doing what we are doing, and the international condition will incrementally and automatically evolve into "virtual world government."

As popular as it is, this scenario is a dangerous delusion. Certainly it is true that the institutions and activities today associated with the term "global governance" are leading toward a better world. But progress through these existing channels is slow and halting, always in danger of breaking down entirely. There have in fact been certain disturbing political developments in the recent past—two examples being the election of Donald Trump to the presidency of the United States, and the decision of the United Kingdom to depart the European Union—that suggest that the appeal of old-fashioned nationalism is by no means inconsequential in today's world. To some minds, these developments will be taken as further evidence of the impracticality of world government. But to more perceptive minds, they are evidence that some appropriate form of world government could be a valuable offset to such dangerously retrograde tendencies. In sum, it would be imprudent to rely on global governance as it is known today, when the possibility exists of a properly designed, limited global government that could do anything and everything that global governance is doing now—only better.

The probability of long-term success would be significantly improved if humanity moves forward in the near future to set up a federal world government subject to various critical limitations (free exit, independent militaries, and so on), via the same sort of international conference that set up the League of Nations in 1920 and the United Nations in 1945. No doubt the kind of world government that would be acceptable to the nations of the world today would be relatively weak—although not altogether powerless. Its principal advantage is that it would create a more reliable institutional foundation on which to base further progress. Therefore, as used herein, the phrase "evolutionary world government" refers to the gradual evolution from a relatively weak and ineffectual world government in the short run, toward a highly authoritative and effective—yet benign—world government in the long run. It is not a matter of *evolving into* the equivalent of a formally established federal world government, it is a rather a matter of *evolving from* the formal establishment of an initially severely limited federal world government.

The argument will be developed in this book via the analogy between "evolutionary socialism" and "evolutionary world government." Just as the concept of evolutionary socialism at the turn of the twentieth century had a profound effect on developments throughout that century and beyond, perhaps the concept of evolutionary world government at the turn of the twenty-first century will have a profound effect on developments throughout this century and beyond. What, therefore, is the meaning of "evolutionary socialism"?

Without doubt the single most influential codifier of the socialist critique of capitalism during the nineteenth century was Karl Marx (1818-1883). In Marx's view, "socialism" means one and only one thing: the replacement of private ownership of the non-human factors of production (land and capital) with public ownership. And there is one and only one way to achieve this goal: violent revolution. Violent revolution was assured by the fact that the condition of the working classes under capitalism would continue to deteriorate indefinitely, until a revolutionary explosion became inevitable. This uncompromising viewpoint came to dominate the socialist movement during the second half of the nineteenth century.

However, toward the end of the nineteenth century, serious questions began to be raised within the socialist movement concerning the validity of these Marxist tenets. Compelling evidence was emerging that the condition of the working classes was improving rather than deteriorating. Perhaps violent revolution would not be necessary after all to achieve the fundamental goal of socialism, which is no more and no less than a decent quality of life for the laboring masses. And perhaps this goal could and should be pursued through such reforms as business regulation, progressive taxation, and welfare programs, these reforms to be attained via peaceful democratic channels. These fundamental departures from the original Marxist orthodoxy came to be known as "evolutionary socialism"—as opposed to "revolutionary socialism."

Evolutionary socialism saved the socialist concept from probable extinction within the economically advanced, industrialized countries. In Western Europe and throughout much of the world, social democratic parties, while continuing to label themselves "socialist" and "Marxist," became evolutionary socialist rather than revolutionary socialist, and by virtue of this, became active participants in political processes throughout the twentieth century. Their leaders often rose to positions of great influence and authority. Numerous social democratic reforms were implemented. Impressive progress was thereby made toward improving the economic condition of working class people—as well as that of middle class people.

Meanwhile, hardline Marxism got its chance when the Communist party gained control of the Russian empire in 1917. At the time of Communist revolution, Russia and its dependent territories were not part of the economically advanced, industrialized world. Although Communist Party control of the Soviet Union ultimately enabled dramatic progress in some areas, such as industrial development and military capability, the road to these advances was long and hard. The welfare cost to the Soviet people was enormous. In the early 1990s, the Soviet people rose up and ousted the Communist Party from the position of political and social domination it had occupied for most of the twentieth century. This dramatic failure of hardline Marxist socialism in the USSR has left the world socialist movement mostly under the influence of the kinder, gentler form of socialism known as "social democracy."

My purpose in this book will be to demonstrate that a close parallel exists between Marx's original hardline thesis of pure public-ownership socialism through which all forms of economic exploitation would be definitively eliminated, this goal only to be achieved through violent revolution, and the hardline world federalist thesis of a politically unified world from which international war had been definitively eliminated, this goal only to be achieved through the military subjugation of all nations to the authority of an omnipotent world state. Of course, conventional world federalists of today do not preach violent revolution as a means to the desired end of a peaceful world. But the kind of drastic attitudinal shift they envision would indeed amount to a kind of "psychological virtual revolution."

Just as hardline revolutionary Marxism, with its insistence on violent revolution as the only means of achieving pure socialism, was dethroned by what came to be called "evolutionary socialism," it is my hope that hardline world federalism, with its insistence on the omnipotent world state as the only means of achieving a war-free world, will be dethroned by "evolutionary world government." At the present time, it would be an obvious exaggeration to describe the remaining vestiges of world federalist activity as a "movement." If not completely dead, world federalism is virtually moribund in today's world. But just as the abandonment of revolutionary socialism and its replacement by evolutionary socialism engendered a rebirth of the socialist movement and the eventual attainment of many of its goals throughout the twentieth century, so too perhaps the abandonment by world federalists of the omnipotent world state goal and its replacement by the goal of a limited world government along the lines of the proposed Federal Union of Democratic Nations, will engender a rebirth of the world federalist movement and the attainment of many of its goals throughout the twenty-first century.

Social democratic socialism has certainly not produced quasi-utopian conditions even in those nations most strongly influenced by it. The various business regulations, progressive taxes, and welfare programs associated with social democracy have not led to an idyllic condition of perfect economic, political, and social bliss. Clearly social democracy has not led to utopia—nor will it ever lead to utopia. But if we compare the overall quality of life for most people in most nations as of 2000, relative to what it was in 1900, only the most contrarian mentalities would maintain that there has not been significant improvement.

Similarly, it cannot be sensibly maintained that a limited federal world government, should one be created along the recommended lines, would lead to an idyllic condition for the world's population. World government would not lead to utopia—nor could it ever lead to utopia. But if a limited world government were to be established, and if it were to persist to the year 2100, significant improvements would be realized over what would most likely be the case if we continue with national sovereignty as the reigning principle of international relations. If there were to be a comparison of the overall quality of life for most people in most nations as of 2100, relative to what it was in 2000, most likely only the most contrarian mentalities would maintain that there had not been significant improvement—and that world government had not been an important facilitating factor in the improvement.

There have always been vociferous critics of the social democratic program, people who have dogmatically forecasted the downfall of human civilization should various social democratic proposals be implemented.[3] Subsequent history has routinely demonstrated the invalidity of these jeremiads. The proposals were implemented, and life not only went on—it went on better than it did before. Therefore it has been established beyond a reasonable doubt that social democracy does not lead to dystopia. It does not lead to utopia—but it also does not lead to dystopia.

At the present time, world federalism is not a sufficiently significant political force to elicit "vociferous" criticism. But if the world federalist movement ever does become a significant political force, it can be predicted with great confidence that vociferous critics will emerge, who will dogmatically forecast the downfall of human civilization should a federal world government be established. Just as subsequent history discredited vociferous critics of social democracy, so too subsequent history will most likely discredit vociferous critics of world government. It will be established beyond a reasonable doubt that world government does not necessarily lead to dystopia. It does not lead to utopia—neither does it lead to dystopia. It may not lead to salvation, but it certainly does not lead to damnation.

The avoidance of damnation, however, is critically dependent on the world government being "properly designed." Given the existent realities of the contemporary world, "proper design" means that the reserved national rights of free exit and independent military forces must be integral and essential features of the overall world government blueprint. There exists a wide range of acceptable institutional forms for the world government—but whatever specific institutional forms are adopted, these reserved national rights must absolutely be part of the overall plan. While it may be true that after a sufficient period of time, measured at least in decades and possibly in centuries, these reserved rights will become virtually forgotten dead letters, for the immediate future they are absolutely indispensable if there is to be any hope of bringing world government into being within the lifetimes of the current generation of humanity.

Implicit in the retained national right of secession from the world government is the principle that the formation of such a government should be considered as a *tentative and provisional* step, as an *experimental* venture. It is impossible for anyone to predict confidently, on the basis of currently available evidence, whether a world federation established at this point in human history, would be a success or a failure. If pessimistic skeptics are proved correct, a world government will create more problems than solutions. Instead of being an integral part of the solution of global problems, it will only aggravate these problems. If this does indeed happen, there would be no need for a formal decision to terminate the world government's existence. Instead it will be informally terminated, quickly or gradually as the case may be, by the departure of its member nations. In other words, a natural "exit strategy" is built into the organizational plan. Thus a decision to establish a world government is not an irrevocable, all-or-nothing decision. If necessary—if the world government is developing poorly—the decision could be reversed.

However, given that the world government is properly designed and incorporates key retained national rights, principally the rights to free secession and independent militaries, there are no compelling grounds for pessimism. In science and technology, it is axiomatic that the one true path to reliable knowledge is through experimentation. This same principle could and should be applied in the area of international organization. Of course, experimentation on this scale is unprecedented in human history, But there are numerous aspects of contemporary global civilization that are unprecedented in human history.

## Outline of the Essay

As befits a large-scale essay on a large-scale topic, this book covers lot of ground. Just as road maps can be useful to people undertaking a long journey, so too an introductory outline of the remainder of this book might be helpful to readers. The following provides brief descriptions of the gist of each chapter section and sub-section. Chapter titles and section titles are in bold; sub-section titles are in italics.

## Chapter 2: A Pragmatic Blueprint

**Need for Specificity.** It is impossible to evaluate judiciously the general concept of world government without having a clear understanding of the specific form of world government under evaluation. This is because the practical pros and cons of world government depend critically on the practical institutional details envisioned for that government. If the underlying concept of world government is the "omnipotent world state," then for most people the arguments against world government are compelling. But if the underlying concept is instead taken to be a limited federal world government along the lines herein advanced, the arguments for world government are significantly enhanced.

**Federal Union Fundamentals.** The proposed Federal Union of Democratic Nations, founded on the basis of a Federal Union Constitution, would be a genuine, legitimate state entity with a permanent and continuous governmental structure, the power to levy taxes and enact binding legislation, and the authority to maintain standing military forces under its direct command. The Federal Union constitution would at a minimum contain two critical limitations on the Federal Union of Democratic Nations: (1) all member nations of the Federal Union are to possess the permanent and inalienable right to withdraw from the Federal Union at any time at their own unilateral discretion; (2) all member nations of the Federal Union are to possess the permanent and inalienable right to maintain whatever military forces they require, equipped with whatever weaponry (including nuclear weapons) they deem appropriate.

**Major Issues.**

*Representation and Voting.* Incorporated into the Federal Union Constitution would be a "dual voting" system within the federation legislature, according to which measures would have to be approved by a majority on two different bases: the population basis, and the material basis. In the population vote, the weight given to the vote of each particular Union Representative would be proportional to the population of his/her Union district, relative to the total population of the Federal Union. In the material vote, the weight given to the vote of each particular Union Representative would be proportional to the financial revenues derived from his/her Union district, relative to the total financial revenues of the Federal Union.

*National Right of Secession.* Perhaps the most fundamental objection to the Federal Union proposal is that any state entity that was not prepared to forcibly prevent the departure of its subsidiary units would lack the most essential characteristic of a state: that it be absolutely determined to preserve its existing territorial integrity. However commonplace this viewpoint might be at the present time, it is not valid. Consider the example of Canada, which for decades has confronted the possibility of secession by the province of Quebec. No knowledgeable person expects that if Quebec does in fact ultimately declare its independence, the national government of Canada will employ its armed forces to keep Quebec within the Canadian federation. But the expectation that potential secession would not be suppressed by force does not mean that Canada is not a legitimate state.

*National Right of Armament.* The conventional world federalist view up to now has been that the foundation of the world state must be accompanied by the total disarmament of nations. The problem with this is that if disarmament of the nations is made a precondition for world government, then the conclusion seems inevitable that world government is indeed impossible—now and into the foreseeable future. Therefore, it is an absolutely essential element of the Federal Union proposal that the member nations possess a permanent and inalienable right to maintain whatever military forces and weapons—including nuclear weapons—that they feel it necessary to maintain, for as long as they feel it necessary.

*Supernational Armament Authority.* It is customary that state entities possess military forces: these military forces protect the citizen body from outside aggression and they also deter (at least potentially) the citizen body from engaging in warfare among itself. Aside from its utilitarian purposes, the possession of a military force carries potent symbolic significance as a key defining characteristic of a political entity. Therefore is it essential that the Federal Union of Democratic Nations possess a substantial military force under its direct control, to be designated the Union Security Force (USF).

*Religion and Language.* The general rule in pursuing the long-term goal of ever-increasing peaceful cooperation and psychological solidarity among the citizens of the Federal Union of Democratic Nations is to maintain perpetual flexibility and toleration with respect to all matters in which diversity is either inevitable, or has no seriously adverse bearing on practical economic and political issues, but to work gradually toward uniformity in other matters. An important example of the former is religion. An important example of the latter is language.

*Trade and Migration.* A primary task of the Federal Union during its early decades would be to oversee the full and comprehensive dismantling of various national impediments (tariffs, import quotas, and so on) to the free flow of physical commodities and financial capital between member nations. On the other hand, the immigration barriers that have been established by the rich nations to restrain the flow of migrants from the poor nations must be kept in force until a higher level of economic homogeneity throughout the world has been achieved.

**A Complementary Proposal.**

*The Economic Problem.* That global economic inequality poses a threat to global political stability seems intuitively obvious to most people, although opinions vary widely on both the nature and extent of the threat. The existence of economic inequality naturally arouses emotions of envy and hostility in the "have-nots" while at the same time it elicits emotions of psychic discomfort and anxiety in the "haves."

*A Global Marshall Plan.* The problem of world economic inequality and poverty did not fully register upon the consciousness of humanity until the middle of the twentieth century. In reaction, the idea was born that the economic inequality problem ought to be tackled by means of a massive, coordinated effort by all the nations of the world, large and small, rich and poor. The major real-world input into the development of this idea was the Marshall Plan from 1948 through 1952, which greatly accelerated the economic recovery of the Western European nations from the ravages of World War II. The original Marshall Plan has continued to inspire visions of a gigantic global version to be implemented in the future. Such a vision is incorporated into the complementary economic proposal described here (a complement to the political proposal for a Federal Union of Democratic Nations) for a "Global Marshall Plan."

An influential argument against undertaking a real-world Global Marshall Plan on the gigantic scale envisioned, is that there is no meaningful evidence that such a program would be successful. The substance of this section is a summary of some computer simulation experimentation by the author (an economist by trade), using a small-scale but fairly comprehensive economic model of the world economy, that constitutes just such evidence. Benchmark simulation of the model with a Global Marshall Plan in operation shows the possibility of significant equalization of living standards throughout the world even though the economic growth of the rich nations is not reduced by any appreciable extent.

However, owing to the unavoidable fact that there is a non-negligible probability that an actual Global Marshall Plan would be extremely *inef-*

fective in attaining its goals, the proposal of this book is that such a program be initiated *on a tentative and experimental basis*. What it means is that the program should be initiated with a clear understanding on the part of all participants, that continuation of the program beyond an experimental period of perhaps 10 to 20 years will depend on the achievement of tangible, dramatic progress in terms of rising living standards within all parts of the populations of the poorer nations.

## Chapter 3. Brief History of World Federalism

**Origins and Development.** A great many proposals for a formal political organization to prevent additional warfare were put forward throughout modern history, some of them from historically important individuals. Although these numerous proposals are generally considered "prototype world state" plans today, in actual fact most of them did not envision a world government as generally conceived at the present time. In many cases, the plans called merely for consolidation of the Western European nations, for something along the lines of today's European Union. However, the substance of some of the more territorially ambitious proposals was indeed eventually realized in the real world in the form of the League of Nations and its successor organization, the United Nations.

*The League of Nations.* The League of Nations, formed in the aftermath of World War I, was humanity's first attempt at a universal political organization among nations. Its brief history was notably unsuccessful, partly because of the failure of the United States to become a charter member, and partly because of the aggressive nationalism of several great powers during the interwar period: Germany, Italy, and Japan.

*The United Nations.* In terms of organization and purposes, the United Nations, established in 1945 at the end of World War II, was very nearly a replication of the League of Nations. However, there were certain important distinctions. First and foremost, no major world power was to be missing from membership in the United Nations. Despite its larger membership and higher aspirations, the fundamental defects of the United Nations were obvious from the start. The United Nations may have made some contributions to the maintenance of peace throughout the more than half-century of its operation, but if so they have not been dramatic and unmistakable.

**The Postwar World Government Boom.** In the immediate aftermath of World War II, the dissemination of technical information regarding the tremendous power of nuclear weapons, together with wide circulation of narrative accounts, photographs and newsreels of the devastation at the unfortunate Japanese cities of Hiroshima and Nagasaki, had a very sobering impact. Numerous respected authorities and acknowledged geniuses, exemplified by Albert Einstein, proclaimed that the sovereign nation-state system was far too dangerous in the nuclear age, and that this new threat to humanity must be immediately contained through the establishment of a powerful and authoritative world federation. There occurred a sudden proliferation of organizations working energetically toward a federal world government. Despite all this, the postwar world government boom quickly went into precipitous decline, a victim of the rapidly escalating Cold War between the Soviet Union and the Western allies. Very soon the conventional opinion on world government had reverted to the time-honored belief that whatever might be the theoretical pros and cons of world government, it was so wholly impractical in the real world as to be unworthy of serious consideration.

**The Cold War and Beyond.** The post-World War II expansion of communism, first in the forcible incorporation into the Soviet bloc of the Eastern European countries overrun by the Red Army, and then in the revolutionary communization of China and other Asian countries, generated acute apprehension in the noncommunist world that the Soviet leadership had always, from the beginning of its control over Russia in 1917, envisioned a worldwide socialist republic as the final destination of human civilization. While this interpretation of Soviet intentions was exaggerated, what the Soviet leadership did indeed envision was a world in which all or most nations subscribed to Karl Marx's vision of public-ownership socialism, and were therefore inclined toward a harmonious relationship with the USSR. This objective was of course unacceptable to the noncommunist nations. Early in the Cold War, U.S. President Harry Truman proclaimed the policy of containment, which remained bedrock U.S. foreign policy throughout the Cold War.

*Postwar Blueprints.* Owing to their abundance, it would be impractical to consider here any significant number of postwar world government proposals. Therefore this section describes only three of the best-known proposals, which may be taken as typical of the entire range of conventional proposals: (1) the proposal of Giuseppe Borgese for a Federal Republic of the World; (2) the proposal of Grenville Clark and Louis Sohn for a strengthened United Nations; and (3) the proposal of Philip Isely for a Federation of Earth. These three "conventional" world government proposals are compared and contrasted with the Federal Union of Democratic Nations. The intention is to demonstrate clearly the critical distinctions between the typical postwar world government proposal, and the Federal Union proposal.

*Since the Soviet Collapse.* The collapse and dissolution of the Soviet Union had a dramatically beneficial effect on international relations. No longer were the two leading superpowers of the world locked in an intractable ideological struggle. The threat of nuclear holocaust receded to a level many people considered inconsequential. This world-altering transformation revived hopes among the few remaining world federalists that just as the end of World War I witnessed the birth of the League of Nations, and the end of World War II witnessed the birth of the United Nations, perhaps the end of the Cold War would witness the birth of a genuine world government.

These early hopes were disappointed, and throughout the quarter century since the Soviet collapse, the sovereign nation-state system has continued onward without any fundamental change. Although the ideological issue has been greatly muted, other issues remain. The superpowers still require massive armed forces, and international squabbles, great and small, still continue on a regular basis. Nevertheless, in the post-Cold War era, there has been something of a resurgence of interest in world government among a handful of academic specialists, foremost among whom is Alexander Wendt, who in 1993 published a professional article with the attention-grabbing title: "Why a World State Is Inevitable." Wendt's utilization of the philosophical concept of teleological development to support his contention that world government is inevitable is a reflection of the fact that the discipline of philosophy has been much involved in the contemporary debate over the practicality and advisability of world government.

## Chapter 4. Brief History of Socialism

**Origins and Early Development.** Early socialist ideas ranged over a wide spectrum from the communal schemes of Charles Fourier to the "enlightened capitalism" of Robert Owen. Prior to the emergence of Karl Marx, the term "socialism" was not necessarily associated with violent revolution. In the earlier part of the nineteenth century, most socialists believed that their projects for the betterment of society could be attained by peaceful means.

*Karl Marx's Codification.* In *The Communist Manifesto* (1848, co-authored with Friedrich Engels), Karl Marx dismissed the main body of his predecessors as "utopian socialists," as unrealistic and impractical dreamers. Marx asserted that the poverty of the proletariat and the wealth of the capitalistic bourgeoisie was the consequence of a mechanism he described as "surplus labor exploitation." Inevitably the proletariat would eventually rise up and topple their capitalist oppressors in a bloody revolution. All nonhuman factors of production in land and capital would pass into public ownership. By the 1870s, Marx's hardline vision of public-ownership socialism achieved through violent revolution had become dominant within the socialist movement.

*The Great Schism.* Throughout the latter nineteenth century, a good deal of the revolutionary basis for hardline Marxist socialism was eroded away by gradual but steady improvement in the condition of the working class. A fundamental rift in the socialist ranks occurred when the "revisionists" under the leadership of individuals such as Eduard Bernstein, renounced the Marxian doctrine of the necessity of violent revolution. In the view of the revisionists, it was preferable to work politically within the framework of democratic capitalism to obtain power peacefully and legally. Thereby, through such reforms as business regulation, social insurance, and progressive taxation, the underlying objectives of the socialist movement could be effectively pursued and achieved. This "social democratic" concept of socialism gradually became dominant throughout Western Europe and most of the rest of the world—with the notable exception of the Soviet Union.

**The Soviet Era.** The influence of the harsh early-Marxist version of socialism might have faded out of modern history altogether if it had not been for the Bolshevik revolution of 1917, which gave this version of socialism something it had never enjoyed before—the practical and moral support of an important nation-state. Among the first official actions taken by the Communist government of the Soviet Union was the total dispossession, without any compensation whatever, of both the landed aristocracy and the capitalist class in Russia and its peripheral territories. Such drastic transformations galvanized the resistance to the Communist regime and led to almost four years of bitter civil war.

Marx's original thesis had been that the first sparks of the revolution would be ignited in the most advanced capitalist nations, wherein the contradictions of capitalism had reached the most aggravated state. In the early days of the USSR, therefore, the Soviet leadership was hopeful that Communist revolutions would occur in Western Europe and elsewhere in the world. Nothing of the sort happened, and it soon became apparent that for the time being at least, Russia would have to remain alone in the vanguard of the world socialist revolution.

*Stalin's Dictatorship.* Under the leadership of the increasingly dictatorial Joseph Stalin, during the late twenties and early thirties, a great Russian economic development effort was launched, consisting of two core components: collectivization and modernization of agriculture, and a crash industrialization program under the guidance of a state planning authority. Although impressive progress was made in terms of economic growth, the effort placed a tremendous strain on the Russian people. Thus there occurred in the mid-to-late thirties an event that dimmed appreciably whatever glory had been achieved in the economic realm: an intemperate purge of the Communist Party carried out at the instigation of Joseph Stalin. The party purge was an early manifestation of an unparalleled tyranny that would persist until Stalin's death in 1953.

*Western Attitudes.* Initially Western attitudes toward the Soviet Union tended to be on the condescending side. Many believed that "socialist blundering" would soon bring about its early collapse. By the end of World War II, however, the Soviet Union had progressed from a wobbly infant to a military colossus. The Western noncommunist world now viewed the Soviet Union, and its expanding sphere of influence in Eastern Europe and Asia, as an extremely serious threat to both political democracy and the capitalist economic system throughout the world.

*The Post-Soviet Era.* Despite several decades of strict control by the Communist Party, the deficiencies of Soviet-style socialism eventually became too much for the Soviet people to bear. In hopes of gaining the advantages of democratic capitalism as exemplified by the West, they rose up and threw off Party dominion in a remarkably non-violent revolution. In the long run, these advantages may eventually be realized, but it will not have been a quick and easy process.

*Socialism in China.* Although Soviet-style socialism eventually collapsed, Chinese-style socialism shows no signs of doing likewise in the immediate future. Through its renunciation of Soviet-style planning in favor of a variety of market socialism, as well as other policy innovations (for example, the adoption of draconic population control), the People's Republic of China has registered remarkable growth in per capita income over the last several decades. The PRC may well eventually follow the example set by the USSR in throwing off the political domination of the Communist Party, but there is no telling when that day might come.

## Chapter 5. Learning from the Past

**Evolution – Not Revolution.** The notion that violent revolution, which forcibly replaces the existing government structure with a new one, is a viable and attractive method for improving society, probably reached its apogee in the early days of the French Revolution of 1789. Well over two centuries have elapsed since that epochal event, and throughout that interval the appeal of political revolution has been gradually but steadily declining. Preference for evolutionary transitions over revolutionary transitions has been steadily gaining ground. Seemingly there has been an over-abundance of "revolutions gone wrong" throughout modern history. Marx's formative years were spent in the long shadow cast by the French Revolution. Thus he came naturally to the conclusion that just as much blood had to be shed for the capitalistic bourgeoisie to wrest power from the feudal landholders, so too much blood would have to be shed in order for the proletarian masses to wrest power from the capitalists.

**Origins of Evolutionary Socialism.** Throughout the latter part of the nineteenth century, real-world developments in Europe and elsewhere continued to erode the basis for the hardline Marxist forecast of public-ownership socialism brought about by violent revolution. As real-world conditions evolved, questions began to be raised concerning the validity of the Marxist vision. One of most prominent questioners was Eduard Bernstein, one of the founders of the German Social Democratic Party.

*Bernstein's Contribution.* Owing to its critical importance, this section provides a fairly detailed analysis of Bernstein's book *Evolutionary Socialism*. It is important to emphasize that Bernstein did not argue that Marx's prediction of proletarian revolution was necessarily and definitely invalid, but rather that there was so little evidence to support its imminence that the socialist movement will be better off if it proceeds on the assumption that this revolution might well never actually occur. Moreover, the spread of the franchise, and the more enlightened and accommodating attitudes among the powerful, were steadily reducing the need for violence to achieve the central objective of socialism, which is no more and no less than significant improvement in the economic condition of the working population.

*World War I and After.* Bernstein's revisionist vision of "evolutionary socialism" became increasingly influential during the early years of the twentieth century, but it was not fully accepted and adopted by the German Social Democratic party until after World War I. It is safe to say that the traumatic—and completely unanticipated—experience of World War I had a major impact on human thinking on a variety of issues, of which one was the meaning and purposes of socialism. Ironically, at the same time that the social democratic version of socialism was becoming dominant within most European nations, the hardline Marxist version of public-ownership socialism gained the support of an important nation-state when the Bolshevik Revolution transformed the Russian empire, previously a stronghold of reaction, into the Union of Soviet Socialist Republics (USSR), whose avowed mission it was to bring about the triumph of Marxism throughout the entire world. A schism that had previously been confined to a relatively academic dispute among socialist theoreticians, now became an important part of the real-world history of socialism throughout the twentieth century.

**Application to World Government.** The development of the revisionist socialist approach in the early part of the twentieth century immensely strengthened the socialist idea as a generally positive force toward the improvement of global human civilization. Perhaps an analogous transition will occur in the early part of the twenty-first century. Perhaps "hardline world federalism" will give way before "revisionist world federalism." Whereas "hardline world federalism" insists that the omnipotent world state is the only meaningful and worthwhile form of world government, "revisionist world federalism" holds out a practical alternative, as exemplified by the proposed Federal Union of Democratic Nations.

## Chapter 6. Could It Be Done?

**The Chicken or the Egg?** The well-known question "Which came first—the chicken or the egg?" provides the basis for a critical insight into the possibilities for establishing a meaningful world government within the lifetimes of the current generation of humanity. What makes this question absurd, and therefore humorous, is that *neither* the modern chicken nor the modern egg came first. The modern chicken-egg-chicken progression is the result of millions of years of slow, evolutionary development with roots in the primeval slime. Those who argue that it is necessary to have a high level of social uniformity throughout the world prior to having an effective world government are equivalent to those who would argue, in response to the chicken-egg question, that since chickens come out of eggs, then the egg came first. The problem with this argument, obviously, is that it is also true that eggs come out of chickens.

If we take social and attitudinal homogeneity to be the egg, and the effectiveness of the state organization (for example, a world government) to be the chicken, the relevance of the chicken-egg question becomes clear. A population which is politically united within the same state organization tends to become, over time, more socially and attitudinally homogeneous. Similarly, as a given population becomes more socially and attitudinally homogeneous, its state organization tends to become more effective. There is an ongoing, progressive, interactive, mutually reinforcing, snowballing process between the social and attitudinal homogeneity of a given population, and the effectiveness of the state organization within which it is politically united.

Owing to the constitutional restrictions on its power proposed for the Federal Union of Democratic Nations, in its early years this federation might be metaphorically deemed the equivalent of the first primitive chicken which produced the first primitive egg. Just as a long period of evolutionary development separated the primitive chicken from its modern counterpart, so too a long period of evolutionary development (albeit not quite so long!) will likely be necessary for the transformation of the early Federal Union into the authoritative yet benign world government we hope to achieve in the future.

**The Nationalism Issue.** A convenient categorization of the major impediments to world government includes the following three factors: (1) ideological conflict; (2) economic inequality; (3) nationalism. There are certainly other impediments, of which the three that come most readily to mind are race, religion, and language. But these others are less important. While ideological conflict, economic inequality, and nationalism are conceptually distinct, they are closely interrelated in a practical sense. Specifically, the nationalistic fervor of any particular national population is positively related to the degree it feels ideologically threatened by other nations and/or economically threatened by other nations.

In historical context, nationalism has been a stabilizing and unifying force to a greater extent than it has been a destabilizing and disunifying force. Those who would argue today that nationalism will forever prevent the formation of a viable federal world government because mankind is incapable of developing anything beyond national loyalties, are comparable to those who, several hundred years ago, would have argued that local and regional loyalties would forever prevent the formation of a viable nation-state.

*Sovereignty and Freedom.* The argument that the nationalistic impediment to world government is insuperable is sometimes expressed along the lines that any kind of world government would necessitate severe and unacceptable constraints on national sovereignty. But a realistic appreciation of history and contemporary civilization clearly manifests that "national sovereignty" is in fact necessarily limited both internally and externally. Thus the formation of a world state would not necessarily manifest the abrogation of national sovereignty, nor would the continuation of national sovereignty necessarily imply an absence of sovereignty on the part of the world state. The world state and the component nation-states would each have their respective areas of sovereignty.

*Internationalist Tendencies.* Although the United Nations of today is a far cry from the Federal Union of Democratic Nations under consideration, it should be appreciated that the very existence of the U.N., as well as that of several other thoroughly grounded real-world international organizations, provides indirect evidence that a functioning world government within the relatively near future might not be beyond the bounds of possibility. A great deal of attention, for example, has been focused on the European Union. We examine here the extent to which the existence of the European Union supports the feasibility of a world government. While the European Union can certainly be deemed a success story insofar as reducing war risk among the Western European nations is concerned, it is still a long way from becoming the long-imagined "United States of Europe." Moreover, the conditions under which the European Union has developed are drastically dissimilar to the conditions under which the potential future Federal Union of Democratic Nations would develop. For example, the European Union has endeavored to implement certain policies that would likely be completely unsuitable for a global federation. The bottom line seems to that the European Union does not provide as much encouragement toward a real-world global federation as might seem at first glance.

The Heterogeneity Bugaboo. Throughout the perilous Cold war era, the possibility of world government was routinely dismissed on grounds of the ongoing geopolitical conflict between the communist and noncommunist blocs of nations. The collapse and dissolution of the Soviet Union in 1991 greatly reduced the importance of ideological conflict as an impediment to world government, but it did not directly affect the global economic inequality problem. The populations of the wealthy nations can easily imagine the horrific outcome if an omnipotent world state were democratically controlled by the teeming masses of impoverished people in the Third World: the establishment of a global welfare state with generous benefits—for which they would be forced to foot the bill. Once again, a properly limited federal world government provides a safeguard against this possibility, as also would the inauguration of a Global Marshall Plan designed to eliminate, once and for all, the problem of excessive global economic inequality.

According to predominant international relations opinion, the existence of a high degree heterogeneity among nations in today's world rules out any sort of effective global government. Ideological conflict and economic inequality are the most prominent contributors to heterogeneity, but there are several others: such as race, language, culture, and religion. But so long as we envision a properly limited federal world government, none of these factors presents an insuperable obstacle to this form of government. In fact, several successful nations in the contemporary world manage to get along quite well despite significant heterogeneity within their populations.

*Religion.* Religion is an especially important component of culture, and merits consideration in its own right. The historical record is filled with religiously based conflicts, both within and among nations, perhaps the prime example being the tortured history of relations between Islam and Christianity. However, most nations today encompass substantial religious minorities, and most national governments today proclaim a strict policy of religious toleration and neutrality. Obviously, it is essential to its success that a future world government follow the lead of most national governments today in terms of religious toleration and neutrality. This should be easier for a world government than for any national government, because at the world level no single religion commands the allegiance of a substantial majority of the population.

## Chapter 7. Should It Be Done?

**A Scientific Approach**. On the basis of the presently existing evidence, it cannot be predicted with absolute certainly that either the political proposal under consideration herein (the Federal Union of Democratic Nations), or its economic complement (the Global Marshall Plan), would, if implemented, be successful. Neither can the opposite be predicted with absolute certainty. The only means of gaining compelling evidence concerning the success or failure of these initiatives would be to apply the same method that has been responsible for scientific and technological progress throughout the history of mankind: the experimental method. The Federal Union of Democratic Nations, and the Global Marshall Plan, should be regarded as no more—and no less— than experiments. Gigantic experiments—and expensive experiments, to be sure—but experiments nonetheless.

**Global Governance**. Among extreme world government skeptics, it is customarily assumed that a world state would immediately take the form of a hideously repressive tyranny. However, among the majority of informed, sensible people, this outcome is not necessarily assumed— nevertheless, it is believed that there is too high a risk of hideously repressive tyranny for a world government to be seriously considered. According to current conventional wisdom, our faith should therefore be put in "global governance" as opposed to "global government." It is argued here that the standard "global governance hypothesis" (that effective global governance is possible in the absence of effective global government) is very doubtful. The prevalent belief in this hypothesis is not only misguided, it cultivates a complacent attitude, fosters inertial conservatism, and deters progressive thinking toward a qualitatively higher form of global government—through which genuinely effective global governance might actually be achieved in the real world.

**A New World Order?** The downfall of Soviet communism in the early 1990s has created what some describe as a "New World Order." The question is whether this order will be benign—or otherwise. It would be imprudent to assume that future developments will necessarily be in a positive direction. Distrust and hostility among independent nations existed long before the Russian revolution of 1917 initiated a global communist movement, and they will continue to exist after the abatement of this movement. The collapse and dissolution of the USSR resulted in no fundamental alteration in the sovereign nation-state system. Under this system, each nation is obligated to think first and foremost of its own national interests, and if these interests are perceived to be in serious conflict with the interests of humanity as a whole, then normally national interests must take precedence. This situation has provided fertile grounds for hundreds of wars throughout modern history. To believe that this powerful tendency will now be reliably halted by the introduction of nuclear weapons into the military mix, may represent little more than wishful thinking. One disturbing possibility is nuclear terrorism. Just as the assassination of an Austrian archduke and his wife by a Serbian terrorist on June 28, 1914, initiated a chain of events leading to World War I, so too a nuclear outrage perpetrated upon an American city by contemporary terrorists might initiate a chain of events leading to World War III.

**The Boat Metaphor.** In the absence of a global government equipped with a reasonable and appropriate degree of political authority, the circumstance of humanity in today's world may be compared to that of a group of people gathered together in a large boat—a boat lacking both a rudder and an engine—that is drifting down an unknown river. At the moment the river is broad and quiet, drifting is pleasant, and the people in the boat feel quite safe and secure. But an unknown river may contain deadly hazards in the form of churning rapids or huge waterfalls capable of smashing the boat to smithereens and drowning its occupants. A good metaphor for the intention of world government is that of attaching a rudder and installing an engine in a boat that is drifting down an unknown river. The idea is to improve the degree of control over the boat, so that there is less likelihood that it will be destroyed if rapids or a waterfall are encountered.

No analogy is perfect, and a world government skeptic would immediately object that this particular analogy is completely misleading. But when stripped to essentials, the skeptic's argument is basically that because a world government *might* turn out to be undesirable in the future, establishing a world government in the present *is* undesirable. The sensibility of this argument depends critically on the characteristics of the world government to be established. If the world government is to be the omnipotent world state envisioned in traditional world federalist thinking (hardline world federalism), then considerable weight attaches to the argument. On the other hand, if the world government is to be a limited government along the lines of the Federal Union of Democratic Nations, then this argument falls far short.

## Chapter 8. Prospects

**Summary of the Argument.** The currently prevailing concept of world government, among both the large majority of world government skeptics and the small minority of world government advocates (the "world federalists"), is that of a very strong state entity that would stand in relation to its component member nations much as the federal government of the United States stands in relation to the fifty component states. This concept of world government is descriptively referred to herein as the "omnipotent world state." Apart from the small minority of world federalists, it is almost universally assumed that there is no credible transition path, of a peaceful nature, from the current international status quo to the omnipotent world state. This essay does not challenge this consensus opinion. However, it does challenge the widespread view that no federal world government short of the omnipotent world state would be a worthwhile undertaking.

The basis of the challenge is the proposition that there exist viable world government possibilities (exemplified by the proposed Federal Union of Democratic Nations) whose authority and effectiveness would lie somewhere between that of today's relatively ineffectual United Nations, and that of the omnipotent world state, and that these intermediate possibilities would both significantly improve the processes of global governance in the proximate future, as well as laying a secure foundation for further gradual, evolutionary progress over the long term toward a highly authoritative and effective—yet democratic and benign—world government. In other words, a limited world government, as opposed to an unlimited world government, is both achievable and desirable.

In support of this proposition, this essay explores the analogy between "evolutionary socialism" and "evolutionary world government." In the final years of the nineteenth century, Eduard Bernstein came forward with a proposal that the socialist movement of his day turn away from its dangerously counter-productive obsession with ideal socialism achieved instantaneously through bloody revolution, toward a more practical and promising vision of the essential goals of socialism achieved through gradual, peaceful reform efforts within the existing socio-political system. He proposed, in essence, that "revolutionary socialism" be replaced by "evolutionary socialism." With broader support, the socialist movement was significantly strengthened, and thereby became capable of achieving tangible, worthwhile, real-world reform objectives.

A close analogy exists between this historical redirection of the socialist movement and a potential future redirection of the world federalist movement away from its traditional focus on an omnipotent world state achieved instantaneously through some quasi-miraculous political enlightenment, toward a more practical and promising vision of the essential purposes of world government achieved through gradual, peaceful reform efforts within the existing international system. Contemporary world federalists, of course, do not preach violence of any sort, revolutionary or otherwise. Yet it is difficult to imagine how their ideal of an omnipotent world state—a government that would necessarily include all the nations of the world and would monopolize all significant military power—could come about in the absence of violence.

**Weighing the Risks.** This book is concerned with one especially important choice out of the multitude of choices confronting humanity at the present juncture in our history: the choice between maintaining the status quo situation under which the United Nations remains the highest level of international organization in the world, or to proceed beyond the United Nations to establish a genuine and legitimate—albeit limited—world government along the lines of the proposed Federal Union of Democratic Nations. There is no escaping the fact that whatever we do, whether we establish a world government or do not establish a world government, we will confront very serious risks.

The argument of this book is that the entire question of relative risk hinges critically on *what kind* of a world government is intended. Among most of that tiny minority of the population that currently favors world government, the envisioned world government would be so powerful that no single nation, nor any group of nations, would be able to challenge its power. Personally, this author concurs with the majority that such a world government, established in the contemporary world, would be excessively risky. It would be far too likely to abuse its power. For most people at the present time, consideration of world government terminates at this point. But this conclusion represents profound error. It is error because there is *no need* for a federal world government to be "extremely powerful," such that its power would be comparable to the power currently exercised by the national governments over their component parts. There is nothing in the laws of nature, logic, or mankind preventing an appropriate *sharing* of power and authority between the national governments and the world government, so that there would be adequate guarantees for the legitimate rights of nations and adequate safeguards against the world government evolving into a monolithic tyranny and/or a crushing bureaucracy.

**No Plausible Scenario?** The major difficulties impeding the initiation of world government at this point in human history do not lie in the real world—rather they lie in the persistence of various preconceptions and misconceptions regarding the probable nature and characteristics of world government that are currently deeply embedded in the minds of so many people. Beliefs and attitudes that may have been perfectly sound and reasonable two hundred years ago, or even one hundred years ago, have been rendered perverse and dysfunctional by the march of time. What may have been plausible in the past is no longer plausible in the present.

What is needed might be described as a "campaign of enlightenment"—a campaign to make the majority of humanity aware of the fact that whatever may have been the case in the past, at the present time there is a reasonable preponderance of evidence in support of the practicality and desirability of a properly designed federal world government. What are the odds that a sufficient amount of enlightenment can be achieved within the foreseeable future to make world government a practical possibility within the lifetimes of the current generation of humanity? Obviously, a precise answer to this question cannot be provided. But it is reasonable to suppose that the odds on this are significantly better than is commonly appreciated at the present time.

Humanity confronts today a puzzling and portentous dilemma. Modern history has witnessed a plethora of deadly and destructive violent conflicts among nations and blocs of nations. Although the technological advance of weaponry has made these conflicts steadily more terrible, they have continued to occur. In the light of this history, still another conflict—this time involving nuclear weapons—is not at all impossible even though it would obviously be terrifically destructive. Common sense suggests a solution: form a supranational federal government composed of an overwhelming preponderance of nations. This government would suppress conflict among the nations in the same way that national governments suppress internal conflict among their citizens. But alas, there are severe obstacles to this common sense solution. The nations of the world are extremely heterogeneous: therefore, if one nation or a small group of nations gains control over the world government, and that government possesses a monopoly on heavy armament, then it would be likely to try to impose its own preferences on all nations—preferences that would be intolerable to millions if not billions of its citizens.

But the assessment of relative risk is fundamentally altered if instead of imagining an extremely powerful world government that would be essentially equivalent to a typical national government of the present day, we envision a limited federal world government that, although exhibiting all the essential characteristics of a state organization and being in fact a genuine state organization, would nevertheless share a considerable amount of effective power and authority with its member nations. Such a potential world state organization is represented by the proposed Federal Union of Democratic Nations.

The purpose of world government in this new vision is hardly to achieve in one fell swoop a millennial condition of perfect peace, prosperity, and happiness. There are no utopian delusions. It is rather merely to establish firm foundations on which to build future progress. The proposed Federal Union of Democratic Nations, even if we imagine it established with great panoply and high expectations, could not quickly abrogate all the problems of the world. What the Federal Union could do, however, is to put into the hands of humanity a new political tool that would significantly foster and facilitate gradual, evolutionary progress toward—perhaps not the abrogation—but at least the substantial amelioration of these problems. The next great step in the political evolution of human civilization upon earth could and should be the foundation of such a union.

# 2

# A Pragmatic Blueprint

## Need for Specificity

In his 1975 article "A New Paradigm for International Legal Studies: Prospects and Proposals" in the *Yale Law Journal*, the eminent international relations authority Richard Falk advised against offering "blueprints for a future world order system" on the basis that such blueprints represent "the fallacy of premature specificity."[1] A considerable period of time has elapsed between 1975 and today, and conditions are much different. Back in 1975, the Cold War was still raging, and most people in the West were fearful that if a world state existed, the USSR would attempt to take it over and utilize it as an instrument with which to impose communism on the entire world. For their part, communists in the USSR and elsewhere were fearful that a world state might be used to impose capitalism on the entire world. With the collapse of communism in the USSR in the early 1990s, these particular fears have greatly subsided. What was premature in 1975 might not be premature now.

More importantly, Falk issued his "premature specificity" injunction in the context of a discussion of Grenville Clark and Louis Sohn's *World Peace through World Law* (3rd edition, 1966): a magisterial but ultimately ineffectual appeal for world government through the mechanism of a "strengthened United Nations."[2] Clark and Sohn went through the existing United Nations charter, expanding it in great detail, and providing voluminous commentary on the expansions. Quite possibly the work of Clark and Sohn amounted to *excessive* specificity, but that is not the same thing as *premature* specificity. The fundamental problem that Falk had with the Clark-Sohn effort was that, despite its representation as a mere "strengthening" of the United Nations, it actually envisioned the transformation of the U.N. into a variety of "omnipotent world state." Clark and Sohn were insistent that the member nations must be completely disarmed, and that all heavy weaponry, especially nuclear weapons, must be concentrated under the sole control of the world government. Reasonably enough, Falk assumed that there was no possibility that the nations of the world would voluntarily disarm themselves in favor of an all-powerful world government, and he therefore dismissed the Clark-Sohn proposal as politically impossible.

This was the real problem Falk had with Clark and Sohn: it was not so much a case of their proposal being prematurely specific, as it was a case of their proposal being politically impossible. And it must be acknowledged that despite the ending of the Cold War as it existed in 1975, it is still the case today that the nations of the world will not turn over control of their weapons and armed forces to a world government. For world government to be politically feasible, it must not require this. What is needed now is a plan for world government—a blueprint, if you will—that is *not* tied to disarmament of the member nations. Such a blueprint is hardly premature at this point, rather it is vitally necessary if there is to be any significant advance within the foreseeable future beyond the contemporary international status quo. While we don't want *excessive* specificity, we do need *appropriate* specificity.

Prior to the successes of the Wright brothers and others in the early years of the twentieth century, it was a fairly commonplace speculation that the problems of heavier-than-air flight were too great ever to be overcome by human ingenuity. No less a scientific authority than William Thomson Kelvin (1824-1907), better known as Lord Kelvin, is reputed to have proclaimed in 1895: "Heavier-than-air flying machines are impossible."[3]

There are several problems involved in flight: lift, control, propulsion, power. Prior to the pioneers of the early twentieth century, several unsuccessful designs had been offered. A critical pre-condition for the successful solution of the overall problem was the development of small gasoline engines with a high ratio of power to weight. This solution to the power problem, in conjunction with solutions to the problems of lift, control and propulsion (wings, ailerons and rudders, propellers), made flight as we know it today possible. Whether or not heavier-than-air flying machines were possible could not have been determined on the basis of speculations employing the general scientific principles of the early twentieth century. It required a workable design involving solutions to the various problems of lift, control and propulsion, in combination with specific technological advances, to demonstrate conclusively that heavier-than-air flying machines were indeed possible.

Much the same is true with respect to world government. Whether or not a world government is possible and desirable cannot be determined on the basis of general principles from political and other social sciences. The fact that these principles suggest that some world government schemes are unworkable does not necessarily establish that all world government schemes are unworkable. As gasoline engines turned out to be the solution to the power problem of flight at the turn of the twentieth century, possibly the technological advances that have produced contemporary communications and transportation will turn out to be the solution to the analogous "power problem" of world government at the beginning of the twenty-first century. Even the most convinced world government skeptics have to concede that modern communications and transportation have rendered null and void the coordination problems of large-scale political organizations in the distant past. But instantaneous communications and rapid transportation do not, in themselves, make world government desirable or even possible. There are other problems that may or may not be solvable by means of a specific institutional design.

In current discussions of world government in the international relations literature, there is very little attention paid to specific institutional characteristics of world government. Perhaps this has something to do with the above-mentioned 1975 injunction against "premature specificity" of Richard Falk. Or perhaps it is because the editors and referees responsible for the professional literature have a low tolerance for institutional specifics pertaining to hypothetical world governments. If so, this is a dysfunctional attitude, in that specific design elements are indeed critical to a proper evaluation of whether world government could or should have a future in human history.

Past appeals for world government have sometimes been accompanied by specific institutional proposals, but more often have not. Some of the best-known, most elaborate and most adamant appeals for world government from the post-World War II period, such as *The Anatomy of Peace* (1945) by Emery Reves and *The Commonwealth of Man* (1952) by Frederick Schuman, are entirely devoid of any specific institutional proposals.[4] These works lambaste in great detail and most unmercifully the notion that reliable international security may be achieved by any means short of world government—and yet they are completely silent on how that government ought to be organized.

In perusing the works of Emery Reves and Frederick Schuman, as well as others of a similar nature, one might well be reminded of Karl Marx's intemperate 19th century tirades against the capitalist economic system, tirades that were unaccompanied by any significant development of a specific socialist alternative. Marx disdained the task of "writing recipes for the social chefs of the future" on grounds that any socialist system was bound to be superior to the capitalist system, and furthermore, that the appropriate institutional structure of the socialist socio-economic system would be transparently obvious to the architects of the revolution once the revolution had been successful. The subsequent history of socialism in the USSR under Stalin, and in China under Mao, clearly demonstrated that the socialist cure may well be worse than the capitalist disease. It is possible, of course, that there could be forms of socialism that would perform better than did the Soviet system under Stalin and the Chinese system under Mao. Indeed, if the social democratic definition of socialism is accepted, then socialism in this sense has performed very successfully, both economically and politically, in many nations around the world throughout the twentieth century and beyond. Be that as it may, what the experiences of Soviet Russia and Red China have demonstrated beyond reasonable doubt is that socialism, in and of itself and defined (according to most dictionary definitions) as public ownership of all or most capital property, is by no means *sufficient* to establish a social system preferable to the capitalist social system. Certainly the socialist cure *could* be worse than the capitalist disease.

In the same way, world government is by no means sufficient to establish global conditions preferable to those currently prevailing under the sovereign nation-state system. Clearly, the world government cure *could* be worse than the international anarchy disease. It follows, therefore, that any appeal for world government that is not based on a specific blueprint for world government, is likely to be quite unpersuasive. In order to avoid this problem, the present analysis will be based on a fairly detailed world government proposal. Although appeals for world government unaccompanied by specific proposals outnumber appeals that are indeed accompanied by specific proposals, there has in fact been a sufficient number of the latter put forward throughout the course of modern history as to constitute an important obstacle to focused consideration of world government. The assets and liabilities of one particular plan of world government might be very much different from those of another.

In point of fact, world government proposals are not all created equal. Some proposals, if implemented, would result in a higher probability of eventual global tyranny; other proposals would result in a lower probability. When compared to the better-known proposals for world government enunciated since World War II, the proposal under consideration herein for a Federal Union of Democratic Nations, would, if implemented, result in a very low probability of eventual degeneration into global tyranny. The originality of this particular evaluation of world government is therefore rooted directly in the originality of the proposed blueprint for a Federal Union of Democratic Nations. This implies the need for a clear and explicit understanding of this particular blueprint.[5]

## Federal Union Fundamentals

Our objective is to formulate a plan for an international political entity that would go qualitatively beyond the United Nations of today, an international organization which is primarily a mere debating society composed of ambassadors from fully sovereign nations, but at the same time would be significantly less centralized and cohesive than is the typical nation-state of today. We want to achieve a happy medium between the competing objectives of a world state sufficiently powerful and authoritative to have an important impact on the future evolution of global governance, and at the same time a world state sufficiently limited and constrained as not to represent a serious threat of degenerating into a global tyranny. In other words, we must absolutely avoid the "omnipotent world state" concept which has hitherto dominated all thinking about world government, favorable as well as unfavorable.

The terms "world government," "world state" or "world federation" are typically utilized to designate the concept under consideration here. "Global government," "global state," or "global federation" are synonymous terms less often utilized. All of these terms will be used interchangeably in this book, plus an additional term which (to my knowledge) I myself coined in prior writings: "supernational federation." This last term is somewhat more accurately descriptive than the others, especially with respect to the specific world government proposal being put forward. The problem with using "world" (or "global") as modifiers of "government," "state," or "federation" is that they imply universal membership of all nations in the world (or on the globe). But one of the fundamental characteristics of the present proposal is that it does *not necessarily* involve universal membership from the outset. The modifier "supernational" (as opposed to "international" or "supranational") clearly implies a state entity superior to the nations—yet not necessarily including all the nations in the world (or on the globe). The modifiers "world" and "global" will continue to be employed, however, to facilitate continuity with previous discussions.

Let us commence our consideration of a potential supernational federation with some fundamental matters of descriptive nomenclature and formal organization, in the understanding that these are purely tentative suggestions designed merely to foster practical conceptualization. Many of these details would likely be substantially revised in the future.

The proposed name of the federation would be the Federal Union of Democratic Nations (FUDN). The Federal Union of Democratic Nations would be a supernational government founded on the basis of a Federal

Union Constitution.

The name of the union implies that the member nations would all be democratic in nature. A fairly generous interpretation of the word "democratic" may be necessary, lest too many nations be denied membership on the basis that they are not sufficiently democratic. In a general sense, "democracy" implies that the government is responsive to the preferences of the people. But more specifically, it implies that high government officials are elected by the citizens in regular, open, contested elections, and that citizens enjoy strong and effective rights of free speech, free press, and free political organization. A substantial number of nations in the world today—even some that proclaim themselves to be "democratic"—do not exhibit these characteristics.

For example, the People's Republic of China is today regarded by many people as a political oligarchy under the effective control of a handful of high officials of the Communist Party of China. But it would be inadvisable to exclude a nation as large and important as China from the Federal Union on grounds that it is insufficiently democratic. If China is a member nation of the Federal Union of Democratic Nations, there would be stronger and more effective psychological pressure on the leadership to implement democratic reforms. The same is true of smaller nations that at the present time are not internally democratic in a strong sense. The long-run objective would be to have every nation maintaining very high domestic standards of democratic accountability of the government—but this long-run objective will be better served if considerable flexibility is practiced in the short run.

Prior to the Enlightenment period of the eighteenth century, the consensus of informed, educated opinion was that democracy, as we know it today, would be an unworkable political system. If the unwashed masses were granted significant power in political decision-making, in all likelihood they would soon succumb to irresponsible demagogues preaching the radical leveling of society—the outcome from which would surely be catastrophic civil war. In the interest of security and stability, therefore, some form of dictatorial or oligarchic government (for example, absolute monarchy or constitutional monarchy) was essential. As we know, this conventional wisdom gradually eroded as time proceeded and societies evolved, so that in our time the virtues of democratic governance seem so obvious to most informed, educated people as hardly to be worth debating. In line with this dominant consensus, I will forego attempting to justify the desirability of implementing the democratic principle in global governance. However, as will be apparent in the discussion to follow of "dual voting" in the global legislature, some modification of "pure" democracy is perceived to be necessary to deal with existing global economic inequality. Such a level of extreme inequality, however, is manifestly unhealthy, and in fact its reduction would be one of the primary objectives of the Federal Union during its early period.

The proposed Federal Union would be a full-fledged, genuine, legitimate state entity with clearly defined geographical boundaries (assuming some non-member nations), a permanent and continuous governmental structure, the power to levy taxes and enact binding legislation, and the authority to maintain standing military forces under its direct command. As the name suggests, it would be a federal rather than a unitary form of government. This means that the member nations would maintain their separate identities, governments, and cultures, and would retain substantial independence, autonomy, and sovereignty in all matters that do not impinge significantly on the welfare of other member nations.

The Federal Union Constitution would comprise five principal sections: (1) nature and purposes of the Union; (2) the three branches of government (legislative, executive, and judicial); (3) powers and responsibilities of the supernational government; (4) rights and responsibilities of nations; (5) rights and responsibilities of citizens. Two absolutely essential components of the articles concerning rights and responsibilities of nations would be: (1) the permanent and inalienable right of a member nation to withdraw peacefully from the Federal Union at its own unilateral discretion; and (2) the permanent and inalienable right of a member nation to maintain whatever military forces and armaments, including nuclear, it deems necessary to its national interests. These two substantive rights would be the practical, de facto guarantors of other national rights. As central elements of the world government proposal under consideration, they will be discussed in some detail below.

As a full-fledged state entity, the government of the Federal Union of Democratic Nations would incorporate the standard tripartite structure of legislative, executive, and judicial branches. It is suggested that world government elections be held on a quinquennial basis (every five years), and that the highest officials of all three branches of government be democratically elected directly by the citizens. Elections would either be "0 year elections" (2020, 2030, etc.) or "5 year elections" (2025, 2035, etc.). In "5 year elections," each of the Union Districts would elect its Union Representative to a 5-year term, and 5 seats on the 25-seat Union High Court would be up for election to 25-year terms. The "0 year elections" would be the same as the "5 year elections" except for the fact that in the former, the entire population of the Federal Union would also elect a single Union Chief Executive to head the executive branch for a 10-year term.

The legislature would be a unicameral body, designated the Union

Chamber of Representatives, consisting of approximately 200 Union Representatives. The Union Chamber would have the power to make laws and issue policy directives within its area of authority, as well as the power to alter and amend the annual financial budget prepared by the executive branch. The Union Chief Executive would be responsible for preparing budgets, for enforcing laws and implementing policy directives approved by the Union Chamber of Representatives, and (through direction of the Union Security Force) for maintaining the internal peace and external security of the Union. The Union High Court would serve as a court of last appeal on those matters within its area of authority, including the constitutionality of legislation and policy directives approved by the Union Chamber of Representatives.

## Major Issues

### Representation and Voting

Although a unicameral legislature is envisioned for the supernational federation legislature, some of the virtues of bicameralism—without incurring its inherent unwieldiness and divisiveness—would be captured by the proposed "dual voting system."[6] Whenever a vote is taken in the Union Chamber of Representatives, the measure being considered would have to be approved by a majority, possibly by more than a 51 percent majority, on two different bases: the population basis and the material basis. In the population vote, the weight given to the vote of each particular Union Representative would be proportional to the population of his/her Union district, relative to the total population of the Federal Union. In the material vote, the weight given to the vote of each particular Union Representative would be proportional to the financial revenues derived from his/her Union district, relative to the total financial revenues of the Federal Union. Union Representatives from the rich nations would be disproportionately represented in the material vote, while Union Representatives from populous poorer nations would be disproportionately represented in the population vote. Since measures would have to be approved on both the material basis and the population basis, only measures on which rich nations and poor nations could achieve a reasonable degree of consensus would have a chance of being approved by the Union Chamber of Representatives. This would protect the vital national interests of both the rich and the poor nations. Either category could in effect veto a proposition favored by the other category.[7]

The dual voting mechanism combines two intuitively appealing principles: the population vote would implement the principle of political egalitarianism underlying universal suffrage in the modern democracies; while the material vote would implement the equally sensible principle that those who pay more to support a government's activities should have a proportionately larger say in determining that government's activities. The latter principle, of course, however "sensible" it might be, is contrary to the principle of political egalitarianism, and as such has rarely been formally implemented in real-world political institutions. Informally, however, the essence of the concept has often been implemented through property restrictions on the voting right. In addition, there has been throughout modern political history a number of examples of an "upper house" of a bicameral legislature representing the interests of that minority of the population on whom heredity has bestowed aristocratic distinctions.

The most obvious short-term motivation for the dual voting principle is to impede possible efforts by populous poorer nations to impose radical redistribution on the rich nations through a "global welfare state," and also to impede the rich nations from passing legislation that is unacceptable to the poor nations—for example, because it would recreate the exploitative conditions of the colonial era. But it is important to realize that if the per capita income among the various member nations of the Federal Union were relatively comparable, then the proportion of Union revenues raised in a given District would become proportional to the District's population, and no systematic differences would be observed between the population and the material votes. This is the long-run aspiration of the economic complement to the political Federal Union proposal: a Global Marshall Plan. (The Global Marshall Plan proposal will be described and evaluated later in this chapter.) Until the economic equalization objective has been achieved through the operation of the Global Marshall Plan, the dual voting provision provides some of the benefits of bicameralism, in terms of ensuring adequate representation of different interests, without incurring the ponderous unwieldiness and inherent divisiveness of bicameralism.

An obvious skeptical reaction to the dual voting proposal is that it would lead to legislative gridlock: the failure of the legislature to pass anything beyond the most trivial and unimportant legislation. Granting that this is a definite possibility, the question remains why this would be inferior to the present situation, in which any kind of global legislation at all is impossible because there is no such thing as a global legislature. If the rich nations and the poor nations would be unable to agree on anything even if they were united within a world government, it seems inescapable that they will also be unable to agree on anything if they are fully autonomous states under the sovereign nation-state system. At any rate, such extreme pessimism is clearly unwarranted. Even under the sovereign nation-state system of today, an appreciable amount of consensus has been achieved—on some issues—among the rich nations and the poor nations.

The regional components of the Federal Union would comprise approximately 200 Union Districts. These Union Districts quite possibly would have little or no administrative significance, but might merely be regions from which legislators are elected. Some large nations would contain several Union Districts; on the other hand, several smaller nations might be needed to comprise a single Union District. For the most part, nations in the same Union District would be territorially contiguous—but not necessarily. In some cases, historical, economic, or cultural factors may override geographical proximity.

As of the early 2000s, there were something over 200 sovereign and independent nations in the world. The above-proposed number of Union Districts is approximately 200. The juxtaposition of these two numbers might suggest that it would be natural to define each Union District as corresponding to a single nation. However, owing to the tremendous disparity of populations over the contemporary nations of the world, such an arrangement would seem patently absurd to most people. It would mean that there would be one Union Representative from China, a nation with a population well over one billion persons, and at the same time one Union Representative from Monaco, a nation of less than 50,000 persons. Therefore, it is envisioned that Union Districts would *not* coincide with nations. In the case of larger nations, more than one Union District would be encompassed within the national boundaries. In the case of the smallest nations, several nations would be required to form one Union District.

On the other hand, we would probably not want the Union Districts to be defined in such a way that they all have approximately the same population. For if we were to do this, the most populous nations would be disproportionately represented. To illustrate, at the present time the People's Republic of China contains over 20 percent of the world's population. If the Union Chamber of Representatives were to number 200 representatives from Union Districts of approximately equal population, there would be approximately 40 representatives from China. This seems to be too high a number from a single nation, even if that nation is by far the most populous in the world. Another problem with requiring all Union Districts to have nearly the same population is that it would mean that a great many nations would not have even one complete Union District within their boundaries. World population as of the year 2000 was estimated to be approximately 6 billion persons. If we assume 200 Federal Union Districts, the average population over the Districts (had there been a Federal Union in existence in 2000) would have been 30 million persons. As of 2000, of the 200-odd sovereign and independent nations in the world, only 36 had populations of 30 million or greater.

One possibility would be to specify that every nation with a population over a specified minimum (such as 5 million) would have at least one complete Union District within its borders, while for nations with populations substantially over 5 million, the relationship between population and number of Union Districts would be specified in such a way that the number of Union Districts would be a positive but diminishing function of population (a "concave" function). For example, if we divided each national population (for the year 2000) by 5,000,000, raised the result to the power of 0.35, and rounded the result downward to the nearest integer, then China and India would each have 6 Union Districts, the United States 4, the next 7 most populous nations would have 3 Union Districts each, the next 21 most populous nations would have 2 Union Districts each, and the next 79 most populous nations would have 1 Union District each, for a total of 158 Union Districts. This would allow 117 nations to have at least one full Union District within their borders. The remaining 42 Union Districts would be allocated over the remaining nations, which number approximately 90.

In cases where smaller nations have to "share" their Union Representative with other nations, obviously every effort should be made to ensure that the nations thus sharing one representative will be homogeneous in important respects, so that their national interests would be relatively uniform. Nevertheless, it is certainly conceivable that some nations would decline to join the Federal Union of Democratic Nations on grounds that owing to their small populations, they would not have representatives in the Union Chamber of Representatives devoted exclusively to their own national interests. If this is an issue for a substantial number of small nations, one way to deal with it would be to inflate the number of Union Districts, and hence the number of Union Representatives in the Chamber. The obvious problem with this is that the more individuals are in the legislature, the more difficult it will be for them to achieve consensus and make operational decisions.

In the final analysis, it must be recognized that there is no possible way to determine representation in the Chamber, and voting weights of Union Representatives, in such a manner that every citizen of every potential member nation will be completely happy. Quite possibly a significant number of nations will in fact decline membership in the Federal Union for one reason or another—including issues of representation and voting weight. This need not compromise the effectiveness of the Union as far as its larger purposes are concerned. If some small nations stay out of the Union because they are worried that their interests will not be adequately served, this is not necessarily a serious problem. According to World Bank data, there were 55 nations as of 2000 that had populations less than 1,000,000, while 19 nations out of this 55 had populations less than 100,000. If a number of these small nations were to stay out of the Union, the Union could operate effectively without them.

## National Right of Secession

One of the most fundamental objections to the proposal for a world federation under consideration herein is that any state entity that was not prepared to forcibly prevent the departure of its subsidiary units would lack what is perhaps the most basic and essential characteristic of a state. It is quintessential, in this view, of a state entity that it be completely determined to preserve its territorial integrity at all costs. However commonplace this viewpoint might be at the present time, it is not valid. A state, whether it be at the national or the supernational level, can be a legitimate, genuine, authentic, and effective political organization in the absence of any determination to utilize force to suppress independence movements in subsidiary regions.[8]

Think, for example, of the nation of Canada. A very large and important province in Canada, the province of Quebec, has been toying seriously with the possibility of independence for several decades. The major basis for this separatist leaning is the fact that the predominant language among the population of Quebec is French, whereas the predominant language among the population of the rest of Canada is English. No knowledgeable person, either in Quebec, or in the rest of Canada, or in the rest of the world, expects that if Quebec does in fact ultimately declare its independence, the national government of Canada will employ its armed forces to keep Quebec within the Canadian federation. But the expectation that potential secession would not be opposed by military force does not mean that Canada is any less a nation. If Quebec leaves Canada, Canada would carry on as a nation with its 11 remaining provinces and territories, which together account for approximately 85 percent of the Canadian land area, and approximately 75 percent of the Canadian population. Although the loss of 15 percent of its land area and 25 percent of its population would not be a happy event for most English-speaking Canadians, one consolation might be that it would no longer be necessary for the nation to maintain two official languages.[9]

What I would suggest is that if and when it is founded in the future, the Federal Union of Democratic Nations should regard possible secessions by individual nations much as the English-speaking population of Canada presently regards possible secession by the province of Quebec: as an unfortunate and undesirable eventuality that is certainly to be avoided if at all possible—but nevertheless as survivable and certainly not worth the costs that would be involved in its forcible prevention. There is actually no alternative to taking this attitude if the world government is to be established. The membership door must be left permanently open, and traffic must be permitted to move freely through this door in both directions.

If the Federal Union evolves as intended, within a relatively brief period there would be strong economic, social, political, and psychological links between the member nations and the supernational federation. Leaving the federation would be by no means costless to the nation, even though it would not have to fight for its independence. For one thing, leaving the Federal Union would take the newly independent nation out of the common market within the Union. As a non-member nation, its exports to Federal Union member nations would be subject to some degree of tariff imposition. We have seen, in the evolution of the European Union, the decisive importance that access to a free trade area can come to have even to nations with a strong nationalistic tradition.[10]

Admittedly, it may require a certain amount of mental flexibility and imagination to fully comprehend how a world government could be tolerant and flexible with respect to its membership, and yet be a meaningful and effective state organization. When we reflect on the concept of "independence," a variety of images and scenarios come to mind, based on both historical and current events. These images and scenarios certainly do not suggest that the condition of independence is ordinarily either won or lost in the absence of military conflict.

Individual citizens, of course, do not have the right to declare themselves independent of the political authority of the locality in which they reside. Occasionally, small groups of citizens who hold personal ownership rights over a certain area of land will proclaim a sovereign and independent state entity located on that area of land. This is typically a form of protest against prevailing laws or taxes. If the "founding fathers" of these micro-states do not soon desist, they usually end up either in prison or mental asylums. Normally such endeavors are not viewed very sympathetically by the majority of citizens. Clearly, if such endeavors were tolerated and thereupon proliferated on a large scale, society might soon devolve into a quasi-anarchic condition.

When it comes, however, to large political entities declaring their independence from still larger political entities in which they had previously been incorporated, this is no trivial matter. Human history is filled with wars fought to gain or prevent independence. Contemporary viewpoints on specific wars of independence vary depending on both the individual and on the circumstances of the war. For example, most American citizens today regard the Revolutionary War of 1775 to 1783, which secured the independence of the thirteen original American colonies from Britain, to have been an unquestionably beneficial episode not merely for the United States but for world civilization as a whole. British citizens today, while not usually inclined to dispute the benefits, understandably tend to be less enthusiastic about them. Meanwhile, most American citizens today regard the U.S. Civil War of 1861 to 1865, which forcibly prevented the Southern states from leaving the Union, to also have been an unquestionably beneficial episode not merely for the United States as a whole, but for the Southern states as well. Citizens of the Southern states today, while not usually inclined to dispute the benefits, understandably tend to be less enthusiastic about them.

More often than not throughout history, wars of independence have been fought by the populations of certain regions against those large political entities known as "empires." The American Revolutionary War, for example, was fought to attain the independence of the American colonies from the British empire. Throughout history, both the construction and the destruction of empires have typically been accompanied by violence and bloodshed. One of the major obstacles to the formation of a world state in our time is the extremely widespread preconception that a real-world world state would be equivalent to an empire. According to the standard dictionary definition, an "empire" is a political organization incorporating a wide diversity of peoples and subsidiary political units. The standard dictionary definition does *not* state that an empire governs without the consent of the governed, engages in exploitation of most of the incorporated peoples, and relies heavily on force and the threat of force to maintain compliance with its dominion. Nevertheless, the word "empire," in the minds of most people, carries strong connotations of exactly these characteristics.

Thus it is obvious that a world government will only be possible if most people can be convinced that such a government would be nothing like any of the numerous empires which have come and gone throughout human history. The critical distinction between the Federal Union of Democratic Nations envisioned here, and the typical historical empire, is that the former would be democratically accountable to the entire population of the Union. The right to vote would be held by every adult citizen in good standing. All three branches of government (legislative, executive, and judicial) would be headed by individuals elected by the citizens in free and open elections. Empires, on the other hand, have been democratically accountable only to a small minority of their populations—if any at all. In extremely centralized cases, which have been the rule rather than the exception, empires were governed by "emperors" equivalent to kings in the era of absolute monarchy, or to dictators in the modern era.

An interesting "what if" historical question, in this context, is the following: Would the American Revolutionary War have taken place if elected representatives from the American colonies had been seated as voting members of the British Parliament? Quite possibly not, in view of the fact that one of leading slogans of the restive colonists, during the years leading up to the Revolutionary War, was "No taxation without representation!"[11] There were two principal problems with adding Members of Parliament from the American colonies during that era. The first was distance: the American colonies were physically separated from the British government in London by the Atlantic Ocean, the crossing of which entailed a dangerous ocean voyage of several weeks' duration. Therefore, it would have been clumsy obtaining input from the American colonies on legislation applying in both the British Isles and the American colonies.

The second problem was that the democratic principle was still quite feeble and undeveloped in the era of the American Revolution. Property requirements for the franchise kept all but a small minority of the population of the British Isles from voting in Parliamentary elections. Parliament itself was still relatively weak vis-a-vis the monarch, and the reigning British monarch of the time, George III, was determined that policy toward the American colonies should mainly be set by the monarchy rather than Parliament. Therefore, there were never any voting representatives from the American colonies in the British Parliament, the American Revolutionary War commenced, it ground onward for several years, at its conclusion Britain recognized the independence of the American colonies.

When we compare the circumstances of the American Revolutionary War with those which would prevail were a world government to be established along the lines of the proposed Federal Union of Democratic Nations, we recognize that it would be virtually impossible for the circumstances which led to the American Revolutionary War to be replicated. There are two main reasons for this. First, the world government would be democratically accountable to its entire population throughout the world via free and open elections. There would be no such thing as "taxation without representation." Owing to the tremendous advances in transportation and communications since the time of the American Revolutionary War, there would be no problems of coordination in having representatives from all parts of the world sitting in the Federal Union's legislative body. In today's world, representatives from even the remotest nations could travel to the Federal Union's capital city in one or two days. Moreover, communications among all parts of the world are virtually instantaneous.

Second, all member nations would hold an explicit constitutional right to secession (withdrawal) from the world federation. It is hardly unimaginable that the world federation—despite being democratically accountable, or perhaps even *because* it is democratically accountable—would implement legislation and policies unacceptable to some nations. The fact that certain legislation and policies are desired by a substantial majority on both the population voting basis and the material voting basis by no means guarantees that they would be not be completely unacceptable to the populations of some nations. If that happened, these nations would be able to peacefully depart the Federal Union. It is difficult to imagine that the American colonies would have been impelled to fight for their independence in 1775 if they had had voting representatives in the British Parliament at that time. It is even more difficult to imagine that if Britain had had a written constitution in 1775 which stated that the American colonies had a right to declare their independence at any time, and the American colonies had chosen to exercise that right, the British government would nevertheless have employed military force to try to block independence.

Let us now move the time frame of U.S. history forward to the 1860s. The U.S. Civil War of 1861-1865 was one of the bloodiest and most destructive wars of the 19th century. For skeptics of world government, the U.S. Civil War provides an instructive lesson on the probable fate of a future world government. Prospects for the success of the United States in 1788 (the year of the final ratification of the present U.S. Constitution) were highly auspicious. The thirteen original states of United States shared a common language, a common heritage, geographical contiguity, and had cooperated closely in waging the war for independence. And yet, despite all of these advantages, after only a little over seven decades of operation, the United States was engulfed in a bitter civil war brought about by the effort of the Southern states to establish their independence. How clear it is, therefore, say skeptics of world federation, that if such a federation were established, it would eventually dissolve and degenerate into bitter civil war.

There are two major flaws in the argument that a world government would necessarily follow the path followed by the United States into the Civil War of 1861-1865. First, the constitution of the world federation considered here (the Federal Union of Democratic Nations), in contrast to the United States Constitution, would explicitly allow member nations to declare their independence from the world federation at any time they desire. The U.S. Constitution was silent on the issue of whether member states would or would not be permitted to secede peacefully from the United States. Had the U.S. Constitution explicitly stated that any move by a state toward independence would be forcibly suppressed, it is quite possible that the Southern states, being fully aware of the fact that they would have to fight hard to achieve independence, would have been more conciliatory and susceptible to compromise. At the time the U.S. Constitution was formulated, however, there was a great deal of apprehension about the federal government being too strong, and therefore putting into the Constitution an explicit anti-secession provision might have eliminated any possibility of ratification.

On the other hand, had the U.S. Constitution explicitly stated that any move by a state toward independence would be unopposed by the federal government, it is quite possible that the Northern states, being fully aware of the fact that they would have no legal right to oppose secession, would have been more conciliatory and susceptible to compromise. Whether the U.S. Constitution had explicitly forbidden secession or explicitly condoned secession, quite probably the conflict between the Northern and Southern states would not have escalated to the point where secession actually occurred. It follows, therefore, that the provision in the Federal Union constitution explicitly allowing secession by member nations will, in all likelihood, prevent the escalation of conflicts to the point where actual secessions occur. And this provision, at the same time, makes it highly unlikely that in the unfortunate event that secessions *do* occur, they will be opposed with military force.

The second flaw in the argument that a potential world federation will follow the path the United States followed into civil war, is that it neglects the overriding role that the institution of slavery played in the degeneration of relations between the Northern and Southern states to the point of secession and civil war.[12] What was not foreseen by the U.S. founding fathers was that the rise of cotton cultivation for export in the Southern states, during the early decades of the republic, would greatly enhance the profitability of slavery, thus giving that reprehensible institution a new lease on life. At the time the U.S. Constitution went into effect, it was widely assumed that the United States would fairly quickly follow the lead of the rest of the civilized world and abolish slavery. It was assumed that the abolition would be peaceful, because of the marginal profitability of slavery.

Unfortunately, the invention of the cotton gin by Eli Whitney greatly changed the business calculus of slavery. Soon, the manifest conflict between the political ideals of liberty and equality on which the nation was supposedly founded, and the economic self-interest of the Southern plantation owners, resulted in continuing acrimonious controversy which bedeviled the young republic. The slavery issue became a bitter moral issue, with each side accusing the other of base and unworthy motivations. When the Southern states eventually declared their independence, it was not because they were in immediate fear that slavery would be abolished by the new Republican presidential administration of Abraham Lincoln, but rather because they simply could not tolerate any more questioning and criticizing of slavery—and Lincoln's administration would certainly engage in a great deal of questioning and criticizing of slavery. And when the Northern states went to war to prevent Southern independence, it was not primarily to preserve the Union, as such, but rather to thwart the selfish determination of the Southern gentry to perpetuate the evil and demeaning institution of slavery. It was the incendiary issue of slavery which made the U.S. Civil War of 1861-1865 inevitable—not the innate unwillingness of state entities to permit subsidiary entities to establish their independence.

At the present moment in world history, there is no political issue on the horizon that will be as controversial and emotional, over the next several decades, as was the slavery issue in American politics in the decades leading up to the Civil War. There is no nation on the face of the globe, of course, in which slavery is legal. This is hardly to say that full racial equality has been achieved in every nation of the world. But the principle of full racial equality is accepted by almost all properly educated people, and gradual progress is being made in most nations toward the practical implementation of this principle. In addition, most of humanity seems to have made peace with itself on the matter of religion. None of the major organized religions in the world today has on its official agenda the suppression of all other religions throughout the world. Even in the handful of nations in which governance is dominated by clerics, there is no serious policy or intention to export this system to other nations. Until very recently, the ideological controversy between communism and noncommunism was a major factor in world politics. In fact, if at some point during the Cold War from the 1950s through the 1980s, accident or miscalculated brinkmanship had ignited a nuclear holocaust which hobbled global human civilization, ideological disagreement over the issue of social ownership of capital property could have been plausibly cited as the decisive factor in bringing about the catastrophe. It can certainly be said that from the world perspective, the issue of socialism was just as pivotal and potentially explosive during the latter half of the twentieth century, as was the issue of slavery in the United States during the first half of the nineteenth century. But with the abandonment of socialism and communism by the USSR in the 1990s, ideological controversy has become a dramatically less important factor in international politics. Even within the handful of nations that continue adhering to communistic socialism, there is apparently no intention of exporting this socioeconomic system to other nations.

The fact that there are no political controversies in the world today comparable to the slavery controversy in the nineteenth century and the socialism controversy in the twentieth century, makes it much less likely that a world federation established at the present time will follow the same path that the early United States followed to the Civil War of 1861-1865. This does not imply, however, that worldwide human civilization in the future will remain forever free of political controversies within or among nations of such intensity and emotionalism as to generate armed conflict. In fact, one important reason why we should form a supernational federation now—while we have the chance—is to forestall the development of such controversies in the future. The Federal Union of Democratic Nations would be a major force for the peaceful elimination of unacceptable institutions and practices (such as slavery). At the same time—still more importantly—it would be a major force for the permanent maintenance of toleration and flexibility in areas where no compelling evidence exists for the superiority of one form over another: examples include the varieties of religion, and social versus private ownership of capital property.

## *National Right of Armament*

The standard view among "world government traditionalists" is that the establishment of the world state would be accompanied by the immediate and total disarmament of nations. Most weapons of mass destruction (such as nuclear weapons) would be dismantled and destroyed, but a small proportion would be taken over by the military arm of the world government. With the nations deprived of heavy armament, presumably the world government would not require a great deal of military power to maintain peace and order. No longer would human civilization lie in the shadow of nuclear holocaust. The problem perceived by the vast majority of the human population with this scenario, however, is that while human civilization would no longer lie in the shadow of nuclear holocaust, it *would* now lie in the shadow of global tyranny imposed by a totalitarian world government.

Therefore, it is an absolutely indispensable component of the present proposal for a Federal Union of Democratic Nations that the member nations possess a permanent and inalienable right to maintain whatever military forces and weapons—including nuclear weapons—that they feel it necessary to maintain, for as long as they feel it necessary. The hope is that slowly and gradually, nations will voluntarily disarm, until at some future point the armaments of nations will be reduced to a very low level which could legitimately be described as inconsequential. But the objective of major disarmament (as opposed to "complete" disarmament—which may forever be impossible) would be a very long-term goal of the Federal Union, to be pursued in a relaxed and unhurried manner.

The idea of reducing the threat of war through formal disarmament treaties among nations came into prominence in the latter part of the nineteenth century. The immediate impetus to this was the arms competition which developed among the major European powers in the wake of German unification at the time of the Franco-Prussian War of 1871. The German people, personified by Kaiser Wilhelm II, were determined that newly united Germany be just as much feared and respected as the three historic superpowers of the European continent: Britain, France and Russia. Thus it became necessary for Germany to have overseas colonies, and a strong navy to protect its overseas interests, and a strong land army to deter the foreign armies which for centuries had marched with impunity to and fro over German territory. The balance of power established by the 1815 Treaty of Vienna following the defeat of Napoleonic France, was thrown into disarray. Other nations found it necessary to build up their own forces lest Germany start dictating unacceptable terms. By 1900, all the major European powers, not just the superpowers, found it necessary to maintain large-scale military forces armed with increasingly sophisticated and destructive weaponry. To the more perceptive and prescient people of the period, the arms competition, in and of itself, was increasing the threat of war. And, of course, if war *did* occur among nations with such formidable military forces, the costs could be horrific.

Toward the end of the nineteenth century, therefore, appeals for international measures to slow or even halt the accumulation of military power were becoming increasingly common. But it was not until the leader of a major European power, Czar Nicholas II of Russia, called for an international conference to control armaments that one actually took place. In fact, two Hague Disarmament Conferences were held, in 1899 and 1907. A planned third conference was cancelled, however, because the would-be conferees were busy fighting World War I (1914-1918). World War I did not terminate human civilization, as had been warned by some alarmists, but it certainly imposed a great deal of pain, suffering, death, and destruction upon human civilization.

Although all of the major military powers had participated in the Hague Conferences of 1899 and 1907, little of substance had been accomplished. The two Hague Conferences not only did not forestall the advent of World War I, but they did not noticeably reduce the carnage of that conflict. No agreements were reached limiting machine guns and other automatic weapons, artillery, bombs, airplanes, capital ships, or submarines. No agreements could have been reached regarding tanks, which were invented later on, during the course of World War I. Despite an agreement not to use poison gas, poison gas was in fact utilized. A ban on aerial bombardment from balloons was observed, but this was only because airplanes and dirigibles proved to be far more effective means for the delivery of bombs than unpowered balloons. Even if detailed provisions for the limitation of weapons had been agreed to at the Hague Conferences, it is doubtful that they would have had any effect. There was no provision for the enforcement of any of the agreements reached, and amid the increasing rancor and tension among the major European powers in the years just prior to 1914, the agreements would most likely have been ignored.

The futility of the Hague Conferences provides a lesson on the limited effectiveness of disarmament efforts—in and of themselves—in those situations where nothing is done (or can be done) to alleviate the root causes of hostility and conflict among nations. In medical terms, disarmament efforts are an effort to treat symptoms of the disease, as opposed to treating the disease itself. The disease in this case is the normal suspicion, distrust, hostility, and conflict that naturally emerges from a system of sovereign and independent nation-states, all of whom are keenly aware of their rightful and legitimate national interests, and all of whom are determined that deadly force can and will be utilized against any nation which presumes to challenge these interests. Arms races are a consequence of bad attitudes.

The post-World War I history of the twentieth century provides further evidence on the limited effectiveness of disarmament efforts in the absence of progress toward the amelioration of basic sources of conflict.[13] During the two decades separating World War I (1914-1918) from World War II (1939-1945), the major powers, shocked by what they had done to themselves in 1914-1918, endeavored to forestall a repetition of the catastrophe. Unfortunately, they left fully intact the root cause of the "Great War": the sovereign nation-state system. They established a League of Nations, but this was not a functional world government, but merely a formalized and institutionalized international alliance. The long history of international alliances in human affairs had demonstrated their frailty when one or more major participants—as normally occurs in the evolving course of events—decides that it is no longer in their immediate national interest to participate. The United States decided, for example, even before the League was formally established, that participation would not be in its immediate national interest. The fact that the United States was not a member of the League of Nations hobbled that organization from the beginning.

In retrospect, one of the more fatuous projects of the interwar period was the Kellogg-Briand Pact of 1928, signed by a host of nations, large and small, renouncing war as an instrument of foreign policy. (Many nations attached qualifications regarding defensive wars and/or wars to pre serve "vital national interests.") Among the 63 signatories to the Kellogg-Briand Pact were Germany, Italy, and Japan, nations which a short while later instigated World War II. The fact provided an object lesson in the fact that solemn statements of commendable principles may have little or no effect on the outcome, presuming no change in the substantive conditions which tend to generate violations of these commendable principles.

The interwar period also witnessed several multilateral disarmament conferences in the tradition of the Hague Conferences. These were held variously in Washington, London, and Geneva. The Washington conferences of the early 1920s endeavored to set limits on the number of battleships in the navies of the great powers. These capital ships were regarded by the disarmament experts of the time as especially promising candidates for arms limitation agreements, owing both to the tremendous costs of construction, and to the virtual impossibility of concealing these huge ships. A 1924 treaty established a 5-5-3 ratio as between Britain, the United States, and Japan. That is, for every 5 battleships possessed by Britain and the United States, Japan could have 3 battleships. When in the 1930s, the Japanese government was swept away by the concept of a Japanese empire in Asia (the "Greater East Asia Co-Prosperity Sphere"), it withdrew from disarmament negotiations and commenced building all the battleships it wanted. In any event, naval warfare in the Pacific theater during World War II established the dominance of the aircraft carrier, a type of capital ship ignored by the naval disarmament conferences of the 1920s. Those conferences also neglected submarines, which were another major factor during World War II.

In 1932, after nearly ten years of preliminary discussions under the auspices of the League of Nations, a World Disarmament Conference was commenced in Geneva. The intention was to establish numerical limitations on all types of weapons: land, sea, and air. Any and all hope quickly foundered on the determination of Germany, controlled from January 1933 onward by Adolf Hitler, to throw off the arms limitations imposed by the Treaty of Versailles following World War I. Hitler ordered the German delegation home from the Geneva disarmament conference, withdrew Germany from the League of Nations, and commenced a massive and comprehensive rearmament drive.

The aftermath of World War II was, in important respects, a carbon copy of the aftermath of World War I. Humanity was shocked and horrified by what it had just done to itself, and was determined to avoid future repetitions of catastrophic warfare. The advent of nuclear weapons intensified the sense of urgency. Prior to nuclear weapons, few had taken seriously the warning of peace advocates that civilization itself could be destroyed by modern warfare. In light of what atomic bombs had done to the Japanese cities of Hiroshima and Nagasaki in 1945, these warnings were taken far more seriously than ever before. Despite intensified apprehensions regarding the potential consequences of unrestricted warfare, however, humanity regretfully concluded that no viable alternative existed to the sovereign nation-state system. The post-World War I League of Nations was replaced by the post-World War II United Nations, an organization based on essentially the same principles as the defunct League. The only major difference was that the United States was a charter member and driving force behind the United Nations, whereas it had declined to join the League.

Just as hopes for major disarmament in the interwar period eventually foundered on German intransigence, hopes for major disarmament in the postwar period foundered on Russian intransigence. Germany had been forcibly disarmed after World War I, and more than a decade passed before it commenced the rearmament program which contributed to the onset of World War II. Russia, on the other hand, was a member of the victorious "Grand Alliance" of World War II. At the end of the war, it was armed to the teeth, and owing to the vituperative ideological conflict with the non-communist nations in which Russia was embroiled, it was most disinclined to disarm. By 1950, Russia was a nuclear power, and by 1960 it was well advanced in missile technology. By the early 1960s, the basic groundwork had been laid for instantaneous nuclear Armageddon.

For more than 30 years, humanity lived in the shadow of nuclear destruction, of catastrophe far beyond anything experienced in the past, of an unimaginable setback so comprehensive and devastating as quite possibly to set humanity sliding irretrievably back toward barbarism or even physical extinction. As in previous times, disarmament negotiations were undertaken among the superpowers in an effort to reduce the risk.[14] Some progress was made in the limited nuclear test ban treaty of 1963, the nuclear nonproliferation treaty of 1968, the first Strategic Arms Limitation Treaty of 1972. The SALT agreements were signed and implemented while the Cold War was still at its height. (Although SALT II was never formally ratified by the U.S. Senate owing to the 1979 Soviet incursion into Afghanistan, its provisions were respected by both sides.)

Two factors seem to have been instrumental in making these agreements possible. First, the development of very capable surveillance satellites made it unlikely that either the United States or the Soviet Union could successfully cheat on the imposed missile limitations. Second, it was generally believed by both sides that the existing sizes of nuclear arsenals, in view of the destructive power of these weapons, was more than adequate to deter the other side. Although the SALT treaties were definitely a step in the right direction, their significance should not be over-estimated. Just as the naval arms limitation agreements of the 1920s had little apparent impact on the destructiveness of the Second World War, quite possibly the nuclear weapons agreements of the 1970s would have had little apparent impact on the destructiveness of the Third World War—had one occurred.

The rapid decline of the Cold War in the aftermath of the collapse and disintegration of the Soviet Union in 1991 certainly improved the prospects for substantial arms reduction by the two nuclear superpowers, the United States and the Russian Federation, either with or without benefit of formal treaties. The various START treaties (Strategic Arms Reduction Treaty) of 1991, 1993, and 2010 ("New START"), between the same two nuclear superpowers as the SALT treaties, are quite ambitious, but have not yet been fully ratified and implemented. Even were the most optimistic objectives of these treaties to be realized, there would still be an adequate sufficiency of operational nuclear weapons available to inflict catastrophe on human civilization should they be utilized.

The same underlying rationale that justifies the United States and Russia maintaining large nuclear arsenals, despite the demise of the Cold War, would justify various other nations adopting the same rationale. Several nations have already taken the step. Hindu India and Muslim Pakistan have been at odds over Kashmir ever since independence and partition in 1948. Relations between India and China have also been fraught over the years. China, as the number two power in the communist camp, felt it needed nuclear weapons—for the same reason that Britain and France in the non-communist camp felt they needed them. Since China had nuclear weapons, India felt it needed them. Because India had nuclear weapons, Pakistan felt it needed them.

Israel needs nuclear weapons to deter the surrounding Arab nations. Therefore, the surrounding Arab nations may need nuclear weapons lest Israel become expansionist-minded. Bosnia may need nuclear weapons to protect itself against Serbia, and vice versa. And so it goes. Most nations of the world have signed the Nuclear Nonproliferation Treaty of 1968. But that treaty is a slender reed on which to depend, because for a number of nations there are compelling reasons to acquire and maintain at least a minimum nuclear capability. These nations may not be dissuaded forever from taking this route.

This is a difficult situation, and I am certainly not saying that the establishment of a world government along the lines of the Federal Union of Democratic Nations would quickly and radically improve the situation. The proposed Federal Union would allow its member nations to maintain whatever armaments they desire under their own direct control. At the same time, there is no guarantee that the Federal Union would succeed. Quite possibly, after a brief "honeymoon period," the various conflicts of interest among the member nations—conflicts of interest that we see constantly at work in the world today—would reassert themselves and cause the departure from the Union of several important member nations. If secession were to become sufficiently prevalent, this could well lead to the remaining Federal Union dissolving itself in despair. Under the circumstances, nations today could not place undue reliance on the Federal Union to protect them against both historical and potential adversaries. It seems inevitable, therefore, that many militarily powerful nations—even if they join the Federal Union with a certain amount of commitment—will exercise their right to maintain substantial military forces. We can expect the nuclear powers to remain nuclear powers.

This is not a problem—in the sense that it is not an argument against world government. We are confronted with a choice between an armed world without a world government in operation, or an armed world with a world government in operation. The hope of every informed and reasonable person in the world today is that as international hostility and tension gradually fade, the level of armaments maintained by the nations will gradually decline. Both the threat of war and the potential destructiveness of war, it is hoped, will slowly subside. The argument put forward here is that an operational world government will increase the probability of this potential outcome. The world state would facilitate the processes of communication and accommodation among nations that further the cause of benign global governance. At the same time, it would provide a potent symbol of the brotherhood of mankind and of the high aspirations of human civilization. With a functioning world government in operation, we would have a better chance of realizing, within a reasonable period of historical time, our natural aspiration toward a world without war, and without the fear of war.

## Supernational Armament Authority

It is customary that state entities possess military forces: these military forces protect the citizen body from outside aggression and they also deter (at least potentially) the citizen body from engaging in warfare among itself. Aside from its utilitarian purposes, the possession of a military force carries potent symbolic significance as a key defining characteristic of a political entity. It is therefore proposed that the Federal Union of Democratic Nations possess a military force, to be called the Union Security Force (USF). The USF would be administered by a civilian authority: the Ministry of Security, an agency of the executive branch.

Of course, the disposition of armed force by a political entity is intended to preserve peace and security, it is intended to deter aggression and violence perpetrated from within or without, it is intended to be of a preventive rather than a curative nature. It is a bitter irony when, as often has happened throughout human history, these intentions fail, and the military forces and armaments which were supposed to maintain peace, are instead unleashed in war. The death and destruction that ensue in the course of warfare are then directly proportional to the size and armaments of the military forces involved. The paradox is that the greater the size and strength of military forces, the higher will be their deterrent effect against armed conflict—but in the event that war occurs despite this deterrent effect, the more horrific will be the slaughter. In the past, this paradox has not been considered a serious argument against national governments maintaining substantial military forces. Neither should it be considered, in the future, a serious argument against a potential supernational government maintaining a substantial military force.

Therefore it should be taken as a given that the Federal Union of Democratic Nations would possess a substantial military apparatus. But exactly how large its military forces should be, exactly what sort of weaponry they should possess, and exactly how the USF should be organized and administered, are difficult questions requiring a great deal of reflective deliberation. The Federal Union would be a unique and unprecedented political form in human affairs. In addition, there are many questions about its circumstances and conditions that cannot be answered at the present time. For example, how many nations will choose to become charter members of the world federation, and what forces will they choose to maintain under their direct control? What military forces will be maintained by those nations not choosing to become charter members of the world federation? How much economic progress will be made at the world level? What will be the course of religious and ideological developments: will increasing toleration and flexibility be the rule, or might

there be retrograde movements which will intensify religion and/or ideology as contributing factors to hostility, suspicion, and strife among
humanity? And so on and so forth.

We must also take into account, in designing the military component
of the world state, the fears and apprehensions that are so widespread
among humanity at the present time that such a state would tend to become, gradually or quickly as the case may be, an instrument of oppression and tyranny. The following suggestions are merely tentative and
provisional: they are intended merely to provide a basis for discussion.

The Union Security Force of the Federal Union of Democratic Nations would comprise land, sea, and air forces, and it would be armed
with the entire range of weaponry from small arms through to strategic
nuclear weapons. The number of military personnel in this force, and the
quantity of weaponry with which they would be armed, would be substantial—but exact numerical figures cannot be specified in advance, as
the exact numerical figures would depend on prevailing conditions and
circumstances at the time the supernational federation is established. An
especially important question concerns nuclear weapons. I would suggest
that the nuclear capability directly controlled by the Federal Union be of
more than a token level, but less than the capabilities of the nuclear superpowers of the present day, the United States and the Russian Federation. An appropriate capability might be on the order of the present-day
nuclear capabilities of Britain and France.

With respect to outside aggression, the ultimate objective of the Federal Union would of course be universal membership by all the nations of
the world, and were this objective to be eventually achieved there would
be no danger of outside aggression by other nations. However, even if
the human race were to achieve complete political unity, there will always exist the possibility, however remote, of conflict with intelligent
nonhumans emanating from other solar systems. Although most of the
abundant "war of the worlds" speculation produced by science fiction
writers from H. G. Wells on down seems patently preposterous, there is
perhaps just enough substance to these scary visions to postulate a Ministry of Security and a Union Security Force as permanent components of
the supernational state, even were complete participation in the Union
and full internal harmony to be achieved.

In the near term, however, such a force might more plausibly be necessary to deter aggression against member nations by non-member nations. It is of course fairly probable that not all nations of the earth will
join the Federal Union upon its formation. Moreover, member nations of
the Federal Union would be guaranteed the right of secession from the
Union, so that some nations might withdraw from the Union at some

point after initially joining it. Until the goal of universal membership has been achieved, the threat of aggression by non-member nations against member nations would continue to exist.

It is proposed that any and all military forces financially supported by national governments at their own discretion be considered, in a pro forma sense, component units of the Union Security Force. In addition to nationally funded military units not subject to direct control by the Federal Union government, the Federal Union would financially support some Union Security Force units of its own, these latter units being subject to direct control by the Federal Union government. The uniforms, insignia, code of conduct, and basic weaponry would be very similar across all units of the Union Security Force, including those supported by national governments and those supported by the supernational government. Common uniforms, insignia, etc., would be in the interest of pro moting psychological feelings of unity and common purpose among both military personnel and the general civilian population.

One of the important purposes of a nation-state is to deter armed conflicts between subsidiary governments representing component localities. Thus, for example, the national government of the United States would not allow the different component states to go to war with one another. If necessary, United States military forces commanded by the federal government would be employed to suppress such a conflict. But to those who are personally familiar with life in the contemporary United States, the notion that the state governments would contemplate making war on one another is simply inconceivable. The ideal of national unity has become so strongly rooted in the United States that state leaders never in their wildest dreams imagine using armed force to resolve various disputes and controversies with other states. It is simply taken for granted that these disputes and controversies will be resolved peacefully by some type of negotiation, arbitration, or adjudication. This psychological attitude is possible because the citizens of the United States harbor very little emotional allegiance to their respective states: rather their emotional allegiance is almost entirely bestowed upon the nation. Thus, armed conflicts between states are not so much deterred by the existence of the United States military forces which would forcibly suppress such conflicts were they to occur; rather they are principally forestalled by the absence of emotional allegiance in citizens to their respective states.

Moreover, the strong spirit of national unity which is common to the populations of all the states guarantees that all the other states—embodied in the federal government of the United States—would come to the assistance of any one state threatened by aggression from a foreign nation. It is virtually impossible for other nations to "divide and conquer," as far as the individual states of the United States are concerned. This unity of purpose and mutual resolution greatly enhances the safety and security of each one of the 50 individual states comprising the United States.

The long-term goal of the Federal Union of Democratic Nations would be to achieve an analogous situation in the international sphere: that is, to bring about a condition under which the citizens of the Union would harbor rather little emotional allegiance to their respective nations, but would rather bestow most such allegiance upon the Federal Union as a whole. A strong spirit of supernational unity would operate very much as does a strong spirit of national unity: it would render armed conflicts among member nations of the Federal Union extremely unlikely, while at the same time it would render the member nations of the Federal Union highly impervious against the threat of military aggression by non-member nations. If a point is reached at which it is obvious to any non-member nation that an attack on any member nation will incur the full military weight of the Union Security Force, including all national as well as supernational component units, then no such attacks will be contemplated. The lengthy process of evolution by which such a condition might eventually be achieved would involve a complex interplay between real factors (such as the supernational federation's military forces) and psychological factors (the important symbolic impact of the very existence of the supernational federation).

The use of military force by the Federal Union of Democratic Nations to protect member nations against aggression by non-member nations is the most obvious and non-controversial use of force. But what about the use of Federal Union force to suppress large-scale military conflicts among or within member nations of the Federal Union? In the long run, such potential conflicts would be forestalled—assuming the world federation evolves favorably—by the prevalence of peaceful and cooperative attitudes among the populations of all the member nations. But in the short run, such attitudes would not be well-developed, and could not be relied upon to forestall all conflicts within the Union. The most realistic answer to be given at this point in time, to the question of whether the supernational government's military forces should be used to suppress armed conflicts among or within member nations of the Federal Union, is that it would depend on the circumstances.

The most difficult question regarding the use of force by the Federal Union of Democratic Nations concerns possible applications of force outside the boundaries of the Federal Union. Should the military power of the Union Security Force be used to suppress large-scale armed conflicts within or among *non-member* nations? Throughout the Cold War era and beyond, there have been a number of humanitarian disasters throughout the world: some of the nations involved include Cambodia, Somalia, Bosnia-Herzegovina, Rwanda, Iraq and Syria.[15] None of these conflicts involved international aggression, but rather intense civil wars motivated by various ideological, economic, religious, ethnic, and other factors. These episodes witnessed complete disregard for and abrogation of all civilized notions of human rights. Should the world stand by quietly while peaceable, innocent people are dispossessed and dispersed, tortured, and murdered?

This question has been asked at the time of each and every major humanitarian disaster over the last few decades. Generally speaking, intervention in such situations by outside forces under specific nations, or under such multinational bodies as NATO or the United Nations, has been rather limited. Notions of a universal brotherhood of man transcending national boundaries have not developed sufficiently for the people of any given nation to accept significant casualties among their own military to protect the natural rights of peoples in other nations, especially when these other nations are geographically distant. Only as long as casualties are relatively light, will intervention be continued.

If we look forward to a future in which a supernational federation along the lines of the proposed Federal Union of Democratic Nations has become an existent, functioning component of international relations, then if and when humanitarian disasters in non-member nations occur, it is inevitable that many citizens of the Federal Union will demand that the Union Security Force be utilized to restore peace and order in the affected nations. Notwithstanding that these calls reflect worthy ideals and commendable principles, I would strongly suggest that any and all calls for military intervention be examined in an extremely cautious and conservative manner. Intervention should only be undertaken if there is strong evidence that the costs would be relatively minor. The thing to be avoided at all costs is for the populations of large and important member nations to begin to believe that their own soldiers are being used heedlessly as cannon fodder by incompetent and callous officers from other nations. If this feeling were to grow to the point where these nations withdraw from the Federal Union, then the long-run costs to human civilization would far outweigh any short-term benefits from intervention.

For those who would decry a passive stance by the supernational federation toward humanitarian disasters occurring in non-member nations, I would offer two consoling considerations. First, these episodes provide useful instruction in the persistence and harmfulness of those negative human characteristics and motivations which it is the long-run purpose of the Federal Union to bring under a satisfactory level of control. There is much good in human nature; but there is also much evil. If there were only good in human nature and no evil, then quite possibly we would need no government whatsoever, either at the world level, the national level, or any lower level. Humanitarian disasters provide a potent reminder of those evil tendencies within humanity which it is the purpose of governments at all levels to curb.

The second consoling consideration is that a passive stance, in the event of humanitarian disasters in non-member nations during the early years of the Federal Union, is only a temporary expedient to get the world federation over the difficult early period during which its stability and permanence would be problematic. Later on, once the spirit of supernational patriotism has achieved the critical minimum at which no further serious doubt would exist on the feasibility and desirability of world government in the long term, then that government might well become far more activist and willing to make significant sacrifices to protect human rights anywhere in the world. Paradoxically, the willingness to absorb large casualties to maintain peace and order throughout the world might reduce the actual number of casualties suffered. A major reason why some civil wars become so vicious and unrestrained is that neither side can imagine that the conflict will ever be suppressed by overwhelming outside military force. But if such intervention were quite likely, then those tempted to violent conflicts with other factions within the nation might be more inclined toward peaceful compromise.

## Religion and Language

The general rule in pursuing the long-term goal of ever-increasing peaceful cooperation and psychological solidarity among the citizens of the Federal Union of Democratic Nations is to maintain perpetual flexibility and toleration with respect to all matters in which diversity is either inevitable, or has no seriously adverse bearing on practical economic and political issues, but to work gradually toward uniformity in other matters.

An important example of the former is religion. Whether this is the result of divine purpose or human nature, humanity has developed a large number of diverse religious systems: Judaism, Christianity, Islam, Hinduism, Buddhism, and Taoism, to name only some of the more important. Within each of the major categories there are normally several subcategories. It is almost definitional that religious belief systems cannot be confirmed or contradicted by any conceivable appeal to either logical reasoning or empirical reality. Many if not most religious belief systems offer the believer some form of solace against the apparent personal extinction implied by the physical realities of death and decay: for example, that the spiritual soul's awareness, perception, and reasoning will continue onward into an afterlife following the death of the physical body. In view of the fact that personal survival may be at stake, religious beliefs are often accompanied by strong emotions and great determination to suppress opposed religious beliefs. No doubt it would be desirable, from the point of view of peace and tranquility, if humanity were to organize a universal ecumenical council with the purpose of specifying the tenets of a single "true" religion acceptable to all people. The futility of such an undertaking will be obvious to most informed individuals.

What this means is that if it is to survive and prosper, the Federal Union of Democratic Nations must exercise complete impartiality and neutrality with respect to religion, now and forever. It must practice an uncompromising separation of church and state. A strong basis for religious toleration has already been laid in the modern world. Centuries of history have taught humanity that religiously based conflicts are not only extremely costly, but also very unlikely to yield long-term advantages even to the winning side.[16] Moreover, the contemporary individual is far more aware of the multiplicity of established, organized religions in the world than were individuals in past centuries. This in itself has weakened faith in the concept of a "single true religion," and has weakened the determination even among sincere believers in a particular religious system to convert others to that system. In the modern world, all the great religious systems have achieved a degree of accommodation with each other—none of them aspires to "world domination," as it were. None of them, therefore, are likely to perceive in a world state an instrument toward the universal imposition of a single religion.

While religion is an example of a matter in which diversity seems inevitable, but which need not have any adverse effect on the practical economic and political operations of the Union, language is an example of a matter in which considerable diversity exists at the present time, but this is a form of diversity which is neither inevitable nor neutral in its effects on economic and political operations. This is an area in which the Federal Union should indeed press forward—albeit at a gradual and unhurried pace—toward less diversity and more homogeneity. History has clearly demonstrated that a common language is a powerful force in support of both political unity and economic prosperity. It has equally clearly demonstrated that different languages are frequently a potent divisive force: more often than not, the curse of separatism (as in Canada's province of Quebec) is linguistically based. As a speaker of English, my own judgment on this matter is possibly biased. Nevertheless, it is certainly arguable that in view of the present widespread dissemination of the English language throughout the world, there are compelling arguments of practicality and expedience in favor of the adoption of English as the official language of the Federal Union of Democratic Nations.[17]

My own proposal is that not only should English be *an* official language of the Federal Union of Democratic Nations, it should be the *sole* official language of the Federal Union. There are several languages besides English that are widely spoken throughout the world, which would make it very difficult to specify the second official language. And once a second official language had been allowed, the arguments would be endless for a third, a fourth, and so on. The operations of the Union would be in danger of bogging down in a multilingual morass.

A possible compromise to facilitate the adoption of English as the sole official language of the Federal Union might be to require schoolchildren in English-speaking nations to study some other language to the same intensity that schoolchildren in other nations study English. According to the ancient proverb, "Misery loves company": thus the knowledge that schoolchildren in English-speaking nations were being subjected to the mental stress and strain of studying another language no less than their own children, might provide a sufficient amount of psychological solace to non-English speakers to induce them to accept English as the sole official language of the Federal Union of Democratic Nations. Even if this compromise were to be acceptable to most nations, it would probably require a period of many decades, if not several centuries, before the overwhelming majority of humanity becomes fluent in a single language. In this area as in others, patience must be the watchword.

## Trade and Migration

It is a conventional policy of a modern nation-state to maintain a free trade area within its national boundaries. The close ties which this policy facilitates between all parts of the nation are not only economically beneficial, but they also augment psychological feelings of unity and shared purpose. Despite decades of multilateral conferences and bilateral negotiations, first under the GATT rubric (General Agreement on Tariffs and Trade) and now under the WTO rubric (World Trade Organization), the various legal and financial impediments erected by individual nations against international trade and investment remain a very significant drag on the development of the global economy. Therefore a primary task of the Federal Union during its early decades would be to oversee the full and comprehensive dismantling of various national impediments (tariffs, import quotas, and so on) to the free flow of physical commodities and financial capital between member nations.

This will not necessarily be an easy task, since in some cases tariff revenues constitute a significant source of national government revenue, while in other cases protection against foreign competition is very much in the financial interest of influential individuals and organizations. Owing to these factors, it may require a substantial period of time before the domestic free trade objective is achieved. However, progress in this area would probably be more rapid than has been the historical rate of progress under the sovereign nation-state system. The Federal Union might also participate in the processes of travel and trade by building and/or maintaining international highways and railroads, as well as airports and seaports.

It is also a conventional policy of a modern nation-state to maintain a high level of internal population mobility. This is also economically beneficial, both to individual citizens and to the nation as a whole, as well as augmenting psychological feelings of unity and shared purpose among the population. Unfortunately, this particular characteristic of the typical modern nation-state cannot be quickly and easily emulated by the Federal Union of Democratic Nations. The immigration barriers that have been established by the rich nations to restrain the flow of migrants from the poor nations must be kept in force until a higher level of economic homogeneity throughout the world has been achieved. The opinion is almost universal among professional economists that the abolition of immigration restrictions, under the current condition of wide economic disparities between nations, would lead to a massive wave of migration from the poor nations to the rich nations, and that the probable result of such a massive wave would be a drastic reduction in the average living standards of the rich nations. In other words, it is believed that the effects of free migration would be basically equivalent to those of a global welfare state.[18] The potential dangers from unrestricted immigration may be exaggerated but they certainly cannot be ignored. Therefore the elimination of barriers to human mobility within the Federal Union will have to await successful completion of the Global Marshall Plan to be discussed below. This will probably entail a period of at least several decades.

Although the elimination of immigration barriers will have to await long-term success in the area of equalization of living standards across nations, existing barriers to commodity mobility and capital mobility should be removed as quickly as possible. Economists generally believe that the elimination of such barriers would be beneficial to all parties in the long run, even though the realization of these benefits may impose substantial hardships and costs on some individuals and groups in the short run. The incentive to undertake these hardships and costs within the context of supernational federation would not merely be to capture relatively narrow economic benefits, but in addition to further the cause of supernational unity, in the expectation that the triumph of this cause would yield very substantial economic and psychological benefits over the long-term future course of human development.

# A Complementary Proposal

## *The Economic Problem*

Apart from the natural apprehensions induced by the daily possibility of instantaneous nuclear Armageddon, the decades of the Cold War instilled in humanity far greater consciousness than ever before of the global economic gap, of the tremendous gulf that separates the high average living standards in the minority of rich nations from the low average living standards in the majority of poor nations.[19] This economic gap was a major factor in the geopolitical situation during the Cold War, as both the wealthier capitalist nations and the communist nations endeavored to win over the nonaligned Third World nations to their respective sides of the ideological struggle. In some Third World nations, such as Cuba and Vietnam, the appeal made by the international communist movement to the natural resentments among the poor against the rich, was obviously effective. On the other hand, most Third World nations avoided communist political takeovers. There is little doubt, however, that communist ideology was a divisive force within these nations, and also contributed to strained and distrustful relations between these nations and the wealthy First World nations.

Now that the ideological impediment to world government has declined to what many would consider a vestigial level, the relative importance of the economic impediment has become paramount. During the Cold War, the noncommunist nations were leery of world government on grounds that it might be subverted by the communist nations and transformed into a tool of communist expansionism. At the same time, the communist nations were leery of world government on grounds that it might be subverted (from their point of view) and transformed into a tool of capitalistic reaction. Now that the Cold War has faded into insignificance, the rich nations are leery of world government on grounds that it might be controlled by the poor nations and transformed into a tool for the radical transfer of current income from the rich nations to the poor nations. At the same time, the poor nations are leery of world government on grounds that it might be controlled by the rich nations and transformed into a tool for the reestablishment of colonial-style economic exploitation of the poor nations. The principal obstacle to world government has in effect shifted from the East-West ideological conflict to the North-South economic gap.

Not that this situation is recognized and openly acknowledged within either the rich nations or the poor nations. At the present time, discussion of the world government possibility among the intelligentsia, the political leadership, and the general public is so limited as to be virtually nonexistent. People are so deeply convinced that world government is a utopian pipedream that they deem it unworthy of thought and discussion. Nevertheless, it remains the case that if world government is indeed a utopian pipedream, there should be plausible reasons why it would be undesirable. It contradicts the rationality of humanity to hold that world government is a utopian pipedream in the absence of plausible reasons why it would be undesirable. What, then, are these reasons? If required to respond to this question, the typical person would respond to the effect: "If there existed a world government to which my own nation was subordinate, foreign interests would impose oppressive conditions upon my nation and myself." But what, exactly, would these "oppressive conditions" entail? A citizen of a poor nation will tend to define oppressive conditions in terms of the reestablishment of colonial-style exploitation: the plundering of natural resources, the hindering of self-sufficiency and industrialization, and so on. Meanwhile, a citizen of a rich nation will tend to define oppressive conditions in terms of enforced redistribution of substantial amounts of goods and resources from the rich nations to the poor nations: an extravagant global welfare state. Oppression, for both, means primarily *economic* oppression.

This is not to deny that other forms of oppression are imaginable and even possible. Conceivably a world government dominated by Christian fundamentalists might outlaw all non-Christian religions. Conceivably a world government dominated by Islamic fundamentalists might require women to be veiled in public. But it is highly implausible that an actual world government would contemplate such policies. Neither Christian fundamentalists nor Islamic fundamentalists are so numerous within the overall world population, nor so fiercely self-righteous and zealously determined, as to desire to and succeed in imposing such policies on a democratically accountable world government with a broad electorate. Economic issues, on the other hand, are quite a different matter. A great many citizens of the poor nations might naturally be predisposed in favor of redistributional policies—policies that might generally be viewed as economic leveling in the rich nations. At the same time, a great many citizens in the rich countries might naturally be predisposed in favor of free trade and free capital mobility—policies that might generally be construed as colonial-style exploitation in the poor nations.

According to World Bank statistical data, most of the Third World nations made respectable gains in per capita income during the latter part of the twentieth century and into the twenty-first, the exception being some nations in sub-Saharan Africa. On the other hand, economic growth has, on the whole, been stronger in the richest nations, with the consequence that the gap between the richest nations and the poorest nations has been getting wider. These points are illustrated by Figures 2.1 and 2.2, based on data from the World Bank's *World Development Indicators* database. Figure 2.1 shows economic growth in terms of per capita income (PCY) from 1960 to 2013 for China and India, where per capita income is defined as Gross National Income (GNI) per capita in constant 2005 U.S. $. Both the Chinese and the Indian plots show apparently healthy upward trends, albeit Chinese growth has obviously been considerably stronger over the latter part of the period.

However, Figure 2.2 shows economic growth in terms of per capita income from 1960 to 2013 for China, India, the United States, and Japan. Owing to the different units of measure on the vertical axis, the plots for China and India in Figure 2.2 appear to be almost horizontal. This shows that when the economic situation of low-income nations such as China and India is directly compared to the economic situation of high-income nations such as the United States and Japan, as is done in Figure 2.2, the magnitude of the problem becomes quite obvious. Not only is the existing economic gap very wide, but the gap is getting wider.

One might entertain reassuring thoughts about this situation. For example, the customary measures of national income and output exaggerate the economic gap because they take inadequate account of non-market production and consumption, and non-market production and consumption are relatively more important in the poorer nations. But such thoughts may well manifest little more than wishful thinking. While purchasing power parity (PPP) measures of per capita income show somewhat smaller differentials between the rich nations and the poor nations than the customary measures, the differentials are still extremely large.

Practical evidence of the extent and significance of the economic gap is found in the fact that the immigration services of the rich nations are engaged in a terrific struggle to curtail immigration from the poor nations. Few people doubt that if the restrictive immigration policies of the rich nations were relaxed, there would occur a tidal wave of immigration from the poor nations to the rich nations. Of course these policies, as

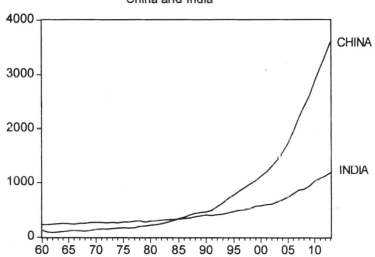

Figure 2.1: Measured PCY Growth, 1960-2013, China and India

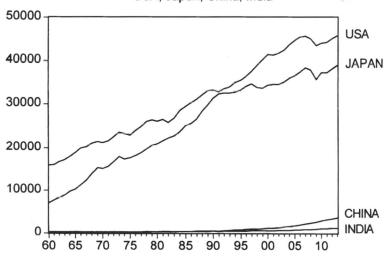

Figure 2.2: Measured PCY Growth, 1960-2013, USA, Japan, China, India

necessary as they may be to preserving the prevailing living standards within the rich nations, are a perpetual thorn in the side of relations between poor nations and rich nations.

Granting that a great deal of economic inequality exists among the nations of the contemporary world, however, the question remains of just how serious a problem this is. A great many historians and social analysts will argue that while existing world economic inequality is unfortunate and regrettable, it does not represent—in and of itself and in the larger scheme of things—a major hazard to the future prospects of human civilization.[20] Various evidence might be cited in support of this proposition. To begin with, history provides an abundance of examples of warfare among peoples and nations that were quite homogeneous in terms of economic circumstances. For example, at the outbreak of World War I, living standards in the contesting nations of France and Germany were quite comparable. Indeed, the example of World War I, among others, suggests that geographical contiguity is a far more significant factor in the outbreak of warfare than economic inequality. Other factors that have apparently contributed to hostility and warfare in the past include racial differences, religious differences, ideological differences, and cultural differences. In light of all these other contributory factors, the role of economic inequality might have been relatively minor.

Clearly this argument possesses a degree of merit, to the extent that it makes us aware of the fact that economic inequality is only one of several contributory factors to international tension, hostility, conflict, and warfare. On the other hand, the fact that economic inequality is only one of several factors does not translate into the proposition that economic inequality is unimportant. History is full of plundering expeditions by poorer peoples desirous of appropriating the material possessions of richer peoples. One thinks of the barbarian invasions of the Roman empire, of the Viking depredations of the coastal areas of Britain and other European nations, of the Mongol invasions of China and Russia.

Nor is the economic incentive to aggressive warfare exclusively confined to the earlier periods of human history. The critical catalytic factor in the two world wars of the twentieth century was Germany's self-perception as a "have-not" nation. The critical factor in the buildup of tension that culminated in World War I was Germany's desire to possess an overseas colonial empire equivalent to that of Britain and France. The critical factor in the buildup of tension that culminated in World War II was Nazi Germany's desire to carve a huge land empire out of Eastern Europe and the Soviet Union, an empire which would have been equivalent to the overseas colonial empires of Britain and France. As a matter of fact, living standards in Germany just prior to both World War I and

World War II, were equivalent to those in Britain and France, and they were certainly higher than those in Eastern Europe and the Soviet Union. This did not prevent Germany from considering itself a "have not" nation in relation to such "have" nations as Britain and France, and consequently from inculcating such hostility toward these latter nations as ultimately to precipitate warfare. If nations that are deprived only in a psychological sense, as opposed to a legitimate material sense, can inculcate such emotions of (in their view) legitimate resentment, how much greater might this tendency be in nations which actually are seriously deprived in a legitimate material sense.

Historians and social analysts inclined to deprecate the role of economic inequality in generating international instability might acknowledge the significance in past history of plundering expeditions by poorer societies against richer societies, but they will argue that such expeditions are no longer feasible in the contemporary world owing to technological developments in weaponry. These developments have endowed the military forces of the rich nations with tremendous superiority over those of the poor nations. They might cite the Persian Gulf War of January-February 1991—in which the technically superior and better trained forces of the U.S.-led coalition slaughtered Iraqi forces with impunity—as an example of what would assuredly happen if a poor nation were ever imprudent enough to invade a rich nation.

Even assuming that this is true at the present time, and without commenting on the morality (or lack thereof) of this somewhat arrogant attitude, there are at least two important counterpoints to be made. First, this attitude neglects the continuing financial costs of supporting a military establishment sufficiently strong to deter aggression by poor nations for a prolonged period stretching into the indefinite future. Military expenditures by the rich nations have indeed declined significantly since the demise of the Cold War, but they have not declined as much as would have been possible in the absence of the large economic gap. If all or most nations had roughly equivalent per capita income, and thus the tendency toward economically-inspired aggression were much lower, it might become possible for the rich nations to reduce military expenditure to only one or two percent of Gross National Product. The second point is that it is imprudent to assume that the military situation that holds today will persist indefinitely into the future. It is not impossible that a relatively poor nation will become a military superpower in the future.

Indeed, the People's Republic of China is an obvious candidate for this status. There are some interesting parallels between the PRC and Japan. When Japan joined the Axis in the 1930s and embarked upon its career of aggressive expansion that contributed to World War II, it was an "up and coming" nation that deemed itself, despite its ever-increasing material prosperity, a "have-not" nation. The fateful "Greater East-Asia Co-Prosperity Sphere" represented an effort by Japan to escape what it considered to be economic subservience to foreign interests. Should the PRC determine to pursue its economically defined national interests more aggressively in the future, history might repeat itself (albeit not in exactly the same way), with consequences that might be even worse.

In current discussions of the threat to worldwide security and equity represented by the relative poverty of such a large proportion of the world population, the possibility of armed aggression by the poorest nations against the richest nations is rarely considered, owing to the fact that the implicit time horizons of these discussions are very short, and do not allow for significant changes in current conditions. To the extent that all-out nuclear world war is envisioned, it is in the context of the poorer regions of the world generating localized wars in which the superpowers might become embroiled. An example of what might eventually happen in the future is suggested by the Persian Gulf War of 1991. Iraq, under the dictatorship of Saddam Hussein, lusted for the lucrative oil wells of Kuwait. Less generously endowed with oil resources than Kuwait, Iraq's 1990 per capita income in current U.S. dollars (according to World Bank data) was $2,170, relative to Kuwait's per capita income of $12,590. On the pretext of a long-defunct historical claim, Iraq invaded Kuwait in the modern equivalent to a plundering expedition. Clearly the motivation in this case was entirely economic. The United States and its allies came to the rescue of Kuwait, and expelled the Iraqi forces in a "short, victorious war."

But let us imagine that in 1991 Iraq had had a military alliance with the Soviet Union analogous to the military alliance that Serbia had with Russia in 1914, an alliance that turned out to be one of the critical linchpins into World War I. Let us further imagine that in 1991 the Soviet Union was not on the verge of dissolution, but was still very much the same as it had been in 1970 or 1980. In that case, the Soviet Union might well have accepted the Iraqi historic claim to Kuwait, have taken the position that the Iraqi invasion of Kuwait was an "internal matter," and have demanded that the United States and its allies desist from their intervention. Ultimatums may well have ensued. The outcome could have been nuclear world war. Persistent inequality among nations might generate analogous situations in the future.

Leaving aside such apocalyptic visions, humanity confronts very serious threats aside from nuclear disaster. The population explosion throughout the world over the last century is putting ever-greater pressure on both the natural resource base and the purity of the physical environment. The AIDS crisis has reminded us of our potential vulnerability to catastrophic epidemics of contagious diseases. Drug abuse has become a major contributor to crime and a major threat to the social fabric. These are global problems in that they have important ramifications in almost every nation on Earth. The extent to which humanity will be able to cope effectively with these problems is critically affected by the predisposition among nations toward mutual respect, trust, and cooperation. The economic gap may be seriously reducing this predisposition. The wide gulf between living standards in the rich nations and those in the poor nations naturally generates a certain amount of hostility and resentment in the latter against the former. This in turn creates a reluctance in the poor nations to do "favors" for the rich nations.

The United States wants Mexico to exert more effort to stem the flow of illegal migration from Mexico to the U.S., but to Mexico this migration reduces its own unemployment problems, and brings into Mexico a considerable amount of U.S. currency from illegal aliens in the U.S. to their families in Mexico. It might seem to the Mexicans rather selfish of the U.S. to want to keep out Mexican migrants, when U.S. per capita income is more than eight times that of Mexico ($31,996 in 2000 relative to $3,819). The United States also wants Columbia to exert more effort to curtail the flow of illegal drugs from Columbia to the U.S., but to Columbia this traffic provides a substantial amount of both domestic employment and foreign exchange. It might seem to the Columbians rather selfish of the U.S. to be so insistent on Columbian assistance in fighting the U.S. drug war, when U.S. per capita income is almost fourteen times that of Columbia ($31,996 in 2000 relative to $2,290). Many rich nations throughout the world want Indonesia to exert more effort to suppress slash and burn methods among its subsistence farmers, because these methods result in augmented atmospheric pollution. One major constraint on the Indonesians in acceding willingly to this desire, however, is the low per capita income of Indonesia ($994 in 2000).

To some extent it is a problem of lack of resources. It requires police resources for Mexico to impede the flow of its migrants into the U.S., for Columbia to suppress drug production and marketing, for Indonesia to deter its subsistence farmers from engaging in slash and burn agriculture. But also to some extent it is a problem of lack of will. It is perhaps not unreasonable for a poor population, with a standard of living that would be considered grinding poverty in the rich nations, to be reluctant to commit significant resources to policies the major benefits of which accrue to the populations of the rich nations, who are already enjoying lavish living standards. It is perhaps not unreasonable that these populations, and their political leaders, experience a strong temptation to rebuff representatives from the rich nations who come to them with transparently self-serving advice and recommendations. The rich nations are generally uninterested in various proposals put forward by the poor nations toward reducing the economic gap. It is perhaps unfair, therefore, to expect the poor countries to happily embrace policies that are more obviously beneficial to the rich nations than they are to the poor nations.[21]

## A Global Marshall Plan

Possibly a major reason why so many people, not only among the general public but also among the intelligentsia and political leadership, have such a difficult time perceiving the true depth and significance of the world economic inequality situation, is that they are absolutely convinced that there is little or nothing that can be done about it. Resignation is a virtue, and psychologists agree that it is unhealthy to dwell upon serious problems that have no solution. Thus if the world economic inequality situation actually is impermeable, then it would be perfectly reasonable to ignore it or minimize it. On the other hand, if plausible means exist toward the amelioration or elimination of a serious problem, resignation is no longer a virtue but is rather a vice. Let us consider, therefore, whether any plausible means exist toward the amelioration or elimination of the world economic inequality problem.

From a purely technical standpoint, it would be possible to set up a global welfare state that would assure every living individual a substantial guaranteed minimum income, with the program financed from a progressive personal income tax. Clearly the costs of the program would fall mostly upon the populations of the rich nations, while the benefits would go mostly to the populations of the poor nations. In prior research, I examined the numerical implications of this policy, for which I coined the term "Crude Redistribution." Although the numerical implications of a global welfare state engaged in Crude Redistribution vary depending upon assumptions (e.g., concerning the disincentive effects of income taxation), even in the most optimistic scenarios, the tax rates necessary to finance such a program for any meaningful level of guaranteed minimum income, would be astronomical by current standards.[22] Crude Redistribution is clearly politically impossible. Only if the rich nations were under military occupation following defeat by the poor nations, would they accede to such a program.

However, my purpose in demonstrating numerically the impracticality of Crude Redistribution was not to imply that the problem of world economic inequality has no solution. It was rather to compare and contrast, in a tangible way, the policy of "Crude Redistribution" with the policy of "Common Progress." Whereas Crude Redistribution envisions equalization of post-tax-and-benefit living standards across nations at a relatively low level somewhere between those of the rich nations and those of the poor nations (but closer to the latter), Common Progress envisions equalization of average national living standards at a high level even beyond those currently prevailing in the rich nations. The rationale for the term "Common Progress" is that economic progress be common to all nations, rich and poor alike. This concept could provide the basis for a politically feasible route toward equalization of average living standards across nations.

The concept could be implemented by means of an international foreign development assistance program on an unprecedentedly large scale. Basically the idea is simply that of a "Global Marshall Plan" (GMP), albeit on a far more ambitious scale both geographically and financially than the program that assisted the reconstruction of Western Europe after World War II.[23] Another descriptive name for such a program is the "World Economic Equalization Program" (WEEP). Although WEEP and GMP are conceptually interchangeable, in my more recent writing I have gravitated toward the latter term. As an economist by profession, I have personally contributed a significant amount of preliminary research on the concept, comprising to this point two professional books and four professional journal articles.[24]

The research involves computer simulation of a numerically implemented model of the global economy. These contributions demonstrate the distinct possibility that a sufficiently massive Global Marshall Plan might achieve a veritably dazzling level of success within a relatively brief period of historical time on the order of 40 to 50 years. My most recent contribution on the subject is a book entitled *Global Marshall Plan: Theory and Evidence* (2014). The numerical results described in the following are derived from this latest iteration of the research.

Whether designated the World Economic Equalization Program (WEEP) or the Global Marshall Plan (GMP), the program must be based absolutely on the principle of Common Progress. Common Progress (the capitalization of the initial letters is deliberate) is the diametric opposite of Crude Redistribution. Crude Redistribution would involve increasing the living standards of the poor nations at the cost of decreasing the living standards of the rich nations. Equalization would take place at a level somewhere between that of the rich nations and the poor nations—closer to the latter than the former. Common Progress, on the other hand, envisions that living standards in *both* the rich nations and the poor nations would continue to increase, so that equalization would take place at a level *higher* than the current level in the rich nations. The intention is that the rate of increase of living standards in the rich nations would be slightly diminished in order that the rate of increase of living standards in the poor nations could be dramatically increased. The populations of the rich nations would be protected against any declines in their current living standards. Progress would then be "common" to the rich nations as well as to the poor nations.

Another key feature of the envisioned Global Marshall Plan would be that it would be regarded from the start as a *tentative and provisional* project, whose continuation beyond a trial period of perhaps 10 to 20 years would depend on dramatic material progress being observed in most participating nations. Of course, the conventional wisdom at the present time is that such a program would be doomed to abject failure: it would merely provide an opportunity for corrupt bureaucrats and dishonest businessmen to enrich themselves, and little or no improvement would occur in the living standards of the great mass of the population.[25] Of course the possibility exists that this belief is merely a shallow rationalization for a policy of short-sighted selfishness, and as such is unworthy of the higher qualities within human nature. But if after a fair experiment, the pessimists are vindicated in their judgment of the uselessness of large-scale foreign aid, then the GMP would be quickly and permanently shut down, and the pessimists would then have ample opportunity to crow and gloat over their own wisdom and prescience.

The research reported in *Global Marshall Plan* utilizes conventional quantitative economic methodology. A production function is specified for each nation giving total output as a function of labor (proxied by population), generalized capital (which incorporates plant and machinery, social overhead capital, and education/training inputs into the labor force), and the total factor productivity coefficient. Output is then allocated to four uses: domestic consumption, domestic investment in generalized capital, military expenditure, and (in the case of the richer nations) a contribution into the "total transfer fund." The total transfer fund is then allocated over the poor recipient nations on the basis of poverty and population. For a given level of population, the lower the per capita income of the recipient nation the larger its share of the transfer fund; and for a given level of per capita income, the higher the population of the recipient nation the larger its share of the transfer fund. Transfer fund shares of the recipient nations are used to expand their generalized capital resources.

The dataset used for GMP model validation purposes was taken from the World Bank's *World Development Indicators* databank. This dataset consists of annual values from 1980 through 2010 (31 years inclusive) for total population $P$ and for four comparable per capita income (PCY) measures for the 146 nations that were listed in the data source as having populations of one million or more in 1980. It was found from experiment that qualitatively the results from the simulations are virtually the same regardless of which particular World Bank measure of per capita income is utilized.

Once the mathematical structure of the model has been specified, a set of benchmark numerical parameter values are determined. These numerical values are set so as to achieve as close a fit as possible between the observed behavior of per capita income across nations over the "validation interval" extending from 1980 through 2010, and the computed behavior of per capita income from the GMP model simulation over the same interval. Although the GMP model does not track short-term fluctuations in national per capita income, for most nations it does a respectable job of estimating long-run trends between 1980 and 2010. The policy simulations, illustrated by Figures 2.3 and 2.4 are "what-if" experiments covering 2010-2050. Most of these years lie in the future.

The 1980-2010 validation simulation assumes that no GMP is in operation (none of the rich nations makes any contribution to the transfer fund). The policy simulations, on the other hand, assume that such contributions might be made, and covers the interval from 2010 through 2050. Therefore, the policy simulations estimate what might have happened had a Global Marshall Plan been commenced in 2010, relative to what is likely to happen if no such plan is initiated. The central implication from the research is that very rapid acceleration in the average living standards of the poor nations might be possible without excessive diminution of the rate of rise of average living standards in the rich nations.

Figures 2.3 and 2.4 show projected per capita income growth (in terms of Gross National Income per capita in constant 2005 U.S. $) over the policy interval from 2010 to 2050, for four nations (the United States, Japan, China, and India), with and without a Global Marshall Plan in operation. Figure 2.3 shows the situation without a Global Marshall Plan; Figure 2.4 shows the situation with a Global Marshall Plan. Obviously the perfectly smooth curves shown in these graphs will not be observed over the coming decades. The GMP model does not incorporate the manifold sources of random variation that are encountered in the real world.

But the good fit between the GMP model results and the observed empirical results over the 1980-2010 validation interval gives us solid grounds for expecting that if random variation is suppressed, the real-world results might be well tracked by the model results. What Figure 2.3 suggests is that without a Global Marshall Plan in operation, we can expect continued widening of the economic gap between rich and poor

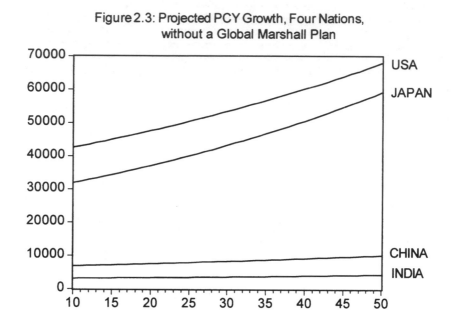

Figure 2.3: Projected PCY Growth, Four Nations,
without a Global Marshall Plan

Figure 2.4: Projected PCY Growth, Four Nations,
with a Global Marshall Plan

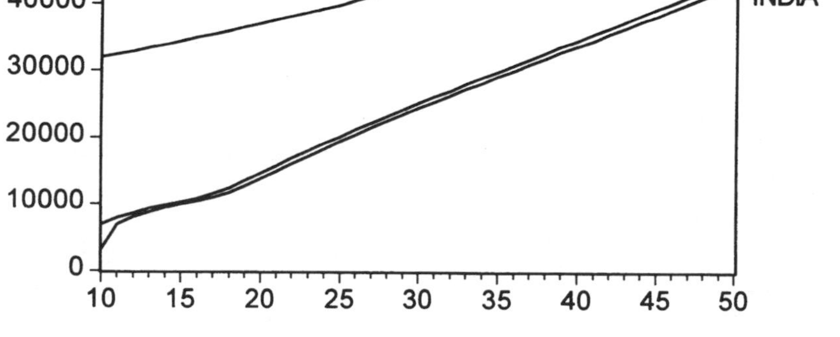

nations. What Figure 2.4 suggests is that with a Global Marshall Plan in operation, there could be a remarkable narrowing of the economic gap within just a few decades. Furthermore, this narrowing would not be at the cost of a significant reduction in the rate of PCY growth in the rich nations.

The conventional viewpoint in the world today, particularly within the richer nations, is that a very large-scale economic development assistance program along the lines of the envisioned GMP would inevitably be a very expensive failure. Such a program would impact heavily on economic growth in the rich nations, reducing it very substantially. At the same time, improvement in the poor nations would be at best modest and at worst negligible. The natural reaction to the benchmark GMP model result described above stemming from this conventional viewpoint is that these results are simply too good to be true. Either the GMP model itself is in error (does not represent an adequate approximation to actual variables and relationships), or else the benchmark parameter values are in error (do not represent adequate approximations to actual numerical parameter values). As for the model, it will have to suffice here to state that it is based on conventional and widely accepted economic principles (detailed technical arguments to this effect are provided in *Global Marshall Plan*, Chapter 3). The benchmark numerical values of the model's parameters are another story—it cannot be reasonably maintained that these values are "very conventional and widely accepted." The fact is that the theoretical content of contemporary economics is far more substantial than its empirical content. Whatever actual numbers are utilized for economic model parameters are normally subject to a considerable amount of uncertainty and error.

Therefore, in assessing the policy implications of any particular economic model, considerable weight is normally placed on sensitivity analysis: on the investigation of how changes in the parametric input into the model simulation affect the numerical output. The question addressed is: How robust are particular qualitative policy indications against changes in parameter values? Do these qualitative policy indications change dramatically if parameter values are changed slightly? If so, we deem the initial policy indications to be non-robust. On the other hand, do these qualitative policy indications remain basically intact despite substantial variation in the numerical values of the parameters? If so, we deem the initial policy indications to be robust. In the case of the present research, the initial policy indication is that a Global Marshall Plan would be highly beneficial. The sensitivity analysis utilized in this research explores in considerable detail the extent to which this indication is robust against parametric variation.

As described, for example, in Chapter 4 of *Global Marshall Plan*, for most of the 14 parameters of the GMP model, substantial variation in the numerical parameter value around the benchmark value does not materially affect the extremely favorable outcome. However, there are two principal exceptions to this rule, exceptions that were not unexpected. One of these relates to $\xi$, the parameter that determines the extent to which initial differentials in per capita income PCY are the result of differentials in total factor productivity $A$, as opposed to differentials in generalized capital stocks $K$. According to critics of foreign aid, a major reason for its ineffectiveness lies in the economically dysfunctional institutional and cultural characteristics of the recipient nations. This translates into the proposition that most of the observed differences in economic output among nations are not owing to differences in generalized capital resources, but are rather owing to differences in total factor productivity, itself a function of the institutional and cultural characteristics of the respective nations. Numerically this implies that the $\xi$ parameter takes on a relatively high value. The other principal exception relates to $\chi$, the parameter that determines how much of the recipient nation's share in the total transfer fund is effectively converted into generalized capital. The familiar proposition that foreign aid is mostly diverted by corrupt bureaucrats and dishonest businessmen into their own pockets and therefore generates very little benefit for the general population in the poor nations, translates into a relatively low value of the $\chi$ parameter.

The benchmark value of $\xi$ is 0, indicating that *all* per capita income differentials are the consequence of $K$ differentials rather than $A$ differentials. This would be the most favorable case. As $\xi$ increases toward 1, the model simulations demonstrate that the effectiveness of the GMP in reducing world inequality by raising output in the poor nations steadily diminishes. If $\xi = 1$, indicating that *all* per capita income differentials are the consequence of $A$ differentials rather than $K$ differentials (the least favorable case), then the GMP is in fact a complete failure: it has virtually no impact on world inequality. However, there are two important points revealed by the simulations with increasing $\xi$ values. The first is that the $\xi$ value has to become very large for the GMP to be completely ineffective. The second point is that the cost to the rich nations of the GMP program, in terms of reduced economic growth, is minimal whatever the value of $\xi$. In other words, the implication is that *if* the Global Marshall Plan is indeed a failure, this would be manifested in the poor nations failing to make significant economic progress, not in the rich nations experiencing a significantly lower rate of economic progress.

Results for the $\chi$ parameter are analogous to those just described for the $\xi$ parameter. The simulations for $\chi$ variation show that $\chi$ has to take an extremely adverse value to render the GMP completely ineffective in raising output in the poor nations and decreasing world inequality; they also show that regardless of the $\chi$ value, the cost of a GMP to the rich nations, in terms of reduced growth, would be minimal. On the whole, therefore, it can be said that the qualitative conclusion that a Global Marshall Plan would be beneficial to humanity is quite robust against parametric variation of the GMP model.

No one is more aware of the limitations of economic models than economists themselves. In legal terms, any evidence forthcoming from either analytical or computational economic analysis must be considered "circumstantial." Nevertheless, results forthcoming from economic analyses are entitled to more weight than are the speculations, informed by prejudice and preconception, on which so much of human decision-making is actually based. Critics of foreign aid regard it as a "proven fact" that foreign aid is ineffective. They point to the fact that billions of dollars of foreign aid have been disbursed over the last half-century— and the poor nations are still poor. This is analogous to saying that modern medicine is ineffective because people still inevitably die. The fact is that with the single major exception of sub-Saharan Africa, the Less Developed Countries (LDCs) have made considerable economic progress over the last half-century, and there is no compelling evidence that foreign aid was not a significant contributor to this progress. For example, several "Asian tiger" nations which registered truly dramatic progress, such as South Korea, were major recipients of foreign aid during the initial phases of their growth.

For most LDCs, obviously, not as much economic progress has occurred as we would have preferred. Why is this? The suggestion which I offer is that the *amount* of effective foreign aid (netting out military aid and less beneficial aid forms such as food aid) has simply not been adequate to produce definitive success. Just as in nuclear physics a critical mass of uranium is required to commence a chain reaction, so too in development economics a critical mass of foreign aid is required to achieve a high degree of economic equalization across nations. In the past, the foreign aid effort of the rich nations fell far short of the necessary critical mass. "Billions and billions of dollars" of foreign aid is not necessarily so impressive when one reflects that there are billions and billions of poor people living in the contemporary world.

Among other things, the GMP model simulations compute for each contributor nation the percentages of GNP which the transfer fund contributions would represent. These percentages are much larger than what has been witnessed in the past, but they are by no means unmanageable. For example, according to the benchmark GMP model simulation, over the first 25 years of operation of the GMP, the United States would contribute approximately 3 percent of its GNP to the transfer fund. Between 2000 and 2010, United States defense outlays averaged slightly under 4 percent, well down from its Cold War high of 9.7 percent, set in 1968 at the height of the Vietnam War. Throughout the post-World War II era, the United States has devoted a substantial proportion of its national output to deadweight military purposes, and not merely has economic catastrophe been averted but the long-term economic growth of the nation has been quite strong. This is compelling evidence that the United States could devote a substantial proportion of its national output to foreign development assistance over the next few decades without incurring unacceptable economic costs. If the United States is capable of this, so too are most if not all of the wealthy nations in the world.

The Global Marshall Plan and the Federal Union of Democratic Nations are complementary proposals. Of course, many of those with more conservative predispositions, even if they could be persuaded to seriously entertain the possibility of a Global Marshall Plan, would probably advise that the establishment of a world government be postponed until the success of the GMP had been demonstrated. That, in their view, would be the safer course. But as long as the world state under consideration incorporates the limitations previously discussed (the right of member nations to maintain military forces, and to secede at their own discretion, plus the dual voting system in the federation legislature), it would be sufficiently safe against the threat of Crude Redistribution. The existence of an operating Federal Union of Democratic Nations would contribute to a spirit of supernational patriotism throughout the world (if only weakly at first), and this spirit would enhance the likelihood that the Global Marshall Plan would be pursued long enough and vigorously enough to achieve final success.

It does not require the prescience of a biblical prophet to predict that the single most contentious issue within the Federal Union during its early years, would be the contributions made by the rich nations to the GMP transfer fund. Many if not most conservatives within the rich nations will be predictably appalled and outraged by the egregious waste and futility of these expenditures, and will continuously demand that they be drastically reduced or eliminated altogether. It is also more or less inevitable that the rich nations, sooner or later, will encounter the economic adversity of business recessions. The economic stress placed on the populations of the rich nations by these setbacks will render them even more susceptible to the arguments and demands of the conservatives. If, at the time of this greater stress, anxiety, and uncertainty, there existed a viable and visible world government, with a capital city, a flag, buildings, and personnel, this tangible symbol of human solidarity and community would significantly increase the likelihood that the difficulties would be surmounted and the advance continued.

The Federal Union and Global Marshall Plan proposals are complementary in the sense that the existence of the Federal Union would increase the probability that the Global Marshall Plan would be pursued successfully, and at the same time the existence of the Global Marshall Plan would increase the probability that the Federal Union would survive and thrive in the long run. If either half of this two-pronged plan to lay the basis for a better world were omitted, this would significantly reduce prospects for ultimate success. In much the same way that a person would be significantly hampered by having to hop along on one leg—as opposed to walking along on two legs.

# Brief History of World Federalism

## Origins and Development

In his book *World Citizenship and Government: Cosmopolitan Ideas in the History of Western Political Thought* (1996), Derek Heater traces the roots of the world government concept back to the ancient Greeks. But this refers to the *roots*. Professor Heater is quite clear that the contemporary concept of a world government did not begin to develop until the modern era, commencing approximately around 1500. In ancient and medieval times, the philosophical notion of the "oneness of man," the political implications of which were ambiguous at best, coexisted with the notion of a universal empire, initially established by conquest, but thereafter governed with such wisdom and benevolence as to command the voluntary support and allegiance of its citizens.[1]

As for the ancient Greeks, much of their political history is the story of jealously sovereign and independent city-states, often at war with one another. In the *Nicomachean Ethics*, Aristotle ventured the opinion that the optimal population of a single political organization could not exceed 100,000, lest there be inadequate social cohesion and political stability. On the other hand, a large number of small political units, each one of which might be desirable in terms of minimal internal strife, multiplies the opportunities for external strife, as dramatically witnessed in the Peloponnesian wars that devastated the Greek peninsula starting in 432 BC. Historical events of this sort may have prompted Aristotle's isolated and unamplified remark, in the *Politics*, that the Greek people possess the intelligence that would enable them "to attain the highest political development, and to show a capacity for governing every other people—if only they could once achieve political unity." This statement suggests the optimal political organization, all things considered (external security as well as internal tranquility), might well comprise more than 100,000 inhabitants. But the statement hardly prefigures a universal state based on contract. Rather it suggests the Greeks conquering and then ruling the world for their own security and benefit—albeit in a wise and tolerant manner that would command the peaceful consent of the various non-Greek populations.

The Greek city-states were eventually united in the kingdom created by the conquests of Philip II of Macedonia, whose son, Alexander the Great (356-323 BC), went on to establish by conquest a huge (by the standards of the time) but extremely ephemeral empire. Professor Heater describes the controversy among modern historians concerning how much, or how little, overlap exists between the ambitious dreams of Alexander the Great in his ascendancy, and the modern concept of a world state. One piece of relevant evidence consists of a lengthy epistle on prudent imperial policy, possibly written by Aristotle to his former pupil Alexander, which contains the following passage.

> I know that if mankind in general is destined to true felicity within the duration of this world, there will come about that concord and order which I shall describe. Happy is he who sees the resplendence of that day when men will agree to constitute one rule and one kingdom. They will cease from wars and strife, and will devote themselves to that which promotes their welfare and the welfare of their cities and countries.

The epistle survives only in Arabic translations dating from the medieval period, and its authenticity as an actual work of Aristotle is subject to doubt. Despite doubt as to its origin, the passage eloquently expresses a vision which clearly *might* have inspired Alexander as he pursued his route of conquest across much of the known world of his day. That such a vision was in fact operative in Alexander's mind was argued in the 1930s by Sir William Tarn, a noted Hellenistic scholar, based on detailed analyses of such events as the "feast of reconciliation" staged by Alexander in 324 BC to gain a military alliance with the Persians in support of greater internal stability and external expansion.

Is it possible that the modern concept of a world state possesses such an ancient lineage, and was entertained by renowned historical personages such as Alexander the Great? Unless "concept" is defined extremely loosely, this is most probably not the case. The putative epistle of Aristotle quoted above uses the critical phrasing: "men *will agree* to constitute one rule and one kingdom." But will this "agreeing" take place before or after most of them have been conquered by some dominant subgroup of the human population (such as the Greeks or the Romans)? A contract is an agreement freely and voluntarily entered, without coercion or the threat of coercion. In our own day, the great majority believes that the nations of today will never freely agree (i.e., voluntarily contract) to establish a world government with significant authority over them. Most probably, the majority who believed that the independent political entities in Alexander's time (city-states, principalities, kingdoms, and empires) would never freely agree to establish a universal government encompassing them all, was even more overwhelming. Then as now, it was certainly possible for people to *imagine* such a thing happening—in the same way that they could imagine the existence of unicorns. But then as now, people were aware of the fact that something that may be imagined may never have existed in the real world, and possibly never could exist in the real world. If, for the sake of argument, Aristotle's epistle is genuine and the passage quoted is accurate, then given that he was advising the conqueror Alexander, it seems most probable that he believed that the agreement of *most* men "to constitute one rule and one kingdom" could only be obtained after they had suffered military defeat and been conquered. But at the same time, it is not a serious argument against a world state based on contract that this basic concept has crystallized in the relatively recent historical past. There are certain things which have become realities in the modern world (e.g., mass democracy, air travel, television, computers) which would have been deemed, by any educated person in earlier times, pure fantasy.

An important document in the post-World War II world government boom (to be discussed in some detail later in this chapter) was a 532-page compilation by Edith Wynner and Georgia Lloyd entitled *Searchlight on Peace Plans: Choose Your Road to World Government* (1944). Wynner and Lloyd undertook to enumerate and briefly describe a large proportion of existing "chartable" theoretical plans for supranational political entities. By "chartable" is meant that the proposer of the plan provided specific, concrete details in all or most of the following categories: type (alliance, league, etc.); membership (universal, regional, etc.); organs of government (legislative, executive, judicial); transfers of jurisdiction (supranational versus national rights and responsibilities); methods of enforcement (individuals versus nations); immediate steps (scenarios toward foundation); territorial changes (revisions in boundaries and jurisdictions); ratification (process of formal approval). In actual fact, however, the process of charting each plan was only applied to world government proposals since 1914. In Part II of *Searchlight on Peace Plans*, which catalogues theoretical plans to unite nations dating up to 1914, Wynner and Lloyd provide only "brief descriptions," as opposed to charts, of the plans. Part II catalogues some 74 plans, from a 1306 proposal of Pierre Dubois to a 1905 proposal of Richard Bartholdt. Apparently Wynner and Lloyd could not find anything earlier than 1306 that constituted a reasonable facsimile to the modern concept of a world state.

Moreover, if one reads through their list of brief descriptions, it becomes apparent that the earlier proposals, starting with that of Dubois, encompassed only the Christian nations of Western Europe, and were largely motivated by a warlike, crusading spirit: a tight political union of the Christian nations would enable a more effective military resistance to and subsequent conquest of the infidel territories, especially those of the Islamic Turks. However, several of the plans provided considerable detail on the mechanisms of political unification among the Western European nations, and these mechanisms, at least in principle, could be extended to encompass other regions of the world.

The first plan listed by Wynner and Lloyd that explicitly incorporates the entire world is attributed to the French monk Émeric Crucé, author of *The New Cyneas* (*Le Nouveau Cynée*), published in 1623. Wynner and Lloyd describe Crucé's proposal as follows:

> Suggested a permanent Council of Ambassadors, meeting in a neutral city to settle all differences between Princes by majority vote of the whole Council. Those refusing to accept the decisions of the Council to be disgraced. Member Princes to defend the Council against resistance by force of arms. Membership to be universal including the Pope, the Emperor of the Turks, the Jews, the Kings of Persia and China, the Grand Duke of Muscovy, and monarchs from India and Africa. A universal police, "useful equally to all nations and acceptable to those which have some light of reason and sentiment of humanity." The Council to exercise legislative power in order "to meet discontents halfway...and appease them by gentle means, if it could be done, or in case of necessity by force." Crucé urged religious toleration, encouragement of scientific discoveries, and of commerce by safeguarding communication and transportation against pirates. Suggested Venice as the place of meeting.

Except for the fact that the term "ambassadors" is used rather than the more appropriate "representatives" (given that the Council is to exercise "legislative power"), this is a recognizably modern proposal, particularly in the fact that all known territories of the world are included. It is perhaps symptomatic that Crucé's work was "ahead of its time" (as the phrase goes) from the fact that it was very little noticed, following its publication, prior to being "rediscovered" in the twentieth century. At least two other factors may also be relevant: (1) unlike several better known proponents of schemes for supranational political unity, at the time he published *The New Cyneas*, Crucé was not a well-known politician, statesman, or intellectual; (2) the notion of extension of political unity beyond European borders may have seemed totally preposterous in the seventeenth century, owing to transportation and communications problems, if nothing else.

On the transportation and communications issue, however, Crucé may have been operating on the basis of a more clear-sighted appreciation of the true nature of the situation than his contemporaries. By the early 1600s, Africa had been circumnavigated, the world had been circumnavigated, trade with the Far East was well established, the Spanish and Portuguese empires in Latin America were well established, and the British, French, and Dutch colonization of North America was gearing up. There may have been large "unknown" areas on maps of North America and Africa, but at least the general location of these areas was known. It may have required a sea voyage of several months to travel from Europe to anywhere else in the world, and this is certainly an appreciable period of time—but it is not the same as several years or several decades. As of the early 1600s, the process of global integration—a process that is continuing apace even today—was well underway. Crucé was exceptional in having a very early vision of the potential global political implications of global economic and social integration. But this vision was not in the same apparent fantasy realm as were accounts in the seventeenth century of voyages to the moon. (Another erstwhile "fantasy," be it noted, that has since come true.)

What is perhaps even more remarkable about Crucé is that despite his clerical vocation, he was insistent upon the necessity and desirability of religious toleration. As already mentioned, the typical supranational unification proposal of the early modern period pertained exclusively to the nations of Western Europe, and this unification was perceived largely as a steppingstone to the defeat of infidels outside of Europe, especially the Turks. Religion was the reigning ideology of Crucé's time, and religious conflicts were the contemporary equivalent of the ideological conflicts of later times. If there was one cause, above all, which men and women around the world agreed was worth fighting for and dying for, it was the cause of religion. As a Catholic priest, Crucé was capable of analyzing doctrinal differences with a professional's eye, and he devoted a great deal of his book to arguing that most if not all doctrinal differences between the major religions of the world pertained to minor issues: for example, whether the supreme being was properly designated "Yahweh," "God," "Allah," etc. With respect to major issues, such as the existence of a supreme being with a benevolent interest in humanity, the main principles of ethical behavior by human individuals, the existence of some kind of supernatural sanctions against unethical behavior, and so on, there was a tremendous amount of overlap between the major religions of the world. There was no sensible basis, therefore, for violent conflict between adherents to different religions. Another factor influencing Cruce's judgment in this matter was the abundance of violent conflict among adherents to each of the major world religions, including the Christian. During the Middle Ages, warfare was perpetual among kings, princes, dukes, and other aristocrats of Western Europe, all of whom subscribed to orthodox Roman Catholicism. Later on, following the Protestant Reformation (initiated in the early 1500s), to these many "traditional" conflicts were added a great many more in which religious differences between Roman Catholicism and the various forms of Protestant Christianity played a major catalytic role. Cruce published *The New Cyneas* in 1623, near the beginning of the Thirty Years' War (1618-1648), the last and perhaps the most devastating of the many religious wars inspired by the Protestant Reformation. He had absorbed the lesson that as far as the maintenance of peace was concerned, it would not be of much help to have the entire world population subscribing to any one religion, whether it be a form of Christianity, or a form of any other of the major world religions.

Although *The New Cyneas* is a remarkable work considering the date when it was published, it prefigures the modern notion of a world state chiefly in scope, rather than in its institutional features. As befits a work published during the rising age of absolute monarchy, it envisions that the subsidiary political units would all be hereditary monarchies of one sort or another. There would be no trace of democracy either at the national level or at the supranational level, since representatives to the Council of Ambassadors would be appointed by their respective monarchs, as opposed to being elected by the citizens. The sole purpose of the Council would be to suppress armed conflicts among and within nations by the adjudication of controversies. The "legislation" referred to in the description of the proposal would not be the passage and promulgation of general legal rules and prescriptions, but rather specific resolutions of specific problems. The Council would not have a permanent executive arm nor armed forces at its immediate disposition. Rather it would marshal the forces of loyal monarchs against those of upstart monarchs (i.e., monarchs refusing to abide by the decisions of the Council). The concept is really that of a universal mutual assistance alliance, later realized in the form of the League of Nations and the United Nations—neither of which were particularly successful in discouraging aggressive war, and neither of which constitutes a genuine world state in the modern sense. Moreover, Cruce's Council of Ambassadors would not be concerned in any way—aside from the suppression of war—with improving the socioeconomic status of the population. Cruce probably assumed that economic living standards were roughly equivalent all around the world—which may not have been far from the truth in the early 1600s. As would naturally be the case with a book published in 1623, *The New Cyneas* is unaware of the tremendous differences in national economic living standards which later developed over the course of the nineteenth and twentieth century. It was therefore oblivious to what is today a major impediment to world government.

In the three centuries of modern Western European history between 1700 and the present time, there were two veritably catastrophic periods of warfare: the "French wars" between 1792 and 1815, and the "German wars" between 1914 and 1945. In both cases, ideological as well as nationalistic factors played a major role in initiating and perpetuating the conflicts. The earlier French wars were precipitated by the French Revolution, a cataclysmic political and social upheaval, extending from the convening of the Estates-General at Versailles in May 1789 to the coup d'état in November 1799 that toppled the Directory and made Napoleon Bonaparte the dictatorial ruler of France. During its first few years, the revolutionary movement in France grew steadily more radical, leading eventually to the execution by guillotine of King Louis XVI in January 1793, and the so-called Reign of Terror from April 1973 to July 1794, during which thousands of "enemies of the Republic" were guillotined. The principal architect of the Terror, Maximilian Robespierre, was himself guillotined in the "Thermidorean reaction" of July 1794. This coup soon led to the Directory, a five-member executive committee in which government authority was largely concentrated, itself overthrown a few years later by Napoleon.

A very serious and sustained effort was made in France, both before and after the advent of Napoleon, to put into practice the revolutionary principles of "liberty, equality, and fraternity." During the tumultuous decade of the 1790s, both the hereditary aristocracy and the Roman Catholic clergy in France were stripped of most of their traditional entitlements and privileges, the monarchy was abolished and a republic established (albeit a short-lived republic), and the natural rights of the common man were exalted. Such sudden and prodigious legal, social, and political transformation quite naturally aroused both intense enthusiasm and intense opposition inside France, as well as intense interest and considerable apprehension outside France. Some felt that the French example should be emulated either wholly or in part, while others looked upon developments in France with shock and horror. Austrian forces invaded France in the summer of 1792, and from then onward until the defeat of Napoleon on the battlefield of Waterloo in June 1815, all of Europe became convulsed in warfare. France itself became an armed camp, ruled from 1799 onward by a military dictator in the form of Napoleon Bonaparte—who proclaimed himself an emperor in 1804. While Napoleonic France in the early 1800s was politically quite similar to the absolute monarchy it had known under the Bourbon kings, the vast legal and social transformations of the Revolution were mostly continued and consolidated.

The French wars from 1792 through 1815 were the most comprehensive, devastating, and destructive wars Europe had known—eclipsing even the Thirty Years' War (1618-1648)—since the chaos attending the fall of the Roman empire to barbarian invaders in the fifth century. The armies were larger and the weapons were more potent than anything witnessed in previous history. In addition, the extravagant fervor elicited by the ideological conflict between the principles of equality and democracy on the one hand, and aristocracy and stability on the other, was equal to anything that had attended the intense religious wars generated by the Protestant Reformation. To many Europeans, the French armies were glorious liberators who might finally release all of humanity from centuries of bondage to an arrogant aristocratic and religious elite. To many others, they were perfidious spreaders of strife, leveling, anarchy, and brutality. The combination of ideological controversy, mass armies, and increasingly powerful weaponry, generated an unprecedented amount of death, disability, disfigurement, and destruction.

Napoleonic France was finally brought down by a coalition of major powers including Prussia, Austria, Britain, and Russia. At the Congress of Vienna, convened from September 1814 to June 1815, the great powers restored the Bourbon monarchy in France, and redrew national boundaries in Europe in such a manner as to hopefully achieve a stable balance of power, under which no one nation could become strong enough to threaten aggression against other nations. However, restoring the Bourbon monarchy in France did not entirely undo the revolutionary transformation of French politics and society, and the Bourbon monarchy's final demise occurred in the disturbances of 1830. Most historians are complimentary toward the work of Metternich and other diplomats at the Congress of Vienna, in that the territorial boundaries devised there, in addition to the Concert of Europe (periodic meetings of national representatives to discuss and resolve emerging conflicts of interest), is generally thought to be responsible for a century of relative peace in Western Europe between the end of the French wars in 1815 and the beginning of the German wars in 1914. Of course, estimates of the long-term stability of the balance of power, as supplemented by irregular meetings of diplomats, had to be revised downward drastically in light of the unprecedented carnage of World War I (1914-1918).

It has sometimes been observed that proposals for supranational political organizations, up to and including literal world states, flourish most abundantly in periods beset by large-scale warfare.[2] A numerical indication of this phenomenon is contained in the Wynner and Lloyd catalogue (Part II) of theoretical plans to unite nations from 1306 to 1905. Of the 74 plans from this 600-year interval enumerated and briefly described in the catalogue, some 28 date from 1792 through 1821, a period of 30 years. Thus approximately 38 percent of the plans date from an interval covering only 5 percent of the total time span. Some notable historical figures are to be found among the proposers of the 74 plans put forward between 1306 and 1905: in addition to those already mentioned, Dante Alighieri, Desiderius Erasmus, Pope Leo X, Hugo Grotius, William Penn, Jeremy Bentham, Johann Fichte, Immanuel Kant, Thomas Paine, Czar Alexander I, Count Henri de Saint-Simon, Napoleon Bonaparte, Simon Bolivar, Charles Sumner, Baroness Bertha von Suttner, William T. Stead. No implication is intended that these individuals advocated a world state as presently understood. To begin with, most of the plans are extremely vague as to organization and procedure. In many if not most cases, the plans merely call for political unification of the Western European nations, i.e., for something along the lines of the European Union of today. Moreover, many of these regional plans, especially those earlier in the period, are inspired by a dubious vision of a politically united Europe conquering, or at least dominating, the rest of the world. Finally, in many if not most cases, the plans conceive "political unification" in terms merely of a formally recognized super-alliance: for something along the lines of the League of Nations of the interwar years and the United Nations of the post-World War II years. Few plans extended qualitatively beyond the alliance concept to the state concept.

For example, perhaps the best-known today of the plans from this period is that of Immanuel Kant, the renowned philosopher of the late Enlightenment period. His influential essay, *Perpetual Peace*, was published in 1795, when the European wars generated by the French Revolution were already in full swing. Inspired by the American and French examples, Kant recommended that all nations should become some form of democratic republic. But he was explicit that these nations should not be organized into a federation, but rather into the much looser form of a confederation, on grounds that a federation would be too susceptible to developing into a tyranny. Thus, while today Kant is widely deemed an important contributor to the historical development of the idea of world government, in fact he advised against it. Indeed, his fundamental skepticism toward world government manifests a predominant attitude that has come down through the years to the present day. For example, John Rawls, another philosopher who is considered one of the most influential practitioners of his discipline of the twentieth century, wrote: "Here I follow Kant's lead in *Perpetual Peace* (1795) in thinking that a world government by which I mean a unified political regime with the legal powers normally exercised by central [national] governments—would either be a global despotism or else would rule over a fragile empire torn by frequent civil strife as various regions and peoples tried to regain their political freedom and autonomy."[3]

Kant's recommended world confederation would not be formed all at once but rather gradually, over an extended period of time. The confederation would function through a Congress of States attended by ministers and ambassadors, a body very similar to Crucé's Council of Ambassadors, except that the nations represented were to be republics rather than monarchies. As was the case with Crucé's Council, the principal function of Kant's Congress would be to mobilize military containment of aggressive nations (such as France was when Kant wrote *Perpetual Peace*). The basic idea was to achieve a more quick, efficient, and reliable way of dealing with aggressive nations than the slow and haphazard formation of temporary coalitions. Kant's essay contains lengthy ruminations on the oneness of mankind, the moral imperative to hospitality, and so on and so forth—but these philosophical ruminations, as such, had little immediate bearing on concrete questions of political organization.

Despite their wide diversity and serious limitations, there is one key and critical element that unites practically all of these plans: the idea that the supranational political entity is to be founded upon contract rather than upon conquest. Almost all of the plans specify that the adherence of the nations to the supranational political entity is to come about owing to free and voluntary decision on the part of each one of the member nations. This is fundamentally in opposition to the imperial concept, according to which nations (or other subsidiary regions) are initially brought into the imperial domain by means of military conquest. The imperial concept can itself be subdivided into the "liberal empire" concept, according to which, following conquest, the loyalty of the component regions is to be assured mainly by wise and benevolent governance, and the "authoritarian empire" concept, according to which, following conquest, the loyalty of the component regions is to be assured mainly by stern and forceful discipline. These various proposals for supranational political organization, illustrated by the 74 plans from 1306-1905 enumerated by Wynner and Lloyd, are qualitatively different from both the liberal empire concept and the authoritarian empire concept. They mark a definite forward progression in the evolution of human thinking on the potential role of a supranational government.

While it was customary for critics of supranational political organization from 1306-1905 (and by extension, of the specific type of supranational political organization known today as a "world state") to ridicule each and every one of the 74 proposals enumerated by Wynner and Lloyd, as thoroughly utopian and patently preposterous, in actual fact the substance of many of these proposals was in fact eventually realized in the real world in the form of the League of Nations, established in 1920 by the Treaty of Versailles. Clearly, the proposers of these schemes for international unity were not such fuzzy-minded dreamers as their critics alleged. They may have been "ahead of their time," to use the standard cliché, but they were not wrong.

During the horrific carnage of World War I, an inspirational slogan emerged that this was going to be "the war to end wars." At the end of the war, a supranational political organization was established known as the League of Nations, whose purpose it was to make a reality of this slogan. The League of Nations was in fact a real-world implementation of the typical pre-1914 proposal for supranational political union: a super-alliance of such power and resources that no non-member nation would dare attack a member nation. The League, obviously, was unsuccessful not only in preventing World War II, but also in either shortening the duration or moderating the ferocity of that conflict. The League was hobbled from the beginning by the fact that two of the major participants in World War I, Russia and the United States, did not join it upon its foundation. Russia was wracked by revolutionary turmoil and its government was calling stridently for worldwide proletarian revolution—obviously, therefore, it was not fit company in a supranational organization dedicated to peace, stability, and the preservation of the status quo. For its part, the United States succumbed, after the war, to a deep-seated isolationist mentality according to which America should not allow itself to become entangled in periodic foreign bloodlettings—and especially in those on the politically devious and morally corrupted Western European continent. But even if Russia and the United States had been charter members of the League of Nations, it is far from certain that this would have deterred Hitler and the German people from their revanchist policies and objectives during the interwar period.

## The League of Nations

The League of Nations commenced its short, unhappy career on January 16, 1920, with a brief Council meeting in Paris to appoint a commission to ascertain the boundaries of the Saar. Established by a Covenant of the 1919 Treaty of Versailles, the League convened its first Assembly meeting at its permanent headquarters in Geneva, Switzerland, in November

1920. By this time it was clear that the United States would not be taking membership. Although the League had been the special enthusiasm of President Woodrow Wilson, a resurgence of American isolationism following the nation's brief but costly involvement in World War I, induced the U.S. Senate to reject the Treaty, and with it United States membership in the League. This was by no means the only inauspicious note as the League commenced its activities. Many if not most of the leading nations of the world harbored serious reservations about both the Treaty and the League. France felt betrayed because in the Treaty negotiations she had given up her claim on territory on the east bank of the Rhine on the presumption that American participation in the League would guarantee her security against future German aggression. The Japanese were aggrieved that the Covenant did not include a declaration on racial equality. The Italians were disappointed that they were not awarded African mandates. Germany and Austria, initially excluded from the League, regarded the Versailles peace terms as intolerably harsh, as veritably sadistic. The Russians remained uninvolved owing to internal revolution and civil war. And so on. Little confidence existed that the League would provide effective security against a recurrence of major warfare. The member nations continued to play the time-honored balance of power game, and regarded the League as merely a minor adjunct to their traditional foreign policy. Possibly this was a case of a self-fulfilling prophecy, but within a very brief period of historical time the League did indeed prove its ineffectiveness beyond a reasonable doubt.[4]

The League of Nations was comprised of four component bodies: (1) an Assembly in which all member nations were equally represented; (2) a much smaller Council in which the major powers had permanent seats, with additional seats allocated to smaller nations on a rotating basis; (3) an administrative Secretariat guided by a Secretary-General; and (4) a Permanent Court of International Justice intended as a supplementary body to the Permanent Court of Arbitration established in 1899 by the first Hague peace conference. The Assembly fielded a supporting network of committees and subcommittees in six general areas: legal and constitutional matters, technical organization of the League, reduction of armaments, budgetary and financial matters, social and general matters, and political matters. The Assembly met once a year for a month at a time, and passed a series of resolutions concerning matters it wanted addressed by the Council and the Secretariat. The Council was obligated to meet once a year but normally it met more or less continuously. According to Article 5 of the League Covenant, decisions and directives of the Council had to be approved unanimously by all members in attendance at the meeting—in the light of subsequent history, this provision is now generally considered to have been fatal to the League's effectiveness as a guarantor of peace.

The League had a superficial resemblance to a typical national government since the Assembly might be considered analogous to the lower house of a legislature, the Council analogous to the upper house of a legislature, the Secretariat as the executive branch, and the Permanent Court of International Justice as the judicial branch. But it lacked three essential characteristics of a national government: (1) it possessed no military forces under its direct control; (2) it did not possess the authority to levy taxes; and (3) it was separated from any direct connection with the populations of the member nations because delegates to both the Assembly and the Council were appointed by the national governments of the member nations rather than being elected by the populations of the member nations. Thus in practice the League was merely an assemblage of ambassadors, the creature of the national governments. Citizens of the member nations did not have the sense of being citizens of a higher political authority than that of their respective national governments, of participating in a qualitatively higher form of international cooperation. Very little effective power and authority was delegated by the member nations to the League. The Assembly of the League of Nations was merely an advisory body to the Council, just as the Council was merely an advisory body to the national governments of the member nations. Member nations were torn between their visions of being protected against foreign aggression by the overwhelming combined military force of the League membership, and their apprehensions that the League would become either an instrument through which many other nations would "gang up" on them and hinder the reasonable pursuit of their legitimate national interests, or an instrument through which they would be "dragged into" devastating warfare unrelated to their legitimate national interests.

The fragile and insubstantial nature of the League's authority was reflected in its judicial arm, the Permanent Court of International Justice. The Permanent Court of International Justice (popularly known as the World Court) did not replace but rather supplemented the Permanent Court of Arbitration (popularly known as the Hague Tribunal), established earlier (1899) by the first Hague peace conference. Except to international lawyers, the distinction between the World Court and the Hague Tribunal is rather vague, and it is further blurred by the fact that both were (and remain) located in the city of The Hague in the Netherlands. After World War II, the League of Nations was replaced by the United Nations and the Permanent Court of International Justice was replaced by the International Court of Justice (ICJ). Just as the United Nations was very close to being a carbon copy of the League of Nations in terms of basic organization and functions, so too the International Court of Justice was similarly very close to being a carbon copy of the Permanent Court of International Justice. A minor difference between the two tribunals is that the World Court (now the ICJ) hears only cases in which the disputants are both national governments, whereas the Hague Tribunal hears cases in which one or both of the parties is a private individual or organization. But the principal distinction between the World Court and the Hague Tribunal is roughly the distinction between adjudication and arbitration. In arbitration, the two parties to a dispute submit it to a panel of impartial arbitrators and agree to abide by the arbitrators' decision. In adjudication, on the other hand, formal legal principles are invoked by one or both parties to a dispute. Within nations, adjudication is further distinguished from arbitration by the fact that the court may call upon the criminal justice system to enforce its decision. Any party to a dispute who ignores the adjudicated decision of a court becomes subject to arrest and imprisonment for contempt of court. In arbitration, on the other hand, there is no direct enforcement of the arbitrators' decision. However, if one party ignores the arbitrated decision, the injured party may bring suit in a judicial court over the same dispute, and if the judicial panel then affirms the arbitration panel's decision, compulsory enforcement could then be brought to bear. Therefore, in principle, adjudication is a large step beyond arbitration.

Thus at the time of its foundation in 1920, it was hoped that the World Court would represent a significant advance over the Hague Tribunal, since it would go beyond the realm of arbitration into the realm of adjudication. However, there was one critical element missing: a means of compulsory enforcement. Although called a "court," the Permanent Court of International Justice associated with the League of Nations lacked those critical powers of enforcement wielded by courts within nations. Theoretically, if a nation ignored its ruling, the Permanent Court could have appealed to its parent organization, the League of Nations, to impose sanctions against the errant nation—possibly even to launch military operations against it. But this was never done. For one thing, the issues involved were too minor. For another, the League of Nations did not have the necessary solidarity and determination even to entertain such a notion. After all, even when it was a case of outright military invasion of one nation by another, the League either looked the other way altogether, or merely issued statements of mild remonstrance. It never mustered military action against errant nations. Therefore the Permanent Court of International Justice was not really a substantive advance beyond the Permanent Court of Arbitration.

The League of Nations had the misfortune of operating during an interval of time that in the longer historical perspective is perceived as little more than an uneasy truce separating the two "German wars": World War I (1914-1918) and World War II (1939-1945). The basic problem was that the peace terms imposed on Germany and her allies by France, Britain, Italy, and the United States after World War I were excessively harsh given that the German defeat had not been sufficiently decisive. Unlike the situation after World War II, the entire German nation was not placed under military occupation. Most of the First World War had been fought on French soil and Russian soil, and that in conjunction with the fact that aerial bombing was in its infancy, meant that the German people had been spared the worst horrors of modern warfare. In the immediate aftermath of the Versailles Treaty, demagogues such as Adolf Hitler put forward the theory that if Germany had persisted she would have won the war, but instead the nation had been done in by "a stab in the back" administered by cowardly civilian government officials in the capital city of Berlin. The theory appealed greatly to the wounded pride of many Germans. The economic suffering and social dislocation generated by the Great Depression of the 1930s gave the German Nazi party of Adolf Hitler the chance it had been waiting for throughout the 1920s. Hitler gained dictatorial powers over the German government early in 1933, and immediately launched into a vigorous program of "national regeneration."

The principal key to German national regeneration, in the minds of the Nazis, was the rectification of the terrible injustice done to Germany by the 1919 Treaty of Versailles. Therefore, one of Hitler's first actions, upon gaining power, was to repudiate the arms limitations imposed by the Treaty of Versailles and commence a crash program of rearmament. At that time, the League of Nations was promoting multilateral disarmament negotiations, but these broke down soon after Hitler withdrew Germany from the League in October, 1933. Germany enlisted as allies certain other non-democratic nations that were dissatisfied with the post-World War I international status quo, principally Italy and Japan. Japan concentrated on extending its influence in Asia by invading the Chinese province of Manchuria in September, 1931, and eventually establishing there a puppet regime known as "Manchukuo." The League sent an investigative commission to Manchuria, but by the time the League Assembly adopted the commission's report condemning the Japanese invasion, the conquest had been completed. Although no action was taken by the League beyond verbal condemnation, Japan announced its withdrawal from the League in March, 1933. Subsequently, Japan assiduously furthered what it termed the "Greater East-Asia Co-Prosperity Sphere," the pursuit of which entailed a full-scale invasion of China in 1937. In 1935, Italy invaded and conquered Abyssinia (now known as Ethiopia), a member in good standing of the League of Nations and one of the few independent nations in Africa at that time. In response to the invasion, the League imposed economic sanctions on Italy, but they were ineffective in preventing the conquest, and as soon as the conquest had been completed the sanctions were lifted on grounds that since the conquest of Ethiopia was now a fait accompli, no further useful purpose was served by the sanctions. (At the time, Britain and France were still hoping to enlist Italy in a united front against Nazi Germany.)

Meanwhile, Hitler had not been idle. Under Hitler's complete control, and emboldened by its rapidly growing military power, Nazi Germany remilitarized the Rhineland (1936), absorbed Austria (spring, 1938), annexed part of Czechoslovakia (fall, 1938) and then conquered the rest (spring, 1939). Protestations against these aggressive actions in the League of Nations were ineffective. When Britain and France finally declared war on Germany in September, 1939, after the invasion of Poland, it was on the basis of their mutual defense treaties with Poland and not on the basis of resistance to aggression organized by the League of Nations. There then followed the so-called "sitzkrieg" along France's Maginot Line from the fall of 1939 to the late spring of 1940. Although they had declared war on Germany, Britain and France were reluctant to have matters escalate into a shooting war. Their restraint was not rewarded. Too impatient to wait for a negotiated peace, Hitler invaded and conquered France in May, 1940, and drove the remnants of the British military forces from continental Europe. Flushed with success, Hitler followed this up with the miscalculation that eventually doomed him: the invasion of the USSR in June, 1941. The Second World War, which lasted almost six years from September, 1939 to August, 1945, rewrote the record books established by the First World War: it was far worse in terms of scale, extent, cost, destruction, injury, and death.

In view of its inability to forestall World War II, it is easy to be contemptuous of the League of Nations. But contempt ought to be tempered with a certain amount of respect for this pioneering effort to establish an institutional underpinning for the principle of collective security and active cooperation among the nations. What doomed the League of Nations in general was the fact that it did not represent an adequate advance beyond the sovereign nation-state system that had preceded it, and what doomed it in particular was the dissatisfaction of several large and powerful nations with the international status quo, especially Germany, Italy, and Japan. Of the three, Germany was clearly the principal catalyst. Had Germany been treated more generously following World War I so that repudiation of the Versailles Treaty had not been an issue, conceivably the League of Nations would have compiled a record comparable to that of the United Nations in the post-World War II era.

## The United Nations

Somewhere around the middle of the terrible years between 1939 and 1945, as inconceivable economic resources where being devoted on both sides to destroying enemy property and lives, resulting in the maiming and killing of millions, but at a point where the Allied powers were starting, slowly and painfully, to get the upper hand over the Axis powers, an idea commenced to gain support: that of a new and greatly improved League of Nations to be known as the United Nations. The name "United Nations" is generally attributed to U.S. President Franklin D. Roosevelt, although as far back as 1918, one Theodore Harris had put forward a detailed blueprint for a world government to be known as the "United Nations of the World."[5] The first official use of the term "United Nations" was in the Declaration of the United Nations of January 1, 1942, in which 26 nations pledged themselves to continue the war effort against the Axis powers until final victory was attained, and not to make peace separately under any circumstances. The first official statement of the need for a new international organization to replace the League of Nations was the Moscow Declaration of October 30, 1943, issued by China, Great Britain, the United States, and the USSR. Specific proposals for the new organization were drafted by representatives of these four nations at the Dumbarton Oaks Conference from August to October, 1944. These proposals were refined at the Yalta Conference in February, 1945.

The founding conference, attended by all 50 nations that had subscribed to the Declaration of the United Nations and had declared war on Germany or Japan by March 1, 1945, was held at San Francisco from April 25 through June 26, 1945. The final United Nations Charter, having been approved unanimously by all national delegations to the San Francisco Conference at a ceremony in the San Francisco Opera House on June 25, 1945, was then ratified by the required number of nations on October 24, 1945. October 24 has thus been declared "United Nations Day," but it is symptomatic of the disappointed hopes aroused by the United Nations that October 24 is an official holiday in few of its member nations. The charter members of the U.N. included the majority of independent nations of the time, one of the few important exceptions being Switzerland. The first meetings of the General Assembly and the Security Council took place in London, respectively on January 10 and January 17, 1946. The U.N.'s first Secretary-General, Trygve Lie of

Norway, was designated by the Security Council on February 1, 1946.[6]

In the minds of those who designed and implemented it, the first and foremost distinction between the United Nations and its little lamented predecessor, the League of Nations, would be that no major power would be missing from membership in the former organization. Specifically, the United States would not only be a founding member, but it would be a driving force in this new attempt to achieve collective security by means of a permanent, well-organized, and generously staffed super-alliance. The extent of its commitment to the United Nations may be gauged from the fact that the United States agreed to meet no less than one-third of the U.N.'s operating expenses. The aspiration toward near-universality implied that the defeated Axis nations would be admitted fairly soon after the war, once the remnants of fascism within them had been eradicated. Italy was admitted in 1955 and Japan in 1956, although owing to Cold War complications, specifically the partition of Germany into the non-communist West Germany (the Federal Republic of Germany) and the communist East Germany (the German Democratic Republic), the two parts were not admitted to separate U.N. membership until 1973. Effective with the accession of the German Democratic Republic to the Federal Republic of Germany in 1990, Germany has had one seat in the United Nations.

In addition to virtually universal membership, the United Nations, in contrast to the League of Nations, would make a far more systematic and determined attempt to eradicate the roots of warfare by fostering economic, political, and social progress throughout the world. In other words, the United Nations would undertake a "peace-building" mission as well as a "peacekeeping" mission. The theme of "a new beginning" was reinforced by abandoning the somewhat stodgy League of Nations headquarters in Geneva and opening a shiny new glass-and-steel skyscraper, built on a parcel of high-priced real estate (donated by John D. Rockefeller Jr.) on the East River in New York City, to serve as U.N. headquarters. Consisting as it does of large quantities of uplifting prose ("We the peoples of the United Nations, determined to save succeeding generations from the scourge of war, which twice in our lifetime has brought untold sorrow to mankind..."), the U.N. Charter is a far more elaborate document than was the old League Covenant. The Charter was soon supplemented by the Universal Declaration of Human Rights, adopted by the General Assembly on December 10, 1948. While this document has been described by some as a "pious wish list," it nevertheless clearly delineates the kind of human condition within world society to which any and all rational persons of good will aspire.

But although its membership was larger and its goals more ambitious, the United Nations was virtually a carbon copy of the defunct League of Nations in terms of institutional structure. The "Assembly" of the League of Nations became the "General Assembly" of the United Nations. The "Council" of the League of Nations became the "Security Council" of the United Nations. The distinction between the permanent seats on the Security Council of the major powers and the rotating seats of the smaller powers was continued, as was the requirement that decisions of the Security Council be unanimously approved by the permanent members (thus, any major power could veto a decision of the Security Council). The "Secretariat" of the League of Nations became the "Secretariat" of the United Nations. The "Secretary-General" of the League of Nations became the "Secretary-General" of the United Nations. The "Permanent Court of International Justice" of the League of Nations became the "International Court of Justice" of the United Nations. The United Nations did, however, add two new councils to supplement the Security Council: the Trusteeship Council and the Economic and Social Council. The purpose of the former was mainly to oversee the devolution of the colonial empires, a purpose largely completed by the 1960s. The purpose of the latter has been, and continues to be, fostering material, institutional, and cultural progress throughout the world. But despite various superficial efforts to differentiate the United Nations from its toothless and ineffective predecessor, from the moment of its origin in 1945 there was not a great deal more confidence in the U.N. as a guarantor of peace than there was in the League of Nations at the time of its origin in 1919. The two organizations were too much alike in structure and mission. And the various pressures toward antagonism and conflict among nations were, if anything, far worse in 1945 than they had been in 1919.

    First and foremost, the one nation in the world incapable of abiding the capitalist economic system and determined to overthrow that system all over the world, namely the USSR, had progressed from being a wobbly infant in 1919 to being a military colossus in 1945. The hopes and intentions underlying the United Nations almost immediately foundered on the deadly reef represented by the polarization of the world's nations into two hostile camps: the camp of communism and the camp of capitalism. Among the optimists at the time of the U.N.'s formation, it was intended that the new international organization would have substantial, permanent military forces under its direct control, and Article 47 directed the formation of a Military Staff Committee, composed of the Chiefs of Staff of the five permanent members of the Security Council, to develop formal agreements that would have put specific military units of member nations under the direct command of the Security Council. But unfortunately, owing to the inability of the representative of the USSR in the

Military Staff Committee to reach agreement with the representatives of the other four major powers on the Security Council, nothing came of this idea. The same split nullified the efforts of two other special bodies established by the Security Council: the Atomic Energy Commission, and the Commission on Conventional Armaments.

At the time the United Nations was established, in the eyes of its charter members the principal function of the organization was the preservation of international peace, i.e. to strengthen deterrence against the sort of very obvious and straightforward military aggression practiced by the Axis nations prior to World War II. It was hoped that the existence of the United Nations would make it easier to quickly muster an overwhelming military coalition against any nation that launched a full scale military invasion of a member nation. In the judgment of the principal noncommunist nations, the most likely candidate for launching such invasions was the USSR, and their most likely target would be the Western European nations still wobbly from the vicissitudes of the War. The intention was to deter Stalin from trying to follow in the footsteps of Hitler. In fact, neither Stalin nor his successors did try to follow in Hitler's footsteps, although the reason for this was not so much the existence of the United Nations as it was the NATO alliance, the possession of nuclear weapons by the United States, Britain, and France, and a substantial U.S. military presence in Western Europe (the "tripwire" force).

There was little or no intention at that time of having the United Nations intervene in civil wars within nations, especially if the foreign involvement was limited and confined mainly to the provision of arms and material, as opposed to combat personnel, to one side or the other. There is no specific provision in the U.N. Charter under which intervention in domestic conflicts is authorized. Nevertheless, the great majority of actual U.N. peacekeeping missions have in fact involved predominantly domestic conflicts. For the most part, however, the U.N. forces involved have been fairly small, especially when compared to the military capabilities of the major powers.

When conflicts arose in which important interests of the major powers were involved, the United Nations kept out of it, as for example in the case of the Soviet suppression of the Hungarian uprising of 1956 and the Czechoslovakian independence movement of 1968, and in the Falkland Islands war between Britain and Argentina in 1982. The United Nations was also excluded from a number of conflict situations in Asia, such as the Chinese occupation of Tibet, the Sino-Indian and Sino-Soviet border conflicts, the war in Indochina and Vietnam, the Vietnamese action in Kampuchea, and the Chinese action against Vietnam. The United Nations also stayed out of the Iran-Iraq War of 1980-1988, a border war that is estimated to have cost the combatants 1 million dead and 1.7 million wounded. Neither side appealed to the U.N. for assistance during the course of the conflict, but given the magnitude of the conflict and the fact that it was confined to border regions, together with the fact that both combatants were significant military powers, it is questionable that the United Nations would have been willing to take sides.

There have been only two occasions in the history of the United Nations in which the vision that initially inspired the organization was actually realized: the rapid mustering of large-scale military forces to oppose a conventional invasion. The first was the Korean War of 1950-1953, and the second was the Persian Gulf War of January-February, 1991. In both of these cases, the invading nation argued that the conflict was an internal affair outside the jurisdiction of the United Nations. In 1950, the dictator of North Korea, Kim Il-Sung, maintained that the purpose of the conflict was to achieve national unification in the face of intolerable provocations from hostile separatist elements in South Korea. This allegation was rejected, and the U.N. Security Council authorized military action against North Korea. The authorization succeeded because of the fact that the Soviet representative happened to be absent from the meeting. But had the Soviet representative been present to veto the Council resolution, there is little doubt that the United States and its allies would have proceeded anyway. The ensuing three-year Korean War resulted essentially in a military stalemate.

In 1990, the dictator of Iraq, Saddam Hussein, maintained that the purpose of the conflict was to achieve national unification in the face of intolerable provocations from hostile separatist elements in Kuwait, a claim that rested on political circumstances prevailing under the Ottoman Empire, a state organization defunct since 1918. The allegation was considered specious by most people outside of Iraq. The real reason for the invasion of Kuwait was Iraq's financial problems incurred during the prolonged border war with Iran (1980-1988), which Saddam Hussein hoped to ameliorate by taking over Kuwait's enormous income from petroleum exports. Hussein's reputation as one of the most brutal and repellent dictators in the contemporary world did not help the cause of Iraq. The invasion of Kuwait greatly alarmed Iraq's neighbors in the Middle East, especially equally oil-rich Saudi Arabia, whose government proposed military action to the United States and other nations for the purpose of ousting the Iraqis from Kuwait.

On August 2, 1990, the day following the Iraqi invasion of Kuwait, the United Nations Security Council called for Iraq to withdraw from Kuwait, and on August 6 it imposed a worldwide ban on trade with Iraq. Hussein responded on August 8 by formally annexing Kuwait. On November 29, the Security Council authorized the use of force against Iraq unless it withdrew its forces from Kuwait by January 15, 1991. Ten or twenty years previously, such resolutions would almost certainly have been impossible owing to opposition by the communist permanent members of the Security Council, Russia and China. But by 1990, the Cold War was in rapid decline, and the superpowers were no longer always being forced into opposition against one another on general ideological principles. Hussein ignored the U.N. demands, continued to build up the Iraqi commitment in Kuwait, and warned that if there was foreign intervention, Iraq's enemies would be annihilated in the "mother of all battles." By January, 1991, an Allied coalition of 32 nations, including the United States, Britain, France, Saudi Arabia, Egypt, and Syria, had fielded a force of 700,000 combat troops and support personnel, of which the U.S. contribution was 540,000.

On the night of January 16-17, 1991, Operation Desert Storm launched a massive air offensive against Iraqi military, production, and infrastructure targets. After more than a month of intensive bombardment, Operation Desert Saber was commenced on February 24, unleashing an overwhelming ground offensive into Kuwait and southern Iraq. The ground war lasted only four days, within which time the Iraqi presence in Kuwait was completely eliminated. In the wake of the defeat, there were popular uprisings against Saddam Hussein in Iraq, which the dictator put down with considerable difficulty. There was some discussion at this time among the Allies about pushing onward to a military occupation of Iraq and the removal of the Hussein regime. But the idea was discarded on grounds that it would have exceeded the official U.N. mandate, and in any event, in the face of such disastrous eventualities Hussein would probably soon be overthrown by internal opposition forces. But internal opposition forces had been greatly weakened by Hussein's longstanding policy of physically eliminating anyone who uttered one word of doubt or dissension (a policy previously employed by such notorious twentieth century dictators as Adolf Hitler and Joseph Stalin). Hussein therefore weathered the storm, and remained in control of Iraq until 2003.

Whatever the shortcomings and limitations of the United Nations in terms of lowering the probability of nuclear holocaust and/or of reducing the incidence of localized civil war, on the basis of the Gulf War episode, it could certainly be argued that the U.N.'s existence operates as an effective deterrent against one specific type of conflict: aggression against smaller nations by somewhat larger nations that are still well short of superpower status. The 1991 U.N. intervention against the Iraqi invasion of Kuwait may have provided a cautionary example to potential aggressors, of what the U.N. is increasingly capable of accomplishing, especially now that the Cold War is over. If the Iraqi invasion of Kuwait had occurred in 1970 at the height of the Cold War, quite possibly the Soviet Union would have vetoed intervention simply because it was favorable to almost any kind of disruption and destruction in the capitalist world. Of course, it is fully possible that the United States and its NATO allies in Western Europe would have dealt firmly with a hypothetical Iraqi invasion of Kuwait back in 1970, even in the absence of U.N. endorsement. Nevertheless, U.N. endorsement of military intervention endows it with greater legitimacy than it would otherwise possess. The greater the likelihood of obtaining U.N. endorsement against aggressive actions such as the Iraqi invasion of Kuwait, the more likely it is that military intervention will take place, and consequently the greater will be the level of deterrence against this particular type of aggression. To the people of small nations such as Kuwait, this is definite progress.

During the 1990s, in the wake of the Gulf War, there occurred something approaching a proliferation of U.N. peacekeeping missions. Up to and including 1990, some 17 peacekeeping missions had been mandated by the United Nations. From 1991 through 1999, some 39 additional missions were mandated. A few of these missions were unmitigated disasters and very high-profile failures. Although the 1992 mission to war-torn Yugoslavia had an authorized strength of 45,000, that turned out to be completely inadequate to the control of a desperate civil war fueled by ethnic hostilities nurtured over centuries. The outnumbered and outgunned U.N. peacekeepers only managed to survive by staying out of the way of the warring forces; in some cases they were literally held hostage. It goes without saying that the humanitarian purposes of the mission went unfulfilled.

A 1993 mission to Somalia, with an authorized strength of 28,000, was even more disastrous in a public relations sense. World public opinion had been outraged by extensive media coverage, prominently featuring photographs of starving children, of the man-made famine in Somalia caused by worsening civil strife. Once again the strength of the United Nations forces was completely inadequate to the task of disarming the combatants and restoring order. On October 3, 1993, a gun battle in the streets of Mogadishu between a U.S. unit and adherents to Mohammed Farah Aideed, whom the unit was attempting to apprehend, left 18 American soldiers dead and their bodies abused by hostile mobs. Photographic coverage of that event provoked outrage throughout the United States against presumably callous U.N. commanders employing U.S. soldiers as cannon fodder against hopeless odds. The U.N. mission to Somalia was quickly reduced to immediate humanitarian objectives (as opposed to the restoration of peace), and was fully withdrawn in 1995. World public opinion had created the mission to begin with, and world public opinion also pulled the plug on it when it became apparent that it was going to entail significant losses. Somalia was left to its fate, which predictably enough was bleak. If Somalia served any useful purpose thereafter, it was simply as an object lesson in the horrific consequences of anarchy.

Although it is now generally agreed that United Nations intervention, at force and casualty levels that are politically acceptable, is unlikely to be adequate to quell severe civil strife such as occurred in the former Yugoslavia in 1992, in Somalia in 1993, and in Rwanda in 1995, it is also fairly well accepted that U.N. peacekeeping missions can be a positive factor in less severe cases by placing on the scene an "impartial" military force not pre committed to one side or the other. Such forces can sometimes appreciably facilitate the achievement of ceasefires and/or political settlements. Among the several "U.N. success stories" are the missions to West New Guinea in 1962, to the Indian-Pakistani border in 1965, to the Sinai Peninsula in 1973, to the Afghanistan-Pakistan border in 1988, to Namibia in 1989, to El Salvador in 1991, to the Iraq-Kuwait border in 1991, and to Cambodia and Mozambique in 1992, and to the Sudan in 2005. So in some specialized cases a U.N. peacekeeping mission can be an effective instrument of peace.

It would be possible go on at considerable length pondering and debating the question of how much of a contribution, on the whole, the United Nations has made to preserving peace and fostering cooperation in the international sphere. At one extreme are those who assert that the U.N. has been a completely negligible factor in world politics, while at the other extreme are those who assert that it has made a major positive contribution. Obviously the truth lies somewhere in between. It is probably safe to say that the United Nations has made an "appreciable" contribution to peace, although it would probably be excessive to say that it has made an "important" or an "extraordinary" contribution. This level of assessment of the peacekeeping effort of the United Nations is probably applicable also to its "peace-building" effort. That is to say, the United Nations has made an "appreciable" contribution to the economic and social progress of nations, but it has not made an "important" or "extraordinary" contribution.

Just as the U.N. has made only a limited contribution to peace and security throughout the world owing to the unwillingness of the member nations to entrust substantial military forces to it, so too it has made only a limited contribution to global economic development because of the unwillingness of the member nations to entrust substantial foreign development assistance resources to it. The World Bank, through which a substantial part of the current foreign aid flow to the LDCs is channeled, is considered a "specialized agency" of the United Nations, but this is more in the nature of a courtesy gesture than a practical reality. Neither the General Assembly nor the Security Council nor the Secretary-General have any direct control over the World Bank, and the World Bank budget is not included in the United Nations budget. Even if the U.N. were spending its entire budget on economic development (in actual fact it spends only a small fraction of its budget for purposes that have anything to do with economic development), it would not account for a substantial share of the total foreign aid flow. Another way of putting the U.N. budget into perspective is to compare it with the government budgets of the larger member nations. For instance, the total United Nations budget in the latter 1990s was about 0.58 percent of the total U.S. federal government budget (a little over one half of one percent), and was 3.6 percent of the U.S. national defense budget. If the United Nations has not yet "solved world problems," including the problem of global economic inequality, it is not difficult to see why. One cannot construct mansions with the resources appropriate for the construction of shacks.

Questions about the practical effect of the United Nations on global realities might be debated endlessly without approaching any meaningful resolution. But there is an important distinction to be drawn between the practical impact of the United Nations and the psychological impact, as well as between the short-term impact and the long-term impact. The fact that the U.N.'s short-term practical impact has not been dramatic does not necessarily mean that it has not been effective in a psychological sense as a symbol of human unity, and that it will not ultimately prove to have been, in the long run, extremely important in a practical sense as well. It could be quite important simply that the United Nations is an existent organization, that it has an impressive headquarters on the East River, that it has a flag, that its "blue helmets" have appeared at many times and in many places over the last several decades, that it represents a foreshadowing of the federal world government that humanity may and possibly will establish in the not-distant future. The cumulative psychological impact of this symbol could be decisive. Taking the League of Nations and the United Nations together, their history covers four fifths of the twentieth century. Throughout four fifths of the twentieth century, these organizations stood as clear indications of humanity's persistent desire for a benign global political unity that will effectively eliminate the human tragedy and material waste associated with warfare, and will raise human civilization to new heights.

## The Postwar World Government Boom

Given the virtually immediate polarization of the world along ideological lines in the aftermath of the Second World War, the fundamental defects of the United Nations were obvious almost from the very beginning to both the "realist" majority and the "visionary" minority. The realist majority viewed the U.N. mainly as just another tool for the pursuance of national interests, but far less important as such than foreign ministries and war departments. The visionary minority—those people responsible for the ephemeral "world government boom" in the immediate aftermath of World War II—saw the U.N. as a hollow shadow of the federal world government that it ought to be. The realists envisioned the indefinite continuation of time-honored balance of power politics, U.N. or no U.N. They also saw no reason why the advent of nuclear weapons should fundamentally alter this game. True, nuclear weapons were far more destructive than anything witnessed in the past—but in a way this was good because the threat of nuclear holocaust would reduce the incentives in nations toward provocative and belligerent behavior. So the increase in the destructiveness of weapons was counter-balanced by a decrease in the probability that they would be utilized. Since humanity was presumably no more threatened by warfare than it had been before the invention and dissemination of nuclear weapons, there was thus no compelling reason for a substantive departure from the familiar balance of power politics of the pre-nuclear age.

The visionaries were far less optimistic on this point. According to them, the development of nuclear weapons immeasurably increased the overall threat to human civilization embodied in warfare. While the prospect of nuclear destruction might somewhat reduce the propensity toward provocative and belligerent behavior among nations, it would by no means eliminate it, and sooner or later some nation would stray over the line separating peace from unimaginably devastating warfare. What was obviously needed, in the view of the visionaries, was a world government with direct control over a large and dominant military force, with the power of taxation, and guided by officials subject to direct democratic accountability to the people through free and open elections. For a brief period, this idea gained an appreciable amount of currency, and it was seriously entertained far more widely than had ever been the case in the past. But the post-World War II world government boom quickly fizzled, a victim of the intractable Cold War conflict among the communist and noncommunist blocs of nations.[7] In very short order, the realist viewpoint was completely dominant that whatever might be the attractions of world government "in theory," it was completely infeasible "in practice," because of the yawning, irreconcilable ideological gulf between communists and noncommunists.

Even if ideological disagreement had not been a factor in the postwar world, there were various weaknesses in the design of the United Nations that militated against its becoming a highly effective participant in international politics. To begin with, any involvement of the U.N. in military resistance to aggression depended on (and still depends on) a unanimous vote by the permanent members of the Security Council. The possibility that the United Nations, in and of itself, would become an important deterrent to aggression was (and remains) considerably reduced by the veto rule within the Security Council. It is a truism that in collective decision-making, true unanimity is very difficult to achieve. Collective security becomes rather nebulous if a single major member of the super-alliance can block joint action by the super-alliance. Not that this *necessarily* makes much difference. Those members of the alliance who believe that military action is advisable could go ahead without those who do not. Alternatively, those members of the alliance who believe that military action is *not* advisable can simply depart from the alliance when called upon to provide assistance. After all, this has been the way of alliances throughout human history, pre-modern and modern.

Public receptiveness toward the general concept of world government attained a sharply delineated pinnacle in the half-decade that separated the end of World War II in the summer of 1945 from the beginning of the Korean War in the summer of 1950.[8] However, the sudden and dramatic ascent in public receptiveness toward world government was almost immediately followed by an equally sudden and dramatic descent. No doubt a decisive factor in the rapid deflation of world government hopes and aspirations was the obstructionist, confrontational, and uncooperative attitude of the Soviet Union in the years following the close of the Second World War. But it is by no means certain that if the Soviet Union had been a capitalist nation—even a democratic capitalist nation—that a genuine world government would have been possible at that time. Quite possibly, the highly ephemeral post-World War II world government boom was largely a shock reaction to the first use of nuclear weapons in warfare—the atomic bombings of Hiroshima and Nagasaki in August, 1945. Human beings are remarkably resilient and adaptive, mentally and emotionally as well as physically. Within a remarkably short space of time, most people had filed away the threat of dying in a worldwide nuclear holocaust in the same compartment as the threat of dying in an automobile accident. It was a regrettable but inevitable hazard of daily life—therefore there was nothing to be done about it. Life went on as before, and the nuclear arms race between the superpowers steadily continued apace.

If one had to select the single most dramatic indicator of the postwar world government boom, it would probably be the remarkable commercial success enjoyed by a book entitled *The Anatomy of Peace* by Emery Reves, published by Harper and Brothers in 1945, shortly prior to the conclusion of the war.[9] The thesis of the book was simply that collective security, as pursued by the League of Nations and the United Nations, was a dangerous delusion, and that the only way to stop, once and for all, an endless succession of devastating wars, was for the nations of the world to establish a strong and effective world government. The thesis was presented in a lively, passionate, and highly readable (if somewhat breathless) style.

In a *New York Times* book review, Orville Prescott wrote: "The logic of *The Anatomy of Peace* is simple and eloquent. It might be a good thing for the world if ten or twenty million persons read and discovered it." The Associated Press review, distributed to 1600 newspapers, declared: "Few books about the causes of war are as stirring as this one about the causes of peace." On October 10, 1945, the following statement, signed by such major luminaries as Mortimer Adler, Thomas Mann, and Senator William Fulbright, appeared in the *New York Times* and 50 other leading U.S. newspapers: "At this anxious moment in our history a book has been published which expresses clearly and simply what so many of us have been thinking. That book is *The Anatomy of Peace* by Emery Reves. We urge American men and women to read this book, to think about its conclusions, to discuss it with neighbors and friends, privately and publicly." Albert Einstein, whose genius fathered the nuclear age, called *The Anatomy of Peace* "*the* political answer to the atomic bomb." *Reader's Digest* serialized a condensation of the book over three issues, and arranged 23,000 discussion groups across the United States to study it. The book was translated into 25 languages and distributed in 30 countries. Pocket Books published a paperback edition for a mass market. Total sales of *The Anatomy of Peace*, over its eight editions, approached half a million copies.

Despite the remarkable success of the book (or perhaps partly because of it), some writers on world government have been inclined to dismiss it as empty rhetoric which merely generated casual interest in world government—but did not sustain that interest. The fundamental complaint was (and remains) that there is little or nothing in *The Anatomy of Peace* that sensibly addresses the organizational specifics necessary to make world government viable in the real world. For example,

Fremont Rider, a contemporary of Reves and author of *The Great Dilemma of World Organization*,[10] had this to say (pp. 6-7):

> Now, every would-be planner of world organization is well aware of the existence of this Dilemma [the fact that relatively poor people, over the world as a whole, greatly outnumber relatively rich people]. Also he knows in his heart that it is the crux of the practicality of his plan. But, just because it has always seemed an almost insoluble problem, each planner has either ignored it entirely, or has "solved" it only in terms of more or less vague generalities. Take, for example, Mr. Emery Reves' *The Anatomy of Peace*, which has received much comment lately. Perhaps it is unfair to call this book a "plan" at all, for it is rather an appeal for a world-state than a definite proposal for one, an appeal making up in apostolic fervor what it lacks in definiteness. What is its solution for the Great Dilemma? So far as its author gives one it appears in the following sentences in his two concluding paragraphs: "We shall have to organize peace independently of the Unholy Alliance stillborn in San Francisco or else we shall delude ourselves until the inevitable march of events into another and greater holocaust teaches us that equal and sovereign power units can never co-exist peacefully... After a disastrous half a century of antirationalism, we must return to rationalism... The task is by no means easy. There is no other fate for us than to climb the long, hard, steep, and stony road guided by reason."
>
> The trouble with this sort of thing is that it doesn't get us anywhere. Little appeal needs to be made for the world-state as a theory: in the abstract almost everyone is already in favor of it. It is the world-state in whatever concrete form it has so far been put that has failed to win adherents. Yet, until it has been put into concrete form, has been made a definite proposal, all argument in favor of it is bound to be more or less *words*. The peoples of the world are demanding, not vague generalities, but an extremely definite, and profoundly reasonable, answer to this question: "What exactly is to be the voting power of each of the nations in your world organization, and by what formula is this voting power arrived at?" Until they get such an answer they are not going to give up their national powers to any new order whatsoever, no matter how persuasive the arguments in favor of their doing so may seem to be.

Rider himself presented a carefully considered, highly specific proposal for world government (albeit in a rather short book)—and perhaps as a consequence of this specificity, his book received little attention. Later on, Derek Heater had this to say about *The Anatomy of Peace* (*World Citizenship and Government*, 1996, pp. 158-159):

> It is the extraordinary success of the book which commends it to our at-

tention, rather than the quality of the thought. The text contains nothing original—the ideas were commonplace in the world federalist literature of the inter-war and wartime years. The text contains no advice about how a world state might be created—except for a few brief paragraphs in the Postscript to the 1947 edition. Here the author identifies five steps from "the conception of the idea" through the election of representatives to the ad hoc solution of the world's problems. There seems little doubt that Reves' success lay in the mood of the time, a splendid publicity campaign, a robust denunciatory style, passionate optimism and vagueness in detail in order to avoid criticism.

Although Reves himself eschewed specifics, in the few postwar years during which *The Anatomy of Peace* remained a widely discussed and highly inspirational appeal for world government, numerous groups and individuals did indeed endeavor to provide specific, concrete blueprints for a viable world government. Fremont Rider was only one of many—although he was among the relatively small minority whose proposals were actually published. Probably the best-known of these blueprints was the "Preliminary Draft of a World Constitution," the product of a group of distinguished citizens styling itself the "Committee to Frame a World Constitution." Not only did the committee include a number of well-known academics, writers and public figures, it was chaired by one of the most illustrious names in American higher education during the twentieth century: Robert Maynard Hutchins.

Although his overall reputation was somewhat on the unconventional side, in the immediate post-World War II years, Robert M. Hutchins was widely recognized as a very solid citizen (presumably the Chancellor of the University of Chicago could not be anything less). In the immediate aftermath of the atomic bombing of Hiroshima and Nagasaki, along with many others, he expressed the opinion that if mankind failed to establish a world government within the very near future, there was a very high probability that human civilization would be destroyed in a global nuclear holocaust. Soon after he made this opinion known, Hutchins was approached by two senior members of the University of Chicago humanities faculty, Richard McKeon and Giuseppe Borgese, with a proposal to form a study group to write a draft constitution for an actual world government.

Hutchins enthusiastically agreed to help form the study group. The Committee to Frame a World Constitution, composed of about a dozen "blue ribbon" individuals, most of them senior University of Chicago faculty members and administrators, with Hutchins as chair and Borgese as secretary, commenced regular meetings in the fall of 1945. From the approximately 4,000 pages of discussion papers and minutes produced by the Committee over the next two years, there eventually emerged the "Preliminary Draft of a World Constitution," published as a booklet by the University of Chicago Press in 1948. The principal architect of the finished product was Giuseppe Borgese, who included it as an appendix to his 1953 book *Foundations of the World Republic* (also published by the University of Chicago Press).[11]

By the time the Preliminary Draft was published, however, relations between the Western democracies and the Soviet Union had deteriorated to the point where serious questions were being asked about the loyalty and/or common sense of those interested in world government. When the *Chicago Tribune*, a traditional stronghold of America-first patriotism and isolationism, obtained an early version of the Draft Constitution, its editor quickly alerted the *Tribune*'s readership to the ominous news that a "super-secret constitution" was being produced by "one of a rash of militant globalist organizations which have sprung up in the United States and England since the United Nations has demonstrated its uselessness." Meanwhile, Moscow Radio harshly condemned the Draft as an effort "to justify the American Empire plan for world supremacy," and maintained that "the program of the Chicago world government embodies the ambitions of the American warmongers." Nevertheless, the Draft Constitution was translated into 40 different languages, and an estimated million copies were circulated around the world. Reactions, pro and con, were so abundant that the University of Chicago Press for two years published a special monthly journal, entitled *Common Cause*, as a venue where proponents of world government could respond to and debate their numerous critics.

In his highly influential critical study of world government, Gerard J. Mangone, possibly out of respect for its origins in one of the leading U.S. universities, was gentle with the Preliminary Draft, describing it as follows (*The Idea and Practice of World Government*, 1951, p. 167): "One of the most commendable efforts of recent years, especially among a spate of nonsensical diagrams, has been the document produced by several savants of Chicago and elsewhere entitled 'Preliminary Draft for a World Constitution.'" However, in the same paragraph, Mangone refers to the "inescapable omnipotence" of the proposed world government, and dismisses it as manifestly unworkable: "Unfortunately, the peoples of the world do not have the remotest prospect of such a *de novo* creation, but at the moment are still fumbling along with the shambles of traditional international law."

While the best-selling author Emery Reves drummed up support for the general concept of world government, and academics such as Robert

Hutchins and Giuseppe Borgese worked busily on trying to develop a practical plan for world government, still others applied themselves to the practical organizational work of building mass support for world government. Henry Usborne, a member of the British Parliament, and Harold S. Bidmead were instrumental in establishing a parent association to coordinate the activities of the "rash of militant globalist organizations" described by the editor of the *Chicago Tribune*: the association was designated the World Movement for World Federal Government (WMWFG). It held its first World Congress in Montreux, Switzerland, in 1947, and issued a Declaration describing in considerable detail what the delegates deemed the necessary characteristics of a world state. Most adherents at that time to the WMWFG expected that the world state would be formally established and ratified by actions of the various national governments.

Henry Usborne, for example, tried to enlist his colleagues in the British Parliament in the world government movement. In the United States, Fyke Farmer, a member of the Tennessee state legislature, secured a resolution to send delegates to a world constituent assembly which would endeavor to draft a constitution for a world government. The high tide of this endeavor was an assembly designated the People's World Convention, held in the Palais Electoral in Geneva, Switzerland, commencing on December 30, 1950. Although there were more than 500 representatives in attendance from more than 47 nations, only four delegates had been properly appointed by duly authorized government bodies—three from the state of Tennessee, and one from Nigeria. The convention continued on for seven days while the delegates argued themselves to a standstill on all substantive matters. The World People's Convention not only did not adopt a world government constitution, it could not even agree on when and where to hold future conventions, and on how delegates should be elected or appointed to them.

Although numerous luminaries at the dawn of the nuclear age in 1945, including Emery Reves, Albert Einstein, Robert Hutchins, and many others, immediately proclaimed the urgent need for world government in light of what had happened to Hiroshima and Nagasaki, it soon became apparent that government officials—especially national government officials—were not going to be very helpful toward this end. The United Nations, established at San Francisco in October, 1945—and little more than a renamed League of Nations with the added membership of the United States and the Soviet Union—was as far as they were willing to go. In the eyes of world federalists, this was not far enough. There developed among some world federalists a strong suspicion that national government officials would tend to be especially skeptical and obstructionist toward world government because such a government could and probably would reduce their own personal power and prestige. The "common people," it was hypothesized, would be more receptive toward world government because it would not be so threatening to their private interests. It might even be necessary, in the extreme version of this viewpoint, for the people to circumvent the national governments entirely—to hold a world constitutional convention and establish a world government without any participation of representatives of national governments. In a less extreme version, the national governments could eventually be brought into line—but only by virtue of massive pressure toward world government exerted by the general population.

One of the best-known and most colorful exponents of the direct-to-the-people approach was Garry W. Davis. Davis had been a bomber pilot in the World War II and had experience as a Broadway actor. His flair for the dramatic attracted a considerable amount of attention to the world government cause in both the U.S. and the international press. With all the fanfare he could muster, Davis appeared at the American embassy in Paris on May 25, 1948, turned in his U.S. passport (contrary to some reports, he did not burn it or tear it up), declared that he was renouncing his U.S. citizenship, and proclaimed that he was henceforth a "citizen of the world." As intended, this led to numerous quasi-comedic encounters with border guards and customs officials nonplussed by his inability to produce anything beyond a "world passport." In his 1961 autobiography (*The World Is My Country*), Davis describes his normal predicament in the following terms: "I had no papers which would permit me to enter any other country... Here I called myself a citizen of the world, but I was being told by national bureaucrats either to seek asylum on another planet, die, become a perpetual mariner living in international waters, or go to jail permanently."

His most successful stunts took place in the fall of 1948. At that time, the United Nations General Assembly was meeting in the Palais de Chaillot in Paris. The grounds of the Palais had been declared "international territory" by the French government, and Garry Davis—in his mind quite legally as a "citizen of the world"—pitched a tent on those grounds. Unfortunately for Davis, he attracted less sympathy from the U.N. delegates than attention from the Parisian press: he was declared by U.N. officials to be a trespasser, and the Paris police were called in to haul him back to "French territory." Soon released from jail, on November 19, with the assistance of Robert Sarrazac and Albert Camus, Davis appeared in the gallery of the General Assembly meeting hall and commenced a speech of admonition to the delegates for neglecting the true interests of the "people of the world." Immediately hustled away by the

Paris police, Davis' speech was completed for him by Robert Sarrazac, a former leader of the French resistance during the Nazi occupation.

The following summer, Davis, as "World Citizen Number 1," was the featured speaker at a world government rally, attended by 15,000 people, in the Vélodrome d'Hiver in Paris. This was followed by his address to a standing-room-only meeting at the Salle Pleyel. Written and telegraphed greetings were read from Albert Einstein, Albert Schweitzer, Sir John Boyd-Orr, and many British MPs. Davis was supported on the speaker's platform by Albert Camus, André Breton, and several other prominent Frenchmen. This event marked the high point of his success. Afterwards, he settled down to more conventional methods of proselytizing. In 1953, he founded the World Service Authority to issue "world passports" (not recognized as valid by any nation) to those who want them—an organization that carries on to this day.

Another organization with roots in the postwar world government boom that carries on to this day is the Streit Council, formerly the Association to Unite the Democracies (AUD). Of all the proposals enumerated from the 1914-1944 period in Wynner and Lloyd's 1944 compendium *Searchlight on Peace Plans*, certainly the most famous in its time was that of Clarence K. Streit (1896-1984), an American journalist and writer. Clarence Streit was born in California but spent many of his early years in Missoula, Montana. After serving with the American Expeditionary Force in France, he was appointed to the American delegation to the Paris Peace Conference (1918-1919). During the interwar period, he worked as a foreign correspondent for the *New York Times* and other newspapers, covering the League of Nations. Appalled by the ineffectiveness of the League against fascist expansionism, he published *Union Now: A Proposal for a Federal Union of the Leading Democracies of the North Atlantic* in 1939, just as Hitler's adventurism was coming to fruition in the form of World War II. The book was a bestseller and established Streit as an important visionary, but had no perceptible impact on events, even though the basic concept was enthusiastically seconded in Britain by William B. Curry in *The Case for Federal Union* (1939). Two years into the war, Streit published *Union Now with Britain* (1941), which confined the federation concept to the United States and Britain. Again the book was a bestseller, but again had no noticeable effect on events. Streit's proposal was categorized by Wynner and Lloyd as an "ideological" plan because it specifies that membership in the union would be available only to democratic nations. The envisioned federation would eventually encompass all nations—but each prospective member of the union would have to become internally democratic prior to joining. Streit's proposals were creditable and commendable, but that did not alter the fact that by the time they were put forward, the disaster of world war had already befallen humanity. To use the standard cliché, they were "too little and too late."

Following World War II, a revised and expanded edition of *Union Now* was published: *Union Now: A Proposal for an Atlantic Federal Union of the Free* (1949). Emphasis now was on a combination of the United States and Canada with the Western European NATO nations. At about the same time, Streit collaborated with Owen J. Roberts and John F. Schmidt on *The New Federalist* (1950), which appeared under the pseudonym "Publius II." The book argued that the federalist principle, on which the United States of America had been founded in 1788, could be utilized—with certain relatively minor modifications—as a basis for a supernational federation. The extent of public interest in Streit's ideas at that time may be gauged from the fact that he was the subject of a *Time* magazine cover story on March 27, 1950. That milestone might be considered the last gasp of the postwar world government boom.

It is testimony to Streit's reputation that a sympathetic forward to *The New Federalist* was provided by John Foster Dulles, shortly afterward the U.S. Secretary of State in the Eisenhower administration. It is also testimony to Streit's reputation that he managed to keep alive for a great many years among the more internationalist members of the U.S. Congress a project for an Atlantic Union, tentatively designated "Atlantica." Working through the Federal Union organization that he founded in 1940, and its main publication *Freedom and Union*, Streit orchestrated a long series of statements, resolutions, and proclamations both in the United States and other potential member nations. In addition to John Foster Dulles, numerous other reputable public figures expressed tentative interest, including George C. Marshall, Harry Truman, Paul-Henri Spaak, Estes Kefauver, Hubert Humphrey, Christian Herter, Nelson Rockefeller, and John F. Kennedy. As preparations for an Atlantic Convention proceeded, Streit published his last book on the Atlantic Union concept: *Freedom's Frontier: Atlantic Union Now* (1961). An Atlantic Convention was actually held in 1962, attended by many authorized representatives of the potential member nations, but all it managed to accomplish was the issuance of a vague resolution calling for increased cooperation and referring the matter to the foreign ministries of the participating nations for implementation. This resulted in nothing. Federal Union carried on with its proselytizing work into the 1970s, but Congressional support in the U.S. was ebbing, and the end of the line was finally encountered in April, 1973, when a bill for creating an Atlantic Union Delegation was defeated on a procedural motion. Federal Union carries on today, long after Clarence Streit's death in 1984, as the Streit Council, on whose Website will be found online versions of all Clarence Streit's writings, as well as much documentary material pertaining to the long but ultimately fruitless effort to create a Union of the Free.[12]

It will never be known with certainty whether a genuine world government would have been founded in 1945 if it had not been for the ideological conflict between the Soviet Union and the Western capitalist nations. Aside from the ideological impediment, there was an economic impediment to world government, and that particular impediment was almost as important in 1945 as it is today. The economic impediment alone might well have precluded genuine world government in 1945, even if the Soviet Union had been a democratic capitalist nation similar to the United States, Britain, France, and others. And even aside from the economic impediment, there is the basic issue of nationalism which, according to some, would be virtually as important as it is now even if all the nations of the world were extremely homogeneous in terms of economics, politics, religion, culture, language, etc. Be that as it may, certainly the most dramatic and obvious impediment to genuine world government in the postwar years was the increasingly hostile confrontation between the Soviet Union and the Western democracies—the rapidly developing Cold War.

While a virulent ideological controversy over the respective virtues and vices of democratic capitalism versus communistic socialism set the stage, the immediate impetus to the rapid degeneration of international relations after World War II was the status of the Eastern European nations which had been overrun by Soviet military forces during the final phase of the War: the Baltic nations, Poland, Czechoslovakia, Hungary, Rumania, and Bulgaria. In the calmer hindsight of today, it is widely accepted that the communization of the Eastern European nations was not in fact part of a detailed plan whose objective was the attainment of Russian global hegemony within a brief period of time. It is now seen as more of a defensive maneuver than an offensive maneuver: Russia had just suffered a devastating invasion by Nazi Germany (only the most recent of a long series of invasions from the West throughout Russian history), and Stalin wanted communist governments in the Eastern European nations to provide a "buffer zone" against possible future repetitions. Be that as it may, the distinction between military offense and military defense is often rather subtle.

Nor was the communist threat confined to the Soviet Union and the Eastern European nations. The Soviet Union also took control of a substantial part of defeated Germany (East Germany) through its militarily enforced establishment of the German Democratic Republic. In Asia, several nations were communized in the latter 1940s: North Vietnam,

North Korea, and most importantly China. These communizations were carried out by indigenous movements without direct support of Soviet troops, but with the assistance of arms and other war material provided by the Soviet Union. It all looked very much like what had gone on in Western Europe during the rapid ascent of Nazi Germany in the latter 1930s. An effective response to those inclined to argue in the postwar years that Stalin, Mao, and the other leaders of the communist nations, were not *really* serious about communizing the entire world was: "That's what they said about Hitler!"

## The Cold War and Beyond

In 1947, U.S. President Harry Truman proposed that the world communist movement be "contained" until such time as it desisted from its perverse, misguided, and extremely hazardous global messianic mission. The containment policy remained a cornerstone of Western foreign policy throughout the long and perilous decades of the Cold War. In its early years, containment involved military assistance to the eventually victorious noncommunist forces in Greece and Turkey, the Berlin airlift, the Korean War, worldwide stationing of American military forces, and the nuclear arms race. World War III seemed just around the corner, and it would be generated by the same sort of geopolitical-ideological conflict that had generated World War II. Only this time the villain would be communism instead of fascism.

The tensions introduced into international relations by the strategic maneuverings of the two superpowers, the United States and the Soviet Union, each espousing diametrically opposed ideologies, were drastically exacerbated by the rapid escalation of the nuclear peril. The Soviet Union exploded its first atomic bomb in 1949, thus terminating the short-lived U.S. monopoly in nuclear weapons. Hardly had atomic bombs been perfected when they were superseded by hydrogen bombs of far greater destructive power. Both the United States and the Soviet Union soon accumulated thousands of nuclear devices. In the latter 1950s and early 1960s, the competition between the superpowers turned to so-called "delivery systems"—especially to the development of nuclear-tipped long-range missiles equipped with very accurate inertial guidance systems. Prior to the development of these missiles, nuclear weapons could have been delivered by conventional bombers of the type that had been used in World War II. World War II had clearly demonstrated that even with highly effective air defense, it was impossible to completely avert bombing attacks by a determined enemy. By the early 1950s, therefore, the possibility of mass destruction of the major cities of the world by airborne nuclear bombing was no longer a nightmare of the distant future—it was rather an existent reality. With the advent of ballistic missiles in the 1960s, the length of warning time prior to a nuclear holocaust was further shortened—from hours to minutes. People everywhere in the world took a deep breath, reassured themselves with the thought that no one would be stupid enough to start a nuclear war, and carried on as before. But the added psychic strain took its toll.

Among the casualties was any sort of rational thinking about world government. Fear and anxiety ruled out any degree of mental flexibility and imagination with respect to the concept. Both the opponents of world government (the vast majority) and the proponents of world government (the tiny majority) could imagine no world government other than an all-powerful state entity that would assume a complete and total monopoly over any and all nuclear weapons, as well as any and all "conventional" heavy weaponry. Opponents of world government were convinced that such an all all-powerful entity would very quickly produce a global totalitarian condition as bad as anything recently witnessed in the Nazi Germany of Adolf Hitler and the Soviet Union of Joseph Stalin. If the proponents of world government had any qualms on this score, they kept them to themselves. In their view, the basic survival of humanity took precedence over the possibility of tyranny. Not to mention the fact that as bad as global tyranny might be, the only thing worse would be the proliferation of local tyrannies over the entire face of the globe in the aftermath of a nuclear holocaust. No blueprint for a *limited* world government was ever considered, as the Cold War grew and matured, either by the opponents or the proponents of world government. The oppressive tensions of the period effectively shut down the reasoning and judgmental faculties of the human race—at least insofar as these faculties applied to international organization. Even highly sophisticated academic writers could not rise above either-or, black-or-white, night-versus-day thinking.

Gerard Mangone's influential book, *The Idea and Practice of World Government* (1951), distilled the final postwar verdict on world government: a fine and noble idea in principle, but (alas) thoroughly impractical in the real world owing to the great strength of ideological preconceptions and nationalistic prejudices.[13] The negative verdict on world government enunciated by Mangone rapidly achieved consensus status among the vast majority of professional academics, political leaders, and rank-and-file citizens. The basic problem, according to Mangone, is the absence of sufficient consensus within humanity on what constitutes a just and legitimate social order:

If a structure of world government is to be imagined, then its size, strength and shape will be conditioned by the social order it intends to establish. Should there be a genuine consensus among the members on the hierarchy of values within such a community, the coercive element will be minimized; if but little consensus exists, an autocratic leadership would be the obvious recourse for universal conformity.

From whence would come the most urgent pressures for "universal conformity," pressures sufficiently urgent to require "autocratic leadership"? From a variety of sources, answers Mangone, not least of which is the communist leadership of the Soviet Union and its allied nations:

Racists, for example, who rant of "naturally" inferior people, demand every means to compel such a status; the Crusaders, on capturing Jerusalem in 1099, to attest the superior morality of the Christian faith, massacred all the Moslems and burned the Jews alive; and Marxists, certain of the inevitable "victory of the proletariat," are painstaking in their efforts to assure the fall of the bourgeoisie.

This sentence lumps together the likes of Adolf Hitler, a racist who instigated (among other things) the genocide of the European Jews, a genocide involving approximately six million murders, on grounds of racial purity, the Christian Crusaders who in 1099 engaged in mass slaughter on grounds of religious purity, and the mid-century communist leadership who would, given the opportunity, happily engineer a massive extermination throughout the world of opponents of communism, on grounds of ideological purity. Of the three, obviously it was the communist leadership who represented for Mangone the most immediate threat. The Nazi regime in Germany had just been dislodged by the massive bloodbath of World War II, Adolf Hitler and his chief henchmen had been physically eliminated, and the German people, under military occupation, were highly receptive to re-education on the matter of racial toleration. The crusading spirit of militant European Christianity had been pretty much extinct for well over 500 years. As of 1951, only the communist leadership constituted a real and present danger.

It is quite obvious that the mid-twentieth-century communist leadership, owing to its ideological fanaticism, was capable of prodigious slaughter in pursuit of what they imagined would be a socialist quasi-utopia. There is no question that individuals such as Joseph Stalin and Mao Tse-tung had been sufficiently brutalized by their respective struggles for power that they would have outdone Adolf Hitler in the area of mass murder—had they been given the opportunity. What Mangone did not explain is precisely how the formation of a world state would have presented the likes of Joseph Stalin and Mao Tse-tung with the opportunity to fulfill their dreams of mass extermination of all the bourgeoisie and their allies. It would depend on the nature of the world state. There is nothing inherently impossible about the concept of a limited world government in which member nations would maintain their own military forces as safeguards against externally imposed totalitarianism and mass exterminations. Mangone simply assumes that any world state would be sufficiently powerful to impose its will on every member nation. Indeed, the same was assumed by communist ideologues on the other side, who viewed themselves as the likely target of extermination programs should a world state be established.

In fairness to Mangone, the standard conception of a world government among almost all world federalists, throughout the Cold War and beyond, involves what is described herein as the "omnipotent world state": an all-powerful state organization that would monopolize all military weaponry, nuclear and conventional, and which would require the adherence and obedience of every nation in the world. There is no compilation of post-World War II world government proposals comparable to that of Wynner and Lloyd's compilation of pre-World War II proposals. However, it seems safe to say that the accumulation of proposals in the postwar period was at least as great as it had been in the interwar period. There are probably dozens of such proposals—although many of them are either entirely unpublished or else published in very obscure sources. The recent development of the World Wide Web has provided a new means of dissemination of such proposals—although the sheer volume of material available on the Web probably precludes these proposals from having any appreciable impact unless they are also available in traditional print media.

## Postwar Blueprints

Although post-World War II world government proposals are highly diverse, almost all of them adhere in general terms to the Declaration of the first World Congress of the World Movement for World Federal Government (WMWFG), held in 1947 at Montreux, Switzerland. The Declaration puts forward six essential characteristics of an effective world government, as follows:

1. Universal membership: The world federal government must be open to all peoples and nations.
2. Limitations of national sovereignty, and the transfer to the world federal government of such legislative, executive and judicial powers as relate to world affairs.

3. Enforcement of world law directly on the individual whoever or wherever he may be, within the jurisdiction of the world federal government: guarantee of the rights of man and suppression of all attempts against the security of the federation.

4. Creation of supranational armed forces capable of guaranteeing the security of the world federal government and of its member states. Disarmament of member nations to the level of their internal policing requirements.

5. Ownership and control by the world federal government of atomic development and of other scientific discoveries capable of mass destruction.

6. Power to raise adequate revenues directly and independently of state taxes.

Interestingly, it is not specified that the world government be subject to democratic control. It is specified, in point 1, that there be "universal membership" in the sense that membership would be "open" to all the nations of the world. Nothing is specified, however, with respect to nations that join the world federation and then decide at a later date to withdraw. However, a phrase included in point 3 ("suppression of all attempts against the security of the federation") may well be directed against such nations. This would be in line with the well-remembered fact (in 1947) that one of the first indications of the aggressive intentions of Nazi Germany and the other fascist nations was their withdrawal from the League of Nations in the 1930s. At any rate, a "right of withdrawal" would be essentially meaningless if nations had no armed forces with which to back up their decision to withdraw from the world federation. And in points 4 and 5, it is clearly specified that the member nations of the world federation would be deprived of all heavy weaponry (i.e., weaponry beyond the requirements of "internal policing"), both nuclear and conventional.

The Declaration set forth very general principles for a world government, but was unspecific with respect to details. A number of people subsequently came forward with more detailed plans. Since it would be impractical to consider any significant number of these, I will describe only three of the best-known, which may be taken as typical of the entire body of postwar world government proposals: (1) the proposal of Giuseppe Borgese et al for a Federal Republic of the World; (2) the proposal of Grenville Clark and Louis Sohn for a strengthened United Nations; and (3) the proposal of Philip Isely et al for a Federation of Earth.

Giuseppe Borgese was the secretary of a committee of influential concerned citizens (the Committee to Frame a World Constitution, active from 1946 through 1948) chaired by Robert M. Hutchins. Borgese's book *Foundations of the World Republic*, published by the University of Chicago Press in 1953, reflected the committee's deliberations on the urgent need for world government, and contained as an appendix the "Preliminary Draft of a World Constitution" developed by the committee. Grenville Clark and Louis B. Sohn were well-known international lawyers who took upon themselves the task of proposing a revised United Nations charter which would have effectively transformed the organization into a legitimate world government. All three editions of their magisterial tome, *World Peace through World Law* (1958, 1960 and 1966), were published by Harvard University Press. As of the latter 1960s, the idea of world government had become sufficiently disreputable (in a practical sense) that there were no further publications of full-fledged advocacies by major university presses.[14]

The Isely proposal is unique among world government proposals in that a serious effort was made by its originator to implement it in the real world. Philip Isely was for many years Secretary-General of the World Constitution and Parliament Association (with headquarters in Lakewood, Colorado). The Association organized a considerable number of international conferences from the 1960s onwards. One of these conferences, called the second session of the World Constituent Assembly, held at Innsbruck, Austria, in June 1977, ratified the initial version of the Constitution for the Federation of Earth. The document carries the signatures of approximately 150 individuals from many different nations. An amended version was later ratified at the fourth session of the World Constituent Assembly, held at Troia, Portugal, in May 1991, and carries the signatures of well over 200 individuals. Some of the signatories to these versions, such as Linus Pauling of the United States, Tony Benn of the United Kingdom, and Desmond Tutu of South Africa, are well-known figures. However, none of them were operating as authorized representatives of a national government at the time they signed.

Under the terms of the Constitution, a Provisional World Parliament met on several occasions during the 1980s and 1990s, and has passed a number of legislative bills. World Legislative Bill Number One (Sept. 11, 1982), for example, carries the title: "To Outlaw Nuclear Weapons and Other Weapons of Mass Destruction." The bill specifies the establishment of a World Disarmament Agency (WDA), but enforcement of the WDA's decisions is to be left to political units (cities, counties, provinces, states, etc.) within nations whose national governments have ratified the bill. To date, no national governments have in fact ratified World Legislative Bill Number One. Indeed, it is probably fair to say that despite prodigious effort by Philip Isely over several decades, only a tiny handful of people throughout the contemporary world were even aware of the existence of the World Constitution and Parliament Association and its various affiliates, and of those few, many would categorize the participants in these organizations as lunatic fringe political enthusiasts.[15]

The world government possibility has, to date, been rejected by the overwhelming majority of humanity on grounds that such a government would create such a severe risk of tyranny as to outweigh the counter-vailing advantage of that it would reduce the probability of disastrous nuclear war. Obviously, the proponents of the three "typical" world gov-ernment blueprints under consideration here were not completely obliv-ious to the threat of tyranny, nor did they rely solely upon the proposition that tyranny would be the lesser of two evils, compared to the carnage and destruction of a nuclear world war. All of them endeavored to install various barriers and impediments to tyranny within their plans. For ex-ample, they all have in common that the world government would be federal in nature, that the existing structure of national governments would be preserved, that the member nation-states would reserve a cer-tain amount of autonomy and independence, and that their populations would retain certain natural rights not to be infringed by higher levels of government, including the supernational government. They also have in common that there would be a division of power within the supernational government itself, that its authority would be spread over separate legis-lative, executive, and judicial branches, and that it would be subject to democratic control by the citizens through free, contested elections. In addition, they all incorporate provisions designed to safeguard against any one nation, or small group of nations, becoming dominant within any of the three branches of government.

Nevertheless, all three proposals, when examined carefully, involve the combination of two central features: (1) the world government would be militarily dominant over all the nations of the world; (2) the world government would be democratically accountable to the entire world population. In a world of drastic inequality in average living standards among the nations, a potential solution to this problem might entail a drastic redistribution of world income by means of a highly progressive global income tax in conjunction with a relatively generous global guar-anteed minimum income.

A scenario of drastic global income redistribution via a global wel-fare state, entailing the relative impoverishment of the populations of the rich nations to benefit the populations of the poor nations, does not nec-essarily require a megalomaniac dictator "taking over" the world gov-ernment by means of a coup d'état. Quite possibly the enabling legisla-tion would be passed by the large majority of a democratically elected legislature, would be implemented and enforced by a democratically elected executive authority, and would be duly reviewed and approved by a democratically accountable judiciary. The effective implementation of the policy in the rich nations could and probably would require considerable force, but this force might well be deployed by a world government enjoying the high degree of legitimacy conferred by democratic accountability. Of course, rioting and armed resistance throughout the rich nations would generate "emergency conditions" that would greatly facilitate the advent of a dictator.

Although the specific proposals for representation and voting are substantially different as between Borgese, Clark-Sohn, and Isely, they all reduce, in one way or another, to majority rule.[16] Implementation of any one of these three world government proposals would result in a world legislature in which representatives from rich nations would exercise very much less voting power than representatives from poor nations. The Borgese, Clark-Sohn, and Isely proposals are typical of postwar world government proposals in failing to deal realistically with this issue.

The only world government advocate from the postwar era who responded, in the form of an institutional proposal, to the difficulty presented by global economic inequality, was Fremont Rider in his 1946 book *The Great Dilemma of World Organization.*[17] Rider expressed the problem in terms of the gap between the "civilized" and the "uncivilized" nations. The "civilized" nations of North America, Western Europe and so on (i.e., the rich nations) would never consider participating in a world government with genuine power and authority that was subject to majority rule—and that would hence be controlled by the vast, impoverished populations of the "uncivilized" nations. And yet if world government is to be made acceptable to all nations, rich and poor alike, the principle of apportioning voting weight among the nations would have to possess compelling rationality, plausibility and apparent legitimacy.

Rider's proposed solution was to make the respective voting weights of the nations in the world government legislature proportional to their "educational attainments," in terms of total number of years of education completed by their populations. Since the average educational attainment in the "civilized" nations was high, they would enjoy dominant voting weight in the world legislature. But this would be acceptable to the poor nations as well, since it makes good sense to give more voting weight to individuals with more education. Such individuals would presumably utilize their greater voting weight more wisely and intelligently. Rider envisioned arms races being replaced by "education races" as nations enthusiastically threw their resources into educating their respective populations. Their immediate motivation would be to increase their influence in the world government, but this strategy would also increase their economic prosperity, which is largely determined by the productivity of the citizens, which in turn is largely determined by educational attainment.

A strange idea, to be sure, but at least it constituted a sincere effort to deal with a serious problem mostly ignored by other, better known formulators of world government schemes. This problem is addressed, within the Federal Union proposal on which this study concentrates, via the dual voting system in the legislative arm of the supernational government. This is a more plausible, direct, and effective way of dealing with the problem than relying on educational attainment. According to the dual voting system, to reiterate, any proposed measure would have to be passed on two bases: the population basis, and the material basis. In the population vote, a particular Union Representative's voting weight would be equal to the proportion of the population of the entire Union represented by the population of his or her own Union District. In the material vote, that same Union Representative's voting weight would be equal to the proportion of the overall revenue of the entire Union represented by the revenue raised in that Representative's Union District. Thus the richer nations, as providers of most of the Union's revenues, would retain more power in the legislature than would be the case if voting weight were based exclusively on population represented.

The dual voting scheme is important because it would prevent a program of radical, short-term redistribution of world income (or any other policy unacceptable either to the rich nations as a whole or the poor nations as a whole) to achieve the legitimacy of being democratically approved by the world legislature. But in light of "Mao's law" that "all power grows out of the barrel of a gun," we need to be sensitive to the possibility that if the executive branch of the world government succumbs to dictatorial temptations, and simply dissolves what it deems an uncooperative legislative branch, and at the same time maintains the loyalty of the military, then radical world income distribution would be a definite possibility.

Of course, if the member nations of the world state were allowed to maintain their own military forces and armaments, up to and including nuclear weapons (as in the Federal Union proposal), then there would not be such a clear danger that the military forces and armaments of the world state might be utilized to enforce radical redistribution of world income despite the legislature's failure to authorize such a program. But the authors of the three typical world state proposals under consideration here are quite explicit on the point that the overwhelming preponderance of military power must be concentrated under the direct control of the world state.

Giuseppe Borgese puts it as follows (1953, p. 104):

> If the World Republic is defective in power, it will disintegrate as did the Roman unity when it grew weak. Or it will be an empty name from the beginning, as were, more or less, the Christian empire in the Middle Ages and the League or United Nations in our years. Against this danger the World Republic as we see it claims the monopoly of weapons, wields all the sanctions and forces that are needed to repress insurrection and separation.

Grenville Clark and Louis Sohn deal with the matter as follows (1966, p. xv):

> The complete disarmament of all the nations (rather than the mere "reduction" or "limitation" of armaments) is essential for any solid and lasting peace, this disarmament to be accomplished in a simultaneous and proportionate manner by carefully verified stages and subject to a well-organized system of inspection. It is now generally accepted that disarmament must be universal and enforceable. That it must also be complete is no less necessary, since: (a) in the nuclear age no mere reduction in the new means of mass destruction could be effective to remove fear and tension; and (b) if any substantial national armaments were to remain, even if only ten per cent of the armaments of 1960, it would be impracticable to maintain a sufficiently strong world police force to deal with any possible aggression or revolt against the authority of the world organization. We should face the fact that until there is *complete* disarmament of every nation without exception there can be no assurance of genuine peace.

Finally, in the course of his critique of the 1995 Report of the Commission on Global Governance (*Our Global Neighborhood*), Philip Isely writes (1999, p. 103):

> The Commission also recommends a "mandatory Arms Register, and prohibition of the financing or subsidy of arms exports by governments," but seems to forget that under its own nebulous proposal for "global governance," there is no way to make anything mandatory— short of war. We cannot help but observe that having rejected, as "leading to less democracy," any proposal for world government (such as the Constitution for the Federation of Earth, which would require total disarmament to proceed upon ratification), the Commission prefers the

obviously more democratic procedure of wasting $500 billion or more per year on the entrenched benefits of the autocratic military-industrial system under national sovereignty.

These are typical expressions of the conventional viewpoint among world state traditionalists that there can be no sharing of military power between the world government and the national governments—not even in the short run. This rigid and unimaginative stance, more than any other single factor, accounts for the impotence, to date, of the world federalist movement.

## Since the Soviet Collapse

The beginning of the end for the Soviet Union is plausibly dated to the elevation of Mikhail Gorbachev, in March 1985, to the position of General Secretary of the Communist Party of the Soviet Union (CPSU). Gorbachev was a dedicated reformer determined to lift his country out of the economic stagnation and psychic ennui of the late-Soviet era. Throughout the Gorbachev period of perestroika (re-structuring) and glasnost (openness), there were increasingly optimistic indications that both the Soviet people and their political leadership were seriously reconsidering their longstanding commitment to Marxist ideology. Apparently some critical mass of dissent from the traditional orthodoxy was eventually reached, the communist leadership suffered a crisis of conscience, a societal chain reaction ensued, and within an amazingly short period of time, the Communist Party had been ousted from the position of political leadership and social domination it had held since 1917.

In December 1991, the Union of Soviet Socialist Republics transformed itself into the Commonwealth of Independent States (CIS), a loose confederation comparable, at most, to the British Commonwealth. On December 25, 1991, Gorbachev resigned as leader of the Soviet Union and turned over all powers vested in the USSR to its direct successor state, the Russian Federation. The various component states of the ex-USSR, as well as the states of its Eastern European satellite fringe, began busily converting themselves into democratic capitalist nations in the image of the United States and the Western European nations. This astounding transition was all the more remarkable for being, on the whole, non-violent. The policy of containment, enunciated by U.S. President Harry Truman in 1947, had finally succeeded. The costs of a large and permanent military force, the continuing risks of the nuclear arms competition, the human and material losses imposed by the Korean war and the Vietnam war, among many other things, were finally justified.

Of course, the collapse and dissolution of the Soviet Union in 1991 did not totally and completely abrogate the problem of ideology in the modern world. The single most populous nation in the world, the People's Republic of China, containing over 20 percent of the world's population, continues to abide by socialist economic principles (albeit with considerable reliance on free market mechanisms) and oligarchic political institutions. Several other nations in the Far East, together with Cuba in the Western hemisphere, also maintain their allegiance to communist ideology. However, rhetoric in the remaining communist nations concerning the eventual collapse of capitalism and ascendancy of socialism has become very muted, and they have more or less completely forsworn providing covert military support for revolutionary movements within noncommunist nations. What was previously considered a strong moral obligation to proselytize and fight for communism has been virtually forgotten, and the non-threatening policy of "peaceful coexistence" has become dominant. The noncommunist nations are fairly confident that it is merely a matter of time before the remaining communist nations follow the example set by the Soviet Union in 1991, and return to the capitalistic world mainstream.

The remarkable developments of the early 1990s in the ex-Soviet Union and the Eastern European nations have fundamentally transformed international relations. The fact that the dominant superpower of the communist bloc of nations suddenly changed its mind about "burying" capitalism and Western-style democracy, and decided that it wanted these institutions for itself, had a rapid, significant, and highly beneficial effect on international relations. A number of nations, especially the United States and the Russian Federation, quickly commenced programs of deep cuts in military expenditures and armaments. The fears and anxieties that had plagued a generation—that human civilization would be suddenly devastated by a nuclear world war—dissipated virtually overnight.

Throughout the Cold War, conventional wisdom had insisted that the ideological confrontation between the USA and the USSR, in and of itself, was sufficient to abrogate any possibility that there could be established a genuine world government with significant power and authority. It seemed plausible, therefore, that the end of the ideological confrontation would restore a certain measure of sympathetic interest in world federalism. In the early 1990s, there were indeed a few signs of this.

For example, in the July 20, 1992, issue of *Time* magazine, there appeared a two-page essay, basically an op-ed piece, entitled "The Birth of the Global Nation."[18] The piece was written by Strobe Talbott, journalist and author of several books on nuclear disarmament negotiations, at that time an editor-at-large for *Time*, later Under-Secretary of State for the ex-USSR and Eastern Europe in the Clinton administration. Talbott briefly sketched the history of world government thinking and opined that world government would probably be a good thing, as evidenced by the following representative excerpt:

> The human drama, whether played out in history books or headlines, is often not just a confusing spectacle but a spectacle about confusion. The big question these days is, Which political forces will prevail, those stitching nations together or those tearing them apart? Here is one optimist's reason for believing unity will prevail over disunity, integration over disintegration. In fact, I'll bet that within the next hundred years (I'm giving the world time for setbacks and myself time to be out of the betting game, just in case I lose this one), nationhood as we know it will be obsolete; all states will recognize a single, global authority. A phrase briefly fashionable in the mid-20th century— "citizen of the world"— will have assumed real meaning by the end of the 21st.

Talbott did not provide any systematic argumentation to support his claim that world government would be beneficial—not that there would have been sufficient space, in any case, within the confines of two pages for such argumentation. The author admits he may be mistaken, and specifies a very long time frame ("next hundred years"), implying that the case for world government has no short-term relevance. The basic ideas expressed in Talbott's essay had been commonplace in world federalist writing ever since the bombings of Hiroshima and Nagasaki in 1945, and these ideas, per se, had not thus far budged the general consensus among humanity against the formation of a world state. Nor have they done so in the post-Cold War era. Still, the appearance in 1992 of pro-world federalist writing in a leading U.S. national news magazine was unprecedented, and quite likely it was made possible by the collapse of the Soviet Union the year before, and with it the apparent elimination of the ideological barrier to world government.

A handful of new books advocating world government appeared in the early 1990s, such as those by Ronald Glossop, Errol Harris, and James Yunker (all published in 1993).[19] But they were few in number, and none of them achieved widespread recognition even among academics and professionals, to say nothing of the general public. In the hundreds of articles and dozens of books published every year since the early 1990s on contemporary international relations and international organization, terms such as "world government," "global government," "world state," and the like, rarely appear, and when they do, more often than not it is in the course of a cursory dismissal. The following typical example is taken from *The New World Order* (2004) by Anne-Marie Slaughter:[20]

> People and their governments around the world need global institutions to solve collective problems that can only be addressed on a global scale. They must be able to make and enforce global rules on a variety of subjects and through a variety of means... Yet world government is both infeasible and undesirable. The size and scope of such a government presents an unavoidable and dangerous threat to individual liberty. Further, the diversity of peoples to be governed makes it almost impossible to conceive of a global demos. No form of democracy within the current global repertoire seems capable of overcoming these obstacles.

Nevertheless, the historian Campbell Craig, in a 2008 article in *Ethics & International Affairs*, wrote of a recent "resurgence" of interest in world government.[21] What evidence is there for this alleged resurgence? To begin with, during the mid-2000s, perhaps in response to the traumatic 9/11 event, there may have been a spike in the production of appeals for world government from world federalist enthusiasts whose strident "one world or none" message harked back to the 1945-50 world government boom. Examples include Jerry Tetalman and Byron Belitsos (2005), Errol E. Harris (2005), Glen T. Martin (2008), and Jim Stark (2008).[22] Of course, if appeals of this nature went unheeded during the perilous decades of the Cold War, they were even less likely to be effective now that the Cold War is history.

What may be more significant is that a trickle apparently began of more restrained and scholarly world government advocacies from authors with reputable academic credentials, as exemplified by Luis Cabrera (2004), Louis P. Pojman (2006), James Yunker (2007), and Torbjörn Tännsjö (2008).[23] While these more reflective and balanced advocacies are more likely to elicit serious interest in world government among those who are currently skeptical of the concept, the fact remains that they are still very few in number, and none of them made much of an impression on international relations specialists, to say nothing of the political leadership and the general public.

The major emphasis in Craig's "resurgence" article was placed on a very unusual article by the eminent international relations authority Alexander Wendt, provocatively entitled "Why a World State Is Inevitable," published in the October 2003 issue of the *European Journal of International Relations*.[24] Inasmuch as the question of inevitability is only sensibly considered with reference to existent reality, and as world government is not yet part of existent reality, Wendt's proposition is clearly not meant to be taken literally. As Wendt himself pointed out, the allegedly inexorable natural trend toward a world state could be negated instantly by a nuclear world war or a large asteroid crashing into the Earth. Rather the proposition is deliberately provocative: intended merely to elicit additional serious thought about the world government possibility. Wendt's inevitability essay has indeed been cited in a substantial number of contributions.

But whether this attention will lead to a serious challenge to the existing strong consensus against world government remains to be seen. While most of these contributions seem at least somewhat sympathetic toward world government, none of them significantly amplifies or expands Wendt's argument. In fact, thus far the only full-scale engagement with Wendt's "inevitability thesis" has been critical: Shannon (2005), Wendt (2005).[25] Many of the citations fall into the "see also" category. Eric Posner points out the lack of immediate relevance of the thesis: "Wendt is in a very small minority, and as he puts off the creation of world government for at least another century, see id at 492, the possibility has no relevant short-term implications even if he is correct"; while Thomas G. Weiss suggests that there is nothing especially innovative about the thesis: "From time to time a contemporary international relations theorist, like Alexander Wendt, suggests that 'a world state is inevitable' (Wendt 2003, 2005; Shannon 2005), or Daniel Deudney (2006) wishes one were because war has become too dangerous."[26] If indeed the inevitability thesis is eventually recognized as a serious challenge to the mainstream consensus against world government, quite possibly the outcome will simply be a further refining of the conventional "case against world government" that underpins the current consensus.

In support of his argument that a world state is, as alleged in the title of his article, "inevitable," Alexander Wendt marshals an argument based on teleological reasoning. According to teleological reasoning, everything in the universe has a purpose toward which it inevitably tends. Just as human babies tend to fulfill their purpose by developing into human adults, so too global human civilization is tending toward its final purpose: a global state. The argument is clever and fleshed out impressively with concepts and factoids derived from a wide range of human knowledge. As a piece of erudite writing, Wendt's article is quite impressive. But it is more likely to be persuasive to a theoretical philosopher than to the typical international relations professional, let alone to the typical member of the general public.

Be that as it may, Wendt offers skeptical readers of his inevitability essay two pieces of reasonably solid, practical evidence that a world state will eventually be established: (1) the very long-run historical trend toward greater and greater political consolidation that has brought humanity from the tens of thousands of small, autonomous tribal units of pre-history down to the 200-odd nation-states of today, several of which encompass populations in the tens and even hundreds of millions; (2) the fact that a world state would benefit both large nations (lower probability of debilitating wars with other large nations) and small nations (lower probability of being subjected to the oppressive hegemony of large nations). Both of these points are significant and worthy of consideration, but in and of themselves, they are far from conclusive.

With respect to the long-term trend toward ever greater political consolidation, the hard fact remains that almost all of this consolidation was brought about, in one way or another, by means of warfare. In the nuclear age, it seems unlikely that additional warfare offers a plausible avenue toward further political consolidation leading to a world state. One must also take note of the fact that there has been a considerable amount of political de-consolidation in the recent past, ranging from the dissolution of the great European colonial empires to the disintegration of the Soviet Union and Yugoslavia. It is sometimes suggested that perhaps the most plausible scenario toward the creation of a world government is a nuclear world war that would so devastate global human civilization as to finally impress upon humanity the need for a strong world government. However, what may be more likely in the aftermath of a nuclear world war, would be a long period of low-intensity warfare fuelled by persistent bitterness and hostility, among a host of small states presided over by what are today referred to as "local warlords." A retrogressive trend might set in toward the same tens of thousands of small tribal units into which humanity was sub-divided prior to recorded history.

In presenting the consolidation evidence, Wendt mentions the estimate of Robert Carneiro (1978) that in 1000 B.C. there were 600,000 independent political communities on the Earth, whereas today there are only about 200. It is interesting to note that in a more recent contribution ("The Political Unification of the World: Whether, When, and How – Some Speculations"), Carneiro summarizes his views as follows:[27]

> That the world will someday be ruled by a single government has been foreseen by visionary thinkers for well more than a century, and this article quotes a number of these predictions. However, there has been less agreement as to how a world state would be achieved. Some have held that it would occur through peaceful and voluntary means. Others have argued that it could only result -- as have all other political coalescences in the past -- through military means. This article sides with the latter view and cites the war in Iraq as perhaps a small step in that direction.

As of 2004, when the above article was published, the war in Iraq had not yet fully degenerated into the quagmire it later became. In view of the adverse long-term aftermath of the 2003 invasion of Iraq, the notion of an "equivalent world government" through a relatively benign imperial hegemony imposed by the United States and its closest allies (Mandelbaum, 2005; Held and Koenig-Archibugi, 2004), has become even more doubtful than it was to begin with.[28]

With respect to the potential benefits of world government for both the large nations and the small nations, it must be acknowledged that these are definite potential benefits, and need to be taken into account in any sensible evaluation of the world government possibility. But potential benefits have to be weighed against potential costs. The contemporary consensus is that the potential costs of world government (totalitarian tyranny, bureaucratic suffocation, global civil war) far exceed the potential benefits. Simply enumerating benefits, while paying little or no attention to costs, is unlikely to be rhetorically effective, given that the costs are so well known.

Two years following the appearance of Professor Wendt's 2003 inevitability essay, the *EJIR* published a critique (Shannon, 2005), to which the author replied (Wendt, 2005).[29] The critique picked up on a potential flaw in the teleological argument that Wendt had himself anticipated in the concluding paragraphs of the 2003 paper: its potential neglect of the role of agency (human action) in the determination of outcomes. Shannon's complaint is that by casting the debate in terms of the *inevitability* of world government, Wendt is detracting from the more meaningful debate, involving agency and conditionality, concerning the *possibility* (i.e. desirability) of world government. Wendt's reply is that, when terms and concepts are properly understood, it is seen that there is no conflict between agency and teleology.

At possible cost to the subtleties of this exchange, it might be roughly compared to debate over the "free will" objection to "mechanical causation." Since we are unaware of all the multitude of factors pushing us to adopt a particular course of action, we have the impression that we have "free will" and could have, if we wanted, adopted a different course of action. The criminal justice system, for example, is based upon the perception that criminals are not forced, through Calvinist predestination, to commit crimes. The free will question is diverting, and debate over it is good intellectual and rhetorical exercise. But in the end, we are not likely to get beyond the following compromise: While the principle of causation does indeed rule out free will as it is normally understood, we do not know in advance what the principle of causation will bring about in any particular case of human decision-making; therefore, we perceive that we possess free will, and much of the existing social order is predicated upon this perception. A similar formula would apply to agency and world government: While the principle of causation informs us either that it is inevitable that a world state *will* be part of future human history, or that it is inevitable that a world state *will not* be part of future human history, we do not know which of these outcomes will actually take place. Therefore, we operate on the basis that we (humanity in general) can make a free will choice between these two alternatives.

Although there are obvious difficulties with Professor Wendt's "inevitability of world government" article, the fact that the author is a recognized and respected international relations authority, and the fact that the article was published in a reputable, mainstream international relations periodical, are quite significant. It is not too much to suggest that 40 years ago, with the Cold War still raging, no recognized and respected international relations authority would have dreamed of writing such an article, and no reputable, mainstream international relations periodical would have dreamed of publishing it. Therefore, the appearance of this article may be, in itself, an important indicator of increased receptivity toward the concept of world government, at least among academic professionals. Increased receptivity among this group may lead, in due course, to increased receptivity among the general population and the political leadership.

This is not to suggest, however, that "increased receptivity" is likely to extend to the "omnipotent world state" concept of traditional world federalist thinking. The case against the omnipotent world state is as strong today as it ever has been. But increased receptivity may enable more individuals to take seriously the possibility of a *limited* federal world government along the lines of the Federal Union of Democratic Nations under consideration herein.

# Brief History of Socialism

## Early Development

By the early nineteenth century, the term "socialism" was well established in common usage. In its earliest and most general form, socialism was perceived as a means by which the adverse socioeconomic consequences of the Industrial Revolution, especially the poverty, misery, and insecurity of the urban proletariat, could be ameliorated. Officially adopted by some of the various reformist groups of the period to describe their objectives, "socialism" gradually became associated with a wide range of such groups. The objectives of these groups were quite diverse, but they were united in their abhorrence for the political and socioeconomic status quo. However, so also were other groups that were not labeled "socialist." Socialists were people who to a greater or lesser extent disagreed with the liberal, laissez faire, individualistic philosophy that was the most successful and influential reformist trend of the nineteenth century.

The liberals, in general, desired the reduction or abolition of the remnants of feudal church and aristocratic privileges, the curtailment or elimination of monarchial power, the reduction of government regulation of and interference with economic affairs, and an increased voice for the non-aristocratic citizen in the governance of the nation. The liberals, at the same time, had a great reverence for property rights—their efforts were directed at eliminating what they considered unjustified infringements on the property rights of non-aristocratic citizens by the traditional aristocratic elite. The socialists—although they agreed with the liberals regarding the aristocracy—were not so confident of the benign social effects of untrammeled property rights. In one way or another, they felt it advisable that the authority of some community or social agency take precedence over these rights, lest their selfish and unwise exercise create an intolerable situation.[1]

Nevertheless, in the pre-Marxian era, the general tenor of socialist writing was relatively gentle. It was Karl Marx who insisted on a bitter class struggle with its inevitable climax in violent revolution. The earlier socialists were generally fairly optimistic that the quality of their schemes for social improvement would be apparent even to the financially privileged. It was indeed often hoped that the owners through voluntary action would bring into being the needed reforms. There need be no compulsion involved.

In the earliest socialist thought, various avenues toward amelioration of the condition of the working class were envisioned. Some reformers, such as Charles Fourier (1772-1837), proposed the creation of relatively small, economically self-sufficient communes. Others, such as Robert Owen (1771-1858), proposed a sort of enlightened capitalism by which the owners, perhaps under the authority of government regulators, would pay their workers more generously and treat them more fairly. This would result in a more contented and cooperative working force whose productivity would vastly exceed what it had been previously. Improving the lot of the poor, therefore, need not greatly impinge on the welfare of the rich—it might even foster it.

Both Fourier and Owen, and many others of similar persuasion, were distressed by the contemporary glorification of the competitive ethic, which they felt was hampering a proper appreciation of the true commonality of interest among mankind. Self-seeking behavior had been sanctioned long before in the theoretical economic realm, most notably in the magisterial *Wealth of Nations* (1776) of Adam Smith (1723-1790). Smith's ideas gradually won out in most minds over the more speculative-seeming, community-minded sentiments of writers such as Jean-Jacques Rousseau (1712-1778). It was not, of course, that selfish aggrandizement was honored for its own sake. Rather the selfish interest of each citizen, interacting peaceably with that of all other citizens, in a social framework that excluded all forms of physical violence and intimidation, would serve to ensure the greatest welfare for all concerned. In seeking to serve themselves, citizens would be forced to serve the whole society. Thus we have an appealingly attractively optimistic view of social relationships that has remained a very influential notion down to the present day.

The early socialists did not share the general faith in the beneficent workings of Smith's invisible hand. To them the hand seemed to work too much to the advantage of the property-owning classes and too little to the advantage of the property-less proletariat. And again, the notion that unbridled laissez faire is hardly the high road to social bliss has come down to the present day. The typical modern viewpoint is indeed a synthesis of the early liberal and socialist creeds. In one sense, many of the most important pre-Marxian socialists were not "socialists" at all, in the more precise meaning of the term codified by Karl Marx. They did not always insist on the abrogation of private property rights in land and capital (the non-human factors of production). What they wanted was restraint put on these rights, their subjection to a higher social responsibility—not necessarily their abolition.

In *The Communist Manifesto* (1848, co-authored with Friedrich Engels), Karl Marx (1818-1883) dismissed the main body of his predecessors as "utopian socialists," as unrealistic and impractical dreamers.[2] First of all, to Marx, many of his forerunners failed to have sufficient appreciation for the industrial accomplishments of capitalism. Often they aspired to a simpler, agrarian world—a feudal life but without aristocracy and manor houses. But it was apparent to Marx that the modern mode of production, with its cities, railroads, factories, and so on, was here to stay. The productive record of modern industry far outshone that of traditional agriculture and handicraft production. Society would have to reconcile itself to urbanization and industrialization.

Furthermore, said Marx, it would have to reconcile itself to violent revolution. Earlier socialists who expected basic human decency, common sense, and goodwill to come to mankind's rescue in his current socially depraved capitalistic state simply had too high an opinion of the intelligence and altruism of the owning class. Rather the bourgeoisie would hang on to its privileges until the proletarian revolution forcibly terminated its stranglehold on society.

The first half of the nineteenth century witnessed the emergence of an explicit, self-conscious socialist protest against the economic institution of capitalism. Ideas do not usually emerge without reference to tangible reality. What were the tangible realities that led to the socialist protest? The most obvious factor is the miserable condition of the early urban proletariat. The average early industrial worker worked incredibly long hours by modern standards, was paid a pittance, and possessed little or no security against sickness, disability, unemployment, and old age. Any modern factory worker transferred back to the early nineteenth century would immediately become an enraged rebel. Of course, such a simplistic view is not completely satisfactory. For example, it is by no means certain that the lot of the early urban industrial worker was materially worse than that of his agricultural brethren.

Quite likely we should not give too much credit to the direct victims of the Industrial Revolution for the genesis of the socialist critique of capitalism. That is, while their plight provided the basic motivation for the critique, its formulation and expression was provided by educated members of the middle class, who were not personally the most abject victims of the system. Reformist urges were rife among the middle class of this period. For most, reform meant the curtailment of the privileged position of the aristocracy. But when people become incensed over the unjustified privileges of one elite group in society, it is typical for at least some to carry the indignation further than the rest, and to become incensed at the privileges of another elite group. In a sense, then, the socialist critique of capitalism road into intellectual history on the coattails of the liberal critique of the feudal aristocracy. The openness of the intelligentsia to reformist proposals, including socialist ones directed against the non-aristocratic but still privileged capitalists, was owing to the vigorous attempts by non-aristocratic capitalists to throw off the dominance of the traditional land-based aristocracy, and to provide a respectable theoretical and ethical justification for this transformation.

## Karl Marx's Codification

Marx's education was in philosophy, and he discerned profound significance in the writings of the German philosopher George W. F. Hegel (1770-1831). The latter in turn was much impressed by the concepts of conflict and change. All reality is imbued and motivated by these forces, according to Hegel. Conflict causes change, change causes conflict, and so on in a never-ending cycle. At any point in any given sphere, temporal or otherwise, there is a thesis, namely a dominant truth or reality. But the thesis is not eternal: it tends to generate from itself an opposed truth or reality, called the antithesis. The conflict between the two is resolved neither totally in favor of the thesis nor the antithesis, but in favor of a synthesis incorporating some elements from both the thesis and the antithesis. But the synthesis is not the end of the story—it sets up as a thesis in its own right, and commences to spawn an antithesis. And so on.

Marx considered himself possessed of a thorough mastery of the dialectical principle and all its ramifications. As a Hegelian, he perceived applications of it everywhere, but particularly in modern history. For example, feudalism is a thesis. It generates its antithesis of capitalism, and the two were now engaged in a titanic struggle. The synthesis that would emerge, however, would be neither feudalism nor capitalism, but rather socialism.

The fundamental social reality, according to Marx, is class struggle. At any point in time, a minority in human society sets itself up in a privileged position from which it dominates the majority of society. Any attempt to topple the elite is met and defeated by the state, which strives at all times to maintain as absolute a monopoly as is possible over the instruments of force. The state, far from being the expression of the common will, is simply an instrument of oppression, whose sole practical purpose is to maintain an unequal social order favoring a self-aggrandizing, self-righteous, and ruthless privileged class. In all previous ages, this elite was some form or another of a hereditary land-owning nobility. But the modern era is witnessing a momentous break in this pattern. The reason for the break was a shift in the underlying structure of production. In all past ages, economic production was dominated by agriculture, and the principal non-human factor of production was therefore land. But during the eighteenth and nineteenth centuries, the balance shifted. Agriculture declined to secondary importance, and the first rank had been taken over by industrial production, involving the non-human factor capital (plant and machinery).

As a subscriber to the materialist basis of history, Marx perceived the whole legal, social, and political superstructure of society to be based on and determined by the underlying economic substructure. Thus a shift in the economic basis of society had to be accompanied by a shift in the political superstructure. The traditional land-holding elite had neglected the new capital forms of wealth, and their ownership had been assumed by a largely non-aristocratic, but wealthy, capitalist class, which Marx termed the "bourgeoisie." Owing to their ownership of the now more important nonhuman factor of production capital, the bourgeoisie possessed the physical power to end the age-old domination of society by the land-owning aristocracy. In its stead they would establish their own dominion, which would be hardly less anti-egalitarian in spite of its abolition of the traditional hereditary aristocratic ranks. The new aristocracy would be that of the property-owning capitalists, and their domination would prove to be no less unenlightened than that of their predecessors in power, the land-owning nobles.

Under capitalism, continuing according to Marx, the capitalist class engages in massive exploitation of the property-less proletariat. However, the mechanism of this exploitation is not nearly so crude and obvious as was the blatant extortion by the aristocracy during the Middle Ages and earlier times. It is, nevertheless, effectively quite as brutal and repugnant. The mechanism may be roughly described as follows.

Labor is the source and producer of all economic value. Labor does not, however, under capitalism receive the full value of the goods it has produced and to which it is rightfully entitled. Rather labor only receives its "cost of production," that is, a subsistence wage, which under free market conditions is its market price. The difference between the value created by labor and its market price, namely "surplus value," is appropriated by the capitalist owners as profit. The latter are enabled to effect this appropriation because of their legal ownership of the capital instruments of production. Labor requires access to these instruments in order to produce the full value of which it is capable. By threatening to withhold this access, which the capitalists are legally entitled to do because of their property rights, they establish an impregnable bargaining position vis-a-vis the proletariat. They in effect gain absolute power over the hapless proletariat, and are enabled to extort the maximum possible. The maximum possible is the differential between total created value and the replacement or subsistence cost of labor. Labor is given just enough to enable it to survive. If it were given any less, it would perish, and without labor to handle them, capital instruments would be inoperative and unproductive, therefore quite sterile and useless to their owners.

This exploitation was of course ethically reprehensible to Marx, but it in itself was not to be the instrumentality of capitalist collapse. Rather that instrumentality was to be the business cycle. Paradoxically enough, it would not be the lavishness but rather the very frugality and parsimoniousness of the capitalists in disposing of their ill-gotten gains that would prove their undoing.

Surplus value provides the capitalists with vast financial resources. If these resources were used to build pleasure palaces and to hire armies of servants, lackeys, concubines, and the like, then quite possibly the exploitative structure of capitalism would survive for ages. But rather than doing these kinds of things, the abstemious capitalists persist in plowing the main part of their ill-gotten gains back into more capital. Continual accumulation of capital is the obsessive theme of the capitalist's career. Meanwhile, the laboring masses continue to receive their subsistence wage, and are hardly able to take advantage of the increase in potential production brought about by the increase in capital stock. Effective demand fails to keep pace with the growth in potential output. Moreover, during the period of rapid expansion of the capital stock, owing to the increasing abundance of capital relative to labor, the competitive position of capital in the free market begins to deteriorate. Against their will, capitalists may find it necessary to give a little more to labor and this further reduces their profits. The improvement in labor's pay, however, is scarcely adequate to purchase the tremendous potential output of the inflated capital stock.

Suddenly, the capitalists become painfully aware of the deterioration of their financial position. Panic seizes them. Investment is cut back to the bone. The multiplier effect causes a fall in national income. Many enterprises are bankrupted because they are unable to meet financial commitments entered upon during the boom period. Production falls and a large proportion of the labor force finds itself unemployed. This unemployment cuts purchasing power still more and intensifies the stress. The economy spirals downward into the pit of business depression.

As the crisis proceeds, a great reorganization of property rights transpires. The smaller capitalists, who are not so capable of withstanding the storm, succumb. Their holdings are purchased at deflated prices by larger capitalists who have managed to remain solvent. Thus the big owners become still bigger and the small owners are forced out of the owning class. The concentration of wealth, already extreme, becomes still more aggravated. The erstwhile capitalists join the growing number of embittered and disaffected middle class people who are destined to provide the leadership of the proletarian revolution.

Capitalism is capable of recovering from a number of business depressions. During the depths of a depression, unused capital wastes away and the competitive position of capital becomes restored. As workers are hired back on, demand expands, and at first the depleted capital stock cannot meet it. Depression is replaced by prosperity; decline by growth. But the same fate of over-expansion lies in wait at the end of the prosperity period, no matter how ebullient and vigorous it might be. The cycles that follow one another become gradually more intense and severe. At the end of each depression, property is more concentrated than before. This increases the inertia of the system, the insensitivity of the capitalists to the warning signals of capital over-expansion. While the prosperity period may thus be extended by the financial insulation of the capitalists, the price to be paid is that the crash that follows it is deeper and more calamitous than ever before.

Eventually the situation will reach the breaking point. The capitalist class will have shrunk down to a tiny minority of society. It will be faced with a heaving mass of social suffering, discontent, and anger. The proletarian masses, led by dissident intellectuals and disaffected ex-capitalists, will rise in a great, cataclysmic upheaval and topple the capitalist class and its state minions into the dust of history. Thus the disappearance of capitalism from the social stage and its replacement by socialism.

Marx did not draw up a detailed blueprint for the socialist society. He believed that it would emerge more or less naturally, and there was minimal need for pre-planning. In his voluminous written work, he was much more concerned to condemn capitalism and to prove the inevitability of its downfall, than to design a successor socialist system. One has the impression, in reading his work, that he believed that *nothing* could be worse than capitalism, so that virtually any system that replaced it would be preferable. Of course, with almost two century's hindsight to rely upon, we can now see how false this belief was.

Karl Marx provided the most influential single statement in the history of socialist thought. The volume and intellectual power of Marx's work far over-shadows that of any other socialist. In a sense, Marx *founded* modern socialism, since many of his predecessors did not in fact emphasize the socialization of capital and land, the abrogation of the private property right with respect to the nonhuman factors of production. To this day, the primary dictionary definition of "socialism" involves public ownership and control of land and capital—in general, of the non-human factors of production. Marx not only insisted on public ownership of land and capital, he expected the abrogation of private ownership in these factors to be attended by violent social upheaval. Obviously there was to be no financial compensation, no coddling of the former capitalist exploiters. Marx expected the fate of the capitalists would be similar to the fate of aristocratic opponents of the French Revolution during the worst period of Jacobin Terror in the early 1790s. In Marx's work, then, the idea of socialization became closely associated with that of violent revolution. An extreme viewpoint thus became the single most important viewpoint within the socialist ranks.

The basic features of Marx's system were first given expression in *The Communist Manifesto* of 1848. They were elaborated and refined in the three large volumes of *Das Kapital* (1867, 1885, 1894), the latter two of which were posthumously published under the editorship of Friedrich Engels (1820-1895), following Marx's death in 1883. Throughout the middle part of the nineteenth century, Marx was active politically as well as intellectually. He was an important figure in the socialist parties of the day. No doubt he hoped that the great proletarian revolution would occur during his own lifetime.

## The Great Schism

Schisms are a common feature of both religious and secular ideologies. Two major schisms in religious history were the division of Christianity into Roman Catholic and Protestant channels in the early 1500s, and the division of Islam into Shiite and Sunni channels shortly after the death of Mohammed in 632. The equivalent schism in the history of socialism was the division of Marxist socialism into two channels, which with the advantage of hindsight we can label the communist channel and the social democratic channel. Socialist parties representing Marxist thinking did not gain power in any country until the Russian revolution of 1917 that brought to power the Russian Bolshevik Party, which shortly afterwards renamed itself the Communist Party of the USSR. On the other side, by 1917 the social democratic channel had become the leading force within the other Western European countries.

Throughout the latter nineteenth and early twentieth century, a good deal of the revolutionary basis for Marxist socialism was being eroded away owing to the gradual, long-term improvement in the condition of the working class. The agitations of the socialist revolutionaries may well have been a fundamental cause of this—along with the great advances in productive technology that continued throughout this era. Technological progress enabled capitalism to improve the lot of its rank and file workers—perhaps the socialist threat induced it to avail itself more fully of the opportunities created by this progress.

The improvement manifested itself both in growing real income and in growing security. Not only did wages and salaries increase, but there were steps in the direction of compulsory unemployment, sickness, and old age insurance. Toward the end of the nineteenth century, what we would today describe as the "social safety net" had taken hold throughout much of Western Europe and the world. Even such undemocratic nations as Imperial Germany, under the guidance of Chancellor Otto von Bismarck, were leading the way in certain areas, such as social insurance. Working class unions played a foremost role in this easing of the material condition of the proletariat. Relations between the socialists and the unionists were somewhat uneasy Many socialists frowned upon what they considered to be modest concessions by the capitalists, for fear that these vestigial improvements would divert the workers away from their resentments and thereby postpone the revolution. Other socialists were more willing to compromise.

A fundamental rift in the socialist ranks occurred when the "revisionists" under the leadership of individuals such as Eduard Bernstein renounced the Marxian doctrine of the necessity of violent revolution. In the view of the revisionists, the manifest improvement in working class conditions and the power of the capitalist state made such a revolution practically impossible. Therefore, it was preferable to work politically within the framework of democratic capitalism to obtain power peacefully and legally. The expropriation of the owners would then have the sanction of the voting public, not that of an unruly mob.[3]

In 1899, the ongoing reorientation of a substantial part of the socialist movement was dramatically manifested by the appearance of Bernstein's seminal contribution. In that year, Eduard (sometimes Edward) Bernstein (1850-1932) published *Die Voraussetzungen des Sozialismus und die Aufgabe der Sozialdemokratie* (*The Preconditions of Socialism and the Tasks of Social Democracy*). In 1911, a somewhat abridged English translation by Edith C. Harvey was published by the New York publishing house B. W. Huebsch under the title *Evolutionary Socialism: A Criticism and Affirmation*. In 1875, Bernstein had been one of the founders of the Sozialdemokratische Partei Deutschlands (SPD – Social Democratic Party of Germany), in which he remained active until his retirement in 1928. Based on a series of articles published in the party newspaper during the latter 1890s, his book explicitly rejected such fundamental tenets of conventional Marxist thought of the time as the inherent immorality and inefficiency of private ownership of land and capital, the inevitable immiseration of the proletariat, and the necessity for violent revolution to overthrow capitalism and inaugurate socialism. Bernstein argued that the condition of the working class was manifestly improving, that such reforms as business regulation, social insurance, and progressive taxation were effective means of achieving the underlying objectives of socialism, and that these reforms could and should be pursued through peaceful democratic means.

From their initial appearance, Bernstein's ideas were recognized as a major contribution to the theory and practice of socialism, eliciting both enthusiastic acclaim and furious denunciation. Among the denouncers was Vladimir Lenin (1870-1924), later to become famous as a prime mover of the successful Bolshevik revolution in Russia in 1917, and afterwards the first head of state of the newly established Union of Soviet Socialist Republics. To Lenin and like-minded critics such as SPD members Karl Kautsky (1854-1938), Karl Liebknecht (1871-1919), and Rosa Luxemburg (1871-1919), revisionist socialism was a craven reformist sell-out of the traditional socialist vision, a sell-out that sought only "crumbs off the table" of the dominant class of capitalist plutocrats. To their minds, the only way to fully achieve the objectives of socialism was through socialism in the pure sense of public ownership and control of the means of production, and such a transformation could only come about through violent revolution.

Although Marx's original view had been that the preconditions for revolution would eventually emerge through ever-worsening business depressions afflicting the industrially advanced capitalist nations, the vicissitudes imposed on the mainly agrarian Russian nation by World War I enabled Lenin's successful Bolshevik revolution in 1917 that established the USSR. But when Karl Liebknecht and Rosa Luxemburg attempted an analogous revolution in defeated Germany in 1919, the revolution failed and its leaders were summarily executed. This outcome seemed to vindicate the position of such centrists as Karl Kautsky that it would probably require a very long period of time to bring about conditions in the advanced capitalist nations under which a socialist revolution would be successful.

As manifested by the attitude of individuals such as Karl Kautsky, Karl Liebknecht, and Rosa Luxemburg, Bernstein's revisionist reformulation of Marxism was not immediately successful. For example, the 1899 congress of the SPD passed a resolution explicitly rejecting Bernstein's ideas. However, the simultaneous motion to expel him from the Party failed to pass. Gradually the revisionist approach to socialism, in Germany and elsewhere, gained ground. Among other things, the fate of Karl Liebknecht and Rosa Luxemburg in 1919 was a further caution against putting too much reliance on violent revolution.

Once the decision had been made to attempt to gain power through the normal legal channels, the temptation existed to water down the program in order to gain electoral support. Thus expropriation tended to be replaced by nationalization with compensation, then economy-wide nationalization by nationalization of "key" industries. Finally, nationalization was often abandoned altogether and replaced by emphasis on such things as progressive income taxation and expanded welfare services (the "welfare state," or "social safety net"). Despite these fundamental shifts in attitudes and tactics, most of the parties and individuals involved did not wish to relinquish the "socialist" label. The term was too sacrosanct ever to be explicitly abandoned. In the meantime, however, it gradually become possible even for wealthy capitalists to call themselves "socialists" without being at all so altruistic as that would have implied if the socialism involved was old-fashioned, hardcore socialism preached by Marx—with its adamant insistence on public ownership and control of the nonhuman factors land and capital.

The influence of socialism for practical purposes might have faded out of modern history altogether if it had not been for the Russian revolution of 1917. This revolution gave the harsh early-Marxist version of socialism something that it had never had before—the support of an important nation-state. If a particular idea is subscribed to by a few random individuals here and there, it is not likely to cause much of a stir in human affairs. But if that idea gains the official support of the civil authority of a sizable sovereign entity in world society, then that idea, whether it be good, bad, or indifferent, becomes something to be reckoned with.

The Bolshevik triumph in Russia was something of an historical accident. If either the Bolsheviks or their opponents had behaved somewhat differently—the variations seemingly well within the range of possibility—the outcome might well have been very different. For example, the late Romanov czars might have been less rigid, and more willing to allow evolution toward a constitutional monarchy. Again, the revolutionary activity which had been so intense in Russia in the late nineteenth and early twentieth century would have been much less so had it not been supported by the nascent industrial capitalist class which was hoping to emulate the accomplishments of the French Revolution. Many of these capitalists failed to notice that the revolutionaries they helped financially and otherwise were as much or more under the influence of Karl Marx as under that of 18th century Enlightenment figures such as Voltaire and Rousseau.

Even all this might have failed to come to a head if Russia had been spared her disastrous participation in World War I. By early 1917, following more than two years of devastating warfare, antiwar feeling among the rank and file of the army and society generally was the most potent single factor in Russian politics. It was used by the Provisional Government to sweep the czar from power. Once free of the incompetent czarist yoke, so the Provisional Government reasoned, the Russian people would be inspired to prosecute the war more vigorously than before, and this time successfully. They were wrong. The damage had already been done, and a political change at the top could not overnight make Russia into an enthusiastic fighting machine. Most people—or at least a very large minority—wanted peace whatever the cost in national pride. The Bolsheviks promised peace. They were willing to promise anything, so long as power was obtained. The other aspects of the Bolshevik program were much less relevant to the fact that they managed to engineer themselves into power. Once in power, they hung on tenaciously in spite of great social turbulence. They kept their promise and got out of the war. The territorial cost was immense, but most of it was recovered once Germany had been defeated by the remaining Allied powers.

Among the first official actions taken by the Communist government of the Soviet Union in early 1918 was the total dispossession, without any compensation whatsoever, of both the landed aristocracy and the nascent capitalist class in Russia and its peripheral republics. Total public ownership of land and capital was implemented immediately, without ceremony, and without apology. Wholesale socialization galvanized the conservative resistance to the Communist regime and led to almost four years of bitter civil war. When it was over, most of the internal opponents of the regime were either dead or in exile. The civil war thus challenged the authority of the Soviet Communist leadership, but the outcome of that war confirmed it.

The socialization of Russia, naturally, greatly concerned the more conservative elements in other countries. Among others, Winston Churchill argued that military intervention should be mounted at once to crush the Bolshevik threat in its infancy. Luckily for the Bolsheviks, the capitalist nations were unable to muster the resolution for more than a small-scale and ineffectual effort at military intervention. The combination of war weariness in the wake of the catastrophic World War I, and the general consensus that socialism was thoroughly impractical—a fact that the Soviet Union would presumably soon discover for itself, precluded a full-scale military invasion of the fledgling Soviet Union by European and American forces.

By the early twenties, the civil war had petered out and the Bolsheviks remained firmly in control of Russia. A new variable had entered the world power equation. There now existed a non-negligible national power that espoused undiluted Marxist ideology. Socialism, whatever its merits or lack thereof, could no longer be shrugged off contemptuously by unbelievers or blithely twisted into nearly unrecognizable mutations by wishy-washy revisionists. Marxist speculation had suddenly become a reality. There had been a revolution, the property-owning classes had been unceremoniously expropriated, and now a great nation was about to move off into uncharted socialist territory. The rest of the world looked on with mixed emotions—curiosity, apprehension, and for some, hope.[4]

## The Soviet Era

It required several years before the Soviet leadership could adjust itself to the reality that for the time being at least, Russia would have to remain alone in the vanguard of the world socialist revolution. Marx's original thesis had been that the first sparks of the revolution would be ignited in the most advanced capitalist nations, wherein the contradictions of capitalism had reached the most aggravated state. Lenin and his colleagues were not unduly troubled by such a technicality. When they recognized an opportunity to take power, they did so. Later on, the ex post facto theory that Russia had been the "weakest link in the world capitalist chain" sufficed to cover the discrepancy between reality and Marx's prediction.

Nevertheless, much of the Bolshevik leadership at the beginning was hopeful that their example would inspire their fellows in the more radical wings of the Western European socialist parties, and the Russian revolution would after all provide the first sparks that would ignite a worldwide revolutionary conflagration. Such hopes were quickly disappointed. The European socialist parties had been much weakened and softened by Bernsteinian revisionism and wartime chauvinism. Their revolutionary spirit no longer sufficed, even if greater opportunities had presented themselves. There was a half-hearted effort at a socialist putsch in Germany shortly after her military collapse and surrender, but it was immediately suppressed and its leaders summarily executed. Not only did the capitalist powers keep order in their own houses, but they seemed dangerously inclined to intervene in Russia to nip the buds of revolution that had appeared there. Some limited aid, human and material, was extended to the White forces during the civil war, but it did not amount to a full-fledged intervention. The socialist parties in Europe still retained enough of their ideals to oppose such intervention. And many of the conservative elements saw no necessity for it—the coming fate of the Soviet Union would soon enough prove the impracticality and inefficiency of social-ism once and for all, thus via actual experiment ending the misguided enthusiasm for the concept on the part of various soft-headed dreamers.

By the time the civil war in Russia had ended, World War I was fin-ished, and the golden opportunity for revolutionary activity had passed. Apparently the initial sparks in Russia would have to smolder for an in-definite period before they would ignite the greater socialist revolution. Enthusiasts within the party for international agitation toward a world revolution were curbed, lest their activities alarm and anger the capital-ists who ruled the rest of the world, and bring about a powerful military intervention that would oust the Soviet government and thereby extin-guish the sparks of socialist revolution.

That left the question of what socialism should properly mean in a country in which the industrial structure was still at quite an early stage of development. Just as the left wing of the party rejected the notion that socialism could be properly developed in an agrarian economy and for that reason insisted that the revolution in Russia be joined and supported by revolutions in the more advanced West, there was a right wing, which while it rejected the practicality of immediate world revolution, also per-ceived little scope for authentic socialism in an isolated, agrarian Russia. The right wing perceived the need for a slow and lengthy industrial de-velopment that would parallel the leisurely industrial development that had transpired in the West.

For several years after the civil war, while the immediate, overriding objective was quick recovery from the ravages and devastation of pro-tracted war, the New Economic Policy remained in effect. This scheme left the economy in a remarkably free and unsupervised state, and more closely resembled free market capitalism than any of the succeeding eco-nomic arrangements prior to the collapse of Soviet communism in the early 1990s. The peasants were freed from the mandatory deliveries of the civil war period, and the industrial managers were permitted to en-gage in commercial production with a minimum of direction by the nom-inal owner, the state. Recovery took place on schedule, and the right wing saw in this general pattern of economic permissiveness the best policy for the indefinite future.

The middle wing of the party, which gradually became dominant under the leadership of Joseph Stalin (1878-1953), did not want to resign itself to long years of development. In the first place, there was too great an external danger. At any time the capitalist industrial powers of Western Europe and America might decide to eliminate the Soviet state. An adequate deterrent against this possibility could only be provided by the rapid development of a formidable internal industrial establishment capable of giving a powerful account of itself in modern warfare. Moreover, this was not, contrary to the opinion of some, a wishful dream. Marx had insisted that socialism, by abolishing business depressions, would burst the productive shackles of capitalism and lead to material wealth that would not have been believed possible beforehand. While Russia's incomplete industrial development at the time of the revolution prevented the immediate enrichment of the citizenry, certainly economic development under socialism, unimpeded by business depressions and guided by the technology already developed in the West, would be astonishingly rapid relative to the tortoise pace set by the capitalist countries during their respective industrial developments.

And thus in the late twenties and early thirties, the great Russian economic development effort, initiated and directed by the Communist Party, was launched. There were two core components of this plan. First, the collectivization and consequent modernization of agriculture would provide the agricultural surplus which hitherto had not been sufficiently abundant to support a major population transfer to the urban factories for the industrial buildup. Second, a state planning apparatus would closely oversee industrial production to ensure the observance of the priorities of the development plan, and to maintain continuous pressure toward high productivity on the part of all echelons of the industrial hierarchy, from unskilled factory hands to the managers of giant enterprises. The priorities of the plan were in steel, machine tools, and electricity. Consumer goods and agriculture were at the far lower end of the priority scale.

The effort of the 1930s placed a great strain on the Russian people. To begin with, a large proportion of the peasantry was opposed to collectivization. Many of them preferred to work independently their own holdings which had been allotted them in the early days of the revolution, and to sell the produce for what they could obtain on the free market. Some of the peasantry had attained to considerable levels of prosperity during the 1920s. Although the Soviet government was the official owner of the land, these farmers felt like and acted like independent proprietors with full legal control over their holdings. Now all this was changed. Large numbers of individual holdings were melded into collectives with centralized administrations. Output was collected and sold commonly, and the proceeds more or less evenly distributed among the membership. The more successful among the peasantry before collectivization resented being lumped together with their less prosperous neighbors. Moreover, the collective would not be able to sell its output for whatever it could get on a free market as in the past, but it would now have to meet compulsory delivery quotas (just as during the civil war), for which the government would pay prices that were well below free market levels. As a result of all this, the living standards of the rural population were drastically reduced by collectivization. Resistance in some areas went as far as armed conflict, and the Soviet state met its severest test since the civil war.

The planners were thoroughly determined, however. In their minds, collectivization was necessary to raise output in the agricultural sector, and this was the basic prerequisite for smooth development in the industrial sector. Once the initial opposition was crushed and the collectivized agricultural sector began functioning normally, output did rise, but not sufficiently to fully justify the optimistic projections of the planners. This agricultural shortfall was at the heart of the unexpectedly large economic sacrifices the Russian people were forced to make during the thirties and thereafter. In the industrial sector, there were close approaches to the ambitious goals of the planners. Russia was in fact succeeding in adding to her industrial power at a rate unprecedented in economic history. But the cost was high. An unprecedentedly high investment rate was required. As more and more of national output was directed into plan achievement in heavy industry and social infrastructure, the consumer goods sector shrank to a bare minimum. The working population was exhorted vigorously to maintain a supreme productive effort, and not to resent the temporary scarcity in consumer goods. But the propaganda effort, however strident and vigorous, was not entirely successful.

## Stalin's Dictatorship

During the great plan-directed industrialization campaign in the USSR during the 1930s, progress was made at an impressive rate—but the cost in social strain was also impressive. It is uncertain whether it was the pressures generated by forced-pace economic growth, or Stalin's paranoid personality, that was more to blame for subsequent events. But for whatever reason, there occurred in the mid-to-late thirties an event that dimmed appreciably whatever glory had been achieved in the economic realm. This was an intemperate purge of the Communist Party carried out at the instigation of the man who had come to dominate it, Joseph Stalin. The purge underscored the monolithic and anti-democratic dominance of the Communist Party in Soviet society. This was the other great, overriding characteristic of the Soviet experience. The first was rapid economic growth; the second was the ruthlessly elitist attitude of the Soviet leadership.

Long before the rise of Stalin, the seeds of his horrific dictatorship had been planted by Lenin. Inspired by the vague references in Marx's work to the "dictatorship of the proletariat," and deeply influenced by the Russian tradition of absolutism in government and the need for party discipline in the long years of struggle before the revolution, Vladimir Lenin elaborated a comprehensive theory of the need for a stringent dictatorship in Russia after the revolution. Lenin was decidedly not a weak-kneed, irresolute man. He full well realized that the capitalist masters would not give up without a fight—and he was fully prepared to take them on. They would savagely resist the socialist revolution with whatever means they could. They would have to be ruthlessly suppressed. Misplaced sentimentalism, chivalry, and lenience were not apropos when the whole future welfare of mankind was at stake. Later on, when socialism was triumphant, there would be time enough for peace, reconciliation, and brotherhood.

Nevertheless, despite these preconceptions, Lenin did not consider himself basically anti-democratic. Democracy is fundamentally the rule of the people, namely the heeding of the desires of the people by the government. Certainly the Communist Party was responsive to the will of the people. In fact, it *was* the will of the people. There was no sense at all in talking about a divergence between the desires of the majority of the people and the desires of the Communist Party. If there ever did occur any resistance to the authority of the Communist Party, it would have to be the work of an obstructionist, anti-social minority.

But while the sovereignty of the Communist Party in all spheres of society was to be clearly recognized, and while the Party itself was to observe strict hierarchical discipline within its ranks, the ideal was to have a liberal, tolerant, enlightened, collegial leadership at the top. Various viewpoints were to have representation in the elite, discussions were to be free and open, and decisions determined by a majority vote of the top Party leaders. Once decisions were arrived at, however, it was the duty of the minority to cease and desist from any resistance or counter-argument, and to carry out the will of the majority as if it were its own will. It later became painfully apparent that the system designed by Lenin with sincere good will did have a natural susceptibility to intolerant and insensitive one-man domination. The dictatorship of Joseph Stalin became so oppressive and capricious that it was afterwards thoroughly repudiated by the Party that had spawned it.

The development task in Russia was interrupted and disrupted by the climactic struggle of World War II. The Soviet government attempted to evade embroilment in hopes that the capitalist powers would exhaust themselves in internecine conflict. But Hitler's intention all along had been eastward expansion, and when he had to his own satisfaction succeeded in neutralizing his enemies to the West, he turned without hesitation on Russia. The ensuing titanic struggle, from the German invasion of the Soviet Union in June 1941, through to the defeat of Germany in May 1945, demonstrated the solidity and power of the Soviet state, but the cost was staggering in both human and material terms.

Taking advantage of post-World War II chaos, Soviet Russia set up satellite socialist states in the overrun eastern European countries, and also supported the Chinese Communist Party in its successful effort to take power in China. As World War I had facilitated the establishment of the first communist state, World War II facilitated a vast territorial and population expansion of the communist empire. The sudden enlargement of the communist sector on the world map deeply alarmed the remainder of the capitalist world. But by now any military intervention to eliminate this threat had become a costly and problematical proposition. The emphasis would now have to be on the containment of further communist expansion. Thus the commencement of the tense and bitter Cold War era. In the Soviet Union itself, the immediate post-war era saw continuation of the industrial build-up, along with more purges.

Following Stalin's death in 1953, the Soviet state commenced a program of gradual, cautious liberalization. In the economic sphere, this meant a better condition for the agricultural working force, and a general increase in the proportion of output devoted to consumer goods. Starting in the 1960s, there were alterations in the planning system to increase the independence and initiative of the industrial managers. While there were no fundamental changes in the traditional patterns of collectivization and state planning, practices were made more flexible and consistent with economic principles in "normal" conditions, as opposed to the conditions of forced-race industrial buildup.

In general, the Soviet experience "proved" only one economic proposition concerning socialism: that public ownership of land and capital, and the absence of a class of private capitalists, does not *necessarily* lead to production so arbitrary and capricious as to induce *speedy* economic stagnation and collapse. The Soviet economy got along without capitalists, without private owners of the nonhuman factors of production, for over seven decades. While no one can say whether the progress was proportional to the sacrifices, or that the Soviet system made as good or better use of its economic opportunities as capitalism would have, the fact remains that the system produced for its citizens a respectable level of material welfare and gained for their country an honorable—if dangerous—position as a formidable competitor in the dog-eat-dog world of military-diplomatic realpolitik. Whatever its demerits and shortcomings, any system capable of putting a particular nation into the key position that Russia held during the twentieth century cannot be dismissed with a contemptuous shrug as merely a soft-headed dreamer's idyll.

## Western Attitudes

The establishment and subsequent history of the USSR had a profound effect on attitudes toward socialism in the rest of the world. Prior to 1917, there had been a tendency for conservatives to view Marxist socialists rather complacently and contemptuously as misguided cranks. For many, the private property right in capital goods was as natural as breathing, and they tended to assume that any society that attempted to abrogate that right would be doomed to speedy economic collapse. Thus socialists must be kept out of power at home because of all the damage they might inadvertently do if they did get into power. But if they took over in some other country— perhaps that would be for the best because it would soon demonstrate, once and for all, the economic futility of socialist schemes.

The Russian revolution demonstrated that it was not wholly impossible for a socialist party to gain political power by means of violent revolution. Of course, the fact that socialists were able to take over from an anti-democratic, absolutist, unloved monarchial regime that was entangled in a devastating and losing war, did not necessarily indicate that they would be able to do the same in more stable, democratic, and economically advanced nations—at least in peacetime. Nevertheless, the Russian revolution alarmed the capitalist nations, and their resistance to socialist thinking became thereafter much firmer than before.

By this is meant the general sentiment among the *majority* of the populations of the capitalist nations. Among certain minorities, attitudes were different. A very small minority of hardline orthodox Marxists applauded Soviet Communism as the wave of the future, as the forerunner of a better world for all. This particular minority started shrinking with the first signs of trouble in the "workers' paradise"— the Stalinist purges of the latter 1930s—and continued shrinking steadily throughout the course of the Cold War. The much larger minority of soft-line social democratic Marxists of revisionist persuasion took care to distance themselves from Soviet Communism from the very beginning. After initially discarding the principle of violent revolution, as the twentieth century progressed, social democratic Marxists also gradually retreated from the public ownership objective. As the emphasis on public ownership gradually receded, political support for social democracy gradually grew, so much so that at certain times within certain countries, social democratic minorities verged on becoming majorities.

It is probably safe to say that the high tide of hardline Marxist socialism in the noncommunist world was reached prior to World War I. Following the Russian revolution of 1917, this brand of socialism was much more on the defensive. To the traditional theoretical arguments against socialism were now added all the defects, real and imagined, of the Soviet Union. The Soviet experiment was viewed with keen and generally critical interest by the capitalist nations. The conviction that Russia's economic system was inferior wobbled somewhat during the 1930s. This decade witnessed the worst recorded business depression in capitalist history. While the West suffered economic disaster, the Soviet Union, albeit painfully, surged ahead in its industrialization campaign. The contrast inspired a reawakening of interest in socialism in the West, although not to the extent of causing a major social transformation. The purges of the late 1930s were welcome news to apologists for capitalism. They seemed to vindicate the viewpoint that whatever progress the Soviet state was achieving was being built on the blood and bones of its people.

The last vestiges of outright contempt for the economy of the Soviet Union were demolished by Russia's impressive performance against the German military machine during World War II. The intent of Nazi Germany, under the dictatorial leadership of Adolf Hitler (1889-1945), had from the beginning been eastward expansion into Russia. England, France, and the United States had no love for Soviet Communism, but they appreciated the vast natural resources of Russia, and assumed that if Nazi Germany gained control over these resources, it would become the premier world power and would be in a good position to carry out its threat of establishing a brutal German-dominated world hegemony. They further assumed that the Soviet state would be unable to mount any significant resistance to a German invasion. Russia's performance during World War I, when Germany's attention had been divided between two fronts, had not been inspiring, and after two decades of socialist blundering, she would hardly be expected to do any better the second time. Thus Germany must not be allowed to expand to the east without confronting western opposition. The line was drawn in Poland, and Nazi Germany's invasion of Poland in September, 1939, initiated the mammoth conflict of World War II. The war ground on for almost six years, killing tens of millions and destroying vast quantities of material goods.

The temporary wartime friendship between the Western allies and the Soviet Union was quickly replaced after the war by natural conflict between capitalist and communist ideologies. The expansion of the communist empire in the post-war world greatly alarmed the remaining capitalist nations. There was no longer a question of contemptuous dismissal of the communist threat. The ideological struggle became part of a strategic conflict along traditional lines of international alliance systems. Most of the developed world became polarized into a communist bloc and a noncommunist bloc. With socialism so closely associated with the great national enemy, hardline Marxist parties and sympathies within the capitalist countries reached a new low in influence, and their chances of gaining political power shrank to almost nothing. As already noted, however, this was not true of revisionist Marxism. So long as social democratic politicians made clear and explicit their renunciation of hardline Marxist principles, specifically the need for violent revolution and need for public ownership of land and capital, their successful participation in governance was not unduly impeded.

The decline of the internal influence of socialism in the capitalist nations—at least as defined in terms of adherence to the public ownership principle—was also fostered by the economic success of capitalism in the post-war period. After World War II, many decades passed without a severe business downturn on the scale of the Great Depression of the 1930s. Accordingly, there has been steadily increasing confidence that capitalism now possesses Keynesian anticyclical tools sufficiently effective to prevent any repetition of the huge economic losses of the Great Depression and earlier crises.

Somewhat flustered by this development, communist apologists during the Cold War endeavored to put responsibility for the long-continued capitalistic prosperity on the large military budget, or the exploitation of the less developed world. Such prosperity, they claimed, cannot be explained in terms of the "natural" internal properties of capitalism. However, their respect for certain attributes of capitalism no doubt increased, and this may account for the greater receptivity toward various economic reforms that reduced the influence of the central planning authorities in the economy. And finally, nearly a half-century following the conclusion of World War II, growing respect for democratic capitalism brought about the definitive end of the socialist experiment in the Soviet Union.

## The Post-Soviet Era

The decade following the dissolution of the Soviet Union witnessed a severe economic downturn. Anyone, either within the ex-USSR or out-

side it, who expected the abandonment of Soviet socialism and the restoration of capitalism to bring about instant prosperity, was sadly disappointed. Throughout most of the 1990s, soon after the Russian people
had joyously liberated themselves from the suffocating shackles of socialistic central planning—at a time when the economic blessings of
democratic market capitalism should have been raining down hard upon
a grateful population—developments were very much contrary to expectation and desire. The economy went into free fall, with prices soaring,
unemployment spreading, production tumbling, and the large majority of
the population desperately coping with scarcities and uncertainties far
worse than anything they had known under the Soviet regime. During
this time, a mordant joke surfaced in Moscow, a joke soon circulated
around the world: "Russia, having discredited socialism, is now going to
do the same for capitalism!" But whatever ephemeral psychic relief may
have been derived from black humor, it did not alter the hard facts. The
economic decline continued on and on, month after month, year after
year. By the latter 1990s, the economic situation in Russia, to most ordi-
nary Russians, was certainly no laughing matter.

According to World Bank data, between 1989 and 1998 Russian real
GDP declined from $869 billion to $485 billion (in constant 2005 U.S.
$), a fall of over 44 percent. In per capita terms, this represented a de-
cline from $5,883 to $3,282. This decline represented a calamitous collapse of production, far worse than that experienced by the United States
during the traumatic Great Depression of the 1930s. (It was not until
2006 that Russian per capita income regained its 1989 level.) The human
costs of this decline were staggering, almost inconceivable—powerfully
affecting even the most fundamental demographic conditions. From 1989
to 1995, the birth rate (per 1,000 people) decreased from 14.6 to 9.3,
while the death rate increased from 10.7 to 15.0. Statistics such as these
convey something of the magnitude of the disaster, although—as cold,
impersonal numbers—they tend to obscure the harsh human realities underlying them. For many if not most people in Russia, going from
planned socialism to market capitalism was like going from the proverbial frying pan into the fire. What had once been mere inconvenience and
irritation had now degenerated into a desperate struggle for survival.

On the other hand, the re-establishment of capitalism in Russia soon
yielded enormous wealth—to a few. For the most part these beneficiaries, far from having been a revolutionary underclass in the now-defunct
Soviet society, had held highly influential positions. They were thus well
positioned to manipulate the reform efforts and transition processes to
serve their own interests rather than those of the general population. In

his article "Russia's Collapse," published in the September/October 1999 issue of *Foreign Affairs*, Anders Aslund, a leading Western authority on post-Soviet economic developments, describes several mechanisms by which insiders subverted the reform movement for their personal benefit. For example, from the late 1980s through the early 1990s, a period that witnessed the final decline and fall of the Soviet Union, managers of state enterprises were allowed to set up privately controlled cooperatives which purchased domestically produced supplies of commodities such as metals and oil at artificially low, state-supported internal prices, and then sold these supplies abroad at the much higher prices prevailing on the world market. The ostensible purpose of the program was to foster exports. But the lavish profits generated by these transactions went not to the state enterprises but rather to the private cooperatives—and from there into the private bank accounts of the managers. The practice, most accurately described as a form of embezzlement from the state enterprises, was hypocritically justified by these managers and their political allies as a necessary means of protecting Russian industry against collapse. Eventually, internal commodity prices were allowed to rise to world levels, thus closing down this particular avenue to dishonestly acquired wealth. But by that time, many managers of state enterprises had lifted themselves out of the ranks of "dreary government bureaucrats" into the charmed circle of privileged multi-millionaires.

Rapid privatization of state-owned enterprises was pushed ahead by the reformers as a means of finalizing Russia's break with its socialistic past. Although some reformers were concerned that the privatization process was neither as efficient nor as equitable as it should be, they rushed ahead with the process in the belief that only the distribution among many millions of Russian citizens of private ownership rights to business enterprises would create an insuperable political barrier to the return of socialism and communism. When the dust had settled, it was found that most large enterprises were under the effective control of their top managers. These managers were no longer subservient to state bureaucracies, nor were they adequately supervised by stockholders, nor were they sufficiently accountable to financial institutions and markets. Essentially uncontrolled, and confronted by severe uncertainty regarding the future, many of these managers put their own interests ahead of those of creditors, stockholders, employees, and the general public. They engaged in practices that in the West would be termed "looting," and which in the West—if discovered and prosecuted—would result in the imposition of lengthy prison terms. In reforming Russia, however, what was once "profiteering" behavior that might have landed a manager in front of a firing squad, was now condoned and veritably encouraged as part of the supposed capitalistic salvation of Russia. This behavior resulted in still more politically influential multi-millionaires—the "oligarchs" of the new era.

Throughout the long and anxious decades of the Cold War, decades fraught with the peril of instantaneous nuclear holocaust, Western experts had continuously exhorted the political leadership and the general population of the Soviet Union that it was in their own self-interest to abandon socialism and central planning. According to these experts, the higher living standards of the United States and Western Europe, relative to those in the Soviet Union, constituted compelling, irrefutable evidence of the economic inferiority of centrally planned socialism to free market capitalism. Communist claims of socialistic superiority over capitalism gradually faded as the years and decades passed and the Soviet Union failed to make significant headway toward its avowed long-term goal of "overtaking and surpassing" the Western capitalist nations, especially the United States. Gradually the West got the upper hand in this protracted "war of ideas," leading eventually to total ideological capitulation by the Soviet Union. By early 1992, the Soviet Union had been dissolved and its successor nations, including the Russian Federation itself, had all officially renounced every aspect of Marxist ideology and communistic practice, and were busily attempting to emulate exactly the economic and political characteristics of the leading Western nations. Optimism ran high that once the necessary institutional changes had been implemented, the Russian people would soon experience a level of economic prosperity and social progress hitherto unknown throughout the entire history of Russia.

Those hopes were bitterly disappointed. When matters go awry, it is a natural human impulse to look for "those responsible." It is far more satisfying, from an emotional standpoint, to blame unsatisfactory conditions on human individuals, as opposed to attributing them to impersonal natural or social forces. Both inside and outside Russia, many people pointed the finger of guilt at dishonest managers and the corrupt politicians and government officials who allowed themselves be bribed into becoming accomplices of these managers.

Some discerned the principal roots of the problem in the seven decades following the Russian Revolution during which Marxist ideology ruled Russian society and governance with an iron hand. This misguided pursuit of a socialist utopia resulted ultimately in both economic stagnation and political paralysis. During those disastrous decades, the Russian people developed a "slave mentality" which stripped them of their individuality, initiative, and moral sensibility. When the chains were finally removed, they reacted like the animals they had become. Other analysts perceive even deeper roots underlying the inappropriate attitudes and motivations of the contemporary Russian population—roots extending back centuries before the Russian Revolution of 1917. An article in *The Economist* (Dec. 19, 1998) on "Russians' Relations with Money" describes the long history prior to the 1917 revolution of Russian governments continually carrying out monetary debasement as a substitute for tax collection, and continually defaulting on their debts, both domestic and foreign. The author comments: "One could be forgiven for making the leap from this almost unbroken history of monetary mismanagement to the conclusion that there is something intrinsically disaster-prone—a 'national character' problem—in Russians' relations with money."

On the other hand, another school of thought held that the central problem is that the Russians tried to accomplish a drastic economic and political transformation far too quickly. Numerous Western experts, such as Anders Aslund and many others, were invited by the Russian reformers to come to Russia and provide guidance and instruction on how to create a free market, private ownership economy which would quickly generate prosperity and growth. Quite a lot of the advice provided by these Western experts was in fact accepted and implemented. When economic conditions deteriorated, the Western experts, of course, did not find anything amiss with their advice and recommendations—rather they blamed the incompetent Russians for failing to implement their advice and recommendations quickly and completely. But the fact remains that a plausible case may be made that the problem was not going too slowly, but rather going too quickly. For example, the Western experts, as a rule, were strongly supportive of laissez faire, and the minimization of legal regulations and bureaucratic controls. Then they complained about such problems as capital flight and embezzlement of enterprise assets—problems of the sort that legal regulations and bureaucratic controls are intended to alleviate.

Although playing the "blame game" is inherently entertaining, it is often an unfruitful if not entirely counterproductive diversion. There is little point in trying to assess guilt because the harm has already been done, and punishment of culprits, even if it could be done reliably, would not undo the harm. Even more importantly, a great deal of the harm stemmed not from the consciously evil behavior of individual human beings, but rather from impersonal socioeconomic conditions and circumstances. One can easily perceive a considerable number of factors that potentially contributed heavily to the economic collapse, but which had nothing to do with such human frailties as greed, ignorance, stupidity, and incompetence.

For example, prior to the dissolution of the Soviet Union, the economies of the Russian Federation and the other republics (Ukraine, Kazakhstan, etc.) were very closely interrelated and interdependent. Once these republics became independent nations, "international trade" complications emerged where none had existed before. Another factor may have been the demobilization of millions of military personnel: many ex-soldiers turned to crime, particularly to the crime of extortion, as a means of making a living. Another problem was uncertainty regarding the proper focus of authority and delegation of responsibility within the critical business enterprise sector. Many enterprise managers were very unclear as to when and where they should be giving orders, and when and where they should be taking them.

Still another factor was the tremendous psychological jolt administered to the entire population when the nation suddenly and dramatically disavowed the Marxist ideology which for more than 70 years had served essentially as the "Soviet religion." Everything which the Russian people had learned from childhood onwards concerning the evils of capitalism and the virtues of socialism, as well as the heroic vanguard role of the Communist Party in the regeneration of worldwide human civilization—all this was now suddenly invalid, reversed, abrogated, cancelled, consigned to oblivion. Back in 1917, at the time of the Russian Revolution, the old regime had been thrown out, abolished, consigned to oblivion—prior to the achievement of any appreciable consensus on what should follow it. The ultimate consequences of that convulsive transformation had been horrific, including as they did the totalitarian dictatorship of Joseph Stalin from the 1930s through the 1950s. Now, for the second time in the twentieth century, Russia cast off the old regime with no clear concept of the appropriate new regime. Understandably, the Russian people were stunned, uncertain, fearful and anxious about what the future held, what would be the accepted standards of behavior, how the economy would evolve, how their personal lives would develop. In such an atmosphere, it is not surprising that many people were motivated to unethical behavior that often strayed over the boundary into criminality.

Nevertheless, problems such as these are inherently ephemeral and transitory. Eventually the economies of the ex-USSR republics reintegrated, eventually the demobilized military personnel found legal, productive employment, eventually the lines of authority within business enterprise became clarified, and eventually the Russian population overcame the psychological shock of transformation and fully embraced the new institutions and philosophies. Economic indicators started improving in the latter 1990s, and growth has been steady throughout the early years of the 21st century. Russia is a huge nation with a rich scientific and cultural heritage, an abundance of natural resources, a well-educated population, and a tremendous national motivation toward success. During the latter half of the twentieth century, Russia's "superpower" status was acknowledged by all, and it is a status which the Russian people naturally desire to restore.

Therefore it seems likely that sooner or later the Russian Federation will boast one of the more prosperous and dynamic economies in the world. Hopefully this will occur sooner rather than later. Until it occurs, there is always the danger of a political reaction that might cast the world backward into the hazardous and wasteful Cold War of unhappy memory. As Anders Aslund pointed out, Russia is too big and too nuclear for its economic failure to be viewed indifferently by the rest of the world. Although the main thrust toward success must be provided by the Russians themselves, the West should be generous in providing capital resources and technical expertise in order to assure success.

## Socialism in China

In the aftermath of World War II, Soviet-style communistic socialism was externally imposed on several Eastern European nations (Poland, Hungary, Czechoslovakia, and so on). Although there had been a few adherents to Soviet Communism among the populations of these nations during the interwar period, they would never have come to power, even in the wake of a devastating war, had it not been for direct force of arms applied by the occupying Red Army. Apprehension and indignation in the West over the externally enforced communizations of the Eastern European nations was the principal immediate impetus to the Cold War, but another factor was the communization of some other nations in which the Red Army was not directly involved. Among these other nations, by far the largest and most important was China.

China had been deeply mired in civil war and social turmoil ever since the overthrow of the Manchu dynasty in 1912. The epic struggle between the Nationalists under Chiang Kai-shek and the Communists under Mao Tse-tung left much of the country in a state of anarchy presided over by an array of competing warlords. The situation was then further complicated by the Japanese invasion of 1937. An uneasy alliance between the Nationalists and the Communists was maintained until the defeat of Japan in 1945. To the consternation of the West, Chiang Kai-shek's Nationalists were then outfought on the battlefield and outmaneuvered in the propaganda struggle for the allegiance of the population, with the result that in 1949 a second great nation was added to the communist bloc of nations: the People's Republic of China (PRC).

The noncommunist world soon observed, to its relief, that national-istic distinctions tended to override the universalistic ideals of Marxist ideology. The Eastern European nations were restive under Soviet do-minion, which is hardly surprising in that communism had been external-ly imposed on them in the aftermath of World War II. But even aside from Eastern Europe, Russia's other ideological allies, especially China, were disinclined to slavishly follow the Soviet Union's prescriptions and preferences. As did the United States during the same period, the Soviet Union found that being the senior partner of a military alliance did not completely insulate it from substantial criticism and opposition from jun-ior partners of the alliance.

In the earliest period of Sino-Soviet disharmony, the major contro-versy revolved around the proper nature and pace of revolutionary social transformation both domestically and internationally—the Chinese ac-cused the Soviets of being inadequately determined on both fronts. The Sino-Soviet conflict was never quite as dire as depicted by some Western propagandists searching anxiously for signs of weakness in the com-munist camp. There was never any serious likelihood of a war between the USSR and the PRC. However, the conflict was serious enough to preclude close cooperation and friendship between the two nations. The tide of radical social egalitarianism crested in the PRC in the Cultural Revolution of 1966-69, nearly 20 years after Mao Tse-tung's accession to power. This turbulent period was followed by a more or less inevitable "Thermidorean reaction," during which the PRC reconciled itself to a certain amount of social distinction and economic inequality.

China's effort to follow the teachings and practices of Marx, Lenin, and Stalin was influenced importantly both by its salient national charac-teristics and its international environment.[5] China is much smaller in ter-ritory than the Soviet Union and much more densely populated. It is a nation with a long history and a complex cultural tradition. At the time of the communist victory in 1949, its industrial sector was even less devel-oped than the Russian industrial sector had been at the time of the Bol-shevik victory in 1917. China followed the Soviet lead in the collectivi-zation of agriculture and also in the initiation of a modernization and in-dustrialization campaign in which central planning of the economy played an important role. However, central planning was never as com-prehensive and detailed in China as it was in the Soviet Union. There is at least one important reason for this: industrialization for purposes of self-defense was never as urgent in China as it had been earlier in the Soviet Union. Unlike the Soviet Union, Red China never had to stand alone against a hostile capitalist outer world. Following its socialist revo-lution, it was able to take shelter under the nuclear umbrella provided by the Soviet Union. In addition, Red China was to some extent able to learn from the mistakes of its predecessor in socialism. Thus for example, when its collective farm sector performed disappointingly, the Chinese government soon fundamentally revised the structure of agricultural production by means of the "responsibility system."

Just as the revolutionary transformation of the Russian empire in 1917 led eventually to the totalitarian dictatorship of Joseph Stalin, so too the revolutionary transformation of China in 1949 led eventually to the totalitarian dictatorship of Mao Tse-tung. And just as the demise of Stalin in 1953 led to an era of reform in which socioeconomic policy moderated, so too the demise of Mao in 1973 led to an analogous era of reform. In both cases, emphasis was placed on decentralization of economic decision-making authority and increased reliance on market forces and individual incentives in the functioning of the economy. Western economists soon became rather scornful of the perennial Soviet economic reform efforts. A succession of well-publicized reform programs were commenced over the years, and one after another they were judged to have "failed" by Western economists as not having had a significant impact on the actual functioning of the planned Soviet economy. Western economists spoke of the Soviet economy as being on a "treadmill of reforms"—much effort, but little progress. Of course the legendary stability of the Soviet system came to an abrupt end in the early 1990s. The political system was indeed radically transformed within a short period of time by the elimination of direct Communist Party control over the state apparatus and the dissolution of the USSR.

Similar efforts of decentralizing economic reform have been undertaken in the People's Republic of China, and perhaps because the economic system there had never been as thoroughly centralized as it had been in the Soviet Union, these reforms were widely viewed in the West as having been more successful. The "responsibility system" in agriculture effectively abolished the system of communal farming which had been the prevailing standard in the communist world ever since the collectivization of Soviet agriculture in the early 1930s. Chinese agriculture blossomed mightily under the responsibility system, and its success in generating a surplus of food laid the basis for the development of all types of industry.

The responsibility system in Chinese agriculture is sometimes characterized as being equivalent to private ownership agriculture as practiced in the West: the land allocations of the Chinese farmer being regarded as fully analogous to the privately owned small family farms which are widely prevalent in Western agriculture. This is a serious misrepresentation of the actual situation. A Chinese farm family working under the responsibility system does not own the land assigned to it. The land is owned by the local commune, which in effect leases the land to the family under a long-term, open-ended contract at a very modest rental rate. In contrast to ownership rights to land in the West, the family assigned a plot of land in China may not choose to allow that plot to remain fallow, it may not sell the plot or sublet it to another family, and if unknown assets are discovered in the land (e.g., mineral deposits), the family has no right to any part of the revenue derived from the sale of those assets. The rights of the family under the responsibility system are limited to the value of agricultural commodities obtained from the land through the family's own personal labor. So long as the family is engaged in good faith tillage of the land, it is subject to a bare minimum of outside intervention in and direction of its production and marketing efforts. The nearest equivalent to Western practices might be a situation of tenant farming in which the landlord is a close relative who requires only a nominal rental payment.

The Chinese responsibility system invigorated not only agricultural production but the economy as a whole, and during the latter part of the twentieth century and into the twenty-first, the Chinese economy became one of the fastest-growing economies in the world. Living standards in China have risen dramatically over the last few decades since the initiation of the responsibility system. This success provides important circumstantial evidence for the economic practicality of market socialism, in that the Chinese experience demonstrates that powerful incentives to effort can be achieved in the absence of legal ownership of the nonhuman factors of production.

Under Western capitalism, a powerful mystique attaches to the concept of private ownership of capital. The same sort of a priori legitimacy of ownership rights which exists with respect to items of personal property such as books and clothing, or to the small tools used by a craftsman such as a carpenter, is supposed to also apply to monetary earnings derived from financial capital instruments such as stocks and bonds. There are of course important distinctions between different types of private property. Unlike books and clothing, stocks and bonds are not directly consumed by the owner. Unlike small tools used by a craftsman, stocks and bonds do not require labor on the part of the owner to produce value. But these distinctions between capital property and other types of property tend to be minimized, if not ignored altogether, by the mystique attaching to private ownership in and of itself. An important practical upshot of the mystique is that private ownership of the business enterprise is deemed essential to its effectiveness. Supposedly only private ownership of a business enterprise can imbue those responsible for its man-

agement with the necessary effort incentives to make the enterprise efficient and successful.

That the private ownership mystique is a myth, and that this particular practical upshot is specious and invalid, is suggested by the success of
the Chinese economy in general, and the Chinese agricultural sector under the responsibility system in particular. Nevertheless, a major hin-
drance to proper appreciation in the West of the circumstantial support
for the potential effectiveness of market socialism currently being provided by the Chinese experience is the unfortunate fact that, despite the
recent improvements, the living standards of the Chinese population are
still relatively low. The people of China are may be better fed and more
prosperous than their counterparts in, say, India—but this may not be
very impressive in the eyes of the typical middle-class citizen of the
United States or the United Kingdom, whose standard of living would be
considered veritably luxurious by most people in China. China's fundamental economic problem is its huge population in relation to limited
land area and scarce natural resources. Given the abundance of humanity
relative to the available natural resources, the impact of the systemic factor (capitalism versus socialism) is relatively minor.

Marxists had traditionally scorned Malthusian concerns about excessive population growth as an exclusively "capitalist problem." Supposedly the revolutionary transformation of capitalism into socialism would so
unchain the productive forces of society that abundance and prosperity
would prevail regardless of the rate of population growth. In addition,
China had the example of its predecessor in socialism, the Soviet Union.
With a huge, well-endowed, and sparsely populated land area at its disposal, the Communist Party of the USSR had never had any qualms
about rapid population growth, and indeed encouraged it on grounds that
it augmented the military strength and productive resources of the nation.
In contrast to the Soviet Union, of course, China did *not* have a huge,
well-endowed, and sparsely populated land area with which to work.
Therefore, the pursuit of pro-natalist policies by the People's Republic of
China for the first twenty years or so of its existence contributed strongly
to its relatively disappointing economic performance. By the time the
Chinese Communist Party leadership realized that population problems
were not necessarily confined to capitalism, and radically revised social
policy to inhibit fertility among the population, a great deal of damage
had already been done. Even now, after decades of anti-natalist policy,
the Chinese population is still growing briskly.

Moreover, population pressure is certainly not the only constraint on
Chinese economic performance. Most of the potential "reasons for Soviet
economic weakness" (other than socialism) have also applied at various

times to the People's Republic of China. Of these reasons, the absence of democratic governance, even if its direct economic impact may not be as important as that of some of the others, is probably the single most important reason why advocates of market socialism are unable to hold up the PRC proudly as a model for emulation. In China as in Russia, the radical transformation of society required by Marxist ideology elicited enormous internal resistance—and this resistance was put down by brute force. The current "human rights violations" in China about which Western governments ritualistically complain are minuscule in comparison with the mass deportations, incarcerations, and executions of the revolutionary period. As Chairman Mao once put it so memorably, "A revolution is not a dinner party." In China as in Russia, the combination of internal dissension with external peril made democracy an unaffordable luxury in the eyes of the Communist Party leadership. It could well be that China will one day follow the lead of the former Soviet Union, throw off the dominance of the Chinese Communist Party, and commence building an open, tolerant, and fully democratic political system. But there is no telling when that day will come.

# 5

# Learning from the Past

## Evolution — Not Revolution

"Revolution" is one of those words, such as "love," "hate," "freedom," "slavery," and so on, that has very different meanings in different contexts, and which also, in some contexts, embodies strong emotional connotations. However, there is one context in which the emotional connotations of "revolution" are minimal: the physical context. In the physical context, a revolution refers to any circular or semi-circular movement, as in the spinning movement of a wheel around its axle, or as in the orbital movement of a planet around the sun. In the technological context, the term is sometimes applied to important changes in the means and methods of production, as in the "Industrial Revolution" or the "microcomputer revolution." In the social context, the term "revolution" is sometimes used to describe important changes in attitudes and customs, as in the "sexual revolution." Particularly in the social context, the term is sometimes used in ways that somewhat devalue it, as, for example, in the recently launched, Internet-based "Fashion Revolution" movement that urges consumers to boycott clothing manufacturers who rely too much on Third World factories in which the labor force is underpaid and otherwise exploited.

In the political context, the term "revolution" refers to the forcible removal of the existing government and its replacement by a new government, in other words, a change of government through force and violence rather than peacefully through hereditary succession, consensual agreement, or elections. In some cases, the "existing government" was imposed or controlled by individuals outside the nation. In this case, exemplified by the American Revolutionary War of 1775 to 1783, what is involved is more accurately described as a war of independence (or liberation), rather than as a "revolution" as normally understood. Historians generally agree, for example, that the American Revolutionary War is more accurately described as the American War of Independence. In the purely domestic context, a revolution involves the forcible replacement of the existing government composed mostly of citizens of the nation, by some other group similarly composed. Although there may be "foreign" elements involved, they are not dominant. The usual connotation of the term "revolution" is that the government overthrown had been controlled by a relatively small minority of highly privileged individuals, while the new government is controlled by a much larger group of unprivileged individuals—or at least less privileged individuals. Such revolutions may bring about significant changes in the existing social order. But in some cases, described by the term "coup d'état, the relatively small minority of privileged individuals is replaced by an almost equally small minority of only slightly less privileged individuals. In these cases, there is no intention toward major alterations in the existing social structure on the part of the instigators of the coup.

The notion that revolution is a viable and attractive avenue toward the improvement of human society probably reached its apogee in the early days of the initial French Revolution of 1789. Even Edwin Burke, soon to emerge as a major critic of the French Revolution, was initially favorable toward it. But within a period of a few years, excessively ambitious policies had been pushed through by the revolutionary government, policies that severely discredited it among a large proportion of the population of France itself, and also among a large proportion of the populations of several neighboring European countries. Internal opposition was met by the Terror under Robespierre, and external intervention was met by a series of foreign wars, commencing in 1792 and not finally concluded until 1815. Robespierre and his main Jacobin associates were executed in the "Thermidorian reaction" of July 1794, an internal coup within France. But it took the combined military might of a coalition of four major foreign powers (Great Britain, Russia, Prussia, and Austria) to bring down Napoleon Bonaparte, who had emerged as France's military dictator and self-appointed "Emperor of France," at the battle of Waterloo in 1815. At the Congress of Vienna, the victors restored the Bourbon monarchy that had been ousted in the early days of the French Revolution, but left intact many of the political, social, and legal transformations implemented within France between 1789 and 1815.

The phrase "evolution – not revolution" describes what is today an extremely widespread preference among sensible, informed people of all ages and social conditions. It is hardly confined to stodgy conservatives of the older generation. Even among the young, who are almost inevitably in a more or less continual state of rebellion against their parents and other authority figures, there is not ordinarily a serious interest in ousting the existing national government and replacing it with another. For most people today, whether young or old, and regardless of nationality, the preferred mode of social progress is definitely via gradual evolution rather than sudden revolution. The notion of revolution as a means of progress has been severely discredited as a result of a number of bad experiences in modern history, starting with the French Revolution of 1789.

The basic problem with government change through violent revolution is that typically there is insufficient consensus among the supporters of the revolution as to what changes the revolution is supposed to accomplish. Prior to the revolution, dissatisfaction with the existing government is likely to be based on several very different grievances. Once the revolution has succeeded in ousting the existing government, disagreement often emerges between different revolutionary elements as to what should be done with government authority. The more radical the transformations envisioned or implemented by the new revolutionary government, the more resistance emerges, leading often toward harsh repression or civil war. The ultimate outcome is often that many of the progressive measures pushed through by the more radical revolutionaries are rescinded once the radicals have been defeated and removed from power. This process can take just a few years, as with the French Revolution of 1789, or many decades, as with the Russian Revolution of 1917.

During the decades leading up to the 1789 explosion, skeptical questions were increasingly raised by influential thinkers and writers of the Enlightenment, such as Voltaire and Rousseau, concerning the legitimacy of the political and social status quo. In today's world, the principle of hereditary monarchy, for example, is generally regarded as nonsensical if not preposterous. How can it be expected, we ask today, that of all the millions of people in a country at a given time, the one most qualified to be head of state is the son, daughter, or other close relative of the current head of state? But in eighteenth century Europe, hereditary monarchy was the rule rather than the exception. It was justified on grounds of stability, as reducing the amount of uncertainty and potential conflict when the current monarch died or abdicated, and competition arose among potential successors. The monarch might be subjected to various limitations imposed by an elected body, as in the case of England's constitutional monarchy, or the monarch might be essentially equivalent to a modern dictator, as in the case of France's absolute monarchy. But whether the monarchy was constitutional or absolute, few questions had been raised about the validity of the basic principle—prior to the Enlightenment.

The idea of getting along without any sort of monarch, as under a republic, was not entirely unknown in the eighteenth century. For example, one of the provisions of the Treaty of Westphalia (1648) confirmed the independence of the cantons of Switzerland from the Holy Roman Empire, and thereafter Switzerland operated without benefit of a monarch of its own. But what made republicanism a serious contender in the realm of political ideas in the late eighteenth century was the success of the American War of Independence, which established within the family of nations one which had explicitly and definitively rejected the principle of hereditary monarchy, and indeed the entire principle of hereditary nobility of any kind. Although the United States of America was at that time still regarded as a mostly uninhabited wilderness far away across a wide ocean, its establishment had an important impact on European political thinking and events.

When in the spring of 1789, the Third Estate defied Louis XVI by breaking away from the Estates-General, declaring itself a National Assembly, and vowing not to disperse until France had a constitution, the lowest common denominator among the vast majority of those subscribing to the insurrection was simply a belief that there should be restraints placed on the traditional privileges of the nobility and the Church, and that France would be better off politically under something other than the existing absolute monarchy. But of what would these "restraints" consist? Perhaps just making noble and clerical landholdings subject to taxation—or perhaps their outright expropriation by the nation? And of what would the "something other" consist? Perhaps a constitutional monarch subject to the modest limitations imposed by a relatively weak elective assembly—or perhaps a republic from which all vestiges of monarchial authority had been eliminated? Whatever the intentions of the National Assembly, the storming of the Bastille on July 14, 1789, by a huge Parisian mob including a large contingent of armed soldiers, put the constituted authorities of the period on notice that the balance of effective power was shifting inexorably toward the revolutionaries.

August 1789 saw the Declaration of the Rights of Man, together with the "August Decrees" which abolished most of the feudal privileges of the nobility and the clergy. France became polarized between those enthusiastically supportive of the Revolution and those bitterly opposed to it. Many nobles sought sanctuary abroad, and began urging their hosts to consider intervening militarily in France to nip this dangerous uprising in the bud. In the summer of 1792, Austria mounted an invasion of France with the objective of restoring the Bourbon regime. The invasion was met and defeated at Valmy in September, but in response to tensions arising from foreign invasion, the Paris mob went on a killing spree known to history as the "September Massacres." The Legislative Assembly dissolved itself and transferred its authority to a new National Convention. The constitutional monarchy called for by the 1791 constitution was abolished and the French Republic declared (the first in a series of five French Republics between 1792 and the present). In December 1792, Louis XVI went on trial for treason, and on January 21, 1793, he was executed by guillotine. By virtue of this action, more than any other, there was henceforth no turning back from the course of radical revolution in France.

From the fall of 1792 through the spring of 1793, numerous members of National Convention lost faith in the Revolution and left Paris, so that more radical elements came to dominate the assembly. In the confusion and uncertainty, the principal wielder of government power in this period became the Paris Commune, a body dominated by enraged sans-culottes and extreme Jacobins. Conservative revolts against the Revolution in the Vendée and other outlying regions of France were violently suppressed. April 1793 saw the initiation of the Committee of Public Safety under the leadership of Maximilien Robespierre, regarded by most historians as an obsessive fanatic. For more than a year, the "Terror" reigned in France, during which thousands perished under the guillotine, including Queen Marie Antoinette. Numerous high officials, heretofore loyal supporters of the Revolution, grew fearful for their lives.

Finally, the paranoia of Robespierre and his main associates brought about their downfall. A conspiracy of high officials was organized, which succeeded in bringing about the "Thermidorian reaction" of July 1794 (so designated according to the short-lived new calendar introduced by the radical revolutionaries). Following Robespierre's execution, a "White Terror" ensued during which many of the most radical elements were purged from power, and either executed or imprisoned.

Under the Constitution of the Year III, approved on August 17, 1795, France adopted a bicameral legislature, but most effective power remained concentrated in the hands of a five-person Directory. In October 1795, a bloody uprising in Paris led by diehard royalists was suppressed with a "whiff of grapeshot" by government troops under the command of a promising young general named Napoleon Bonaparte. Napoleon's reputation as a military leader thereafter advanced steadily owing to successful campaigns in Italy, Austria, and the Mideast. By 1799, popular disgust with the Directory, in combination with Napoleon's growing personal charisma, enabled his successful coup d'état of November 9, 1799, which established the French Consulate, ostensibly a continuation of the First French Republic, but effectively a dictatorship. Subsequently, carried away by megalomania, Napoleon proclaimed himself Emperor of the French on December 2, 1804, and the First French Republic was thereupon officially transformed into the First French Empire. Alarmed by France's increasing hegemony over Europe and the consequent spread of revolutionary ideas, several European powers participated in a series of coalitions against Napoleonic France. France became militarily over-extended, especially owing to the 1812 invasion of Russia, which result-ed in catastrophic defeat. Finally in 1814, the Sixth Coalition forced Na-poleon's abdication. Following a brief exile to the Mediterranean island of Elba, Napoleon returned to France, mustered another army, and led it to defeat at Waterloo on June 18, 1815. This time his exile was to a re-mote South Atlantic island, Saint Helena, where he died on May 5, 1821. Not until Adolf Hitler in the twentieth century would a single man have such an enormous impact on European history.

The French Revolution of 1789 is perhaps the single most significant political milestone in modern Western history. The 1789 revolution might be considered the political equivalent of an earthquake with an 8.0 rating on the Richter scale. Continuing with the analogy, the tremendous 1789 earthquake was followed by a series of "aftershocks" of lesser in-tensity: in 1830, 1848, and 1871. For both the original earthquake and the various aftershocks, the basic pattern was the same: following initial successes, the revolutionary leadership became overly ambitious, which engendered a conservative reaction which deposed it. Some advances were retained, but others were rescinded. It became a case of "two steps forward, one step back." Or perhaps more accurately, "ten steps forward, nine steps back." It is clear that there was much progress throughout the nineteenth century, in France and elsewhere in Europe and throughout the world, toward what is today regarded as a desirable socio-economic and political system. But the progress was hardly smooth—it was slow and halting.

The reason for this was that at any given place and time, the practical objectives of revolutionaries desiring fundamental changes varied wide-ly. To begin with, the desired form of government varied from absolute monarchy through various degrees of constitutional monarchy right up to constitutional republic. Within the general category of constitutional monarchy, preferences ranged from a very strong monarch and a very weak elective assembly at the one extreme, to a very weak monarch and a very strong elective assembly at the other extreme. With respect to the elective assembly, the desired extent of the franchise ranged from very limited, with highly restrictive property or other requirements for voting, to very general, with little or nothing in the way of requirements for vot-ing. At the extreme limit was the idea of universal male suffrage (the extension to full women's suffrage did not become common until the twentieth century).

Aside from the basic form of government, and the desired extent of the franchise for the elective assembly, the economic policies to be pursued by the government were subject to much disagreement. At one extreme were those who preferred extreme laissez faire, with the role of government restricted to the maintenance of internal peace and external security. At the other extreme were those desirous of extensive government intervention in the market economy, with projects involving the extent and incidence of taxation, the regulation of business (e.g., limitations on the length of the working day), and the nature and extent of welfare benefits such as state-supported unemployment insurance and old-age pensions. In addition, there were a number of other areas of concern among nineteenth century revolutionaries: toleration for Catholics, Jews and other religious minorities; abolition of censorship of the press and freedom of speech; elimination of capital punishment; provision of unemployment relief (for example, through the funding of "national workshops"); price controls to prevent profiteering and keep the cost of living down to a manageable level for the poor; elimination of the financial and social privileges of the clergy; secularization of education; state-sponsored free education.

A question of particular interest for present purposes is the relevance of the history of nineteenth century political revolutions in France and elsewhere to socialists of hardcore Marxist views. Recall that Karl Marx's position was that: first, there must be a successful bourgeois revolution through which the traditional agriculture-based aristocratic class would be defeated and supplanted by the new industry-based capitalist class; then, after a certain period of capitalistic domination, the contradictions of the system (periodic business depressions, decline of the petty bourgeoisie, immiseration of the proletariat) would generate conditions favorable to a successful proletarian revolution. The period of time between the successful bourgeois revolution and the successful proletarian revolution was indeterminate. As the nineteenth century progressed, the probable length of the interval between the bourgeois and the proletarian revolutions became a major area of contention among Marxists.

If one accepted as the central goal of Marxist socialism public ownership of the means of production, then the history of French revolutionary disturbances from 1789 through 1871 gave scant evidence that France had ever been on the verge of a successful proletarian revolution. In each of the four cases (1789, 1830, 1848, and 1871), what had happened was in the nature of a bourgeois revolution, each of which advanced the objectives of the bourgeoisie by a certain amount, but none of which ever had any real hope of achieving the public ownership goal. In each case, a public ownership objective was envisioned by only a tiny minority of the overall revolutionary element. In fact, Marx's ideas about a proletarian revolution toward public ownership socialism were entirely unknown to the French revolutionaries of 1789 and 1830, as it was only in 1848 that Marx and Engels published their "pamphlet that changed history": *The Communist Manifesto*. But even among the French revolutionaries of 1848 and 1871, the *Manifesto* was relatively little known and less understood. What actually made *The Communist Manifesto* into a world-altering document was the successful Bolshevik Revolution in Russia in 1917. Had it not been for that event, Karl Marx would probably be no better known today than various other obscure nineteenth century socialist visionaries such as Count Henri de St. Simon, Charles Fourier, Robert Owen, Pierre-Joseph Proudhon, Charles Hall, Ferdinand Lassalle, Louis Blanc, and Auguste Blanqui.

Of the three "aftershocks" from the original French Revolution of 1789, the most traumatic for the French nation were the events of 1871. The chaotic end of Louis-Napoleon's Second French Empire brought about the Paris Commune, probably the closest thing to Marx's vision of proletarian revolution ever to have occurred in nineteenth century Europe. Nevertheless, although the Commune was indeed an extremely radical revolutionary force, few if any of its principal leaders were fully aware of Marx's theories about surplus value, business depressions, etc., and aspired to nationalization of all private property in the means of production, including agricultural land as well as industrial capital. Marx's ideas were simply not sufficiently well-known, understood, and accepted at the time of the Paris Commune to have an appreciable impact on real-world events.

The decline and fall of Louis-Napoleon in some ways mirrored that of his predecessor, Louis Philippe: both men might be deemed victims of the Curse of the Long-Term Incumbent. Just as Louis Philippe's standing among the French deteriorated as the critical year of 1848 approached, so too did Louis-Napoleon's as 1870 approached. In order to bolster his dwindling reputation among his subjects, Louis-Napoleon decided to pick a fight with Prussia, on the principle that nothing takes peoples' minds off their troubles better than a victorious war. The trouble with this tactic, of course, is that if the war is not victorious, the people tend to become even more discontented. Apparently this possibility did not unduly trouble Louis-Napoleon, since back during his famous uncle's time, French armies had been virtually invincible all across Europe.

As it turned out, Louis-Napoleon's military calculations had been seriously flawed. The French military machine had declined greatly since the days of Napoleon I, and France had no allies since its war was generally regarded as frivolous adventurism by the other European powers. The Prussian chancellor, Otto von Bismarck, welcomed war as an avenue for transforming the loose North German Confederation into a tight-knit German Empire under Wilhelm I, king of Prussia. France's armies were decisively defeated within the first few weeks of the conflict. On September 2, 1870, Louis-Napoleon himself was captured by the Prussians at Sedan, and on September 4, the Government of National Defense abolished the Second French Empire, and established a provisional government along republican lines. The national defense government continued the war effort but without success. Paris was surrounded by a Prussian army headquartered at the Versailles palace and intent upon starving the city into surrender. All attempts to raise the siege came to nothing, and the population of Paris suffered terribly as winter advanced. On January 18, 1871, the German Empire was proclaimed in the Versailles palace. On January 28, the French provisional government surrendered to Prussia. Negotiations commenced immediately, but the final Treaty of Frankfort was not completed and signed until May 10. According to its terms, France assumed a huge indemnity, and also lost its provinces of Alsace and Lorraine.

As the negotiations proceeded, radicals in Paris became concerned that the provisional government, under the leadership of the conservative Adolphe Thiers, intended to replace republican institutions with some kind of empire or monarchy. They also blamed the provisional government for its incompetent performance in the war, and its abject submission to Prussia. On March 18, left-wing National Guard soldiers in Paris captured a cannon stockpile, and killed two provisional government generals sent to forestall this. Soon a bloody civil war was in progress, in which the Paris Commune was opposed by provisional government forces mustered from the rest of France. The Commune's leadership was dominated by a heterogeneous assortment of socialists, anarchists, and revolutionaries, but while it enjoyed the loyal support of a majority of the Parisian population, its appeal was weak outside the urban centers. Over the course of two months, the provisional government, in effect the national government of France, gradually gained the upper hand. Both sides were guilty of horrific war atrocities during the conflict, with prisoners being routinely executed without trial. A large number of Catholic clerics, including the respected archbishop of Paris, were murdered. When the Commune was finally suppressed during the *La Semaine Sanglante* (Bloody Week, May 21-28), its defeat was accompanied by thousands of summary executions. During the final days of the revolt, a number of historic public buildings in Paris were wantonly set aflame and destroyed by fanatical Communard diehards. This kind of behavior, of course, did not help the cause of social progress in France.

The Paris Commune from March through May of 1871 was mostly

preoccupied with its struggle for survival, as well as by the organization of public services essential for a city of two million residents. While its consensus was definitely of a progressive and secular nature, it did not survive long enough to implement significant reforms. In any case, its authority did not extend past the territorial limits of the city of Paris. Among the decrees of the Paris Commune were included the following: appropriation of church property by the state; exclusion of religion from schools; remission of rents accumulated during the siege by the Prussian army; abolition of night work in bakeries; pension grants to unmarried companions and children of national guardsmen killed in action; free return by pawn shops of workmen's tools and household items pledged during the siege; postponement of commercial debt obligations and abolition of interest on these debts; the right of employees to assume control of an enterprise if it were deserted by its owner (albeit with compensation); prohibition of fines imposed by employers on their workers. None of this added up to a major social transformation, even if these reforms had been implemented throughout France—which they were not. In any case, most of the Commune's decrees were rescinded following its suppression.

In exile and residing in London at the time, Karl Marx wrote a pamphlet entitled *The Civil War in France*, intended as an official statement of the International Working-Men's Association. Writing of the first edition started in April 1871, and was completed at the end of May, just after the Commune's final suppression. Marx's take on the event was that it represented a very close approach to the successful proletarian revolution that he and his associate Friedrich Engels had been predicting ever since the first edition of *The Communist Manifesto* in 1848. It represented an heroic attempt by the downtrodden proletariat of France to throw off the chains of oppression imposed upon them by the heartless, ruthless, hypocritical, and supremely smug and self-righteous bourgeoisie. In this energetically written polemic, Marx contrasted the nobility and progressiveness of the bulk of the Communards with the treachery and vindictiveness of the Thiers regime. For example, he places responsibility for the death of Archbishop Darboy on Thiers: "The Commune again and again had offered to exchange the archbishop, and ever so many priests in the bargain, against the single Blanqui, then in the hands of Thiers. Thiers obstinately refused. He knew that with Blanqui he would give the Commune a head; while the archbishop would serve his purpose best in the shape of a corpse."

If Marx had any serious criticism to make of the Paris Commune, it was that it lacked the degree of discipline and determination required to achieve success. Auguste Blanqui had been a well-known revolutionary firebrand since the time of the 1848 insurrection, and was especially notable for his insistence on the need for a well-organized, well-disciplined party ready to take charge when the opportunity arose, as a precondition for successful revolution. When the Paris Commune was established in March, it had attempted to recruit Blanqui as its leader. But the Thiers government, recognizing the danger, had him arrested and incarcerated before he could accept the offer. Marx was ever after convinced that if the Commune had had Blanqui as its leader, it might well have won over all of France to its cause, and thereby forestalled the reactionary outcome that actually occurred. In his 1908 commentary, "Lessons of the Commune," Vladimir Lenin echoed Marx's view that the Commune had been an exemplary foreshadowing of the "dictatorship of the proletariat," and that it might have achieved final success had its leadership been more aggressive. For example, in its earliest period, the National Guardsmen of the Commune might have marched on Versailles and routed Thiers' provisional national government. Instead, by waiting passively within Paris, the Commune leadership allowed Thiers to gather the necessary force to suppress it, much of this force being derived from prisoners of war held in Prussian camps, and released by Bismarck only on the understanding that they would be utilized to crush the Paris Commune. Another mistake of the Commune, according to Lenin, was their failure to take control of the national bank located in Paris.

In their respective commentaries on the Paris Commune, neither Marx nor Lenin clearly acknowledged the obvious factor that much of the psychological motivation for the uprising stemmed from France's humiliating defeat by the Prussian army. Marx's theory of inevitable capitalist collapse attributed it to the ever-increasing vicissitudes imposed on the population by ever-worsening business depressions. There was no hint in the original theory that a critical contributor to revolutionary impulses within the population might be its emotional reaction to an unsuccessful war. But just as it was doubtful that the Paris Commune would have occurred had not the Franco-Prussian War preceded it, so too it is doubtful that the successful Bolshevik Revolution in Russia in 1917 would have occurred had not Russia's disastrous participation in World War I preceded it. History strongly suggests that military defeat is a far more important contributor to revolutionary impulses than business downturns.

Although historians customarily date the Third French Republic from the 1870 proclamation of the provisional government, during its first few years there was a serious threat of reversion to some form of monarchy, or even to a military dictatorship along Napoleonic lines. It wasn't until the French Constitutional Laws of 1875 that the republican form of government became fairly thoroughly established. The Third French Republic, with a bicameral legislature and a president serving as head of state, persisted until the Nazi defeat of France in 1940.

Emphasis in the foregoing on the French experience should not generate the misapprehension that only France was prone to revolutions during this period. In fact, there were numerous revolutionary events, of varying degrees of success, all across Europe throughout this time period. The year 1848, the same year in which Marx and Engels published *The Communist Manifesto*, was especially notable for revolutionary disturbances in numerous European countries. In most countries, the revolutionaries attained initial successes, but were eventually defeated by reactionary forces. Even Britain with its renowned constitutional monarchy, generally regarded as a model of political stability during the nineteenth century, experienced some disturbances that came perilously close to violent revolution. For example, the Chartist movement from the 1830s through the 1850s, demanding universal male suffrage and other political reforms, organized mass meetings that might have degenerated into violence. The central Chartist goal of universal male suffrage was not achieved until 1918, but most of the other objectives were achieved earlier than that. The eventual success of most of the Chartist program in Britain is frequently cited as an example of the typical superiority of the evolutionary approach over the revolutionary approach, as an instrument toward progressive reform of society.

Of the numerous revolutionary events throughout Europe from the commencement of the 1789 French Revolution to the suppression of the 1871 Paris Commune, it would seem that in terms of Karl Marx's distinction between bourgeois revolutions and proletarian revolutions, these were far more in the nature of the former than the latter. While it is clear that much of the "muscle" for these uprisings was provided by mobs of urban working-class proletarians, especially if the mobs contained a substantial component of sympathetic armed soldiers, the leadership was mostly provided by educated middle-class people—the sort of people whom Marx derisively described as "petty bourgeois." The essence of this term describes an individual who, although not a wealthy capitalist, is at the same time not a downtrodden worker. He might be a craftsman or a shopkeeper, a doctor or a lawyer, a professor or a student, a mid-level manager or bureaucrat. This individual, while frequently sympathetic toward the downtrodden worker and desirous of improving his lot, at the same time shares the same respect for property rights as the wealthy capitalist. A "petty bourgeois," therefore, wants change but does not want change to go so far as a general abrogation of property rights, either in personal property or in capital property (i.e. in the nonhuman factors of production). The large majority of nineteenth century revolutionaries shared this petty bourgeois mindset. Therefore they were not likely candidates for leading the kind of proletarian revolution envisioned by Karl Marx.

The foregoing describes the main elements of the intellectual history of socialism, in combination with real-world events, as they were known to the generation of Eduard Bernstein. The twentieth century was still in the future, and it is safe to say that no one in the late nineteenth century could have imagined the forthcoming travails of the twentieth century: two devastating world wars in quick succession, the Russian and Chinese revolutions, the rise and fall of fascism and Nazism, the development and use of nuclear weapons in warfare, the prolonged, ideologically-based Cold War that had the world perched at the edge of a nuclear abyss for almost half a century. As far as revolution as a means of permanent progress is concerned, that notion—among the majority of informed individuals—had begun declining in the latter part of the nineteenth century, and the decline continued and accelerated throughout the twentieth century. The horrors of Stalin's USSR and Mao's PRC could be, and often were, presented as the likely outcome of ill-considered revolutions. The idea of "socialism" in the public ownership sense was also deeply implicated in the adversities of Soviet Russia and Red China. Of course, some of the worst atrocities of the twentieth century were committed by Nazi Germany, and despite the term "National *Socialism*," public ownership of capital was never part of Hitler's grand design for Germany and the world. Nevertheless, anyone looking back carefully at twentieth century world history could not fail to be impressed by how strikingly the so-called "law of unintended consequences" seemed to apply to revolutions—and perhaps especially to revolutions intended to bring about socialism in the public ownership sense.

Correspondingly, the notion that long-term, permanent social progress is more reliably attained through gradual, peaceful means, rather than through sudden, violent revolutions, became more and more widely accepted. The phrase "evolution – not revolution" became the dominant preference among the large majority of people in all walks of life, and over all national populations. Few people, even today, will argue that there can *never* be a positive role for violent revolution to play, but the circumstances under which this would be true are regarded as increasingly unlikely, increasingly farfetched.

Returning to the nineteenth century, while no doubt the majority of people in the latter part of the nineteenth century whom Marx regarded derisively as "petty bourgeois," were opposed to "socialistic schemes" as variously understood at the time, some of them, a significant minority in fact, were in fact very much interested in such schemes—depending on their specific content. In the years and decades following the 1848 publication of *The Communist Manifesto*, the specific "socialistic scheme" proposed by Karl Marx and Friedrich Engels became gradually better and better known. According to this particular scheme, the ultimate outcome would be universal public ownership of capital and land, this outcome would necessarily be accomplished by a violent revolution at least as bloody as the French Revolution of 1789, and furthermore, this outcome was literally inevitable on completely irrefutable, solidly scientific grounds. The only open question, according to this hardcore Marxist scenario, was exactly *when* the proletarian revolution would occur that would transform capitalism into socialism. Whether it would occur in one year, or ten years, or a hundred years, was, in principle, a matter to be left open to events.

Assuming one accepted the fundamental correctness of this scenario, there remained important tactical questions: How best to hasten the day of transformation? Should piecemeal reforms of the capitalist system be supported and implemented, because presumably they would be part of the socialist system once it had been fully implemented? Or should they be opposed and blocked, on grounds that any minor improvements in the condition of the working class would likely weaken its revolutionary fervor, and thereby postpone the final revolution? Should socialists participate in elective assemblies as a means of furthering sympathetic interest in socialism among its prospective beneficiaries? Or were these assemblies so much part and parcel of the exploitative capitalist system that they should be shunned, in order that socialists better devote their energies to educational work among the people, preparing them for the revolution that history had declared essential to the ultimate redemption of society? These kinds of questions preoccupied socialists of Bernstein's generation.

## Origins of Evolutionary Socialism

Eduard Bernstein, the seventh of fifteen children, was born into a Reform Jewish family living in the Berlin suburb of Schöneberg, on January 6, 1850. His father's earnings, first as a plumber and later as a locomotive driver, barely sufficed to maintain the family in a state of genteel poverty. Owing to financial constraints, Bernstein's formal education was concluded at the age of sixteen, when he took a position as an apprentice in a Berlin bank. His career as a bank employee continued until his expulsion from Germany in 1878, the result of his increasingly prominent role as a socialist party organizer.[1]

Although most German patriots were exalted by Prussia's military triumph over France in the 1870-1871 Franco-Prussian War, and the ensuing foundation of the German Empire under the guidance of Otto von Bismarck in January, 1871, the minority of German socialists, increasingly under the influence of the teachings of Karl Marx, criticized the war as adventurism which in no way assisted the international working class in its continuing quest for a better life. These criticisms made Bismarck and his nationalist allies sufficiently uncomfortable that some top socialist leaders spent time in jail for sedition. During the early 1870s, two socialist parties competed for the loyalty of the German working class: the Eisenacher (after the German town in which it had been founded), and the Lassallean (after Ferdinand Lassalle, who had died several years earlier in a duel). Although both claimed Marxist pedigrees, Marx himself favored the Eisenachers as adhering more closely to his own vision of socialism. To Marx, Lassalle's idea of working through the state to achieve socialist objectives represented a dead end—especially regarding the central objective of public ownership of land and capital. Lassalle was dismissed by Marx as a craven opportunist willing to limit the legitimate demands of the workers' movement in exchange for exceedingly modest concessions from the capitalists—"crumbs off the table."

Although in the German Reich of the 1870s, the Reichstag was still primarily a consultative body to the Kaiser, elections were regarded as important indicators of the public mood, and the two socialist parties worked hard to elect representatives. It soon became apparent to the leadership of both parties that pooling their efforts might be more productive in terms of Reichstag seats. Bernstein, together with other party leaders such as August Bebel and Wilhelm Liebknecht, organized a "party unification congress" in the German town of Gotha in 1875, which resulted in the formation of the Social Democratic Party of Germany (Sozialdemokratische Partei Deutschlands – SPD). Except for relatively brief periods of suppression (the last one being during the 1933-1945 Nazi era), the SPD has been a major player in German politics ever since that time.

The inaugural program of the SPD called for universal suffrage, freedom of association, limits on the length of the working day, and for various other provisions to protect the health and rights of working people. The program invoked the "socialist" label in stating that "the socialist labor party of Germany endeavors by every lawful means to bring about a free state and a socialistic society, to effect the destruction of the iron law of wages by doing away with the system of wage labor, to abolish exploitation of every kind, and to extinguish all social and political inequality." Although this seems quite a strong position, Marx attacked it in a pamphlet entitled "Critique of the Gotha Program," which accused the Program as being too much under the influence of Lassallean ideas. Among other things, Marx disapproved of the phrase "by every lawful means." Later on, the SPD's program migrated toward more hardline Marxism, as expressed in the Erfurt Program of 1891. The essence of hardline Marxism, then as ever, lies in its insistence upon the need for violent revolution to bring about genuine socialism (i.e. public ownership of capital and land).

The new Social Democratic Party of Germany made a respectable showing in the Reichstag elections of 1877, an indication not to the liking of Bismarck, who regarded the party as potentially a serious threat to stability. When during the following year, two unsuccessful assassination attempts were made on the aging Wilhelm I, King of Prussia and Emperor of Germany, this provided a useful pretext for taking action against the socialists. The first would-be assassin, a plumber named Emil Max Hödel, had once belonged to the SPD, although he had been expelled for his extremist views, and assassination had never been advocated by any party leader. The second would-be assassin, a Dr. Karl Nobiling, may have had some contact with socialist circles during his student days, but no political motivation for the attack was ever ascertained. Despite the unlikelihood that socialist activists were involved in either assassination attempt, Bismarck succeeded in gaining Reichstag approval for the "Anti-Socialist Law" of October 12, 1878. The Social Democratic Party was outlawed, as well as other mass organizations representing the working class. Pro-socialist literature was to be confiscated and destroyed.

Despite the outlawing of the SPD, it was permissible for former members of the outlawed party to run for Reichstag seats as independents, and during the 1880s many did so. Furthermore, Bismarck soon supplemented his "stick" anti-socialist policy with a "carrot" policy that was also aimed at weakening the socialist threat. In November 1881, Bismarck proposed a program he called "practical Christianity," a program that was soon denounced by opponents as "state socialism." Despite the denunciations, the program was soon implemented in the form of the mandatory health insurance bill of 1883, the mandatory accident insurance bill of 1884, and the old-age and disability insurance bill of 1889. For the first two programs, costs were divided between employers and employees, while for the last, the government directly assumed some of the expenses. The irony, of course, is that these landmarks in the evolution of the modern "welfare state" were initiated by a conservative government for the sole purpose of weakening support among the population for the cause of socialist revolution. In 1890, following the accession of Wilhelm II, and owing to the accumulation of various political reverses, the Bismarck government fell, and soon afterwards the "Anti-Socialist Law" was repealed. Thereafter the Social Democratic Party of Germany was allowed to operate freely—until 1933, when it was once again outlawed by the Nazi regime of Adolf Hitler.

Sensing that his strident opposition to the Bismarck government would subject him to reprisals, Eduard Bernstein chose to go into exile in Switzerland even before the Anti-Socialist Law of 1878 went into effect. He accepted a position as private secretary to Karl Höchberg, a wealthy German supporter of social democracy, who had also gone into exile in Zurich. A warrant for Bernstein's arrest was subsequently sworn out in Germany, and he was unable to return to Germany even after the repeal of the Anti-Socialist Law in 1890. All told, he remained in exile, first in Switzerland and then in England, for more than 20 years, until 1901. All through the period of his exile, however, Bernstein remained active in the SPD. He started work as a writer for the party newspaper, *Der Sozialdemokrat (Social Democrat)*, in Zurich in 1880, and shortly thereafter became its editor. When in 1887, the German government persuaded the Swiss authorities to expel Bernstein, he relocated to London, and continued contributing to and editing the *Social Democrat* from there.

Bernstein first made the acquaintance of Karl Marx and Friedrich Engels in London in 1880. His employer at the time, Karl Höchberg, had published an article which greatly displeased Marx and Engels, on grounds that it was awash in fuzzy-minded, reformist idealism, and had nothing whatever to do with a correct interpretation of the Marxist vision. In the company of his close friend and SPD colleague, August Bebel, Bernstein traveled to London to assure Marx and Engels that he had had nothing to do with the writing of the offending article. Despite the inauspicious circumstances of the meeting, Marx and Engels quickly warmed to Bernstein, and he commenced a long-standing friendship with the two founding fathers of Marxism. After Marx's death in 1883, and Bernstein's relocation to London in 1887, he continued in close and friendly contact with Engels as the latter labored on various projects, including the publication of the second and third volumes of Marx's *Das Kapital*. Engels was sufficiently close to Bernstein to appoint him, along with August Bebel, executor of his will, which became effective upon Engels' death in 1895.

By the beginning of the 1890s, Eduard Bernstein was an impeccably orthodox adherent of hardcore Marxism who was thoroughly conversant with the Marxist scenario of capitalist collapse amidst violent revolution, and fully accepted every detail of it as gospel truth, as the secular equivalent of divine revelation. By this time, Karl Marx had been veritably canonized, if not deified, by thousands of disciples throughout Europe. They were still a small minority of the overall European population, yet they represented a significant absolute number. As the 1890s continued, debates proliferated among Marxists on the subject of "what Marx really intended"—especially now that Marx himself, having passed away, was no longer available to participate in them. For example, what exactly was the meaning of the phrase "dictatorship of the proletariat"? And what was Marx's stance on colonies, a topic of renewed interest as the European countries were at that time carving up the African continent among themselves? And now that Bismarck's "state socialism" was a reality in Germany, and numerous SPD members had been legally elected to the German Reichstag, was it really necessary, after all, that a violent proletarian revolution take place, engendered by a catastrophic business depression—as the one and only means of achieving the blessings of socialism? As it happened, the 1890s were a generally prosperous time in Germany and throughout Europe, which cast doubt at least on the imminence, if not necessarily the inevitability, of violent revolution.

It is understandable, therefore, that as the 1890s advanced, and the capitalist system was showing no visible signs of significant distress, a number of Marxist socialists began having doubts about the central Marxist prediction of a bloody proletarian revolution as the only avenue leading to the attainment of socialism. In Bernstein's work, these doubts became crystallized and cogently articulated. No other SPD member of the period could equal Bernstein's credentials, not only as an expert on Marxist thought, but as an individual who had personally met with, befriended, and conversed with the very founders of Marxism. Thus it was virtually impossible to attack Bernstein convincingly as someone who simply "failed to understand" Marxism.

According to Bernstein's later testimony, the key moment in his personal epiphany on the issue occurred in January 1897, when he presented a lecture on the subject "What Marx Really Taught" to the British Fabian Society.[2] By that time his doubts about the need for violent proletarian revolution had advanced considerably, but he was still trying to reconcile these doubts with the master's pronouncements. There came a point when he realized that such a reconciliation truly was impossible: that what he was presenting to the Fabian Society did not express Marx's actual views. The important thing at this point, he decided, was to try to clarify where Marx was correct as far as the future destiny of human civilization was concerned—and where he was incorrect. It represented a form of intellectual liberation once Bernstein concluded that Marx, like most if not all other human beings, was not infallible.

Although Bernstein dated his epiphany to January 1897, he had actually been publishing articles throughout 1896 that raised serious questions about key components of Marxist orthodoxy. Most of these articles were published in *Neue Zeit*, the SPD's theoretical journal edited by the eminent Karl Kautsky. This series of articles continued throughout 1897 and into 1898, eliciting vigorous critiques by various defenders of Marxist orthodoxy. These critiques were countered by equally vigorous rebuttals from Bernstein. Among the critics were Belfort Bax, an early British convert to Marxism, Alexander Parvus, a Russian émigré, and Rosa Luxemburg, a Polish émigré. Both Parvus and Luxemburg, though not originally of German nationality, were active, influential members of the SPD. Among the issues debated were colonialism, labor laws, industrial concentration, capitalist business depressions, and proper political strategy for social democratic parties. At the bottom of most of these exchanges lay the question of whether proletarian revolution was sufficiently imminent for this possibility to significantly affect SPD policy.[3]

In a January 1898 *Neue Zeit* article entitled "The Theory of Collapse and Colonial Policy," Bernstein wrote:

> I frankly admit that I have extraordinarily little feeling for, or interest in, what is usually termed "the final goal of socialism." This goal, whatever it may be, is nothing to me, the movement is everything. And by movement I mean both the general movement of society, i.e. social progress, and the political and economic agitation and organization to bring about this progress.

Inasmuch as Marxist orthodoxy insisted that the "final goal of socialism" was nothing less than the complete destruction of capitalism via violent proletarian revolution, this confession of Bernstein's galvanized his radical opponents and drew down upon himself the concentrated ire of many if not most SPD members. Under pressure, Bernstein issued a brief statement explaining that since the precise outcome of the socialist movement lies in the unknowable future, the emphasis should be on activities which by common consensus are leading in the direction of that outcome. He provided the following restatement of his intention: "The movement is everything to me because it bears its goal within itself." Needless to say, this reformulation did not appease Bernstein's orthodox critics.

The ferment within the party aroused by Bernstein's virtually heretical views reached a head at the SPD party congress in Stuttgart from October 3 to 8, 1898. Bernstein could not attend the conference because a German arrest warrant was still in effect and he remained in exile. Instead he sent a statement to the congress that was read into the record by August Bebel—who quickly added that he was in disagreement with much of what Bernstein was advancing. This statement was utilized as the "Foreword" to Bernstein's book *The Preconditions of Socialism and the Tasks of Social Democracy*, published the following March. In it, Bernstein declares bluntly:

> I have opposed the view that we stand on the threshold of an imminent collapse of bourgeois society, and that Social Democracy *should allow its tactics to be determined by, or made dependent upon, the prospect of any such forthcoming major catastrophe.* I stand by this view in eve ry particular.

This statement elicited little approval from the delegates. Although there were a few expressions of support, most comments were critical. There was no explicit rejection of Bernstein's revisionism at the Stuttgart congress, but the following year, the party congress in Hanover passed a resolution condemning it. However, efforts to expel Bernstein from the SPD were defeated, and when he finally returned to Germany in 1901, he resumed active participation in party affairs, and sat in the Reichstag from 1902 to 1918 as an SPD representative, and again from 1920 to 1928. Following Germany's defeat in World War I, in 1919 the ortho- dox, hardline Marxists split from the SPD to form the German Com- munist Party. With the hardline Marxists gone, the SPD party conference at Görlitz in 1921 had no difficulty adopting a new party platform fully embodying the revisionism that Eduard Bernstein had been advocating for more than 20 years. As is often the case with such major policy shifts, warfare had been necessary to bring it about.

Following the Stuttgart congress of October 1898, August Bebel urged Bernstein to collect the elements of his revisionist thinking into the form of a substantial book that could be used as a reference point for fu- ture debate. Bernstein readily complied with the suggestion and the vol- ume was produced quickly, to some extent because much of its substan- tive content had already appeared in articles published in *Neue Zeit* and other periodicals. Initially published in German under the title *Die Vor- aussetzungen des Sozialismus und die Aufgaben der Sozialdemokratie* (*The Preconditions of Socialism and the Tasks of Social Democracy*) by the Stuttgart publishing house J. H. W. Dietz in March 1899, Bernstein's book had a profound—though not immediate—effect on the develop- ment of the socialist movement into and during the twentieth century and beyond.[4] It is therefore worthy of fairly detailed consideration.

## Bernstein's Contribution

Throughout his seminal contribution, Bernstein made it clear and explicit that while he had great respect for Karl Marx, and regarded him as a visionary genius who correctly foresaw the pressing need for fundamental changes in the existing capitalistic social order, at the same time Marx's specific prophecies as to the nature and timing of the transformation need not be uncritically accepted by Marxists. It was quite possible and appropriate, in Bernstein's view, to consider oneself a loyal Marxist, even though one rejected the prediction that genuine socialism could only be achieved via violent revolution, and that this revolution was imminent.

In Chapter 1 ("The basic tenets of Marxist socialism"), Bernstein draws a distinction between "pure" and "applied" scientific propositions. The former are prima facie acceptable to any intelligent, informed individual, while the latter are more easily modified in light of advancing knowledge. Marx's view that the material methods and relations of production have a dominant effect on the development of human society most likely belongs to the former category. But Marx also concedes that there are other non-economic factors that may be important, and that the relative importance of economic versus non-economic factors varies from time to time and place to place. That the materialist conception of history indicates the collapse of bourgeois society is, therefore, a *hypothesis* not strictly provable on the basis of scientific evidence. This proposition belongs to the category of "applied' science.

In any case, there is no indication in Marx's writing of exactly *how long* it will take for bourgeois society to collapse. Marx writes of a "tendency" toward collapse, not of a "law" of collapse. The late Marxist view of "tendency toward collapse" was elaborated in Engels' *Anti-Dühring* (1878) and other writings. Late Marxist thinking (by both Marx and Engels in their old age) allowed more of a role for non-economic considerations: geographical, traditional, social, institutional, political, legal, religious, etc., in the determination of historical trends and events. Humanity is increasingly knowledgeable about economics and other matters. Therefore, modern society increasingly has the ability to direct economic forces, rather than being carried along by them. The "iron necessity of history" is thereby curtailed, and there emerges greater influence of what might be described as "ideological" factors.

Chapter 1 concludes with a relatively substantial review of the Marxist view of class conflict, the illegitimate bourgeois appropriation of surplus value produced by proletarians, the tendency toward a declining rate of profit, the steadily amplifying cycles of boom and bust, leading eventually to revolution and the transformation of the private property of capitalists into public property owned by all. Following this "briefest possible summary" of the Marxist theory and forecast, Bernstein claims that the main points of the central doctrine laid out in *The Communist Manifesto* of 1848 were gradually modified by Marx and Engels during succeeding decades. For example, he quotes the following statement from their preface to a new 1872 edition of the *Manifesto*: "In view of the gigantic strides of Modern Industry in the last twenty-five years, and the accompanying improved and extended party organization of the working class, in view of the practical experience gained, first in the February Revolution [1848], and then, still more, in the Paris Commune [1871], where the proletariat for the first time held political power for two whole months, this program has in some details become antiquated. Marx and Engels themselves did not address in any detail the presumed modifications and changes needed in Marxist theory to bring it into better alignment with contemporary knowledge and conditions. This task they left to others. Taking up this task, says Bernstein, does not imply abandonment of basic Marxist principles and insights. The amputation of acknowledged errors does not destroy the remaining validity of much if not most of the Marxist worldview.

In Chapter 2 ("Marxism and the Hegelian dialectic"), Bernstein commences by challenging the usefulness of the Hegelian dialectical method as a means of gaining reliable knowledge about the world. The shortcomings of Hegelian dialectics are greater to the extent that the method is applied to more complex problems and issues in the real world. Thus the dialectical prediction that bourgeois revolution will be followed by proletarian revolution is perhaps too facile. Moreover, Marx-Engels apparently envisioned a much shorter time span leading up to the proletarian revolution than would actually be needed: "In his preface to *The Class Struggles*, written towards the end of his life, Engels acknowledged unreservedly the error which he and Marx had committed in estimating the time which social and political development would take. We cannot praise too highly the service he rendered to the socialist movement by this work, which is rightly described as his political testament." But Engels was still a "prisoner" of the Hegelian dialectic, which is the treacherous element in Marxist thought. It led Marx and Engels into errors that need to be acknowledged and transcended.

Bernstein goes on to discuss the relationship between Marxism and Blanquism. Louis Auguste Blanqui (1805-1881), mentioned above in conjunction with the Paris Commune, was a fierce revolutionary figure of the nineteenth century. In his writings, he foresaw a bloody revolution equivalent to the French Revolution Terror as the essential, necessary means of a successful proletarian revolution. But in fact, says Bernstein, in clear-sighted retrospect we see that both in 1848 and again in 1871, real-world conditions were not yet ripe for a successful proletarian revolution. When the revolutionary disturbances became destructive, the bourgeois radicals withdrew their support leaving the path open to reactionary suppression. Marx and Engels were sometimes carried away with fervor and wrote polemics arguing that the 1848 and 1871 upheavals in France could—if managed somewhat differently—have been successful "permanent" proletarian revolutions. For example, they argued that if Auguste Blanqui had led the Paris Commune (he was in prison at the time), it might have been successful. They were wrong about this, just as they had been wrong in their earlier assessment of the 1848 French insurrection.

Chapter 3 ("The economic development of modern society") endeavors to show, through reliable statistical data, that in certain critical respects, the German national economy, and the European national economies in general, were not evolving in the direction predicted by Karl Marx and Friedrich Engels. The chapter commences with a somewhat complicated exposition of Marx's refined theory of value and surplus value as elucidated in the recently published Volume III of *Das Kapital*. The refined theory was developed in response to the "Great Contradiction" advanced by Eugen von Böhm-Bawerk and thoroughly explicated in *Karl Marx and the Close of his System* (1896). The "Great Contradiction" challenges the basis of Marxist thought, the labor theory of value, on grounds that if it were true, as Marx claims, that the source of the capitalist's profit is the workers he hires, then capitalists would not be avid to replace workers with machines. Marx's response, in Volume III, was that total surplus value is extorted from the proletarians as a whole by the capitalists as a whole, and that the sum total of surplus value is then divided up among the capitalists in proportion to their total expenditures, adding together expenditures on labor and expenditures on machines. While this mode of accounting is hypothetically valid, there is no empirical evidence to support it, since empirically, the profits of capitalists are not proportional to their labor expenditures. Whatever the inherent merits or demerits of Böhm-Bawerk's Great Contradiction, and Marx's response to it, Bernstein says that the issue is immaterial, since Marx and Engels never claimed that the immorality of surplus labor exploitation would bring about the collapse of capitalism. That instrumentality was to be ever-worsening business depressions.

Bernstein continues with a brief recitation of Marx's theory of capitalist collapse coming about owing to a cycle of declining rate of profit, panic, crisis, depression, recovery accompanied by further concentration of capital property. He then poses the question: "Now, is all this cor-

rect?" Answer: "Yes and no. It is correct above all, as a *tendency...*"
However, Marx's theory is incomplete, since it does not take adequate
account of "factors which have a limiting effect on the antagonisms described." The clear implication of the basic theory is that over time the
number of capitalists will be continuously declining, while the average
capital wealth of each capitalist will be getting steadily larger. But, says
Bernstein, reliable statistics show the atomization of ownership of very
large enterprises, so that there continues to be a very large number of
capital owners with relatively modest capital wealth—these people are
"property owners" but not in a strict sense "capitalists," since they are
not capable of "living off the interest" from their capital property holdings. Statistics also show that there continues to exist a very substantial
number of middle class people with middle-level incomes. Therefore
Marx's implication that industrial production is becoming steadily more
concentrated, and that society is becoming steadily more polarized into
two classes: the very poor (the vast majority) and the very wealthy (a
steadily shrinking minority)—these implications are not supported by
reliable statistics.

The final section of Chapter 3 discusses the views of Marx and Engels on trade crises: whether they are more sensibly viewed as the result
of under-consumption or over-production, and the extent to which the
duration of the trade cycle may be changing (shortening or lengthening).
Bernstein cites some mentions of mitigating factors (expansion of world
trade, cartels, credit) in their work, but says that Marx-Engels regarded
these as merely short-term factors which would make the eventual crash
even more violent. Against the Marx-Engels implication that a catastrophic crash is just around the corner, Bernstein says:

> No signs of a worldwide economic crash of unprecedented violence
> have been detected, nor can the improvement of trade between crises be
> characterized as particularly short-lived. Rather, a third question aris-
> es—which, incidentally, was already partly contained in the previous
> one—namely, (1) whether the enormous geographical expansion of the
> world market in conjunction with the extraordinary reduction in the
> time required for transport and the transmission of news have not so in-
> creased the possibilities of *leveling out* of disturbances, and (2) whether
> the enormously increased wealth of the European industrial states in
> conjunction with the elasticity of the modern credit system and the rise
> of industrial cartels have not so diminished the reactive force of local or
> individual disturbances on the general state of business, that, at least for
> some time, general trade crises similar to the earlier ones are to be re-
> garded as unlikely.

Bernstein then responds at considerable length to Rosa Luxemburg's assault on the proposition that credit, cartels, international trade, and so on, have rendered modern capitalism impervious—or at least highly resistant to—disastrous crashes. Of course, at the time of their debate on business cycles, neither Rosa Luxemburg nor Edward Bernstein had any inkling that in the fourth decade of the twentieth century (the 1930s), the global capitalist economy would be assailed by the worst business depression in recorded history. Had they had some foresight of this event, both could have derived some support from it. Rosa Luxemburg could have pointed out that the Great Depression of the 1930s gave the lie to Bernstein's optimistic belief that capitalism was on the verge of solving the cycle problem. On the other hand, Bernstein could have pointed out that despite the severity of the Great Depression, and despite the fact that at that time socialism had a role model, of a sort, in the burgeoning economy of the Soviet Union, the Depression did not elicit a proletarian revolution anywhere in the world. The only important political development to come out of it was Germany's descent into Nazism, which was partially caused by apprehensions among capitalist plutocrats aroused by the continuing appeals for proletarian revolution issued by the Communist Party of Germany throughout the 1920s and into the early 1930s. This outcome was consistent with Bernstein's argument that enthusiastic calls for violent socialist revolution were most likely to result in a reactionary backlash.

Chapter 4 ("The tasks and opportunities of Social Democracy") takes up the policy questions confronting the German Social Democratic Party, and by extension confronting analogous parties across Europe and the rest of the world. An essential prerequisite for the establishment of genuine socialism, according to Marx-Engels, is the seizure of political power by the proletariat. Such seizure might be through legal means of exploitation of the franchise to achieve a parliamentary majority, or it might be through violent revolution. The latter means was regarded by Marx and Engels as inevitable throughout their lives, and continues to be regarded as inevitable by many contemporary Marxists (of Bernstein's generation). The standard, hardline view is that the dictatorship of the proletariat would be equivalent to the Terror of the French Revolution, with rampant denunciations of disloyalty and masses of executions of "unreliable elements." The leaders of the French Revolution Terror (Robespierre and associates) utilized mobs of proletarians to sustain their power, but they did not, on the whole, represent the interests of the proletariat, but rather the interests of the bourgeoisie. Also, the excesses of the Terror eventually ended rule by radicals such as Robespierre. If the "proletariat" is defined as those possessing little or no capital property, there is still a wide range of income and status within its ranks. Many of these "proletarians" are materially comfortable—they are not living in desperate poverty and on the brink of starvation. They are certainly not interested in radical transformations of society. In Germany, many of those who vote for socialists of the Social Democratic Party do so because of the short-term goals of the party, not because they want violent revolution and complete transformation of society.

Taking up the subject "democracy and socialism," Bernstein asks "What is democracy?" Democracy (he answers) is the absence of government by the few (e.g., the capitalists). Spreading of the franchise decentralizes political power—it goes toward genuine democracy. The revolutionary rhetoric of Marx and Engels in *The Communist Manifesto* (especially in the term "dictatorship of the proletariat") was based on the violence of the French Revolution Terror. That happened at a time when there was little recourse to democratic decision-making anywhere in Europe. But now, in late nineteenth century Europe, the franchise is spreading and universal suffrage seems an attainable goal in most advanced capitalist countries. For example, the Electoral Reform of 1867 in England, which extended the franchise to urban workers, was a very significant development. Since then, there has been much expansion of publicly supported education. The Electoral Reform did not eliminate privileged classes, but it significantly curtailed their practical power and effective privileges.

Bernstein then delivers the following tirade against "literary advocates" of socialism who continue to harp on the need for revolution:

> And Social Democracy cannot further this work better than by taking an unqualified stand on the democratic doctrine of universal suffrage, with all the resulting consequences for its tactics. In practice, that is, in its actions, it has in the end always done so. However, its literary advocates have often offended against this doctrine in their pronouncements, and such offences still continue. Phrases which were coined at a time when the privilege of property reigned unchecked all over Europe, and which were understandable and even to some extent justified under these circumstances, but which are nowadays only a dead weight, are treated with as much reverence as though the progress of the movement depended on them, and not on direct perception of what can and should be done. Is there any sense, for example, in maintaining the phrase "dictatorship of the proletariat" at a time when representatives of Social Democracy have in practice placed themselves wherever possible in the arena of parliamentary work, in a struggle for a representation of the people which adequately reflects their numbers, and for the struggle for popular participation in legislation, all of which are inconsistent with

dictatorship. The phrase is nowadays so out of date that it can be reconciled with reality only by stripping the word dictatorship of its actual meaning and giving it some kind of diluted signification. All the practical activity of Social Democracy is aimed at creating the circumstances and conditions which will enable and ensure the transition from the modern social order to a higher one—without convulsive upheavals.

Throughout the history of Marxism, its most dedicated adherents have made a fetish of closely examining the written work of Karl Marx and Friedrich Engels in search of quotations that seem to support whatever point they are trying to make. Unfortunately for Eduard Bernstein, his viewpoint had so much departed from Marxist orthodoxy that he was unable to muster much in the way of unambiguously supportive quotes from the works of Marx and Engels to buttress the arguments set forth in *The Preconditions of Socialism*. However, he did find one important exception. In 1864, Marx had written an "Inaugural Address" upon the foundation of the International Working Men's Association, which in the historiography of the socialist movement came to be known as the "First International." The bulk of the address utilized statistics from official British government reports, such as the Sixth Report on Public Health (1864), published by order of Parliament, to prove that the living standards of the bulk of working class families were hardly better than subsistence—despite the fact that government officials were crowing over the spectacular growth of the British economy over the last few decades. However, Marx does acknowledge two "bright spots" in this generally gloomy picture. One of these was the recent passage by the British Parliament of the Ten Hours' Bill. The Ten Hours' Bill, otherwise known as the Factory Act of 1856, was one of a series of acts passed by Parliament during the course of the nineteenth century. The earliest acts in the series had restricted the working hours of women and children in the cotton mills, but as the century progressed they were gradually extended to wider categories of labor, and broadened to include working conditions as well. Marx's Inaugural Address had this to say about the Bill:

> After a thirty years' struggle, fought with most admirable perseverance, the English working classes, taking advantage of a momentary split between the landlords and money-lords, succeeded in carrying the Ten Hours' Bill. The immense physical, moral, and intellectual benefits hence accruing to the factory operatives, half-yearly chronicled in the reports of the inspectors of factories, are now acknowledged on all sides. Most of the Continental governments had to accept the English Factory Act in more or less modified forms, and the English Parliament itself is every year compelled to enlarge its sphere of action. But be-

sides its practical import, there was something else to exalt the marvelous success of this working men's measure. Through their most notorious men of science, such as Dr. *Ure*, Professor *Senior*, and other sages of that stamp, the British bourgeoisie had predicted, and to their heart's content proved, that any legal restriction of the hours of labor must sound the death knell of British industry, which, vampire like, could but live by sucking blood, and children's blood, too. In olden times, child murder was a mysterious rite of the religion of Moloch, but it was practiced on some very solemn occasions only, once a year perhaps, and then Moloch had no exclusive bias for the children of the poor. This struggle about the legal restriction of the hours of labor raged the more fiercely since, apart from frightened avarice, it told indeed upon the great contest between the blind rule of the laws of supply and demand which form the political economy of the bourgeoisie, and social production controlled by social foresight, which forms the political economy of the working class. Hence the Ten Hours' Bill was not only a great practical success; it was the victory of a principle; it was the first time that in broad daylight the political economy of the bourgeoisie succumbed to the political economy of the working class.

Not surprisingly, Bernstein utilized part of the above passage on the title page of *The Preconditions of Socialism*. This is perhaps the clearest, most emphatic statement to be found anywhere within the voluminous written work of Karl Marx to indicate that he was indeed aware of the possibility that significant social progress could be achieved in the absence of violent revolution. Just as the Ten Hours' Bill had not required bloody revolution, so too many other advances might be achieved through peaceful means. The sum total of such advances might, in fact, eventually amount to a reasonable approximation to the idyllic conditions conjured up, in the minds of its advocates, by the term "socialism."

Following publication of *The Preconditions of Socialism* in March 1899, a vigorous debate over Bernstein's revisionism continued in socialist periodicals for a couple of years, before eventually petering out because practically everything that could be said about the matter had already been said. As noted above, it was not until the 1921 SDP conference at Görlitz that Bernstein's revisionism was fully incorporated into the Party program. During the two decades prior to 1921, the principal Party leaders, such as August Bebel, Karl Kautsky, and Karl Liebknecht, remained officially opposed to Bernstein, signifying that they remained believers in the hardline Marxist prediction of eventual proletarian revolution. But the emphasis was now on the word "eventual." The Party leaders were at pains to emphasize that "eventual" could—and probably would—entail a very long period of time: many decades, possibly a century or more. In the meantime, it was appropriate for the SDP to continue its peaceful, day-to-day pursuit of piecemeal reforms by legal means. For the rank-and-file membership, it was basically a matter of indifference whether or not the day would eventually come for bloody revolution. That day was so far off in the remote future that it need not affect activities in the here and now. Besides, keeping their conservative opponents aware of the bloody revolution possibility, might make them more amenable to the various reforms that were the actual operational objectives of the Social Democratic Party of Germany during the early years of the twentieth century.

## World War I and After

On June 28, 1914, "business as usual," for socialists and everyone else in Europe, was rudely interrupted by a wholly unpredictable event: a tubercular teenaged Serbian nationalist by the name of Gavrilo Princip assassinated the crown prince of the Austrian empire and his wife in the Bosnian town of Sarajevo. Within a month, the major European powers were embroiled in warfare. Owing to ongoing tensions over overseas colonial empires (Germany wanted one), amplified by an accelerating arms race, war had been brewing in Europe for many years. Therefore the onset of war was not really unanticipated, and from the enthusiasm with which it was greeted by immense crowds in several nations, it was apparently welcomed by many people. Experiences with wars through much of the nineteenth century had created an expectation that they would be brief, soon settled by negotiations, and would entail relatively minor human and material costs. Moreover, most people expected that their own nation would be on the winning side. What was completely unanticipated at the time of its onset was the immensely long duration and terrible costs of World War I.

Among the early casualties of World War I was the Second International, an organization of socialist and labor parties founded in Paris on July 14 (Bastille Day), 1889. From its formation, the primary mission of the Second International was to instill cosmopolitan sentiments among its working class constituency, and to educate the international proletariat in the commonality of its interests against the international bourgeoisie. As the fateful year of 1914 approached, the European socialist parties viewed with alarm the ominous war clouds on the horizon. There was considerable talk within their ranks about calling an international general strike to avert a war, or even to shut it down once it had started. In the event, such talk came to nothing. Nationalistic fervor trumped socialistic sentiment: most socialists marched off to war just as eagerly as their anti-socialist countrymen. The temper of the times was indicated by the assassination of Jean Jaurès on July 31, 1914, by an enthusiastic French patriot. Jaurès, the leader of the French Socialist Party (which had subscribed since 1902 to Bernstein-style revisionism), had long been noted for his vehement anti-militarism and anti-imperialism. His effort to forestall the oncoming war cost him his life.

In Germany, Eduard Bernstein was one of a handful of Reichstag members representing the SDP who opposed the war. In 1917, the antiwar element of the SDP founded a temporary splinter group that styled itself the Independent Social Democratic Party of Germany (USDP). Upon the war's end, most of the USDP membership, including Bernstein, rejoined the SPD. By that time, the SPD was sufficiently mainstream that it was a major participant in the abolition of the German empire and the inauguration of a republic, styled by historians the "Weimar Republic" from the town of its formation. The Weimar Republic persisted through the 1920s and into the early 1930s, when it was swept away by Hitler's Nazi regime. The first president of the Weimar Republic, from 1919 until his death in office in 1925, was Friedrich Ebert, an SDP member. Bernstein's antiwar stance from 1914 through 1918 had not been as extreme as that of Rosa Luxemburg and Karl Liebknecht, who as early as the summer of 1914 were among the founders of an antiwar organization that eventually styled itself the "Spartacus League," after the famous leader of a slave revolt in ancient Rome. In 1916, Luxemburg and Liebknecht were imprisoned for their antiwar activities.

During the time of their imprisonment came electrifying news from Russia: first the February 1917 revolution which terminated the tsarist regime that had persisted for centuries, and then the November 1917 Bolshevik revolution which swept away the provisional government. In the view of the primary Bolshevik leader of the time, Vladimir Lenin, the February revolution had been a bourgeois revolution, and the October revolution was its logical successor, a proletarian revolution. Past experiences in Europe suggested that the Bolsheviks, as excessively extreme radicals, would not remain in power for long. Indeed, substantial reactionary armed forces were quickly mustered, and the Bolshevik government (which soon renamed itself the Communist government) found itself enmeshed in a desperate struggle for survival. However, this time the outcome was different: the radical revolution was *not* overcome. Unlike the Paris Commune of 1871, the Communist Party of the newly formed Union of Soviet Socialist Republics (USSR) consolidated its power, gradually gained the upper hand in the civil war, and eventually emerged victorious. In order to accomplish this, extreme measures had been necessary: for example, the murder of the entire Romanov royal family in

July 1918. Lenin's real-world version of the "dictatorship of the proletariat" truly was a dictatorship—and an especially brutal one at that.

From the vantage point of her prison cell back in Germany, Rosa Luxemburg, who had been one of the main critics of Eduard Bernstein during the revisionist debate, found much of which to disapprove in Lenin's new Communist regime in the USSR. Although she had been a stalwart defender of the hardline Marxist prediction of the need for a violent revolution leading to a dictatorship of the proletariat, realities in the Soviet Union did not measure up to her personal conception of a proper dictatorship of the proletariat. Specifically, there was insufficient attention being paid to non-Bolshevik viewpoints: in effect, the actual proletariat was not adequately represented in Lenin's Communist government. Luxemburg's position was that while the proletarian government could and should be harshly dictatorial toward its bourgeois opponents, it should also be democratic in terms of its internal decision-making: all legitimate proletarian viewpoints should be given due opportunity to express themselves. Obviously, this is a difficult prescription to fill, especially with a desperate civil war in progress.

An armistice concluding the hostilities of World War I was signed on November 11, 1918. However, another seven months would pass before the war was formally ended by the Treaty of Versailles on June 28, 1919. Understandably, the last months of 1918 and the first months of 1919 were a chaotic time in Germany, which, along with much of the rest of Europe, was reeling from the human, material, and psychological costs of the war. Compounding these costs was the humiliation of military defeat. The German Empire came to an immediate, ignominious end, and without further ado, Kaiser Wilhelm II abdicated and departed for exile in Holland. This left the field open to various political organizations desirous of filling the power vacuum. Foremost among these was the Social Democratic Party, as supplemented by its offshoot, the Independent Social Democratic Party.

However, one of its major competitors for power was the Communist Party of Germany (KPD). Shortly before the November armistice, most of those imprisoned for opposition to the war were freed, including Rosa Luxemburg and Karl Liebknecht. Shortly afterwards they were instrumental in reorganizing the Spartacus League and, in combination with various other Marxist organizations, transforming it into the KPD, formally launched at the end of December, 1918. The Communist Party of Germany remained active until its suppression by the Hitler regime in 1933. However, its first leaders, Luxemburg and Liebknecht, did not survive to see this. Both were summarily executed, along with some of their associates, by a right-wing Freikorps paramilitary unit in Berlin on January 15, 1919.

Ironically, while both Luxemburg and Liebknecht, as notable opponents of Bernstein's revisionism, looked forward to a violent proletarian revolution at some point in the future, when confronted by the immediate prospect of one, they were disinclined to embrace it. Despite the chaos of postwar Germany, conditions were not yet ripe for a successful proletarian revolution. They believed instead that the Communist Party of Germany should participate, along with the Social Democratic Party, in the National Assembly that eventually established the Weimar Republic. But extremists within the KPD believed that Germany might indeed be ripe for the same kind of Bolshevik-style revolution that had successfully taken control of the Russian government in November 1917. As it turned out, they were wrong.

Luxemburg and Liebknecht, in the enthusiasm of the moment, albeit reluctantly and with great misgivings, authorized an armed uprising in Berlin. The uprising was quickly suppressed by forces operating under the authority of Friedrich Ebert, head of the National Assembly, and soon to become the first president of the Weimar Republic. When Luxemburg and Liebknecht were captured, they were savagely beaten and executed without trial. As so often before, advocates of violent socialist revolution themselves met a violent end at the hands of armed reactionaries. For much of the remainder of 1919, revolutionary disturbances continued at various locations throughout Germany. They met with the same fate as the ill-fated Berlin uprising in January. This fate was essentially the same as that which had befallen the Paris Commune in 1871: some initial success, soon followed by brutal suppression.

By the early 1920s, the German Communist Party, as well as other Communist parties throughout Europe and much of the rest of the world, had desisted from efforts to take over their respective governments by force. They contented themselves with "participation" in government, usually as the "not-so-loyal opposition." But following the victory of Communism in the Soviet Union, the adherents of these parties found renewed inspiration, renewed faith that the hardline Marxist prediction of the end of capitalism amid violent revolution would eventually occur after all. Meanwhile, the social democratic component of the socialist movement fully embraced Bernstein's revisionist viewpoint, and thereafter was at pains to emphasize that no longer was a violent end envisioned for the capitalist economic system. According to the social democrats, the capitalist system would either be fundamentally transformed peacefully—or it would not be fundamentally transformed at all.

Eduard Bernstein continued as an SPD representative in the Reichstag from 1920 until his retirement from active politics in 1928. He was witness to the formidable difficulties of the Weimar Republic during the 1920s, not least of which was the ominous rise of Hitler's Nazi Party. The coup de grace to democratic governance in post-World War I Germany was administered by the economic travail imposed by the worldwide Great Depression of the 1930s. The rise in unemployment was just what Hitler needed to put his Party over the top. Bernstein died on December 18, 1932, just weeks before Hitler was appointed Chancellor of Germany, from which position he quickly moved forward to establish an absolute dictatorship. It was perhaps fortunate for Bernstein that he did not live to witness and experience the abyss into which Germany plunged from 1933 to 1945.

## Application to World Government

In the early part of the twentieth century, much if not most of the socialist movement was weaned away from hardline Marxism with its gloomy forecast of violent revolution, and toward the "kinder and gentler" revisionist version of socialism, which jettisoned the need for violent revolution, and insisted that the essential objectives of socialism could indeed be achieved peacefully through the democratic process. The development of the revisionist socialist approach, now usually associated with the term "social democracy," immensely strengthened the socialist idea as a generally positive force toward the improvement of global human civilization. Had not this epochal transition occurred, had the socialist movement remained in thrall to hardline Marxism, had all the socialist parties of Europe shared the mindset of Lenin's Bolsheviks, it seems inescapable that continuous, devastating civil war between fascist forces and communist forces would have been the fate of Europe throughout the twentieth century.

Perhaps an analogous transition will occur in the early part of the twenty-first century—or at least at some point during this century. Perhaps "hardline world federalism" will give way before "revisionist world federalism." Whereas "hardline world federalism" insists that the omnipotent world state is the only meaningful and worthwhile form of world government, "revisionist world federalism" holds out a practical alternative, as exemplified by the proposed Federal Union of Democratic Nations described in Chapter 2 above. Whereas the omnipotent world state concept requires all nations, without exception, to become members of the world federation, and that the world federation monopolize all significant military forces and heavy weaponry, the Federal Union concept allows for non-member nations, and still more importantly, it allows all nations, whether members or non-members of the Federal Union, to

maintain whatever military forces and heavy weaponry they deem necessary to their national interests. If this revisionist alternative to the omnipotent world state option becomes sufficiently understood and appreciated, this might revitalize the world federalist movement in the twenty-first
century in the same way that the development of revisionist socialism
revitalized the socialist movement during the early twentieth century.
Just as the development of revisionist socialism led eventually to the better world we know today, so too might the development of revisionist
world federalism lead eventually to the better world we hope to know
tomorrow.

As Lenin's Bolsheviks discovered in the years following their take-
over of government power in November 1917, they had taken a flying
leap into the unknown. It was not just that the complete and total expropriation of the Russian capitalists and landowners aroused such intense
opposition that they (the Bolsheviks) immediately became involved in a
life-or-death struggle for survival with the armed forces of reaction. It
was also that they did not know exactly what they wanted to do with
their power even if the transition had been effected smoothly and they
were not involved in a desperate civil war. It was well known to all nineteenth century Marxists, hardline and revisionist alike, that the Master
himself had declined to "write recipes for the social chefs of the future."
It eventually became evident, especially following the Bolshevik take-
over of Russia, that this was potentially a very serious omission. It has
long since been generally recognized that it is highly imprudent to abandon existing policies or institutions in the absence of any clear consensus
as to specifically what policies or institutions should replace them.

Marx's intemperate rhetoric against the various "contradictions of
capitalism" carried the strong implication that once the shackles of the
capitalist system had been burst asunder by the proletarian revolution,
immediately the productivity—as well as the equity—of the socialist
successor system would soar to undreamed-of heights. Basically, the
problem of economic scarcity would disappear, would be relegated to
oblivion. Since everyone would then have every material thing they
could possibly want, envy, jealousy, conflict, crime, warfare, etc., would
all disappear. There would no longer be any need for a repressive state
apparatus. Put this way, any reasonable person can immediately perceive
that this is a vision of an impossible utopia. Almost certainly, the problem of scarcity can never be completely overcome. The limitations of the
natural resource base, which includes the natural resource of human intelligence and ingenuity, in conjunction with the indefinite expandability
of human wants (as opposed to human needs), ensures that there will almost certainly never come a time, no matter what future heights are

scaled by global human civilization, when "everyone will have every material thing they could possibly want."

The fatal intellectual consequence of this utopian fantasy of unbounded productivity under socialism, was an inadequate understanding of and appreciation for the economic market. At its heart, the economic market is a mechanism for dealing with the problem of scarcity. As long as scarcity exists, there will be a need for an economic market. Karl Marx confounded "capitalism" with "the economic market," a misapprehension that led eventually to unfortunate consequences for public ownership socialism as practiced in the Soviet Union and elsewhere in the world. Marx studied the economic realities of early nineteenth century Europe, and concluded, reasonably enough, that industrial workers were not being paid enough, defining "enough" as an amount sufficient to support at least a comfortable standard of living for the workers and their families. This situation he attributed not to the combination of low productivity with excessive economic inequality, but rather to the economic market. The only way to rectify the problem, to Marx's way of thinking, was to smash the economic market, to abolish it, to replace it with some type of social planning. But as is now almost universally recognized, Marx was entirely incorrect about this. The problem of low wages during the early Industrial Revolution was eventually overcome by a combination of increasing productivity through technological advances, and government intervention to reduce economic inequality (chiefly through progressive taxes and expanded welfare benefits). It was not the economic market itself that was to blame; it was rather the circumstances under which the economic market functioned in the early nineteenth century.

There have been important real-world examples of socialism in the puristic public ownership sense: most importantly, the Soviet Union, and the People's Republic of China. In neither of these cases was the economic market ever actually abolished. Although the nature and degree of the planning and regulatory overlay on the economic market varied throughout the histories of these two nations, there was never any serious attempt to get along entirely without an economic market. Both in the USSR and the PRC, the Communist authorities soon realized that no large-scale national economy can operate without a market. As a result of various problems in the USSR, one of which was an excessively ambitious planning system overlaid upon the economic market base, the nation's economic performance never measured up to the promises made by the Communist leadership, leading to the eventual abandonment, in the early 1990s, of the entire Communist system there, public ownership socialism and all. The People's Republic of China, on the other hand, has never abandoned public ownership socialism, and its economic growth performance over the last several decades has been one of the strongest in the world. This is because China eventually abandoned most forms of planning and adopted a pure market socialist system. Indeed, market socialism is a well-known economic possibility which combines public ownership of most of the means of production with heavy reliance on the free economic market for everyday economic processes of production and distribution. Back in Marx's time, the term "market socialism" would have been regarded as a ludicrous oxymoron, but today it is widely acknowledged as a viable economic system. Although it has not yet been implemented in any First World nation, it has definitely been implemented—and is doing very well indeed in an economic sense—in the People's Republic of China.

One of the implicit advantages of revisionist socialism, as developed by Eduard Bernstein and others toward the end of the nineteenth century, over the hardline Marxist socialism of that era, was that it did *not* propose "taking a flying leap into the unknown"—of the type that Lenin's Bolsheviks had done when they took power in Russia in November 1917. Prior to 1917, no advocate of socialism had any clear idea of what the proletarian revolution, if and when it occurred, would or could achieve. The expropriation of capitalists and land-owners would lead to a social system that would be a great deal superior to the capitalist system—that much all socialists agreed upon. But the specifics of the successor socialist system were cloaked in a golden haze. Was a reasonable approximation to utopia, to an earthly Eden, really possible? And how exactly would this utopia operate? Not even the most adamant hardline Marxists could produce satisfactory answers to these kinds of questions.

Revisionist socialists did not have to worry about such questions. What they were concerned with were incremental reforms to the existing economic system: for example, greater progressivity in the tax system, shortening the working day, increasing the minimum wage rate, providing more generous unemployment and pension benefits, and so on and so forth. None of these kinds of reforms, if and when implemented, would involve fundamental alterations in the existing economic system. That they were "minor" reforms implied the disadvantage that they would not instantaneously raise working class welfare to undreamed-of heights. But also implied was the countervailing advantage that there was less risk of their having seriously adverse "unintended consequences." These kinds of relatively minor alterations did not run the risk of seriously derailing the economic system, which could potentially result in catastrophe.

At the present time, the traditional, orthodox world federalist objective, what we might term the "hardline" objective, is the omnipotent world state. This world state would be "omnipotent" because it would include all the nations of the world without exception, and moreover, it would directly control all significant military forces and heavy weaponry in the world, including (especially) nuclear weapons. The advantage of such a world state, it goes without saying, would be the elimination of all wars, including (especially) nuclear wars. No one doubts that this would be a very good thing, in and of itself. Nevertheless, only a virtually microscopic proportion of the contemporary world population would want to see the omnipotent world state established in the real world. The fear is virtually universal that such a state would quickly degenerate into an oppressive totalitarian tyranny, probably accompanied by bureaucratic strangulation and cultural homogenization.

The Bolshevik revolution of November 1917 established hardline Marxists, intent upon universal expropriation of the capitalist class, as the rulers of Russia. It is virtually impossible to imagine such a drastic transformation occurring under "normal" circumstances. In fact, the essential "precondition" for Russia's Bolshevik transformation was its disastrous participation in World War I from 1914 through 1917, a participation which imposed tremendous strains on the Russian people. If we envision a roughly analogous transformation of the existing international regime of today into the omnipotent world state, it is difficult to imagine how such a thing could come about unless tremendous strains were imposed on the world population. Such tremendous strains might be imposed by a nuclear world war. It is, in fact, a commonplace speculation that the only feasible scenario for the foundation of a world state would be in the aftermath of a nuclear world war. This is a scenario from which most reasonable people recoil in horror. It is not just that the costs of a nuclear world war are too horrible to contemplate—it is also that the most likely outcome in the aftermath of a nuclear world war would not be a world state, but rather the continuation of the current international system, albeit in a much splintered and diminished form. It has been predicted that World War IV would be fought with bows and arrows. While that seems unlikely, it does seem fairly plausible that World War IV would be far less destructive than World War III—for the simple reason that there would be far less remaining to destroy.

If we think about the transformation of the current international system into the omnipotent world state under "normal" conditions—that is to say, in the absence of a nuclear war—we are forced to think about it as an impossible fantasy, as something which has not even the remotest possibility of occurring within the foreseeable future, given the present status of global public opinion concerning world government. Almost any reasonably intelligent and well-informed person, if asked to think about such a transformation, would respond that it could never happen because most people throughout the world believe that an omnipotent world state would enforce intolerable impositions upon their own nation, and many other nations. Even if by some improbable conjunction of events, a small minority of fanatical world federalists managed to establish an infant world federation armed with a measure of military power, it would immediately crumble to bits amidst devastating civil war.

I have repeatedly emphasized in these pages that I do not contest the view that the omnipotent world state is, at the present juncture in human history, thoroughly impracticable. But I have also emphasized throughout that this virtually axiomatic proposition should not be allowed to terminate consideration of the world government possibility. The omnipotent world state is emphatically *not* the one and only option for establishing a meaningful world government. The proposed Federal Union of Democratic Nations represents a happy medium between the United Nations of today, and the hypothetical omnipotent world state advocated by orthodox, hardline world federalists.

Just as revisionist socialism did not call for reckless leaps into an unknown future, so too revisionist world federalism is the same. Owing to the provision in the Federal Union proposal for free exit at the unilateral discretion of the member nation, and the equally critical proposal for independent control by the member nation of as much military force and armaments as it needs, the foundation of such a world federation would not constitute a dramatic departure from the existing international system. True, there would be important innovations: the administrative structure of a world federation would be formally established, representatives to it would be regularly elected by the populations of the member nations, it would become immediately active in the ongoing operations of global governance. If the supplementary economic proposal for a Global Marshall Plan were implemented, over the first several decades of its operation, the primary objective of the Federal Union of Democratic Nations would be the achievement of a significantly higher level of economic equality over the nations of the world. Not *complete* equality, it must be stressed, but a *significantly higher level* of equality.

Whether or not the Federal Union would actually be able to undertake a Global Marshall Plan, and if so, what level of resources would be allocated to it, cannot be predicted in advance. So too it cannot be predicted what other aspects of global governance might be pursued by the Federal Union, and with what success. This is because of the practical, constitutionally imbedded constraints on the Federal Union's authority. The Federal Union could not do anything that would threaten its existence and viability: that is to say, it could not do anything that would precipitate the secession of a substantial number of member nations. If, for example, a Global Marshall Plan of the sort envisioned here, would be unacceptable to a substantial number of member nations, it would not be undertaken.

Because of the operational constraints on its authority and military power, the inauguration of the Federal Union of Democratic Nations would not represent a dramatic departure from the existing international status quo. Such an inauguration, if it occurred, would represent a marginal, incremental, evolutionary step forward. The primary advantage of the Federal Union would not be manifested immediately; rather it would consist of providing more effective institutional support for the progressive development of global governance into the future. It is certainly conceivable that eventually a reasonable approximation to the omnipotent world state will be achieved. Mutual respect and confidence among the nations would then be such that no nation would feel a need for a significant armed force under its direct control, and all nations would be comfortable having the world federation assume sole responsibility for whatever armed force is deemed necessary by the nations as a whole. At that point a nuclear world war would indeed become virtually impossible. But such a situation would not come about immediately—or even quickly. Several decades of evolutionary development might be required, perhaps a century or two. The important thing is that this ultimate outcome would become *more likely* if the Federal Union is established, than if we continue with the existing international system.

There is a close analogue between this approach and the approach of revisionist socialism. Revisionist socialism did not (and does not) promise giant leaps forward, of millennial progress within a short space of time. What it espouses is gradual progress, through the adoption of a series of measures, each one of which is relatively inconsequential in itself, but which together, in the fullness of time, lead to a qualitatively higher condition of life. If one compares the economic quality of life for most people as it was at the turn of the twentieth century, to what it was at the turn of the twenty-first century, only the most contrarian mentalities will refuse to acknowledge dramatic improvement. A large part of the credit for this improvement lies directly with the revisionist branch of the socialist movement.

At the present time, in the opening years of the twenty-first century, the world federalist movement is feeble to the point of near-extinction. This debilitating weakness is because it is having great difficulty in ridding itself of the invalid belief that the omnipotent world state is the only worthwhile form of world government. Belief in the omnipotent world state among hardline world federalists of today is equivalent to the belief among hardline Marxists in Bernstein's time that only public ownership socialism is a worthwhile form of socialism, that the only means by which this goal can be achieved is through violent proletarian revolution, and that such a revolution is not merely likely but literally inevitable. All three components of this overall belief system (that only public ownership socialism is worthwhile, that violent revolution is necessary to attain it, and that violent revolution is inevitable) were challenged by Eduard Bernstein and like-minded socialists of his generation. The victory of Bernstein's revisionism did not come easily, and it did not come quickly. But eventually it prevailed, and the world was made a better place because of it.

Perhaps our time will see a similar development. Perhaps a limited world government along the lines of the proposed Federal Union of Democratic Nations will be recognized as not only a viable alternative to the omnipotent world state, but as a preferable alternative to it. Perhaps "revisionist world federalism" will supplant "hardline world federalism." Were this to happen, it might revitalize the world federalist movement, empower it, strengthen it, make it into a viable contender in the arena of political ideas and controversy. And were this to happen, possibly the current generation of humanity will be fortunate enough to witness the advent of a legitimate, full-bodied world federation in human affairs.

# 6

# Could It Be Done?

## The Chicken or the Egg?

For the most part, specialists in international organization do not consider that any form of world government will become feasible at any point within the foreseeable future, and therefore deem it unworthy of detailed consideration. Most discussions of world government in the professional and textbook literature are sketchy outlines of the progress of the concept in the history of ideas, to which is appended a cursory dismissal as far as the contemporary real world in concerned. The usual basis for the dismissal is the assertion that the contemporary human population is far too heterogeneous and diverse—economically, religiously, and ideologically—for peacefully attained universal political unity to be feasible. According to this conventional viewpoint, the only kind of state entity capable of encompassing and controlling such diversity would be a ruthlessly totalitarian regime determined to crush and annihilate any and all vestiges of dissent and resistance.

In the well-known formulation of Kenneth Waltz, the degree of coercion necessary to hold a political system together is positively related to the heterogeneity of the population. The current world population is highly diverse—ergo, only a brutal totalitarian regime could hold its various components in check. In the following well-known passage from *Man, the State and War*, Waltz applies the principle to suggest the imprudence of contemplating world government:[1]

> Yet in the international as in the domestic sphere, if anarchy is the cause [of monstrous behavior], the obvious conclusion is that government is the cure... The problem, however, becomes a practical one. The amount of force needed to hold a society together varies with the heterogeneity of the elements composing it. World federalists write as though the only alternatives before us were unity or death. "World government is necessary and therefore possible," Robert Maynard Hutchins avers. But demonstrating the need for an institution does not bring it in-

to existence. And were world government attempted, we might find ourselves dying in the attempt, or uniting and living a life worse than death.

Implicit in this passage, which is typical of the mainstream international relations literature, is an assumption that the essential *precondition* for successful world government is the attainment of a very high degree of socioeconomic homogeneity and psychological consensus among humanity. This assumption fails to recognize two critical aspects of the relationship between social uniformity and political unity: the *continuous nature* of the relationship, and the *interactive nature* of the relationship.

First, the relationship between social uniformity and political unity at any one point in time is a smooth and continuous relationship: the higher the degree of social uniformity achieved, the higher the level of political unity that may be established. To have a *very high* level of political unity in a world government—that is to say, an extremely strong, centralized and authoritative world government (an omnipotent world state)—we would need a very high level of social uniformity. We are not here concerned with any such world government. If we are content with a *reasonable* level of political unity at the global level—that is to say, with a limited world government along the lines of the Federal Union of Democratic Nations—then we would *not* need a very high level of social uniformity.

Second, the relationship between social uniformity and political unity over a period of time is an interactive and mutually reinforcing relationship: the mere existence of political unity, albeit weak in the beginning, tends gradually to generate a higher level of social uniformity, and as social uniformity increases, it in turn permits a higher level of political unity. Thus the relationship over time between social uniformity and political unity is not static but dynamic: a mutually reinforcing, snowballing process is created that over time will tend toward a high (albeit far from "complete") level of both social uniformity and political unity.

Consider the traditional question: Which came first—the chicken or the egg? What makes the question absurd, and therefore humorous, is that *neither* the modern chicken nor the modern egg came first. The modern chicken-egg-chicken progression is the result of millions of years of slow, evolutionary development with roots in the primeval slime. Those who argue that it is necessary to have a high level of social uniformity prior to having an effective state are equivalent to those who would argue, in response to the chicken-egg question, that since chickens come out of eggs, then the egg came first. The problem with this argument, obviously, is that it is also true that eggs come out of chickens.

If we take social and attitudinal homogeneity to be the egg, and the effectiveness of state organization (i.e. political unity) to be the chicken, the relevance of the chicken-egg question becomes clear. A population which is politically united within the same state organization tends to become, over time, more socially and attitudinally homogeneous. Similarly, as a given population becomes more socially and attitudinally homogeneous, its state organization tends to become more effective— among other reasons, because it expends less resources on enforcing the majority will upon recalcitrant minorities. There is an ongoing, progressive, interactive, mutually reinforcing, snowballing process between the social and attitudinal homogeneity of a given population, and the effectiveness of the state organization within which it is politically united.

It is reasonably obvious, to all but the most enthusiastic proponents of world government, that the degree of homogeneity among nations today is insufficient to support a world state with an amount of practical and moral authority over the nations of the world analogous to that, for example, of the national government of the United States today over the 50 state governments. This means that an *extremely* powerful, effective and authoritative world state is an impossibility at the present time. It does not mean that a *somewhat* powerful, effective and authoritative world state is an impossibility at the present time. The constraints which are integral components of the proposed Federal Union of Democratic Nations would make this limited form of world government acceptable to many if not most nations of the world today—if and when they become aware of the possibility. If and when such a Union is established, it would then commence a long-term process of gradual evolution—just as did the United States—toward a higher level of homogeneity among its citizens, and a higher level of effectiveness in its operations.

In terms of the chicken-egg analogy, the "egg" which we have at the present time (the level of social homogeneity throughout the contemporary world), and the "chicken" which is capable of coming forth from this egg (the level of political unity which could be achieved by a world government established at the present point in history), are both fairly primitive versions of what we eventually hope to achieve. The ancient egg and the ancient chicken were virtually unrecognizable relative to their modern counterparts. But we should not (to utilize the well-known adage) allow the best to be the enemy of the good. It is certainly true that the world government that we could establish today would be far short of the ideal that might be imagined. Such a world government would not directly and immediately banish the threat of nuclear holocaust, would not directly and immediately banish such equally serious threats as genocidal outbreaks and accelerating environmental degradation. But these facts should not obscure the very high probability that a world government *would* establish a more secure foundation for long-term efforts toward the reduction of such threats as nuclear holocaust, genocidal outbreaks, and accelerating environmental degradation. Also, the fact that a limited world government would not produce utopian conditions in the short run should be weighed against the equally important fact—in fact, the *more* important fact—that it would be very unlikely to produce dystopian conditions.

The memorable "life worse than death" quote from Kenneth Waltz cited above dates from the Cold War year of 1959, and the sentiment it expresses was echoed by any number of other authorities from that era. Two examples are Inis L. Claude and Stephen Goodspeed.[7]

In Chapter 18 of the 1971 edition of *Swords into Plowshares*, Inis L. Claude subjects the notion of world government to a somewhat more thorough critique than it usually received in the textbook literature. Claude's argument may be summarized as follows: World government would either be useless or it would be intolerable. If it were such a weak federation that it could not suppress wars among member nations, or between members and nonmembers, there would be no value in it. On the other hand, if it were given enough power to suppress wars among nations, it would almost certainly constitute an intolerable tyranny. The latter is seen as the more serious defect, and the point is stated as follows:

> The problem of power looms large with respect to any governmental system adequate to cope with the elements of disorder and discord in the international community. If a global regimen is to have sufficient power to fulfill its task, questions of profound gravity arise: who will exercise and control the force of the community, in accordance with what conception of justice, within what constitutional limits, with what guarantees that the limits will be observed? These are not questions that can be readily answered, but they are crucial for the threat of global tyranny lurks in unsatisfactory answers. In terms of Western liberalism, the problem is not to get just any kind of world government— Hitler and Stalin were only the most recent of a long series of leaders who would have been glad to provide that—but to get a system of world order that is compatible with the political ideals of the democratic heritage.

In *The Nature and Function of International Organization* (second edition, 1967), Stephen Goodspeed explains the impracticality of world government as follows:

> While the arguments of the world government enthusiasts have great

appeal on the surface, a number of them are open to serious question. Those who still demand the immediate remaking of the United Nations into even a limited world government oversimplify the problem by not assessing fully the manner in which governments are made, nor do they recognize the basic meaning of sovereignty. All evil cannot be eradicated simply be revising the Charter or devising a new constitution. Constitutions follow upon a society which has grown used to common institutions, a community attached to certain norms and interests. It is from this communal society that governments and constitutions spring. The community is developed first, and the constitution, the laws, and the administration come afterwards...

The way in which the United States was created is often cited as an argument in favor of the theory of world federalism. When carefully scrutinized, this analogy breaks down. The thirteen colonies meeting in convention did not constitute thirteen separate sovereignties preparing to join together as one. They had fought a war together and possessed the same moral convictions, the same loyalties, a common heritage, and similar political institutions... The colonial people existed as a community before the establishment of the United States, just as a world community must be created before the erection of a world state.

If, in some desperate effort to solve the problems dividing the Soviets and the Western world, the United Nations were to be transformed into some form of world government with the General Assembly made a legislature based on the democratic principles of popular representation and majority rule, could it succeed in the absence of a majority possessed of common values, interests, and goals? The answer is a categorical "no" since struggle between East and West would not dissolve merely because the setting was changed. The possibility of establishing a world government is at the present time as remote as it has been for centuries.

What do these quotations—which are typical of numerous similar discussions of world government to be found throughout the academic and textbook literature on international organization during the Cold War—have in common? To begin with, they are rather unimaginative. Their authors seem oblivious to the possibility that a limited world government—a world government subject to sufficient and adequate constraints to preclude it from establishing an intolerably totalitarian hegemony over the nations of the world—could nevertheless make a meaningful and useful contribution to the future evolution of the international community. On what basis, for example, does Inis Claude assert that unless a world government were to possess a virtual monopoly on heavy weaponry, it would be "useless" as an instrument for the suppression of wars between nations? A world government might not possess a virtual monopoly on heavy weaponry, but it might possess enough of such weaponry to give serious pause to potential aggressor nations. Moreover, the simple existence of a world government, even were several of its member nations to remain heavily armed, would create moral and psychological pressures toward peaceful and cooperative behavior among member nations. Perhaps these negative viewpoints on world government would not have been so pat and complacently dogmatic were their authors to have given any serious consideration to proposals for a properly limited world government. The authors assume that a meaningful world government must necessarily be all powerful—the omnipotent world state—and that an all-powerful government must necessarily be despotic.

Another striking commonality of the above quotations is that they are based firmly on the Cold War conditions which prevailed from the end of World War II in 1945 until the collapse and dissolution of the Soviet Union in 1991. Waltz, Claude, and Goodspeed all take it as a given that a primary problem with world government—if not *the* primary problem with world government—is that communist national leaders would endeavor to subvert the world government and transform it into an instrument for the expansion of communism. None of the authors feel it necessary to explain the disadvantages of communism. They merely assume that their readers are sufficiently aware of recent history (specifically the dictatorships of Adolf Hitler in Germany and of Joseph Stalin in Russia) to be sensitive to the threat of totalitarianism.

With the sentence: "And were world government attempted, we might find ourselves dying in the attempt, or uniting and living a life worse than death," Kenneth Waltz expresses the standard Cold War judgment that it would be better to be dead than Red. With the sentence: "In terms of Western liberalism, the problem is not to get just any kind of world government—Hitler and Stalin were only the most recent of a long series of leaders who would have been glad to provide that—but to get a system of world order that is compatible with the political ideals of the democratic heritage," Inis Claude effectively smears world government by portraying the likes of Adolf Hitler and Joseph Stalin as putative endorsers of the concept. And in answering a rhetorical question concerning the feasibility of world government with a "categorical no," Stephen Goodspeed explains that the "struggle between East and West would not dissolve merely because the setting was changed." Anyone aware of the collapse and dissolution of the Soviet Union in 1991 realizes that in order to retain a reasonable amount of relevance, such quotations as these need to be revised rather substantially. What is really quite surprising, however, is the very limited alteration to be found in typical treatments of world

government in the international organization literature in the years following the Soviet collapse in 1991.

For example, in his one-page discussion of world government, Mark
Amstutz writes (1999):[3]

> A stable world government needs a centralized governmental structure
> and widespread shared values and aspirations. A world federal regime
> will require the creation of both a central authority and strong social,
> economic, cultural, and political affinities. The dilemma of world gov-
> ernment is this: the international system needs world government to re-
> duce the threat of war, but the precondition for world government is
> world community, which can only be solidified through the political
> transformation of the anarchic world system.

Although the general thrust of the passage is obviously that world
government is unlikely, the statement is not quite clear. What, precisely,
is meant by "the political transformation of the anarchic world system"?
If by this is meant "the establishment of a world government," then we
would have a logical refutation of the possibility of world government
along "Catch 22" lines: you can't have world government without world
community, but you can't have world community without world government. This would constitute a sensible interpretation of the word "dilemma," but then the argument could be satirized as follows: "You can't
have a chicken without an egg, and you can't have an egg without a
chicken, therefore chickens and eggs are impossible."

On the other hand, if by the phrase "the political transformation of
the anarchic world system," Amstutz means "the achievement of a high
degree of mutual toleration and cooperation among sovereign nations,"
this is not a "dilemma" but a "problem." More importantly, Amstutz offers no reason why the *present* level of mutual toleration and cooperation
among sovereign nations is not sufficient to the establishment of a world
government—of a limited nature. He cannot cite, as did Goodspeed in
the 1960s, the "problems dividing the Soviets and the Western world."

He could cite, however, the "problems dividing the First World and
the Third World," i.e. the absence of "economic affinities" between the
rich nations and the poor nations. As a matter of fact, although it was
overshadowed during the Cold War era by ideological discord, the economic gap was always just as serious an impediment to world government as was the ideological gap. But even as the ideological gap need not
necessarily have abrogated the possibility of world government during
the Cold War period, so too the economic gap need not abrogate the possibility of world government during the post-Cold War period. What
could have worked then, and what could work now, is a limited world

government along the lines of the Federal Union of Democratic Nations. All that is needed to perceive this possibility is a certain amount of mental flexibility and vision.

Throughout most of the second half of the twentieth century, mankind lived in the shadow of nuclear catastrophe. There were massive arsenals of nuclear warheads and, particularly after the development of intercontinental ballistic missiles, extremely rapid and reliable means of delivery. If the decision had been made by top level officials that total war was necessary, within a few hours, hundreds of millions would have been dead or dying, and much of human civilization would have lain in ruins. Proponents of world government, alarmed by this situation, urged the formation of a world state as a means of reducing this dire threat. But the decision had been taken, by the overwhelming majority in all walks of life within the Western noncommunist nations, that the possibility of nuclear catastrophe constituted an acceptable risk in the interest of preserving the capitalistic way of life ("freedom") and preventing the imposition of communistic totalitarianism.

Proponents of world government were chided by mainstream authorities in the tradition of Waltz, Claude, and Goodspeed because they could provide "no plausible scenario" by which a benign world government could be established within an international community beset by intense ideological controversy. But the mainstream authorities themselves never troubled to provide "plausible scenarios" by which a world government in which the Western noncommunist nations were founding members, could be subverted and turned into an instrument for the abolition of the capitalistic way of life and the imposition of communistic totalitarianism. Of course, the communist leaders were also concerned that a world government would be subverted (from their point of view) and made into an instrument for the abolition of the communist way of life.[4] They also did not bother with constructing "plausible scenarios" by which this (in their view intolerable) outcome would come to pass.

The Federal Union of Democratic Nations described herein could have provided, even at the height of the Cold War, a type of world government which might have been acceptable to both the communist and noncommunist national leaders. Obviously, the founding constitution would have had to be neutral on the issue of capitalism versus socialism, just as most national constitutions throughout the world today are neutral on religion. It would have had to have been specified in the federation constitution that the Union "would make no law respecting the ownership of capital property." Thus the noncommunist nations could have continued to uphold private ownership of capital, while the communist nations could have continued to specify public ownership of capital. This

would not have prevented the communist nations from peacefully arguing the alleged virtues of socialism in an effort to persuade the populations of the noncommunist nations; while at the same time the noncommunist nations peacefully argued the alleged virtues of capitalism for an
analogous purpose. This could have been done in the same way that religious missionary efforts are conducted in the contemporary world.

The practicality of the proposed limited federal world government
under consideration herein is based upon one simple but profound insight: it is possible to create a meaningful and effective federal government without requiring its component political units to be militarily de-
fenseless, and without forbidding them from detaching themselves from
the union if that is their wish. Needless to emphasize, few national governments in the contemporary world would be comfortable about explicitly authorizing their subsidiary units (states, provinces, districts, and so
on) to maintain whatever military forces they desire, and to declare their
independence from the nation whenever they desire. Such liberties are
commonly perceived as contradictory to the core principle of national
sovereignty. The armed forces of subsidiary political units are typically
regarded as potential threats to the authority of the national government.
And history is littered with examples similar to the United States Civil
War of 1861-1865, precipitated by unauthorized declarations of independence by the Southern states. These declarations were regarded as
treasonous and were met with force.

Nevertheless, we need not be imprisoned by the past. We need not be
constricted within an intellectual straitjacket composed of traditional
thinking about government and sovereignty. The fact is that the national
governments of today are not at all comparable to a potential future
world government. A potential future world government would be operating within a very different environment from that confronting the national governments. Therefore its institutional structure and operating
procedures would, quite appropriately, be very much distinct from those
of today's national governments. Human knowledge, understanding and
flexibility is advancing on many fronts. This is—or can be—as true in
the area of political organization as it is in many other areas. The world
is changing, and we need evolving concepts of political organization to
cope with the evolving world in which we live.

The proposal for a Federal Union of Democratic Nations examined
in this book is entirely and fundamentally innovative. Nowhere in the
annals of world federalist thinking will be found a scheme of world government that allows the member nations to arm themselves as they
please, and to secede from the federation whenever they please at their
own unilateral discretion. Or if such ideas have been advanced in the

past, they are now buried in obscurity. The conventional world government scheme of today envisions what is descriptively termed the "omnipotent world state": member nations would be fully disarmed, and any move toward independence by a member nation would be instantly suppressed by armed force. Such a world state, it is true, would virtually eliminate the possibility of a sudden nuclear holocaust of the sort that has haunted the nightmares of humanity ever since the atomic bombings of Hiroshima and Nagasaki in 1945. Unfortunately, such a world state might also quickly degenerate into a totalitarian nightmare equivalent to what Hitler and Stalin inflicted on their respective nations during the worst years of the twentieth century.

In the years following the Second World War, world federalists put the case for an omnipotent world state before the court of global public opinion. The case was quickly and definitively rejected: fear of global tyranny trumped fear of nuclear holocaust. To this day, however, "traditional" world federalists continue to insist that the threat of nuclear holocaust is far more dangerous than the threat of global tyranny. Conceivably they are correct about this, but the only way they will be proved correct is if nuclear holocaust befalls the world. And then, of course, it will be too late. It has sometimes been suggested that only a nuclear holocaust will convince humanity of the necessity for an omnipotent world state. Rather more likely is that the embittered and impoverished survivors of a nuclear holocaust would be fragmented into a host of independent mini-states ruled by brutal warlords thirsting for revenge, who would thereafter make perpetual war on one another with whatever weapons were available, as the human race slides inexorably toward a new dark age. Whatever the aftermath of nuclear holocaust might be, in the absence of nuclear holocaust, it is difficult to imagine how traditional world federalists will get the majority of humanity to change its mind on this issue and embrace the omnipotent world state—especially now that the ebbing of the Cold War has greatly diminished the immediate threat of nuclear holocaust.

Most traditional world federalists today would be inclined to dismiss such notions as the member nations of a world federation arming themselves as they please and leaving the federation whenever they please, as manifestly unworkable. They cannot imagine that such a world government would persist for any length of time and achieve anything worthwhile. They would predict that within a few years—a decade or two at the most—the federation would have splintered into its component nations, and humanity would be right back to where it is today, confronting the possibility of nuclear holocaust brought about by the suspicion and hostility endemic to the sovereign nation-state system.

I would ask: How can they be so sure? How can they be so sure that a limited world government along the lines discussed would be so useless that it is not even worthy of experiment? The establishment of a such a world government would obviously be in the nature of an experiment. If the Federal Union of Democratic Nations soon flies apart from centrifugal forces, there would be no need for a central decision to dissolve it, since it would be effectively dissolved via the independent decisions of its component nations. If pessimistic skeptics are correct, and both the Federal Union (as well as its economic complement, the Global Marshall Plan) are failures, this would be a bad omen for the future of humanity on this planet. But from a practical standpoint, we would be no worse off than we are today. We have little to lose and much to gain. To my mind, therefore, both the Federal Union experiment, and the Global Marshall Plan experiment, are well merited.

## The Nationalism Issue

To some people, nationalism is deemed such a fundamental, immovable, irreducible, ineluctable obstacle to world government that even if we envisioned a world in which the human population was almost completely homogeneous in terms of race, language, ideological convictions, economic living standards, religious beliefs, and cultural traditions—there would still be no hope of political unification at the global level. This is simply because people everywhere are much too loyal to their own respective nations. This loyalty is rooted in whatever accident of birth was responsible for the nationality of any given individual, and is nourished by parental and educational immersion in the tangled web of historical grievances nursed by the populations of any one nation against numerous other nations throughout the world. It results in such deep-seated nationalistic prejudices and preconceptions as to constitute an impervious, impenetrable, adamantine barrier to the foundation of any sort of federal world government, no matter how limited, and no matter how carefully designed.[5]

Upon close examination, this proposition, however popular it may be at the present time, is seen to be untenable—as well as being a veritable insult to human rationality and intelligence. Nationalism is not some primitive, instinctive, quasi-mystical force totally beyond the dictates of reason and rationality, which will forever preclude the development of political loyalty to a state entity higher than the contemporary nation-state. Presuming that the world government in question is a properly restrained and limited state organization, nationalism as it is known in the world today does not represent an insuperable obstacle to the establishment of such a government.

As a matter of fact, in historical context, nationalism has been a stabilizing and unifying force to a greater extent than it has been a destabilizing and disunifying force. Those who would argue today that nationalism will forever prevent the formation of a viable federal world government because mankind is incapable of developing anything beyond national loyalties, are comparable to those who, several hundred years ago, would have argued that local and regional loyalties would forever prevent the formation of a viable nation-state. Indeed, a healthy degree of national pride might in some ways actually facilitate the establishment of a world government. Once the possibility of a limited world government along the lines of the Federal Union of Democratic Nations became widely known, and a critical mass of interest and enthusiasm was aroused, at some point a bandwagon effect might take hold, so that people will demand that their particular nation take up its rightful place in this great human endeavor—and not be left behind with the handful of unprogressive, reactionary, and backward-looking nations that continue to decline membership in the Federal Union.

In considering the nationalistic impediment to world government, we should first take note of the fact that this impediment, while logically distinct from the ideological and economic impediments, is in practice closely associated with them. Depending on the circumstances, the nation-state may be perceived as either the principal line of defense against the external imposition of ideologically hateful social systems, or as a principal instrument for the sharing of ideologically superior social systems with the rest of humanity. Throughout the modern era, and especially in the twentieth century, ideological fervor and nationalistic patriotism have been intimately related. To the traditional role of the nation-state as the champion of ideologically correct social systems, an increasingly important role has been added as consciousness of the economic gap has intensified throughout the twentieth century: the nation-state as the preserver of economic prosperity and welfare against potential inroads by envious and greedy foreigners.

During the modern era, nationalistic spirit has been associated with three major conditions and motivations: (1) religious and ideological ideas and aspirations toward the general reform and progress of human civilization; (2) desires for political unification and territorial expansion; (3) desires for liberation from governments perceived to be remote and oppressive. Some historical episodes show a relatively simple pattern: for example, the British revolutionary period from 1640 to 1688 witnessed an intensification of British nationalism almost exclusively on the basis of the first motivation. The genesis and development of American nationalism in the United States from its inception through the early twentieth century, on the other hand, shows a more complicated pattern involving all three motivations.

The immediate impetus to the American Declaration of Independence and the Revolutionary War was the desire for liberation from the British imperial government in London—a government perceived by most colonists to be remote and oppressive. But the American founding fathers quickly supplemented this immediate motivation with a vision of a new and improved democratic political commonwealth, based upon the natural rights of man and eschewing the aristocratic distinctions and the religious activism of the state which had characterized Europe through its long and difficult history. Finally, American nationalism was further intensified throughout the nineteenth century by the "manifest destiny" of westward territorial expansion toward the Pacific Ocean. The interaction of these three basic correlates of nationalism—in various permutations and combinations—may be observed in numerous other historical episodes: the French Revolution and the Napoleonic Wars, the consolidation of Italy and Germany, the decline and ultimate collapse of the Ottoman and Austro-Hungarian empires, the ideological and military conflicts of the twentieth century involving fascism and communism, and the dissolution of the British, French and other European colonial empires after the Second World War.

The attitudes and emotions which have been associated with nationalism in the past are by no means uniformly and consistently unfavorable to the foundation and operation of a supernational state in the future. In fact, of the three major historical correlates of nationalism, two might easily work in favor of a world government: in other words, these particular motivations to national pride and patriotism might also serve as motivations to supernational pride and patriotism. The Federal Union of Democratic Nations could be seen as an instrument toward the general reform and progress of worldwide human civilization—as an effective means for the extension to all mankind of such values as personal freedom, political democracy, social equality, and economic prosperity. At the same time, the Federal Union could be perceived as a means for the political unification of an extensive and populous territory, and for the possible expansion of mankind out into the solar system and beyond. The third correlate of nationalism is where the potential problem for world government lies: the desire for liberation from remote and oppressive governance.

A realistic appreciation of nationalism clearly shows that in order to be viable in a world still very nationalistically oriented, the world government must not be regarded as remote and oppressive by any substantial proportion of its citizens. As to the specific issue of remoteness, this potential problem has largely been abrogated—relative to 100 or 200 years ago—by amazing technological progress in the areas of transport and communications. There would be no difficulty in maintaining close contact between the individuals and agencies of the supernational government and their constituent citizens. Moreover, in recent decades the methodology of opinion polling has also made great progress, and no doubt this methodology would be relied upon extensively in making judgments as to what the Federal Union should and should not do.

The maintenance of close and continual communication between the Federal Union and its citizens would help to forestall feelings of oppression. In addition, the proposed Federal Union would incorporate numer ous features explicitly intended to inhibit tendencies toward oppressiveness—ranging from the national right of secession to the dual voting principle in the legislative assembly. Among the strongest guarantees of non-oppressiveness is the fact that the government of the supernational federation would be democratically elected by the population of the Federal Union. When we think of oppressive regimes throughout history, from the ancient Roman empire through to Stalinist communism, a unifying feature is the absence of democracy, of democratic accountability of the government to the population which it governs. By virtue of close contact and communication, democratic elections, formal constitutional guarantees, and the good sense and wisdom of the leaders of the supernational federation who will hopefully remain aware of the strong possibility of disaster should they overstep their political and moral authority—it may be anticipated with a reasonable degree of confidence that the Federal Union of Democratic Nations will avoid becoming an instrument of oppression.

## Sovereignty and Freedom

The proposition that the nationalistic impediment to world government is impermeable may be restated as the proposition that any world government would inevitably involve unacceptable inroads into national sovereignty. The term "sovereignty" has an appropriately sonorous ring: it tends to evoke deep and abiding emotions, to elicit intimations of fundamental issues of survival and wellbeing, to generate what might be termed a "mystical" frame of mind in an individual. Once in this frame of mind, it is relatively easy to imagine that the concept of national sovereignty constitutes an insuperable obstacle to supernational federation.[6] Such a federation (according to this reasoning) would constitute an abridgement of and an infringement upon the national sovereignty of its member nations. But nations cannot permit such a "competitor" for their traditional authority to exist and yet remain sovereign states. By the same token, a world government—in order to constitute a proper state entity—could not tolerate the limitations upon its own sovereignty represented by the sovereignty of its component nations. It simply could not allow such significant restrictions on its authority, and it simply could not permit so much competition for the loyalties of its citizens. Therefore, one or the other would have to go: either the concept of national sovereignty, or the concept of supernational sovereignty. Since we cannot imagine the nations of today surrendering their national sovereignty, we are forced to conclude that a world government is impossible.

Such thinking is muddled and fallacious. It manifests an excessively rigid mentality that perceives only black and white rather than shades of gray, that focuses only on the extreme endpoints of the spectrum of possibility rather than looking for the happy medium. The formation of a world government would not necessarily manifest the abrogation of national sovereignty, nor would the continuation of national sovereignty necessarily imply an absence of sovereignty on the part of the world government. The world government and the component nation-states would each have their respective areas of sovereignty: areas in which they would indeed exercise undisputed authority. In some areas the world government would possess sovereign authority, and in other areas the individual nation-states would possess sovereign authority. In the United States today, individual states such as Texas and New York are frequently described as "the sovereign state of Texas" and "the sovereign state of New York." Such phrases are not contradictory to Texas and New York being components of the "sovereign United States of America." At first it may seem paradoxical to think about "areas" of sovereignty and "limitations" on sovereignty—such restrictive notions may seem basically contradictory to the essential concept of sovereignty. But we must take a more sophisticated view of reality. It would be a serious error to think of "sovereignty" as an absolute rather than a relative concept.

In actual fact, the notion of "sovereignty" with respect to a state is closely analogous to the notion of "freedom" with respect to an individual. "Freedom" is of course a marvelous abstraction: it expresses the deepest and most sublime human aspirations toward individual autonomy, discretion, and self-determination. Every rational human being desires to have as much freedom for himself or herself as is conceivably possible. But at the same time, every rational human being also recognizes the many practical and unavoidable constraints which must restrain autonomy, discretion, and self-determination. Some of these constraints are imposed by nature: human beings cannot fly like birds, they cannot breathe water like fish, they require food, drink, and shelter to survive, and despite their best personal efforts to implement the instinct of self-preservation indefinitely, they are all eventually subject to the physical dissolution of death. Some of these constraints are imposed by economic realities: the person of average means, even in the most prosperous nations, is not able to live in a large mansion on an extensive estate, is not able to eat steak and lobster every day, is not able to take six-month tours around the world. Some constraints are imposed by the social enforcement system: theft, rape, murder, and many other actions that may appeal to certain persons at certain times, will normally eventuate in confinement and the Spartan living conditions of prisons. Some constraints are imposed by the political system: even in the most democratic polity, no individual citizen can autonomously specify who shall be the head of state—such as himself/herself or some close friend or relative.

Such constraints, however, do not constitute flat contradictions to a sensible understanding of freedom. It is fully sensible to interpret "freedom" as involving simply a *substantial amount* of personal autonomy, discretion, and self-determination—even if that amount is indeed far short of what could be imagined. We may certainly think of ourselves as free, even though we may be subject to physical limitations and mortality, even though we may be able to afford only a relatively modest standard of living, even though we must avoid criminal behavior or suffer the consequences, even though our own personal influence in determining the social leadership may be minimal. It is the same thing with national sovereignty—or in more general terms, with any type of state sovereignty. Just as it is possible to legitimately describe a person as free even though there may be many practical constraints operative upon his or her individual autonomy, discretion, and self-determination, so too it is possible to legitimately describe a state as sovereign even though there may be various practical constraints on the power and authority of that state, and even though that state must share the loyalty of its citizens with other state entities.

A realistic appreciation of history and contemporary civilization clearly manifests that "state sovereignty," whether that state is a nation-state or some other form such as an empire or a city-state, is in fact significantly limited both internally and externally. Internally, the government cannot ignore the interests and desires of its citizens, or it runs the risk of being ousted by election or overturned by revolution. The externally imposed limitations on the sovereign power are just as important. Throughout human history, the exercise of sovereign power has frequently brought various states into armed conflict with one another, and the possibility of armed conflict constitutes a major constraint on their autonomy, discretion, and self-determination. No national government can afford to entirely disregard the strong national interests of other national governments—sovereignty or no sovereignty. All this is not to deny the existence and significance of the concept of sovereignty. It is rather merely to point out that in practice, sovereignty does not imply absolute and unlimited power.

The political unification of all or most of today's nations within a properly designed federal world government would not entail abrogation of national sovereignty. It would, of course, involve some additional limitations on national sovereignty beyond those that exist today. But these would be reasonable and appropriate additional limitations, and they would apply to all member nations alike. In return, the national populations would reap significant material and psychological advantages from living in a more secure and prosperous world than we have today.

## Internationalist Tendencies.

The proposed Federal Union of Democratic Nations would be an exercise in international cooperation—a very innovative, fundamental and important exercise to be sure—but different only in degree, rather than in substance, from the myriad of past exercises in international cooperation. Throughout all recorded history and into the modern era, there has been a plethora of treaties and alliances among sovereign and independent governments. In the modern era, most of these sovereign and independent governments have been governments of nation-states as we know them today. Each one of these treaties and alliances may be regarded, to a greater or lesser extent, as an exercise in international cooperation, and as imposing various constraints and obligations on the signatory nations. As such, each one of them provides a precedent for the proposed Federal Union of Democratic Nations. Treaties and alliances are closely connected, especially in the sense that most alliances are formalized by means of a treaty. But the distinction is that a treaty is a formal agreement among nations regarding some specific issue, signed and ratified at some specific point in time, while an alliance is a formal association among nations for the purpose of jointly pursuing the common interests of the member nations over some more or less prolonged period of time.

Aside from peace treaties such as those ratified at the Congress of Vienna (1814-1815) following the Napoleonic Wars, and the Treaty of Versailles (1919) following World War I, there are several other types of treaties. General agreements on the conduct of war include the Declaration of Paris (1856), the First Geneva Convention (1864), the second Geneva Convention (1906), the Third Geneva Convention (1929), the 1930 protocol on submarine warfare, the 1948 expanded Geneva conventions on protection of civilians, treatment of prisoners of war, relief of wounded and sick in field armies, and extension to maritime warfare, and the supplementary protocols of 1977 extending the Geneva conventions to wars of national liberation and civil wars. General agreements on the protection of intellectual property include the Paris Convention for the Protection of Industrial Property (1883, with subsequent revisions in 1925, 1958, and 1967), the European Patent Convention (1973), the Berne Copyright Convention (1886, with subsequent revisions in 1896, 1908, 1928, 1948, 1967 and 1971), and the Universal Copyright Convention (1952, revised 1971). General agreements on nuclear and other weapons of mass destruction include the Nuclear Test-Ban Treaty (1963), the Nuclear Non-Proliferation Treaty (1968), the Treaty on Control of Arms on the Seabed (1971), the Convention on the Prohibition and Destruction of Bacteriological Weapons (1971), and the Convention on the Prohibition of Military or Any Other Hostile Use of Environmental Modification Techniques (1976). Agreements on scientific, space and environmental cooperation include the Antarctic Treaty (1959, expanded in 1972 and 1978), the International Telecommunications Satellite Agreement (1964), the Outer Space Treaty (1966), the European Space Agency Agreement (1975), the Bilateral U.S.-Soviet Space Cooperation Agreement (1977), the Convention against Marine Pollution (1972), the Convention for the Prevention of Marine Pollution from Land-Based Sources (1974), the various IMCO (Intergovernmental Maritime Consultative Organization) conventions on marine pollution (1954, 1969, 1972, and 1973), the various agreements developed by the International Whaling Commission established by the International Convention on the Regulation of Whaling (1946). All of these illustrative treaties and agreements remain in effect today, although in some cases a significant number of nations have not subscribed to them.

Treaties represent an effort to create among nations the equivalent of a legal contract among individuals or organizations within nations. They differ from domestic contracts mainly in that the enforcement mechanism is relatively vague, indirect and weak. If a domestic contract is breached, the aggrieved party may bring suit in a civil court, and if the judgment of the court is in favor of the plaintiff, there exists a strong enforcement system. A defendant who ignores a court judgment indefinitely will eventually be arrested and imprisoned. The court decision can thus be imposed effectively on individual culprits. In the case of a treaty entered into by a nation, on the other hand, the treaty may be disregarded or repudiated by that nation at almost any time, and it is most unlikely that the national government officials responsible for this will soon be imprisoned, fined, or otherwise personally punished for what amounts to breach of contract. One of the most dramatic treaty repudiations of the twentieth century was the repudiation of the Treaty of Versailles by the Nazi-controlled German national government in the 1930s. Several high officials of the German national government of the 1930s were eventually hanged in the aftermath of World War II, but this was not for the transgression of treaty repudiation, but rather for crimes against humanity committed during the war.

In a word, treaties among nations, unlike domestic contracts within nations, are non-binding agreements which may be cancelled at any time by any participant. It would be a gross exaggeration, however, to say that international treaties are therefore "meaningless." Any national government that flagrantly disregards a treaty obligation puts itself at a certain amount of risk—albeit that risk is not as strong and direct as the risk incurred by an individual or organization within a nation that flagrantly disregards a formal legal contract. Other parties to the treaty may retaliate in some way against the errant nation; in the extreme case, war may result. The fact that a given nation enters into any treaties at all is evidence of the core reality that it cannot heedlessly pursue its own interests but must rather take into some account the interests of other nations. If a given nation were truly all-powerful, it would not have to enter any treaties at all—it would merely "rule the world" by military force. Of course, ruling an unwilling and uncooperative world by military force would not be a cost-free proposition. Even if it were possible to achieve global military domination temporarily, the costs of the military forces necessary to maintain such control would quite likely outweigh the material benefits forthcoming from the control.

One of the most important examples in the contemporary world of an international treaty is the European Union. In fact, some have perceived in this organization a prototype for world government. Although the E.U. does in fact provide a certain amount of indirect support for the practicality of a limited world government along the lines of the Federal Union of Democratic Nations, it is important that the degree of support not be exaggerated. The circumstances and development of the European Union are a far cry from the circumstances and development of a potential future world government.

From its humble beginnings in 1951 as a limited customs union designated the European Coal and Steel Community (ECSC), at which time it contained only six member nations (Belgium, Germany, France, Italy, Luxembourg, and the Netherlands), the European Union evolved into an extremely important quasi-state political organization encompassing no less than 27 European nations as of 2010.[7] Only Switzerland and Norway, of the core Western European nations, are not yet included. Eventually the E.U. may encompass additional ex-republics of the Soviet Union, even the Russian Federation itself. It may encompass the Muslim nation of Turkey, already a candidate member. Of all the regional organizations in the world, it is clearly the most fully advanced, and indeed, it is beginning to strongly resemble the old "United States of Europe" concept long prevalent in the visionary literature on international organization.

On the other hand, there have always been centrifugal forces operating toward the dissolution of the European Union. These forces came into sharper focus in 2016 when a British referendum approved, by a narrow margin, British withdrawal from the E.U. (the so-called Brexit—for "British exit"). Although the terms of the withdrawal have not yet been determined, speculation has become rife that other member nations will also choose to depart the Union.

The objectives of the European statesmen who founded the European Coal and Steel Community were hardly confined to reaping whatever relatively modest economic benefits may be derived from a customs union for coal and steel products. In actual fact, these economic benefits were secondary and incidental. The main purpose was to initiate a process that would eventually lead to a much higher level of political unity within the European continent, for purposes of erecting both practical and psychological barriers against the resumption of the perpetual internecine conflict and warfare that had plagued Europe throughout its history. Those responsible for the concept and design of the ECSC, Jean Monnet and Robert Schuman of France, and the many European statesmen who thereupon implemented it, such as Paul-Henri Spaak of Belgium, Konrad Adenauer of Germany, and many others, had lived through the horrors of both World War I and World War II. On the basis of this personal experience, they were determined to exert every effort toward preventing a recurrence of these catastrophes.

Since the origin of the European Union lay in a mere customs union, it is tempting to interpret its development as functional cooperation evolving into political unity. There is some truth in this, and certainly the history of the European Union in some respects strengthens the case for world government, as well as providing lessons on how that government should be organized and what it should attempt to accomplish. But it is important not to exaggerate either the degree of support or the usefulness of the lessons. Obviously the European continent during the latter half of the twentieth century was not an accurate microcosm of the world as a whole as it exists at the present time. As far as the attainment of political unity is concerned, Europe had certain key advantages, including relatively homogeneous economic development and culture.

On the other hand, it is important to recognize that Europe also had some significant disadvantages, most prominently the psychological residue from centuries of internal conflict and warfare. Physical proximity may increase the practical need for functional cooperation, but it also lays a firmer basis for confrontation and conflict. Especially when viewed in light of what happened in Europe during the first half of the twentieth century, what was accomplished there during the second half of the twentieth century seems truly remarkable.

In its current form, the European Union is composed of a number of separate entities, of which the most important are the European Commission, the Council of Ministers, the European Parliament, and the Court of Justice. The major force within the Union is the European Commission, consisting of 27 commissioners, all appointed by the national governments of the member nations, supported by a staff numbering approximately 40,000. It has both legislative and executive responsibilities: not only does it conceive and draft legislation for submission to the Council of Ministers and the European Parliament, but it also oversees the enforcement of approved E.U. legislation. The Council of Ministers consists of the ministers of each of the member nations broken down by functional area: for example, one sub-group consists of the finance ministers, another of the education ministers, and so on. The European Parliament consists of several hundred delegates, with the distribution of delegates over the member nations in proportion to population. Neither the Council of Ministers nor the European Parliament has the formal authority to revise or veto legislation proposed by the European Commission.

However, the commission is normally responsive to input received from these bodies on proposed legislation. It is responsive to the parliament since the parliament possesses the formal authority to dismiss the commission as a whole (although so far this has never happened), and it must also approve the president of the commission who, once approved, selects the other commissioners. As for the Council of Ministers, if opposition to legislation among this group is sufficiently intense, the implementation of the legislation could conceivably lead to the departure of some nations from the union (this also has not happened so far). Assuming legislation is approved by all three bodies (the commission, the council and the parliament) it can still be challenged by member nations, organizations, or individuals before the Court of Justice. Although called a "treaty," the Treaty on European Union is in some respects the equivalent of a constitution. "Constitutional" challenges to union legislation, as well as other disputes, are decided by the Court of Justice.

Although the customs union and the efforts toward homogenization and unification of the entire internal market have had an extremely beneficial effect on the material prosperity of most Europeans, not every European has benefited from the transformations. To begin with, whenever and wherever customs duties and other trade restrictions are lowered, at least a few of the industries exposed to greater foreign competition go into serious decline. In the process of homogenizing innumerable commercial rules and regulations, as well as a multitude of social, educational, and other institutions and legislation, a great many Europeans have been at the least inconvenienced and at the most completely ruined. All this leads periodically to ugly street protests and demonstrations. The intensity of the opposition is all the greater because in the view of those who have lost out in the process, all these intolerable aggravations and impositions are owing to the misguided and malevolent machinations of nasty foreigners. Even among the large majority of the population that has been materially benefited by the European Union's policies, there are vague anxieties and apprehensions, no less acute for being hazy and indistinct, that somehow one's own national identity and sovereignty will be completely submerged and lost. In a sense, the experience of the European Union provides as much guidance as to what a potential world government *should not* do, as it does what such a government *should* do.

To the rest of the world unfamiliar with the details of its history and current status, the European Union sometimes appears to be a blandly monolithic expression of a unified public will. But the fact is that the development of the European Union has been accompanied by problems and controversies every step of the way. Not too much confidence should be placed in the predictions of some to the effect that the European Union will soon be a United States of Europe in no fundamental respect different from its cousin across the North Atlantic Ocean, the United States of America. This could eventually happen, of course, but there is still a long distance between the E.U. and a potential USE (United States of Europe) of the future. Our interest in the future direction of the European Union, however, is only incidental to our interest in international organization at the global level, specifically in the idea of world government. What bearing, if any, does the European Union have on the prospects for a genuine, functioning world government in the future?

The foundation and subsequent success of the European Union has clearly established that even very large and powerful nations with proud traditions of absolute independence, and long histories of bitter enmity punctuated at regular intervals by desperate warfare, may be induced to forget the past and surrender a substantial proportion of their autonomy and sovereignty—when there exist compelling economic and political reasons for doing so. However, we must also recognize the fact that from the beginnings of the European Union, the economic status of its component nations has been relatively homogeneous. The difference in per capita income between the richest member nations of the European Union and the poorest member nations has always been a small fraction of the difference between the richest nations of the First World and the poorest nations of the Third World. In a word, the European Union never confronted the very difficult economic impediment to political union that federal world government on a global basis has always confronted, and continues to confront. In addition, throughout the development era of the European Union its member nations have been relatively homogeneous ideologically, politically, and culturally—if not linguistically.

While the European Union, over its several decades of development, has gone a remarkable way toward a unified economy, meaningful political unification is still a long way off. The European Parliament, although directly elected since 1979, still cannot promulgate legislation. Effective legislative and executive power in the E.U. is exercised by a commission whose members are appointed by the national governments rather than being directly elected. The European Union, as such, cannot levy mandatory taxes on member states or their populations, nor does it directly control either a military force or a police force of its own. Although many of the Western European nations comprising the European Union are members of the NATO alliance, their military forces are still very much under the independent control of the various national governments. Considering the amount of dissension and protest that certain of the Union's policies have elicited in some of its member nations, it is rather remarkable how much effective power the E.U. apparently exercises, despite its lack of any military or police power. There is no military or police deterrent to member nations simply ignoring E.U. policies. The main deterrent to such behavior is the threat that the recalcitrant nation will be expelled from the E.U. and will no longer partake of the economic, political, and psychological benefits membership entails. But the desire for these various benefits does not necessarily translate into the emotional allegiance known as "patriotism."

A significant divisive factor within the European Union, as it exists today, is the lack of a common language. Most nations in the contemporary world either have a common language, or at least a dominant language. Countries such as Canada with its two official languages, and Switzerland with its three, are exceptions to the rule. The two meganations in the contemporary world in terms of population, China and India, both deal with a multitude of local languages and dialects. But there are only two dominant languages in China (Mandarin and Cantonese), and similarly only two dominant languages in India (Hindi and English). Almost all of the nations incorporated into the European Union, on the other hand, have their own common language: France has French, Germany has German, Italy has Italian, Britain has English, the Netherlands has Dutch, and so it goes. All of these languages have well-developed literatures and are an integral part of the culture and identity of their respective nations.

To the extent that there is a de facto common language in the E.U. countries, it is English, the same de facto common language that holds throughout the world. If an educated German and an educated Italian wish to converse with one another, most likely they will have to do so in English, the same as if they were an educated Indonesian and an educated Italian. Lack of a common language divides Germans and Italians in the same way it does Indonesians and Italians. Like it or not, language is a divisive factor that impedes the progress of European patriotism, and reduces the likelihood that the European Union will evolve, anytime within the foreseeable future, into a United States of Europe equivalent to the United States of America.

## The Heterogeneity Bugaboo

During most of the second half of the twentieth century, human civilization teetered precariously over the abyss of nuclear Armageddon thanks to an ideologically fueled geopolitical confrontation between the communist and noncommunist blocs of nations. Even during that perilous Cold War period, a limited world government along the lines of the proposed Federal Union of Democratic Nations would have been possible (above all, because member nations would have been able to retain their own independent armed forces), and had such a federation been formed, the better communication and closer cooperation it would have facilitated might well have hastened the end of the Cold War and thereby reduced the terrible threat of instantaneous nuclear holocaust to which humanity had been exposed. But neither the intelligentsia nor the political leadership possessed sufficient vision to perceive the possibility. Instead, assuming that a world state must necessarily be omnipotent and claim a monopoly on large-scale armed force and weapons of mass destruction, the intelligentsia and the political leadership dismissed the possibility of world government on grounds that if the "other side" got control of such a government, they would immediately impose their odious economic and political system on "our side." This assessment was common to both sides: noncommunist and communist. During the Cold War, therefore, the ideological gap was perceived as the primary impediment to world government.

Now that the ideological gap of the Cold War appears dead, and will hopefully never arise again from its grave to haunt humanity, the primary impediment to world government is the economic gap: the tremendous gulf that has opened up between economic living standards in the richest nations and those in the poorest nations. Not that this fact is explicitly recognized and openly acknowledged by either the general public or international relations experts. The latter speak of "heterogeneities" within the human population and the "lack of shared values," while the former are instinctively appalled by the notion that "foreigners" will gain any sort of meaningful control over their lives. Perhaps it is simply too crassly materialistic for the peoples of the rich nations to confess their fear of a global welfare state that will economically despoil them, and for the peoples of the poor nations to confess their fear that the re-imposition of colonial-style exploitation will economically despoil them. Both prefer to think that their apprehensions regarding world government are based on something higher than "mere economic self-interest."

Be that as it may, if we dig down past various superficial rationalizations, it is fairly apparent that the North-South economic gap has now replaced the East-West ideological gap as the primary impediment to world government. Certain fundamental characteristics of the proposed Federal Union of Democratic Nations are designed to cope with the situation, most importantly, the dual voting system in the Union legislature, and the retained national rights to withdraw from the Union and to maintain independent military forces. These are short-term expedients, to enable the world government to be established and to commence functioning. In the long term, the only way to remove the economic gap as an impediment to successful world government, is to remove the economic gap itself—or at least drastically reduce it. This would be the goal of the proposed Global Marshall Plan (GMP) under the direction of a World Development Authority (WDA), an agency of the Federal Union. During its early decades, the top priority of the Federal Union should be pursuit of the global economic equalization effort to a satisfactory conclusion.

Although the existence of large economic differentials among the nations of the world is the primary impediment to successful world government at the present time, there are certain other impediments that need to be considered in assessing the practicality of world government. In a very general sense, any distinction at all within the human species can be perceived as an impediment to political unification. Among the most important of these distinctions are race, language, culture, religion, and nationality. Obviously, some of these impediments are more serious than others. But I would argue that even the most serious of them do not constitute a significant obstacle to federal world government, as long as the envisioned federal world government is properly limited and constrained. The Federal Union of Democratic Nations blueprint under consideration in this book is in fact "properly limited and constrained."

The issue of nationalism has already been considered in an earlier section of this chapter. The fact that race and language, in and of themselves, are not particularly serious obstacles to political unity, is clearly suggested by the many examples of successful nations that are quite diverse in terms of race and language. China and India are probably the most dramatic examples of very large nations within which there are numerous different languages and dialects spoken by substantial proportions of the populations. With respect to race, the United States "melting pot" is probably the single most important evidence that may be cited that considerable racial diversity is not necessarily an insuperable obstacle to political unity. The principal minorities in the U.S. are blacks, Asians, and Latinos. Of these, Latinos are not sufficiently different in a physical sense from white Caucasians to constitute a "racial" minority. The presence of a substantial black racial minority in the United States today is the result of 400 years of slavery, an institution that represents the greatest historical stain by far upon the honor of the nation. It would be a gross misrepresentation of reality to claim that full racial equality of whites and blacks has been achieved in the contemporary United States. However, it would be equally blind to reality not to acknowledge the very considerable progress that has been made in this direction, as exemplified, for example, by the election to the U.S. Presidency of Barack Obama. The examples of China and India, among many others, show that linguistic diversity is not a serious obstacle to world government. The example of the United States, among many others, shows that racial diversity is also not a serious obstacle to world government.

Turning now to culture, we should recognize and acknowledge that most "cultural differences" are quite harmless. What difference does it make that one person prefers classical music by great composers such as Bach, Beethoven, and Brahms, while another person prefers heavy metal rock and roll as provided by AC/DC, Iron Maiden, and Motorhead? What difference does it make that one person prefers representational painting by great masters such as Rembrandt and Monet, while another person prefers abstract paintings by modern artists such as Hoffmann and Pollack? There is an overwhelming variety of diverse musical and artistic expressions available to people in the modern world, not to mention literary and cinematic expressions. Most people relish the abundance of choice and revel in the amazing diversity. While devotees of some of these expressions may experience a certain amount of distaste and distain for devotees of other expressions, it seems absurd to suggest that cultural differences of this sort could provide a significant basis for intense hostility and physical conflict within and between organized groups.

## Religion

When we come to religion, however—often deemed to be an important component of culture—clearly the situation is not as favorable. The horrific events of September 11, 2001, were instigated by Islamic extremists who were obviously motivated, to some extent, by religious enthusiasm. The 9/11 horror demonstrated that religiously aggravated hostility and conflict is hardly extinct in the modern world, despite the general advance of secularism. That event was a particularly dramatic example of a phenomenon that has often appeared elsewhere in the world. For example, India continues to be disturbed on a regular basis by Hindu-Muslim riots. For another example, despite decades of "progress toward peace" in Northern Ireland, violence still occasionally erupts between Catholics and Protestants. Indeed, the matter of religion is sufficiently serious to be worth more extended discussion than that accorded to the more innocuous cultural differences mentioned above.

Prior to the rise in modern history of "secular ideologies" promoting such ideas as democracy and socialism, "religious ideologies" promoting various belief systems such as Christianity, Islam, Buddhism, Hinduism, etc., were very prevalent in human society and human history. The fundamental characteristic of any ideology, whether it be secular or religious, is that the validity of its various propositions (democracy is preferable to oligarchy, Christianity is ordained by God, etc.) cannot be confirmed or refuted by any sort of logical argument or empirical evidence. At the same time, these propositions have a strong bearing on individual welfare, social welfare, or both. Subscribing to the "wrong" religion can cause a person to suffer eternal damnation to the fires of hell. Living under the "wrong" political or economic system can severely limit the achieved level of individual welfare. The combination of critical importance with irreducible uncertainty endows ideological issues with strong emotional overtones. The existence of people who believe otherwise than oneself on these issues inspires in any normal person emotions of dread, anger, and hostility. But sensible people recognize that in the normal course of events, no good can come of such emotions, and that the thoughts that inspire these emotions—namely thoughts about ideological issues—should be suppressed to the maximum extent possible.

The reason why such thoughts should ordinarily be suppressed is that hostility leads to violence and warfare, and history has repeatedly shown that ideologically fueled warfare rarely results in the complete annihilation of those with opposed ideological beliefs. And of course warfare cannot, of its nature, lead to any sort of clarification or resolution concerning the truth or falsity of ideological beliefs themselves. In this sense warfare is futile, despite enormous human and material costs. This lesson has been fairly well absorbed by humanity—although obviously not fully absorbed. Most nations of today exercise some degree of toleration for religious diversity, to a greater or lesser extent as the case may be. Even a "theocracy" such as contemporary Iran does not forbid adherents of non-Islamic religions from setting foot in Iran. A few contrary cases such as Iran aside, the vast majority of national governments today recognize the importance of religious toleration and endeavor to uphold it to the extent possible, given the intolerant attitudes of many of their citizens. Almost everywhere in the world, religious toleration and freedom is perceived as an ideal and a desirable goal to be pursued.

Against this background, it need hardly be emphasized that it is absolutely vital that religious freedom be recognized in the Union Constitution as a "fundamental human right," and that the Federal Union be constitutionally prohibited from passing laws or pursuing policies that favor any one religion over any other. It is not simply a matter of forbidding an established church; rather there must be erected a very high, very strong "wall of separation" between the state and any one religion or group of religions. In some ways this will be easier for the world government to accomplish than it has been for the national governments. This is because the amount of religious diversity over the entire world is much greater than the amount of religious diversity within any one nation. In many if not most nations, one religion has become dominant: for example, Christianity in the United States. Thus there might be a tendency in the U.S. toward extending various favors and benefits toward this religion and not toward others. On the other hand, very general religious categories such as "Christianity" frequently subsume numerous divisions and subdivisions that are very much opposed to each other. In such cases, there is less likelihood of special favors and benefits being extended by the state to any one religious group. At the world level, there is no single religion, even defined very generally, that has achieved such dominance that the world government would be inclined toward favoring it.

Probably the most obvious, dramatic and historically prolonged case of religiously inflamed conflict and warfare has been between Islam and Christianity. The founder of Islam, Mohammed (c. 570-632), was himself no stranger to the role of armed force in religious conversion, and immediately upon his death his successors initiated one of the greatest eras of military conquest in the history of the world, extending far to the east into Persia and India, and far to the west along the north African coast into present-day Spain. This era extended from the death of Mohammed in 632 a full 100 years until the defeat of the Moorish Arabs at Poitiers in 732. The Christian reaction, in the form of the Crusades, covered an even longer period from the launching of the first Crusade in 1096 to the fall of the Kingdom of Jerusalem in 1291. Another era of Muslim expansionism was the rise of the Ottoman empire centered in Turkey. The high point of the Ottoman empire in western Europe was the siege of Vienna (1529), which was broken more by harsh winter weather and the length of the Ottoman supply lines than Hapsburg military action. More recently, the foundation of Israel within Muslim Palestine (1948), has once again inflamed Islamic sensitivities in the Mideast, and has generated no less than four full-fledged Arab-Israeli wars, in addition to numerous Muslim terrorist attacks inflicted on the rest of the world, most notably the 9/11 attack that destroyed the World Trade Center and killed thousands of people. Looking at this unfortunate history, there are some who assert a "clash of civilizations" between Islam and the other major religions, especially the Judeo-Christian, that can only culminate in the destruction of one side or the other.

Such a bleakly pessimistic view is completely unjustified. Although there are indeed some hair-raising passages in the Koran justifying and indeed glorifying warfare between Muslims and various "infidels," these passages need not be taken any more seriously than various passages in the Old Testament of the Bible proclaiming the Israelites as "God's chosen people," and urging them on to the conquest and subjugation of their various enemies. Close reading of the Koran passages about killing infidels indicates that such killing is justified on self-defense grounds in the course of warfare with non-believers. Moreover, there are various admonitions in the Koran toward humane treatment of infidels living peacefully within Muslim societies. There are no urgings in the Koran toward what we would today identify as "genocidal" behavior toward infidels—albeit admittedly resident infidels are to be subjected to adverse discrimination in the form of special taxes.

Although history tends to concentrate on violent episodes because they are inherently more interesting than peaceful periods, we should not lose sight of the fact that there were many hundreds of years, between the various wars between Christian and Muslim societies, during which Christians and Muslims practiced peaceful coexistence. For example, Islamic societies welcomed Christian pilgrims to the holy places of Christianity within their borders for the same reason that nations today welcome tourists from abroad—they bring in foreign exchange and help local businesses to flourish. Furthermore, history records numerous vicious wars among different Christian societies, as well as among different Muslim societies. For more than 100 years following Martin Luther's initiation of the Protestant alternative to Roman Catholicism, Europe was beset by a series of religiously fueled wars and civil wars, culminating in the devastating Thirty Years' War from 1618 to 1648. Most of the wars associated with the Islamic empires were among various sultans all of whom nominally accepted the teachings of Mohammed—just as all the wars of modern Europe, up to and including World War II, were among various nations all of whom nominally subscribed to the teachings of Jesus Christ. In fact, it would be quite difficult to argue from the historical record that there has been any greater propensity toward Christian vs. Muslim war, than toward Christian vs. Christian war or Muslim vs. Muslim war. It would appear that Muslims and Christians are no more fore-ordained to inevitable violent conflict than are, for example, Catholics and Protestants, or proponents of socialism and proponents of capitalism.

With respect to the original Muslim jihad following the death of Mohammed, most historians are inclined to rate the influence of religious zeal on campaigns of imperial conquest as relatively minor. The Greeks and the Romans built their empires through conquest, and their motivation ran to the acquisition of wealth and power on the earthly plane, not to increasing their chances of pleasing God and getting into heaven. The same could be said of the barbarian invasions that overthrew the Roman empire, and the Mongol campaigns that subjugated much of the known world from eastern Europe in the west to China in the east. The European reaction to the Islamic conquests, after an interval of over three hundred years, came in the form of the Crusades. When Urban II preached the First Crusade in 1095, he placed much emphasis on the reward of eternal salvation for liberating Jerusalem from "the heavy yoke of the Turk"—but he also mentioned prominently the potential material spoils of war as an incentive for signing on. Spiritual rewards alone were too nebulous to justify a risky war of conquest. Campaigns of materialistically inspired imperial expansion are not confined to the distant past: the most recent large-scale example being the Nazi effort to establish a Eurasian empire under German control, an effort thwarted by the outcome of World War II. No religious motivations were involved in that event, although Hitler endeavored to enlist secular ideological support for the 1941 invasion of the USSR by alleging that the principal purpose of the invasion was the preservation of European culture against unholy Bolshevism.

New religions are coming along all the time, and only rarely do they quickly get mixed up in wars of expansion. It may well have been an accident of history that the Islamic religion played such a large part in the Arab conquests of 632-732. A campaign of conquest was already brewing, and the new religion merely intensified the campaign. Mohammed was recently deceased, his religion was new and his disciples few in number and highly enthusiastic. No one outside what is now Saudi Arabia had ever heard of Mohammed and his religion. Thus what might have been perceived simply as the "wars of Arab imperial conquest" became the "wars of Islamic expansion." As the Arab armies marched across North Africa and up into Spain, they probably perceived their Islamic religion as a handy tool for establishing control over various peoples and regions. In their view, they were offering the keys to the kingdom to prospective co-religionists and subjects. To the extent that prospective subjects could be persuaded that the teachings of Mohammed offered a sure path to personal salvation, they would be less inspired to resistance. The role of the Islamic religion in the Arab wars of imperial conquest was arguably quite analogous to the role of the Christian religion in the Iberian wars of imperial conquest in Central and South America. To the extent that the indigenous American Indians could be made into docile Christians, there was less risk of disruptive rebellions against the Spanish and Portuguese empires.

Fortunately for the cause of contemporary global human civilization, Islamic jihadists in the image of Osama bin Laden constitute a tiny fraction of the Muslim population of the world. If this particular pathological infection becomes too widespread in the future, of course, it will cause disastrous warfare throughout the world. But it would be the same if Christian fundamentalism, or nationalistic separatism, or communist fanaticism were to become too widespread. In 1095, Christian fundamentalism (of a sort) generated the Crusades. In 1914, Serbian nationalistic separatism motivated the assassination of Archduke Franz Ferdinand that plunged human civilization into World War I. The Cold War that nearly precipitated a nuclear World War III was fueled by communist fanaticism. There is nothing particularly unique about the Islamic fanaticism that inspired 9/11 and thereby led to the ensuing events. We can only hope that just as Christian fundamentalists, nationalistic separatists, and communist fanatics have not thus far precipitated the downfall of humanity, the same will be true of Islamic jihadists. Sensible Muslims throughout the world can see for themselves, in the aftermath of 9/11, the folly of jihadist actions against the United States and the other major Western nations. That terrorist attack led directly to the invasion of two Muslim nations (Afghanistan and Iraq), the overthrow of their national governments, and the deaths of tens of thousands of Muslims, many if not most of them innocent bystanders. Unless jihadist terrorist actions somehow embroil the Western nations in conflicts among themselves, they will probably do more harm to Muslims than to Christians.

Most people think of the various differences of opinion among humanity (e.g., whether the supreme being should be referred to as Yahweh, God, Allah, etc.) as an obstacle to world government. But in the past these same differences were an obstacle to the formation of large nation-states, and yet history records that large nation-states nevertheless came about. An important reason for large-scale political unions is that of discouraging and suppressing the violent conflicts that these differences of opinion often engender among people under conditions where there is no higher authority. That argument is as valid today with respect to supernational government as it was in the past with respect to national governments. A world government would certainly not abrogate these differences in religious opinion—nor would we want everyone in the world to think alike anyway. The important thing is simply that differences of religious opinion not generate armed conflict.

Thus to reiterate, it is essential that the Federal Union refrain from any laws or actions that might be perceived as favoring or disfavoring any specific religion. But this does not imply that the Federal Union should necessarily oppose all such laws and actions within specific member nations. Among the complaints heard about world government is that it would be intolerant of cultural diversity, and would attempt to suppress it by various direct and indirect means. But most cultural differences, in and of themselves, present no problem for world government. The world government would have no incentive, for example, to try to suppress certain types of music (e.g., heavy metal rock and roll) in order to foster other types (e.g., classical music by Bach and Beethoven). Students of culture usually include religion as a very important component of any cultural system. Some cultural customs have a religious basis: for example, the reason why Saudi Arabian women have to cover their faces in public is that the Koran prescribes this—at least in the view of fundamentalists. Some such customs may seem perverse and dysfunctional to people of other cultures. They may seem like a violation of the separation of church and state principle, to the extent that religious documents and doctrines are the basis for these customs. But if the world government were to oppose such customs, even just verbally, this might be interpreted as a form of oppression to people of cultures that value these customs.

The fundamental guarantee that the world government would not oppress any given nation in cultural and/or religious terms, whether that nation be primarily Christian, Islamic, or whatever, is the retained right of member nations to withdraw from the union at their unilateral discretion, along with the right to independent military forces. In the interest of the stability of the world federation, it would be advisable to maintain a high degree of flexibility on culturally oriented church-state issues within member nations. For example, if an Islamic nation wants to prescribe that only mullahs can hold political office in the national government, or to require that women keep their faces covered in public, then so be it. The Federal Union Constitution should specify clearly that the supernational government shall take no action against national customs, so long as these customs do not infringe on basic human rights.

Possibly a line might have to be drawn on some very important issues. For example, it may not be permissible for member nations to impose special taxes on citizens who do not subscribe to the majority religion. Such provisions might cause that nation to be expelled from the Union, or prevent it from joining in the first place. But complete church-state separation at the national level is probably unrealistic. For example, in most Christian nations, Christmas is recognized as a national holiday—yet it is clearly a religious observance in terms of its traditional underpinnings. Non-Christians might complain that declaring a religious observance a national holiday constitutes an impermissible church-state connection. Most Christians would argue that such complaints should be ignored, on grounds that Christmas has become a secularized holiday, and in any event no fundamental human rights are being violated. Analogous arguments could be made in defense of many other religiously inspired customs of certain nations that seem strange to the people of other nations. Clearly, with respect to such matters, a reasonable degree of toleration and flexibility is essential.

# 7

# Should It Be Done?

## A Scientific Approach

Proponents of major social policy innovations in the past have tended to be extremely confident that the benefits of these innovations would far outweigh the costs. If they had any doubts on the matter, they kept these doubts to themselves. They argued the virtues of their proposals with an enthusiasm bordering on fanaticism, and dismissed critics and opponents as either mental incompetents or hypocrites in the pay of "vested interests." If they were heeded and their proposals implemented, then, normally, unanticipated and undesirable consequences would quickly surface, so that the net benefits of the transition would be less than expected, sometimes far less than expected.

In some cases, the proposed cure was indubitably far worse than the disease. One thinks immediately of Karl Marx, who proclaimed the socialist millennium with all the faith and zeal that one normally associates with religious fanatics. Within a few decades of Marx's death, what should have been the workers' paradise of the Soviet Union was transformed into a totalitarian nightmare presided over by Joseph Stalin, who may not have been a monster as a young man, but who had certainly evolved into one by the time of his death. No doubt Stalin, who died comfortably enough of old age in 1953, after slaughtering millions of his own countrymen, never experienced any significant self-doubt. No doubt he convinced himself that his own personal survival and continued undisputed leadership of the Soviet Union was hastening the glorious socialist millennium promised by Karl Marx. From the ideas and idealism of Karl Marx to the concentration camps and firing squads of Joseph Stalin—such can be the disastrous outcome of sympathetic concern for all humanity and innovative social thinking.

As a result of the real-world disaster initiated by the social theories and prescriptions of Karl Marx, as well as a host of similar experiences throughout human history, a large proportion of both the intelligentsia and the general human population have today lapsed into unimaginative conservatism and thoughtless opposition to almost any significant social transformation. This is most unfortunate, since continued social innovation and progress is probably no less important to the further development of human civilization, and to the further enhancement of individual human existence, than continued scientific innovation and progress. However, in light of past history, it is incumbent upon proposers of social innovations to think very carefully about such innovations, to be quite detailed and specific in their formulation, to be quite thorough and balanced in considering possible flaws and problems, and, above all, to be properly circumspect and restrained in presenting the case for these innovations.

Therefore, it needs to be stated here and now, without qualification or equivocation, that no sensible person can be completely certain that the effect of a potential future Global Marshall Plan, or of a potential future Federal Union of Democratic Nations, would be favorable. It is extremely important that if either one or both of these initiatives is actually undertaken in the real world, it should be on a tentative, provisional and experimental basis. It would be useless to deny that a non-negligible possibility exists that a Global Marshall Plan would be a complete failure, that there would be little acceleration in the growth rates of the poor nations and/or a serious decline in the economic status of the rich nations. If that happens (after a reasonable trial period of somewhere between 10 to 20 years), then the program should be cut back drastically or terminated altogether. It would be equally useless to deny that a non-negligible possibility exists that the Federal Union of Democratic Nations might be a complete failure, for a variety of reasons, including continued pursuit of a Global Marshall Plan which is clearly failing to achieve its mission. If that happens (again after a reasonable trial period), nations should withdraw from the Federal Union, until finally, having been reduced to an impotent rump state, the Federal Union voluntarily terminates its own existence. Such a dissolution would be sad and unfortunate, and an ill omen for the future of humanity. But peaceful dissolution would obviously be preferable to violent dissolution.

It is an absolutely central component of this proposal for a world government, therefore, that the world government practice an absolutely pure and unadulterated "open door" policy with respect to membership. The Federal Union must always remain ready to admit new nations to membership in the Union, and it must always remain equally ready to allow member nations to depart from the Union whenever they desire to do so. These principles must be clearly and unequivocally stated in the constitution which establishes the Union. The constitution must not only enshrine the permanent right of each member nation to withdraw from the Union at its own unilateral discretion, but it must also enshrine the permanent right of each member nation to maintain whatever military forces and armaments it desires, including nuclear. These military forces and weapons would provide a practical guarantee and a tangible safeguard for the constitutional right of free secession from the Union. These two interrelated reserved rights of the member nations are essential to the effective initiation of the Federal Union—owing to these reserved rights, a large number of nations, including the larger and more powerful nations, will be willing to join the Union. Conceivably there could even be universal membership by all nations right from the start. Of course, the hope would be that the Federal Union would evolve smoothly and favorably, so that the member nations would become more confident and would gradually reduce the military forces under their direct control. The hope is also that the reserved right of secession would, in due course, become nothing more than an historical curiosity, since the benefits of maintaining membership in the Federal Union would be so clear and compelling to every national population that secession would become virtually unthinkable.

Of course, these hopes might be disappointed. It cannot be assumed that the future evolution of the Federal Union of Democratic Nations would necessarily be smooth and favorable. It is far from impossible that serious problems would in fact emerge, problems so serious that, one after another, the member nations would withdraw from the Union and go their separate ways. Ultimately, the Federal Union might consist of so few member nations that either it will voluntarily terminate its own existence, or else it will have become such a negligible consideration in international relations that it may as well do so. If that happens, then humanity would be back to where we are today—sadder and wiser, but otherwise none the worse for wear.

The preeminent danger of world government, as perceived by most people today, is that the dissolution of such a government would be accompanied by devastating civil war. According to this scenario, the member nations of the world government would become divided into two camps of roughly equal military power: those nations desiring that the Union be maintained, and those nations desiring to depart the Union. Neither camp would be able to intimidate the other into submission, with the result that the two camps would descend into all-out warfare. This scenario extrapolates the historical circumstances of the United States in 1861, at the outbreak of the Civil War, to a potential world government in the future. But this is an inappropriate extrapolation. The Federal Union of Democratic Nations would be founded under very different circumstances from those which obtained at the time of the foundation of the United States of America, and therefore the constitutional framework of the Federal Union of Democratic Nations would be very different from the constitutional framework of the United States of America. Among other things, there would be a far greater appreciation of the danger of civil war, and the constitution of the Federal Union would greatly reduce this danger by means of explicitly and unequivocally guaranteeing to each member nation the permanent and inalienable right to secession at any time. The Federal Union constitution would therefore provide a strong and reliable means for its own peaceful dissolution. If dissolution of the Union did in fact take place, it would not be violent. Of course, dissolution would be an unfortunate outcome, and it would augment the likelihood of devastating international wars in the future. But there would be no violence and warfare directly connected with the dissolution. Or at least, the probability of violence and warfare attending dissolution would be very small.

The formation of a world government along the lines of the proposed Federal Union of Democratic Nations should be looked upon as no more and no less than *a scientific experiment*. Such an experiment is the one and only way we have for achieving truly reliable, convincing and compelling evidence on the potential performance of world government. Whether a world government would be a success or a failure simply cannot be determined, to any reasonably satisfactory level of certitude, by means of theoretical speculations and hypothetical musings based on the past history of human civilization. The current situation is simply too novel, too unprecedented, and too unparalleled for past history to provide more than circumstantial and inconclusive indications. The fact is that the only means by which we may ascertain whether a world state would make a positive contribution to the future development of human civilization is to set up a world state and then observe the outcome. What is needed is not more words but rather experimental *action*.

Whether progress has been achieved, in a fundamental social welfare sense, through the historical evolution of the institutions and operations of human civilization, might be debated by reasonable people. Most of us believe, for example, that the principle of representative democracy does in fact constitute a meaningful advance over the principle of absolute monarchy. But it cannot be proven, in a mathematically or logically rigorous sense, that the average level of human happiness and self-realization is higher today under representative democracy than it was in the past under absolute monarchy. But where historical progress *has* been achieved, surely and incontestably, is in the area of science and technology. It cannot be reasonably disputed that a world in which automobiles and computers exist, is farther along than a world in which these things did not exist. Note that the argument is *not* that automobiles and computers necessarily increase human welfare in any meaningful way (though most of us believe they do). The argument is simply that automobiles and computers represent incontestable scientific and technical advance. And the point is simply that an essential component of scientific and technical advance has always been the experimental method. Throughout the history of science and technology, fruitless abstract disputations over factual propositions have very often been resolved more or less conclusively by means of properly designed laboratory experiments. These disputations could never have been, and would never have been, settled by means of logical argumentation and a priori reasoning, even if that argumentation and reasoning had been continued unto the end of time. In the final analysis, disagreements could only be overcome by making reference to *facts*. Speculations, conjectures, hypotheses, and theories are not necessarily factually accurate. Factual accuracy of abstract propositions can never be compellingly demonstrated in the absence of factual demonstrations. In the absence of experimentation, it is very doubtful that science and technology would ever have been capable of bringing forth such marvels as automobiles and computers.[1]

What this means, in terms of the fundamental thesis of this book, is that we will never be able to compellingly demonstrate either the desirability or the undesirability of federal world government without actually establishing a federal world government. This proposition may seem strange to the reader at first, because neither the proponents nor the opponents of world government in the past have been sufficiently aware of it. Or if they were aware of it, they apparently feared that explicit recognition and discussion of this point would have weakened the case they were attempting to put forward, pro or con, on world government. But upon reflection, the reader will hopefully acknowledge the high level of plausibility which characterizes the proposition. Of course, even if the reader is prepared to assent to the proposition that only a real-world experiment with world government is likely to yield compelling evidence on the performance of world government, he or she might still regard such an experiment as far too risky to be undertaken. What I am attempting to do in this book is to show that a real-world experiment with a *properly designed* world government would not in fact entail excessive risk, especially in view of the great benefits that might be garnered if the experiment is a success.

Of course, it would clearly be dishonest to assert that there would be *absolutely no risk* involved in an experimental foundation of a federal world government, even one as "properly designed" as the proposed Federal Union of Democratic Nations. Risk is unavoidable at all levels of human existence. Whatever course of action (or inaction) is taken, there are inevitable risks. A psychotic person might decide to stay in bed every morning, as a means of avoiding such risks as killing himself by falling in the bathroom, or being killed while driving to work. But as any sane person realizes, this strategy is untenable. Bathrooms are essential to the maintenance of personal hygiene, and commuting is necessary to retaining a job and earning a living. The notion of "avoiding all risks," clearly, is an insane notion. Sometimes we *must* take risks. And sometimes we *should* take risks. So it is with world government. In actual fact, the risks involved in not establishing a world government are greater than the risks involved in establishing a world government.

However, honesty also dictates the acknowledgement of another uncongenial reality with respect to active risk-taking. ("Active" risk-taking is involved in *taking* a certain action; "passive" risk-taking is involved in *not taking* an action.) A calculated active risk, prior to the action being taken, might be completely sensible: the expected payoff to the individual if the action is taken might be very much greater than the expected payoff if the action is not taken. However, owing to purely random bad luck, the actual outcome of taking the action might be disastrous. Thus the sane person who gets out of bed in the morning to go to the bathroom and then drive to work, might kill himself in a bathroom fall—or if the bathroom is survived, he might then be killed in a traffic accident on the way to work.

Equally bad luck might befall human civilization even if humanity does follow the active course which is advocated herein by establishing a federal world government. Despite all the precautions and safeguards, such a government might actually become the mechanism which generates the very nuclear world war it was intended to forestall. I make this point not because I believe that it is a sensible argument against world government, but because I wish to reduce to a minimum the sensibility of the charge that this particular advocacy of world government is based upon "idealistic and unrealistic" thinking. The thinking from which this advocacy of world government proceeds, is in fact solidly rooted in a realistic perception of the facts as we presently know them: the facts of human psychology, the facts of human history, the facts of the planetary habitat, the facts of science and technology, and the facts of decision-making under uncertainty. It is realism to acknowledge that no strategy exists which will absolutely guarantee a favorable long-term outcome for human civilization. It is also realism to acknowledge that under some circumstances, the risks of inaction are greater than the risks of action. Specifically in this case, the risks of *failing* to take the logical next step of forming a world government are greater than the risks of actually forming such a government.

Needless to emphasize, in the past major social innovations have rarely if ever been proposed in experimental terms. Rarely have the proposers of such innovations offered arguments which could be easily satirized as equivalent to: "Try it—you *might* like it!" Neither have the opponents of these innovations considered it advisable to express their arguments in anything less than terms of complete certainty. However, to those in the middle of the dispute, to those whose judgment inclines them in one direction or the other but *not strongly* in one direction or the other, the perception may be that the proposed innovation may be worthwhile as a means of establishing once and for all, by experimental means, whether or not the innovation is, on the whole, beneficial.

It may be found, after the innovation is adopted, that its overall effect is unfavorable. In that case, the innovation could and should be repealed, revoked, discontinued. An interesting case of this sort in United States history was the imposition of a national ban on the production, transportation and sale of alcoholic beverages from 1920 through 1933.[2] The ban was the outcome of long-term, organized efforts, dating back to the early nineteenth century, to limit the consumption of alcohol and thereby to curb the various social problems generated by drunkenness. Major organizations opposed to alcohol included the National Prohibition Party (founded in 1869), the Woman's Christian Temperance Union (founded in 1874), and the Anti-Saloon League (founded in 1893). Section 1 of the proposed Eighteenth Amendment to the United States Constitution, submitted by Congress to the states in 1917, stated: "After one year from the ratification of this article the manufacture, sale, or transportation of intoxicating liquors within, the importation thereof into, or the exportation thereof from the United States and all territory subject to the jurisdiction thereof for beverage purposes is hereby prohibited." The Amendment was ratified by the requisite number of states by early 1919. Enforcement legislation entitled the National Prohibition Act (popularly known as the Volstead Act after Representative Andrew J. Volstead of Minnesota) was passed by Congress on October 28, 1919, over the veto of President Woodrow Wilson. The ban went into effect on January 29, 1920.

Within a short period of time, the costs of "legislating morality" became obvious. Millions of otherwise law-abiding citizens ignored the ban, resulting in a thriving illegal black market supplied by organized crime. Violence erupted in the streets as rival gangs fought to gain control over the illicit but lucrative trade. Corruption spread widely through the enforcement agencies as some of the abundant revenues were diverted to bribes to gain the complicity of the police. The quality of illegal alcohol degenerated, leading to much death and disability among the consuming public. Anyone who wonders what the "war on alcohol" was like during the 1920s has only to look at the "war on drugs" being waged today.

After a decade of experience suggesting that in this case the cure was worse than the disease, the pendulum of public opinion swung against prohibition. By the latter 1920s, anti-prohibition forces were well-organized in the Association Against the Prohibition Amendment (AAPA). The Democratic candidate for President in 1928, Alfred E. Smith, was strongly in favor of repeal of prohibition. Although defeated in the election, Smith's advocacy of repeal legitimized the repeal movement. The onslaught of the Great Depression in 1930 may have put the final nail in prohibition's coffin. To the other arguments against prohibition was now added the assertion that a legal liquor industry would add thousands of new, legal jobs paying taxable income. Another argument at that time might have been that legalized alcohol would help people to cope peaceably with the new economic adversity: clearly, drunkenness might be preferable to the insurrection being preached by the newly socialized Soviet Union. At any rate, by the early 1930s, the repeal movement was in full swing. The Twenty-First Amendment to the U.S. Constitution, whose principal purpose was simply the repeal of the Eighteenth Amendment, was ratified before the end of 1933. And that marked the end of what Herbert Hoover, defeated in the election of November 1932 for U.S. President by Franklin D. Roosevelt, referred to as "the noble experiment."

Whether the episode had been noble or ignoble, Hoover's use of the term "experiment" is informative. Throughout the many decades prior to the 1920s during which the controversy had raged, advocates and opponents of prohibition had speculated endlessly about the probable effects of a national ban on alcoholic drink. Advocates forecast the moral regeneration of a nation no longer plagued by intoxication and alcoholism. Opponents forecast a narrow and joyless existence presided over by puritanical religious zealots. But no one *really* knew what would happen. When the pro-prohibition forces finally got the upper hand and pushed through the national ban, the anti-prohibition forces howled their lamentations. As it turned out, they should have shouted their hosannas. Within ten years, the compelling evidence provided by actual experience with prohibition swung the overwhelming weight of public opinion over to the anti-prohibition side of the controversy. The political strength of prohibitionist sentiment was soon rendered negligible, and the national ban on alcoholic beverages was lifted. Ten years of actual experience with prohibition were worth more than ten decades of speculative controversy.

Opponents of world government today should keep this historical in-

cident well in mind. Assuming they are correct, then very shortly after
the formation of a world government, its disadvantages and liabilities
will begin to manifest themselves in a very clear and obvious manner.
Perhaps, despite all the admonitions and warnings against attempting to
make the world state into an instrument for the radical redistribution of
current income, the high officials of the world state will set themselves
resolutely toward this course of action. Against opposition to this policy,
they will threaten to unleash the military and police forces of the world
state. Clear evidence would then exist that the apprehensions and antici-
pations of world government skeptics were fully on-target. If this were to
happen, then the world state would dissolve very quickly and very completely. Just as prohibition was abandoned as soon as its disadvantages
could no longer be reasonably denied, so too the world state would be
abandoned. It would be a very long time—if ever—before humanity
would ever again consider experimenting with world government.

Of course, I myself do not believe that there is any significant possibility that were a world government to be established, its high leadership
would be so foolish and misguided as to pursue policies which would
inevitably be strongly opposed by substantial national populations. Into
this category would certainly fall the policy of radical redistribution of
current income. I have cited the example of prohibition of alcohol in the
United States from 1920 through 1933 only to suggest that the formation
of a world government need not be a final, definitive, and irrevocable
step. If a potential future world government were to be as unsuccessful in
practice as was the policy of prohibition of alcohol in the United States
during the 1920s, then that world government would quickly follow the
same path as that followed by prohibition—into rapid oblivion.

But at the same time, most students of social policy recognize in the
experience of prohibition in the United States during the 1920s an atypi-
cal case. The general rule is that innovative social policies—policies
which are finally adopted after decades of vociferous controversy and
bitter resistance—are successful rather than unsuccessful. The various
vicissitudes and disasters confidently predicted by conservative opponents turn out to be groundless fantasies. Society carries on much as before, and after a while even most of the conservatives become fully reconciled to the changes, and recognize them to be beneficial not only to
the larger society, but to themselves as well. Of all of the amendments to
the United States Constitution, for example, only the Eighteenth was later repealed because its effects were obviously perverse. The Thirteenth
Amendment, abolishing slavery, has not as yet had to be repealed. Nor
has the Nineteenth, which granted the right to vote to women. If a world
government is established in the real world, I am very confident that it

will very quickly be acknowledged as a positive development by all but a small handful of extremely inflexible and reactionary mentalities. The key point is, however, that my own personal confidence on this score is *not* a vital component of the case to be made for world government. What *is* a vital component of this case is that it would not be impossible, nor even especially difficult, to dissolve a world government which was not developing in a positive way.

## Global Governance

In his 1952 world federalist classic bemoaning the passing of the postwar world government boom (*The Commonwealth of Man*), the historian Frederick L. Schuman offered the following categorization of the perceived difficulties and salient objections to the establishment of a genuine, full-fledged world government: "The antifederalist case, reduced to bare bones, holds that world government, federal or otherwise, is either undesirable or unnecessary or irrelevant or impossible, or all four together."[3] Although the "all four together" phrase is a sarcastic expression of Schuman's personal skepticism toward the overall "antifederalist case," this four-part categorization is quite comprehensive, and remains as relevant today as it was back in the early 1950s.

The first and most important of these four is clearly the proposition of undesirability: that world government would almost certainly lead to such dysfunctional outcomes as civil war, global tyranny, bureaucratic suffocation, cultural homogenization, and so on and so forth. The proposition of "irrelevance," that world government, in and of itself, will not cure the diseases of global human civilization, is less convincing, since a literal interpretation of the proposition implies that world government would not worsen these diseases. If that were the case, world government should be attempted, because of the possibility that it might do some good. The "impossibility" proposition, in and of itself, is also logically weak as an objection to world government, unless it is combined with the "undesirability" proposition. In a literal sense, world government is clearly not impossible: it could be established by the same kind of international conference that set up the League of Nations and the United Nations. Unless it is also maintained that world government is undesirable, to maintain that it is impossible (owing to the ingrained prejudice within the entire human population against any and all schemes of world government) implies the irrationality or ignorance of the human population. But the typical human individual is neither irrational nor ignorant.

The proposition that world government is "unnecessary" holds that global human civilization can attain the maximum amount of international harmony and cooperation without establishing a formal world government. At the time Schuman's book was published in the early 1950s, the Cold War was coming to full maturity, both sides had nuclear bombs and delivery systems, and the possibility of a devastating nuclear world war was no longer merely a figment of science fiction. The overwhelmingly dominant perceived reason for world government at that time was simply to reduce the probability of nuclear world war. But almost as soon as nuclear weapons became a part of reality, a general consensus arose, among the large majority of the population, that no one would be "stupid enough" to start a nuclear war. To some extent, this consensus, which is still prevalent today, manifests wishful thinking. Among other things, a nuclear World War III could occur as a result of miscalculated brinkmanship, the same thing that was responsible for both World War I and World War II. Be that as it may, this consensus is undeniably reassuring. As of the early 1950s, therefore, the operative meaning of "maximum amount of international harmony and cooperation" was merely that nuclear world war would be avoided. At that time, the unnecessity proposition simply meant that world government was not necessary in order to avoid nuclear war.

Since the collapse of the Soviet Union and the end of the Cold War in the early 1990s, anxieties over a possible nuclear Armageddon have greatly subsided. We now think of the "maximum amount of international harmony and cooperation" as involving much more than simply avoiding nuclear war. Even so, the idea that world government is not required to achieve this maximum is still quite prevalent, and finds clear expression in certain extreme versions of the global governance theory.

The sudden and dramatic rise of the term "global governance" in the popular and professional literature on international relations is plausibly attributed to the sudden and dramatic demise of the Soviet Union. Global governance has become one of the leading mantras of the contemporary age. Alternatively known as global civil society, it may be defined as the totality of institutions, policies, and initiatives by which humanity is currently endeavoring to cope with such universal (global) problems as violence and warfare, poverty and exploitation, explosive population growth, natural resource depletion, and environmental degradation. The term was apparently invented in the latter 1980s, and came into wide usage in the early 1990s with the publication of such seminal works as *Governance without Government: Order and Change in World Politics*, edited by James N. Rosenau and Ernst-Otto Czempiel.[4] In 1995, the quarterly professional journal *Global Governance: A Review of Multilateralism and International Organizations* commenced publication to provide an outlet for the burgeoning number of contributions on the subject. In addition, a substantial number of books and symposia have appeared devoted specifically and entirely to global governance. Since the early 1990s, no treatise on globalization, international relations, and/or international organization would be considered complete without substantial discussion of global governance.[5]

The global governance term was officially recognized and sanctioned with the formation of the Commission on Global Governance in 1992. The Commission, consisting of 28 eminent individuals from many countries and walks of life, received a high level of support from the United Nations, several national governments, and a number of private organizations. The extent to which discussion of global government had been veritably purged from the professional literature on international relations may be gauged from the virtually nonexistent treatment of the concept in the commission's report (*Our Global Neighborhood*, Oxford University Press, 1995). Within the 410 pages of this document, there are exactly two references to world government. The first occurs in the chairmen's Foreword:

> As this report makes clear, global governance is not global government. No misunderstanding should arise from the similarity of the terms. We are not proposing movement towards world government, for were we to travel in that direction we might find ourselves in an even less democratic world than we have—one more accommodating to power, more hospitable to hegemonic ambition, and more reinforcing of the roles of states and governments rather than of the rights of people.[6]

To those sympathetic toward world federalism, this definitive pronouncement, supported by no argumentation anywhere in the report, was reminiscent of nothing so much as the calmly complacent dogmatism of a medieval theologian. The second and final reference to world government is perhaps even more arbitrary:

> States remain primary actors but have to work with others. The United Nations must play a vital role, but it cannot do all the work. Global governance does not imply world government or world federalism. Effective global governance calls for a new vision, challenging people as well as governments to realize that there is no alternative to working together to create the kind of world they want for themselves and their children. It requires a strong commitment to democracy grounded in civil society.[7]

The report does not discuss or even take notice of the abundant literature produced over the course of the twentieth century by numerous proponents of world federalism. In a volume which purportedly deals comprehensively with global governance, this arbitrary dismissal is implicitly rather insulting to the many talented and dedicated people who have argued the case for global government.

In justice to the members of the commission, it is fairly obvious that their report was planned, designed, and drafted by a team of professional social scientists and political analysts drawn mostly from academia and government. Any suggestions from commission members that perhaps the idea of global government was worthy of more careful consideration were likely discouraged by the professionals on grounds that any such consideration, even if it tended toward criticism and rejection, would adversely affect the credibility of the report, and hence the odds that any of its specific recommendations would be adopted.

The irony is that without exception the practical proposals of the Commission on Global Governance would in fact involve strengthening the United Nations and moving it slightly closer to a world government, despite explicit assurances to the contrary. Examples of commission proposals include establishment of a permanent U.N. Volunteer Force of 10,000 soldiers under direct U.N. command, increasing the peacekeeping reserve fund to facilitate rapid deployment, establishment of a U.N. Economic Security Council to enable more vigorous pursuit of global economic development, establishment of a Global Competition Office as a U.N. specialized agency, gradual phase-out of the veto power in the U.N. Security Council as well as expansion of its membership, effective budgetary control by the General Assembly, all member nations of the U.N. to accept the compulsory jurisdiction of the International Court of Justice, and so on and so forth.

Needless to say, little if any of this has been implemented. In the end, the commission's disavowal of any world government aspirations did little good. While conservative guardians of national sovereignty immediately dismissed the report as little more than world federalist propaganda, the small minority of world federalists also dismissed it as insufficiently bold and original.[8] It failed to capture the attention and imagination of either the proponents or the opponents of world government, and it had little perceptible impact.

In a strict sense, "global governance" is merely a descriptive term signifying the existing level of international cooperation and coordination, through the United Nations and other organizations, in coping with global problems. This existing level might be very high or very low, depending on the implicit basis for comparison. If the basis for comparison is the level of international cooperation and coordination that would be achieved under the world federalist ideal of the omnipotent world state, then obviously the existing level is very much below this. On the other hand, if the basis for comparison is the level of international cooperation and coordination that held during the "bad old days" of the Cold War, then apparently the existing level is very much above this.

What some world federalists consider objectionable about the "global governance" term is that it implies that the existing level of international cooperation and coordination is comparable to that which would be achieved if an actual, functioning global government were in existence. According to reputable dictionaries, the term "governance" is closely linked to the term "government." In a word, governance *is* what governments *do*. The "global governance" phrase suggests the actuality, or at least the feasibility, of a maximally stable and well-ordered international regime in the absence of a unifying governmental authority.

The phrase possibly represents a case of tendentious terminology. "Tendentious terminology" may be defined as the putting forward of a controversial proposition not by means of direct, explicit statement but rather by indirect, implicit means that utilize certain terms with generally understood and accepted meanings, according to which the proposition would be true. In this case, the controversial proposition is, "The current level of international cooperation and coordination is equivalent to what would be achieved if there existed a functioning global government." Of course, most of those currently employing the "global governance" phrase, especially international relations professionals, would insist that they personally do not endorse this particular proposition. Be that as it may, the current prevalence of the phrase may be contributing to an attitude of complacency that is not justified by the actual realities of the contemporary international status quo.[9]

The essence of any authentic government is that it possesses a significant amount of coercive power over its citizens: the capability and willingness to arrest, convict, and incarcerate those citizens who violate laws. International law differs from domestic law in that there are no effective organs of enforcement. This is another way of saying that there is no analogue to the national government at the international level. Nation A can persuade—or intimidate—nation B to behave in a manner that nation A approves. But in behaving this way, nation B is not abiding by generally accepted rules of conduct enforced by an agency above and beyond nation A.

For example, while it might be desirable for Mexico to resume the control over the American Southwest that it lost at the time of the Mexican-American War of 1848, this is not desirable for the United States, and the military forces of the United States deter Mexico from acting upon any temptations it might harbor on this issue. Clearly this is not a case of governance at work. Rather it constitutes a long-term bargaining agreement or negotiated settlement between the United States and Mexico—a settlement that was originally concluded following the military defeat of the latter back in 1848.

Global governance notwithstanding, the fundamental principle of national sovereignty is not being seriously challenged in today's world. What goes on between nations in today's world, therefore, is more accurately described as negotiation and bargaining based on the potential use of force. The negotiation and bargaining lead to various agreements, treaties, and alliances. In the past, these agreements, treaties, and alliances have not prevented the regular recurrence of large-scale warfare. The situation is essentially the same now as it was throughout the nineteenth and twentieth centuries. It probably does not reflect meaningful governance at the global level, at least according to the conventional definition of the term "governance."

## A New World Order?

That the collapse and dissolution of the Soviet Union has generated a new world order is obvious. The salient question is whether this new world order will be stable and benign—or otherwise. There are many hopeful signs—but also many not-so-hopeful signs. Certainly the most hopeful sign of all is that since the de-communization and dissolution of the USSR in 1991, there is no longer a superpower nation in the world that is vociferously disdainful of the capitalist economic system, and openly declares, as its moral duty, its intention to facilitate the impending collapse of that system. Given that fundamental ideological attitude, official Soviet assurances throughout most of the Cold War concerning its commitment to "peaceful coexistence" were never entirely reassuring.

The second communist superpower of the Cold War, the People's Republic of China, has abandoned Soviet-style central planning entirely in favor of a variety of market socialism that, for the moment, is performing quite impressively. However, the communist leadership of the PRC is also, for the moment, completely uninterested in political reform. They are acutely aware of the unintended consequences of Gorbachev's liberalizing initiatives of the latter 1980s: initiatives that led to overthrow of communist party control of the USSR, and sent the ex-Soviet economy spiraling into a decade-long depression. The political and socioeconomic system of the People's Republic of China is obviously very much different from that of the leading Western nations, but so long as neither side proclaims any aggressive intentions against the system of the other side, peaceful coexistence seems attainable.

On the less hopeful side of the ledger, the accommodation between the communist bloc and the leading Western nations did not entail any fundamental, qualitative change in the world system. The land surface of the planet continues to be divided up among something more than 200 jealously independent and self-righteously sovereign nations. In fact, the breakup of the Soviet Union resulted in several more independent sovereign nations, as did the breakup of Yugoslavia. A substantial number of these sovereign nations are armed with nuclear weapons. While there was considerable nuclear weapons reduction during the 1990s by the United States and the Russian Federation, the remaining stockpiles of these weapons are sufficient—if they are ever utilized in total warfare—to devastate the world.

The Nuclear Non-Proliferation Treaty (NPT) of 1970 recognized five "nuclear weapons states": the United States, the USSR (since succeeded by the Russian Federation), the United Kingdom, France and China. According to estimates published in the *Bulletin of the Atomic Scientists*, the U.S. has approximately 4,000 active warheads, Russia somewhat over 5,000, the U.K. around 150, France around 300, and China around 400. Since 1970, three nations that were not parties to the NPT have conducted nuclear tests: India (approximately 150 active warheads), Pakistan (approximately 50 active warheads) and North Korea (possibly as many as 10 active warheads). Israel declines to confirm or deny that it possesses nuclear weapons, but it is widely assumed that its nuclear arsenal contains between 100 and 200 active warheads. South Africa is apparently unique in being the only nation to have developed an independent nuclear capability, following which it subscribed to the NPT and voluntarily disassembled its small stockpile. Three former republics of the Soviet Union, Belarus, Kazakhstan and Ukraine, inherited nuclear weapons from the USSR, but voluntarily returned them to the Russian Federation in the mid 1990s and subscribed to the NPT.

It may be unduly optimistic to expect significant further reductions in nuclear stockpiles if there are no substantive changes in the world order. For several decades, both the United States and Russia have placed heavy reliance on possessing large nuclear arsenals. Why do these two nations need nuclear weapons? Russia has to consider, for example, the possibility of a resurgent Germany tempted by the huge Russian land area and natural resource base in the same way that Hitler was tempted. A Russian nuclear capability will help ensure that Germany continues to resist such temptations. The United States has to consider, for example, that there are masses of poor people in the world, many of them living in Mexico and the Latin American nations to the south of Mexico. Mexico, of course, suffered what it might still tend to regard as an outrageous territorial injustice at the time of the Mexican-American War of 1848. A U.S. nuclear capability will help to ensure that Mexico does not contemplate redressing that injustice, nor that the impoverished masses of Latin America do not contemplate a forcible redistribution of wealth by means of a land invasion of the continental United States. A U.S. nuclear capability also helps to ensure that various other nations, especially erstwhile ideological opponents such as Russia and China, do not take upon themselves any sort of military resistance when it becomes necessary for the United States to protect its essential national interests by military means on the soil of other nations. In the recent past, following the September 11, 2001, terrorist attacks on New York and Washington, military invasions were undertaken into Afghanistan and Iraq. Others may have to be undertaken in the future to deal with various "rogue states," especially those such as Iran, Syria and North Korea, tempted by the prospect of joining the nuclear club.

Quite frankly, the nuclear superpowers, Russia and the United States, have a tiger by the tail—they dare not let go. Within both nations, therefore, any suggestions of complete nuclear disarmament are arbitrarily dismissed as crackpot nonsense. But among the second tier of nuclear powers, most of them also seem locked into maintaining their nuclear capabilities. Britain and France, nations that developed their nuclear weapons capabilities just in case the NATO umbrella should fail to provide shelter against the USSR, are apparently highly reluctant to dismantle their nuclear arsenals even though the USSR disappeared from the scene more than 20 years ago. After all, Western Europe was nervous about the huge "Russian bear" to its east long before the 1917 revolutionary transformation of Russia into the Soviet Union. Although shorn of eleven SSRs, the Russian Federation, by itself, is still a huge "Russian bear" to the east, and it is well-armed with nuclear weapons. China, India and Pakistan seem frozen into a three-way Mexican standoff. China needed nuclear weapons to defend itself against both the U.S. and the USSR. Then India needed them to defend itself against China. Then Pakistan needed them to defend itself against India. Israel, surrounded as it is by a vast and thoroughly hostile Muslim population in the Mideast, considers its nuclear weapons essential insurance for its very survival. But as long as Israel possesses nuclear weapons, the several Muslim nations in the region will be subject to a permanent temptation to correct this imbalance by developing their own nuclear capabilities.

A major theme in current international security thinking is that of the "rogue state"—a small but nuclear-armed nation whose leadership gets into a bellicose frame of mind and is not afraid to die (e.g., North Korea).[10] The consensus view is that we (the superpowers) need plenty of nuclear weapons to ensure that if these rogue state leaders ever do anything desperate, they will indeed die. But on the other hand, perhaps all these concerns about "rogue states" are greatly exaggerated. It has been seriously argued by Kenneth N. Waltz, by reputation one of the great intellects of twentieth century international relations theory, that nuclear proliferation should be welcomed and encouraged—not opposed—by the current nuclear powers. In a volume co-authored with Scott Sagan, Waltz argued that in a world in which any one nation could destroy any other nation, nations would be compelled to treat each other with proper dignity and respect.[11] During the high Cold War period, Waltz argued (*Man, the State and War*, 1959) that fears about nuclear war *would not* compel the nations of the world to establish a world government. One wonders on what basis he later concluded that fears about nuclear war *would* compel the nations of the world to treat each other with proper dignity and respect. Scott Sagan argued the conventional consensus that the more nations are armed with nuclear weapons, the more likely it is that a nuclear exchange will eventually take place, and thus nuclear proliferation should be opposed by all means possible. Quite possibly Kenneth Waltz was just having fun playing the devil's advocate. Or possibly he was apprehensive that deadly confrontations among the nuclear superpowers might arise based on disagreements about just how far it is permissible to go in order to forestall nuclear proliferation. To the extent that a limited amount of nuclear proliferation is not perceived as unduly threatening, there would be less probability of such confrontations actually happening.

Another obvious source of potential deadly confrontations among the nuclear superpowers would be disagreements about just how far it is permissible to go in pursuit of individuals responsible for terrorist outrages. References to the 9/11 attack have been ubiquitous in the international relations literature ever since that fateful day, and this book is no exception. Special emphasis has been placed herein on the ominous parallel between the 9/11 attack and the assassination of Franz Ferdinand in Sarajevo in 1914: in both cases there was a brutal assault on the national honor of one nation by citizens of another nation. Gavrilo Princip and his accomplices had in common with the nineteen 9/11 hijackers an overpowering, blind hatred against their perceived national enemy, combined with complete indifference to and irresponsibility concerning the larger consequences of their actions. Princip was determined to strike a blow against the Austro-Hungarian empire, the national enemy of his beloved Serbia.[12] Mohamed Atta and the other hijackers were determined to strike a blow against the United States of America, in their view the preeminent national enemy of the entire Islamic Mideast. Of course,

Gavrilo Princip, an undistinguished, tubercular teenager, could not know that his deed would lead to World War 1, and thereby (indirectly) to the communist revolution in Russia, the rise of Hitler during the interwar period in Germany, World War II, and the ensuing Cold War that had the world perched precariously on the edge of a nuclear volcano for the better part of half a century. But had he the capacity to imagine that such a chain of disasters might follow upon his assassination of the Austrian Archduke, it is doubtful that he would have been deterred. Similarly, Mohamed Atta and his accomplices were not deterred by the possibility that such an enormous outrage might somehow spark a nuclear world war. Since they subscribed to the twisted perversion of the Islamic religion purveyed by a handful of unhinged extremists, they believed that the more death and destruction they managed to inflict on infidels, the greater Allah would be pleased and the more generous would be their heavenly reward.[13]

In certain key respects, the world situation is evolving at a glacial pace. Economic progress is widespread, but it is proceeding slowly in terms of the average person's expected lifespan. Political evolution at the international level is at a standstill. The United Nations represented little more than good intentions when it was established in 1945, and so it remains today. More than half a century has passed since the foundation of Israel in 1948 inflamed the Mideast, and the region is still seething. Earth's human population continues to grow precipitously, and the environment correspondingly continues its long-term decline. Among other things, these problems ensure that there will be a steady supply of completely alienated and thoroughly nihilistic individuals long into the future, individuals who are ready, willing, able, and indeed eager to carry out terrorist actions—and the more deadly and potentially destabilizing these actions may be, the better.

Of course, the most ominous possibility is that some well-financed terrorist gang will get possession of an operational thermonuclear weapon, upon which they will happily detonate it in the middle of a city—New York City being the most likely target.[14] In the movies, square-jawed action heroes thwart the terrorist plots of evil masterminds on a regular basis. James Bond alone has saved the world at least a dozen times—or at least in each case a large part of the world. Perhaps because terrorist plots are invariably squelched in the fictional media, or because the plots themselves seem to be part of the same mythical fantasy world populated by hordes of vampires or plagues of zombies, it is extremely difficult for most of us to take seriously such possibilities as a nuclear terrorist attack on New York City. The thing is that vampires and zombies never have existed and never will exist in the real world. In contrast, nuclear weapons exist in the real world, and fanatical terrorists who want to get hold of these weapons in order to destroy large cities also exist in the real world. The case of Osama bin Laden is sufficient to prove that there are also wealthy people in the real world with the capability and the desire to assist terrorists in carrying out their designs.

The Council on Foreign Relations recently sponsored an "online debate" on the topic: "How likely is a nuclear terrorist attack on the United States?" led by experts Michael Levi, author of *On Nuclear Terrorism*, and Graham Allison, author of *Nuclear Terrorism: The Ultimate Preventable Catastrophe*.[15] The experts agree that such an attack is definitely possible, therefore significant effort and expense to prevent it is worthwhile. They offer various disconcerting observations (e.g., there exists much bitter hatred against the United States throughout the world, especially in the Middle East), and various reassuring observations (e.g., getting hold of an operational nuclear weapon is not as easy as buying a handgun in Houston). But in the final analysis, nothing that they have to say on the matter is quantifiable in any meaningful way. Should the United States be spending 50 billion dollars per year on nuclear terrorism prevention, 500 billion dollars, or what? Assuming the United States continues its anti-nuclear terrorism expenditures at the same level they are now, is the probability of a successful nuclear attack on an American city, within the next 25 years, 20 percent, 5 percent, 1 percent, or what? Experts are reluctant to answer specific questions such as these with specific answers, and when they do, they are likely to add the caveat that whatever number they give is "just a guess." Probabilities cumulate, of course. Something that is very unlikely over a short period of time becomes more likely the longer the period of time. For example, if the probability of a nuclear terrorist attack on an American city within the next year is only 1 percent, assuming that probability remains constant, the probability of a nuclear terrorist attack within the next 100 years is approximately 64 percent.

Quite likely a thermonuclear bomb detonated under the Empire State Building in New York City would kill millions of people, some by heat and blast, others by radiation poisoning. The magnitude of such a horrific catastrophe coming about through deliberate human intention would be absolutely unprecedented in the recorded history of humanity. The world wars of the twentieth century killed millions of people, but not so suddenly and unexpectedly. The United States is the virtually inevitable target of such an attack. With great success and power comes great resentment and hostility. Despite the fact that as individuals, the people of the United States are no better or worse than the people of any other nation in the world, the U.S. is the recipient of far more than its fair share of criticism and denunciation. This continual negative hum can and does inflame some of the more susceptible minds in other nations to unrestrained rage and hatred, the type of rage and hatred that generates terrorist attacks. Determined terrorists are not likely to be mindful of the fact that the United States of America is a nation armed with thousands of operational nuclear warheads, and the ballistic and guided missile means to deliver them virtually anywhere in the world. They are not likely to take account of the possibility that if you sting an elephant hard enough, the elephant is liable to go berserk.

Among the extreme religious right in the United States, there are millions of Christian fundamentalists who believe (or say they believe) that mankind is in the end days, that there will soon appear the Antichrist, that a great world Armageddon is imminent, that there will be the Rapture, the Tribulation, the Second Coming of Christ, the Millennium, and so on and so forth. There are several versions of this story and the details can get somewhat complicated, but the nub of it seems to be that "all hell will break loose," the human casualties from which will number in the hundreds of millions. What makes the story so appealing to some is that these horrific events will thoroughly humble and destroy all those unbelieving skeptics and atheists whose sneering doubts are currently making the faithful so uncomfortable. For most normal people, contemplating a near-term "end of the world" scenario is rather unpleasant, but for these people the thought elicits positively gleeful anticipation.

Other right-wing extremist groups in the U.S. are fully secular in outlook, but they share with the religiously oriented groups the interpretation of the "new world order" as a giant conspiracy to enslave the people of the United States. These groups think it would be a sensible policy for the United States to "nuke" anyone or anything that represents a serious threat to U.S. national interests—and they see serious threats everywhere. Thus far these groups have been kept under control. But if an international terrorist organization such as al-Qaeda manages to detonate a nuclear device in New York City, the belligerent attitudes that are today confined to a minority of extremists would spread out among the general population like wildfire. Quite possibly they would spread into the highest corridors of power, to people who exercise significant, immediate authority over the nation's nuclear arsenal. How the United States, as a nation, would react to such an outrage is unknown. It is impossible to predict. Most of us hope that we will not live long enough to find out. But there are those who can hardly wait to find out.

Meanwhile, outside the United States there is much unease over what many perceive as unrestrained U.S. power. The "balance of power," on which all hopes for peace have hitherto depended—is now out of balance. Not everyone perceived in the 1991 Gulf War, for example, a heartening example of international solidarity against aggression by a nation under the control of a mini-Hitler. Some saw it as an ominous portent of global hegemony by the United States alone, or by an alliance among the small minority of wealthy nations. According to this view, the United States and its allies would never have bothered if the victim of the aggression, Kuwait, had not happened to be a major oil exporter. The main point of the exercise was not (in this view) to teach a lesson to would-be aggressors in the future, but to keep the price of oil low. Those who think this way tend also toward the opinion that it is important that "counterweights" be built up against the power of the United States.[16]

The 2003 invasion of Iraq by a "coalition" consisting almost entirely of the United States and (to a much lesser extent) Britain, generated a wave of protest not only in the Middle East but throughout the world. While few of the protesters would have denied that Saddam Hussein had degenerated into a vicious tyrant, and that he represented a "threat to stability" in the Middle East, they doubted that his regime presented such a clear and present danger to the security of the United States and its allies as to justify military invasion. The quick military victory of U.S. and U.K. forces in Iraq intensified apprehensions throughout the rest of the world that the United States, aided and abetted by a handful of its closest allies, was evolving into an international bully that would in future take upon itself the task of preemptively eliminating, via military conquest, all real and perceived threats to its national interests. No doubt those concerned that the United States might evolve into an international bully derived considerable comfort from the fact that postwar Iraq became a sucking quagmire that swallowed up substantial U.S. human and material resources. By general consensus, the United States is the single strongest military power in the world today, possessed of the most formidable nuclear arsenal. Be that as it may, there are several other nuclear powers that may eventually confront the U.S. should it become unduly aggressive in protecting its national interests. It would take only one instance of miscalculated brinkmanship to plunge humanity into a nuclear abyss from which we may never emerge.

In her bestselling book *The Proud Tower* (1966), historian Barbara Tuchman painted a richly detailed portrait of the world in the decades leading up to the outbreak of World War I in August 1914.[17] Knowing what we know now—what the people of that era did not know—such phrases as "marching toward catastrophe" or "sleepwalking toward disaster" come readily to mind. There were a few who were concerned that the combination of testy relations between the major European powers and the increasing destructiveness of military hardware was creating a hazardous situation. But there were many others who did not consider the possibility of warfare to be a serious threat. Indeed, for some of the more pugnacious personalities, warfare was eagerly anticipated since it would provide a welcome opportunity to defeat and humble various enemy nations. After all, warfare (in the view of these personalities) was an integral part of nature's ultimately benevolent scheme for strengthening and improving the human species. For others, the economic interdependencies among nations made warfare such an unviable proposition that assuming the political leaders of the various nations were in the least bit rational, they would never authorize and initiate a war. But most people gave the matter little thought. The world was as it was, and could not be changed. This attitude was shared not just by rank-and-file citizens, but by the highest leaders of the nations. Since there was nothing feasible that might be done to significantly diminish the threat of warfare, one may as well forget about the whole matter and just get on with the business of life. When the Damocles sword finally broke loose and descended upon that hapless generation, people were stunned—how could such a monstrous thing have happened?

The unification of Germany in the aftermath of the Franco-Prussian War of 1870-1871 is normally taken as the starting point of the run-up to World War I. Before that time, the territory that became Germany consisted of several independent principalities (Prussia, Bavaria, Saxony and so on), a circumstance that well suited France since it reduced the potential military power of its German-speaking neighbors to the east. Prussia's rise to dominance in the region was manifested by its quick victory over the Austrian empire in 1866, which gave rise to French apprehensions over a potential German federation under Prussian direction (Prussia had been a major participant in the alliance that brought down Napoleon in 1815). Reacting to the inane (in retrospect) issue of whether or not a Hohenzollern prince should sit on the Spanish throne following the deposition of Isabella II, and fictitious reports of mutual insults exchanged between the Prussian king and the French ambassador to Prussia at the resort town of Bad Ems, France declared war on Prussia on July 19, 1870. The imprudence of this declaration was soon demonstrated. Not only was Prussia by itself militarily stronger than France, Prussia was joined by most of the other German principalities. Well prior to the French capitulation, the German Empire was proclaimed in the Palace of Versailles on January 18, 1871, thus bringing about the very result that the French had intended to forestall by military means. To make matters even worse, the new mid-continent German Empire included two slices of previously French territory, the provinces of Alsace and Lorraine. Added to a large war indemnity owed to the German Empire, and the virtual civil war involved in the rise and fall of the Paris Commune following the siege of the city by the Prussians, this left the French people tasting fully of the bitterness of defeat.

Meanwhile, the German people, puffed up with their triumphant victory, developed a virulent case of nationalism verging on chauvinism. Enthusiasts of "pan-Germanism" envisioned the incorporation into the Reich of several specific territories in other nations in which there were substantial German-speaking populations. Aside from Austria itself, there were substantial German-speaking populations within both the Austro-Hungarian empire (in what later became Czechoslovakia) and the Russian empire (in what later became independent Poland). This is not to mention German-speaking parts of Switzerland. Moreover, many Germans regarded most enviously the enormous world empires under British, French and Dutch control. Coming late to the scramble for African colonial territories, Germany had to content itself with a few leftover scraps such as German East Africa (most of which was to later become the independent nations of Tanzania, Rwanda and Burundi). In the past, wars on the European continent had often eventuated in transfers of ownership over huge colonial areas from the defeated to the victorious nations, and some Germans eagerly anticipated future victorious wars with other European powers that would bring about a great worldwide German empire that would write finis to and put to shame the erstwhile imperial domains of Britain, France and Holland.

Although Germany's various territorial ambitions were the most dangerously destabilizing factor in the pre-World War I era, Germany was by no means the sole source of tension. Competing claims to African territory by Britain and France resulted in the "Fashoda incident" (1898) that nearly precipitated warfare between these two nations, despite their having been allies for decades prior to this. Even more serious was the fact that the "sick man of Europe," the Ottoman empire centered in Turkey, was gradually disintegrating. Among others interested in ownership or control of the newly independent territories were the Russian empire and the Austro-Hungarian empire. The two Balkan Wars of 1912-1913 solidified the reputation of this area of southeastern Europe as the "powder-keg of Europe." Sure enough, the assassination of the Austrian Archduke that lit the fuse to World War I occurred on Balkan soil, specifically in the city of Sarajevo, in Bosnia-Herzegovina, later part of Yugoslavia, and later still, following the dissolution of Yugoslavia, an independent nation. One important argument against excessive complacency in our own time is simply that the Balkan area of the pre-World War I era has much in common with the Middle East of today.

Among those increasingly uncomfortable with the general trend of international relations throughout this era, much optimistic joy and relief was elicited by the appeal for a multilateral "peace conference" issued by Czar Nicholas II of Russia. The purpose of the conference would be to arrive at arms limitations agreements to relieve the great powers of the heavy burden of military expenditures, and also to set up institutions and procedures for the peaceful arbitration of international disputes. The consensus among historians, reflected in Tuchman's *The Proud Tower*, is that the principal motives of the Russian government were not particularly humanitarian. It was more a matter that the economically under-industrialized Russian empire was having great difficulty in keeping up its end of the European armaments race, along with concern that the potential vicissitudes imposed on the Russian population by a war would generate a revolution that would bring down the autocratic Russian regime. Accordingly, the leaders of the other great powers were highly suspicious of Russia's motives and highly skeptical that anything worthwhile would come out of the conference. But since the appeal had come from the head of state of a great power, it could not very well be tossed carelessly into the nearest wastepaper basket. After all, public opinion could not be entirely disregarded, even in that long-ago era. In the event, not one but two Hague Conferences (so named for the Dutch city which hosted them) were held, in 1899 and again in 1907. A planned third conference, scheduled for 1915, had to be cancelled because most of the participants had become embroiled in World War I.

The initial hope of the Russian government of Nicholas II that the Hague conferences might slow down the arms race was entirely disappointed: no significant arms control or reduction agreements of any sort were reached. However, despite the unenthusiastic attitude of most of the conferees, the two conferences did result in some limited agreements on other matters, agreements that were regarded in their time somewhat comparably to the SALT and START treaties of more recent times. For example, Article 2 of the Hague Convention of 1899 states: "In case of serious disagreement or conflict, before an appeal to arms, the Signatory Powers agree to have recourse, as far as circumstances allow, to the good offices or mediation of one or more friendly powers." Of course, the circumstances following upon the assassination of the Austrian Archduke in Sarajevo on June 28, 1914, did not allow recourse to the good offices or mediation of one or more friendly powers. Moreover, once World War I had started, the agreements did nothing to diminish its ferocity. For example, one of the three Declarations produced by the 1899 Hague conference states: "The Contracting Powers agree to abstain from the use of projectiles the object of which is the diffusion of asphyxiating or deleterious gases." This was simply ignored in World War I: following Germany's first use of lethal gas in early 1915, the British followed suit. The only reason why poison gas was not more widely utilized during the war is simply that artillery and machine guns proved more reliable and effective. The Hague conferences are good examples of the limited effectiveness of formal negotiations among sovereign nations that do not like or trust each other.

Among the many influential contributors to the intellectual environment of pre-World War I Europe were Norman Angell of the United Kingdom and Ivan Bloch of Russia. Both men produced books, well-known at the time, that argued the proposition that the overwhelming destructiveness of war fought with the then-modern weaponry of the period made war thoroughly infeasible—something to be avoided at almost any cost. Norman Angell (1872-1967), placed the major emphasis in *The Great Illusion* (1910) on the economic interdependencies among nations that are inevitably ripped asunder by warfare to the detriment of all sides, victors as well as defeated. Ivan Bloch (1836-1902) produced a monumental six-volume work (*La Guerre Future*, 1898) on military technology, strategy and tactics that anticipated some aspects of World War I quite accurately: the necessary commitment of armies numbering in the millions, a tendency toward static trench warfare, the degeneration of warfare into a brutal contest of human and material attrition. Bloch's conclusion was that the costs of warfare had become unendurable to civilized society, thus no effort should be spared to make war virtually impossible. Bloch was an invited participant at the 1899 Hague peace conference, where he distributed copies of his magnum opus to the delegations of 26 participating nations. No doubt they were politely received by various under-secretaries, then ignored by the delegation authorities as misguided alarmism produced by a harmless crackpot. After all, it was the dogma of the period, accepted by almost all, whether high or low in society, that a nation requires armed force to preserve its vital national interests against various provocations and impositions of malevolent foreigners, and that any nation unwilling or unable to wage war in defense of its interests will soon be humiliated and despoiled.

Just as this was unquestioned dogma in the early years of the twentieth century, so too it is unquestioned dogma in the early years of the twenty-first century. Of course, today we have the harsh lessons of the twentieth century to temper our natural proclivities toward warfare. Presumably we are not nearly so prone to escalate disagreements to conflict, and conflict to warfare. There is much wider and clearer realization now, relative to the situation 100 years ago, that because of the development of nuclear weapons, total warfare would almost certainly be immensely and intolerably destructive, and therefore it should be avoided at almost any cost. Almost. But if, God forbid, it should come to pass that irresponsible, malevolent, virtually suicidal foreigners should somehow push us into a corner from which there is no escape other than through the use of nuclear weapons, then so be it.

New tensions seem to be arising all the time, sometimes from the most unexpected sources. For example, the Arab spring of 2011 aroused hopes that many if not most Mideast countries would soon transition into genuine democracies along Western European or American lines. These ephemeral hopes were soon extinguished, but nowhere was the failure more catastrophic than in Syria, wherein a bloody civil war has gone on for several years. Deaths are already numbered in the hundreds of thousands, and a vast out-migration of refugees is having a destabilizing effect extending all the way to the member nations of the European Union. In the United States, after two presidential terms served by the admirably sensible and balanced Barack Obama, the American public elected (by a narrow margin, and only with the help of the outmoded Electoral College) Donald Trump to the presidency of the nation. Trump is not only ludicrously unqualified to be U.S. president, but even more disturbingly, he is an irresponsible demagogue whose campaign pandered to the darkest elements in the contemporary American psyche. Meanwhile, the Russian Federation is currently being guided by Vladimir Putin, who has centralized authority in himself to the degree that he is seriously accused of harboring dictatorial aspirations along Stalinist lines. Thus the two nuclear superpowers in today's world are both being led by men who proclaim as their primary objective to make their respective nations "great again." The potential for miscalculated brinkmanship is obvious, and the flashpoint might well be the suffering nation of Syria. Thus continues the course of an international regime based solidly on the principle of national sovereignty.

It is a standard cliché among world government skeptics to dismiss the concept as a utopian delusion. The use of the utopian descriptor to smear an idea has a long history. For example, in T*he Communist Manifesto* of 1848, Karl Marx ridiculed his various predecessors as "utopian socialists." But if we strictly define the word "utopian" as an "impossible dream," then there is nothing utopian about the plan presented herein for a limited world government to be known as the Federal Union of Democratic Nations. On the other hand, if we interpret "utopian" simply as a "better world" than the world we know today, then one would have to describe the present plan of world government as utopian in that specific sense. Clearly, at the present time, the dominant implication of "utopian" is that of an "impossible dream" and not simply a "better world." Thus it is important to emphasize most strenuously that this plan of world government is not at all utopian in this dominant and generally accepted sense. Far from being utopian, this proposal is absolutely and positively practical, possible, pragmatic, viable and workable. What may indeed be "utopian" in the usual sense of naïve unrealism is the commonplace expectation today that the contemporary quasi-anarchic world system will keep us all safe and sound, prosperous and secure, into the far future.

In Number 6 of *The Federalist Papers*, Alexander Hamilton, in response to the argument that there was no need for a closer political union among the thirteen original states because there was no foreseeable basis for future conflicts among them, wrote as follows (italics added):

> A man must be far gone in *Utopian* speculation who can seriously doubt that, if these states should either be wholly disunited, or only united in partial confederacies, the subdivisions into which they might be thrown would have frequent and violent contests with each other. To presume a want of motives for such contests as an argument against their existence, would be to forget that men are ambitious, vindictive, and rapacious. To look for a continuation of harmony between a number of independent, unconnected sovereignties in the same neighborhood, would be to disregard the uniform course of human events, and to set at defiance the accumulated experience of the ages.

*The Federalist Papers* were written in support of the proposed United States Constitution which was formally adopted in 1789. The 1789 Constitution was intended to provide the basis for a "more perfect union" among the original thirteen states than the relatively weak union specified by the Articles of Confederation (1777). In some ways, the United Nations Charter of 1945 might be compared to the U.S. Articles of Confederation of 1777, while a potential future Federal Union Constitution might be compared to the U.S. Constitution of 1789. Hamilton's 1787 argument concerning the original thirteen states is plausibly extrapolated to the 200 nations of the "global neighborhood" today. Just as Hamilton described skeptics toward the proposed U.S. Constitution as "far gone in Utopian speculation," the same description might apply to skeptics who oppose world government on grounds that it is "unnecessary"—since (they say) there is no good reason why serious future conflicts among nations should arise.

## The Boat Metaphor

Few people doubt that the world today is a much safer place than it was twenty-five years ago. The renunciation of communist ideology by the components and satellites of the ex-Soviet Union has greatly eased tensions. Around the world, military spending and arms stockpiles have been significantly reduced. The possibility of instantaneous nuclear holocaust has been reduced to a level that many consider negligible. Although an impressive degree of desensitization to the nuclear threat had been achieved early in the Cold War, it was never complete and total. Always at the back of people's minds, hidden away in some dark corner, lurked the awareness that "it" might someday happen—and if it did happen, there would be very little warning. Understandably, people are now breathing more easily, especially those living in or near to obvious urban targets of ballistic missiles armed with thermonuclear warheads.

The downside of this development, as far as the future destiny of the human race is concerned, is the loss of a sense of urgency, the growth of complacency, and the dominance of a policy best described as "let's drift and see what happens." Not even the traumatic events of September 11, 2001, and those of its aftermath, have apparently dislodged humanity's strong consensus that the current international status quo situation is—if not the best of all *imaginable* worlds—at least the best of all *possible* worlds. In some ways, the contemporary world is very dynamic. Notwithstanding occasional recessionary "meltdowns," the long-term economic trend, throughout most of the world, has been strongly upward ever since the end of the Second World War. The pace of technological progress, especially in the area of consumer electronics, has been veritably dizzying. Throughout the world, the human population is growing briskly. Unfortunately, the political evolution of the human race at the global level is currently frozen in time, stationary, immobile. The fact that progress in other areas has outpaced progress in global political organization is unhealthy—at best it is slowing down the overall progress attained by humanity, and at worst it may be setting up conditions that will eventuate in ultimate, self-inflicted, planetary catastrophe well within the lifetimes of many people alive today.

In the absence of a global government equipped with a reasonable and appropriate degree of political authority, the circumstance of humanity in today's world may be compared to that of a group of people gathered together in a large boat—a boat lacking both a rudder and an engine—that is drifting down an unknown river. At the moment the river is broad and quiet, drifting is pleasant, and the people in the boat feel quite safe and secure. But of course an unknown river may contain deadly hazards in the form of churning rapids and huge waterfalls capable of smashing the boat to smithereens and drowning its occupants. Should one of these hazards come into view around a bend in the river, the people in a boat unequipped with engine and rudder would be staring doom in the face.

A good metaphor for the intention of world government is that of at-taching a rudder and installing an engine in a boat that is drifting down a broad, quiet river. The idea is to improve the degree of control over the boat, so that there is less likelihood that it will be destroyed if rapids or a waterfall are encountered. Of course, maybe there are no rapids or water-falls ahead on the river, so that if our boat continues drifting down it in-definitely, it will eventually emerge into a deep, blue, quiet, peaceful sea. In this case, the people in the boat would never have needed the engine and the rudder, and installing them would have been a waste of time and energy. Or, perhaps, the engine and rudder that were installed would have been too weak to do any good should the people be unlucky enough to encounter churning rapids or a high waterfall. Once again, the installa-tion of the engine and the rudder would have been a waste of time and energy. But even if either of these two cases happened to be true, these possibilities are not good arguments against installing the engine and the rudder—unless it is assumed that the "wastage of time and energy" would be extreme. The only good argument *against* installing an engine and a rudder is that such action would *worsen* the overall prospects of the boat and its occupants. It is hard to imagine how an engine and a rudder on a boat filled with people that it drifting down an unknown river could possibly be actually *undesirable*, in terms of the interests of the people in that boat.

Of course, no analogy is perfect, and a world government skeptic would immediately object that this particular analogy is egregiously mis-leading. Establishing a world government in the contemporary world (according to the skeptic's argument) is in no way comparable to in-stalling an engine and attaching a rudder to a boat. Engines and rudders are standard equipment on boats, and any group of people intending to descend an unknown river would be quite sure that their boat possessed both an engine and a rudder. On the other hand, global human civiliza-tion has so far been unencumbered with world government—and so far, so good. We have not yet encountered the equivalent of churning rapids and high waterfalls. More to the point, unlike equipping boats with en-gines and rudders which is customary and risk-free, there are definite hazards that would be involved in establishing a world government. Such a government might quickly degenerate into a horrific global tyranny. Or it might imprison humanity in a vast, stifling, suffocating, bureaucratic straitjacket. Or possibly it might manage to do both simultaneously. The unwillingness of some nations to participate in the world government might lead to warfare, possibly nuclear warfare. The plausibility of these adverse outcomes means that establishing a world government would be nothing like putting an engine and a rudder on a boat—it would rather be recklessly risky and highly imprudent.

The skeptic's argument is basically that because a world government *might* turn out to be undesirable in the future, establishing a world government in the present *is* undesirable. One wonders what the condition of humanity would be today if this argument had been decisive ever since the Stone Age. Presumably the condition of the human race would still be very much the same now as it was then. Of course, in itself this is not a particularly weighty observation. In fact, mankind *has* made progress since the Stone Age because mankind *has* aspired toward progress and *has* been willing to take risks toward the achievement of progress. The question at this point is whether mankind should now take another risk, in the interest of progress, of establishing a federal world government?

How much more clear can it be that the answer to this question depends critically on the specific institutions and procedures of the proposed federal world government? Not all world government schemes are equal: some are more attractive than others, in that some plans are more likely to lead to the future we want than others. What we need is the proverbial "happy medium," located somewhere between the weak-as-water United Nations of today, and the "omnipotent world state" preached by conventionally-minded world federalists. On the wide spectrum of political organization between these two extreme points, the Federal Union of Democratic Nations lies at, or very near to, the optimal "happy medium" point. The Federal Union described in these pages would look like a government, talk like a government, and act like a government—it would *be* a government. It would have legislative, executive, and judicial branches, a permanent administrative apparatus headquartered in a capital city, local offices in numerous cities around the world, an armed force, a flag, an anthem. The democratic election of its officials by an electorate composed of a substantial part of the entire population of the planet, possibly the totality of it, would endow its deliberations and decisions with a great deal of legitimacy and authority. At the same time, the Union would operate under the key limitations embodied in the reserved national rights to free withdrawal from the federation, and to the maintenance of independent armed forces of whatever size and nature deemed necessary by the national governments. These reserved rights add up to an "exit strategy" should the Federal Union, once established, be drifting toward policies unacceptably inimical to the national interests of various member nations. Of course, the hope of most people of good will is that after an initial period of suspicion and resistance, lasting perhaps several decades, the increasingly obvious benign evolution of the world government will make these reserved rights mere historical curiosities.

It might be argued that the ingrained prejudices and preconceptions against world government are so overwhelming that it is useless to seek a happy medium plan toward workable world government. Even if a specific form of benign, effective, and progressive world government was indeed fully practical, a form that would greatly increase the security and prosperity of humanity as we advance into an uncertain future, it will never be recognized as such. The negative presumptions and assumptions concerning world government are too strong ever to be challenged. The vast majority of people will simply ignore the case for world government, no matter how rational and plausible it may be in objective terms. Even just thinking about world government is therefore a complete and utter waste of time. I refuse to accept such a pessimistic argument, which merits rejection simply on the grounds, if none other, that it is gratuitously insulting to human rationality and intelligence. While I will concede that today's prejudices and preconceptions against world government are very, very strong, I do not think they are "overwhelming" in the sense that they never can and never will be successfully challenged.

At the present time, the large majority of people believe that benign and effective world government is impossible. But if we go far enough back in the history of humanity, we can find several important examples of things that the great majority believed to be impossible—that were later proved to be possible. Space travel is an example from the technological realm; representative democracy is an example from the political realm. In the light of these kinds of examples, we need to be skeptical of the belief, no matter how widespread, that any sort of benign and effective world government is an impossibility at the current juncture in human history. Perhaps it *is* impossible; perhaps it is *not* impossible. To properly illuminate the question, we need to look carefully at proposed world government blueprints.

Prior to the achievements of the Wright brothers in the early 1900s, many if not most people believed that it would be impossible for human beings to construct powered, heavier-than-air, manned aircraft capable of flying substantial distances at high speeds. The Wright brothers disproved this belief, but to do so they had to carefully consider the many technical design issues involved. It would not have been feasible to prove or disprove the possibility of powered, manned aircraft by means of general speculative discussions that did not address technical design issues. Prior to the Wright brothers, there were numerous unsuccessful aircraft designs, which demonstrates that not just any old aircraft design will be capable of flight. But as became evident in due course, all these unsuccessful aircraft designs did not imply the invalidity of the basic concept of air travel. Similarly, it is not feasible to prove or disprove the possibility of stable and effective world government without carefully considering the various institutional design issues involved. But once these design issues are seriously addressed by informed and competent people, I am confident that a consensus will eventually emerge that stable and effective federal world government in our time is, after all, very much within the realm of possibility.

Until such time as there is virtually universal consensus that nuclear weapons must never be utilized in human conflict, and nuclear stockpiles have been reduced to virtually negligible levels, and consequently nuclear war has truly and literally become "unimaginable," the possibility of nuclear world war will continue to be the single biggest danger confronting humanity within the relatively proximate future (over, say, the next 50 years). Correspondingly, the single most important argument for establishing a federal world government is that it would significantly reduce this danger. I have had much to say about this in the foregoing, and while it is hard to overstate this crucial point, it is necessary to append an important caveat lest the argument seem naïve and unrealistic. This caveat is that owing to the necessary restrictions on the power and authority of the proposed world government in order to make it feasible in today's nationally oriented world (specifically the reserved rights of member nations to free withdrawal and independent military forces), the reduction in the nuclear holocaust threat will obviously be much less than the reduction that could be achieved by the omnipotent world state of conventional world federalist thinking. Recall that under the omnipotent world state concept, all nuclear and other weapons of mass destruction, along with all other heavy armaments, would be concentrated under the direct control of the world government. The implication of conventional world federalist thinking on the matter has also been that the world government would not hesitate to use these weapons upon recalcitrant nations. According to the deterrent principle, however, if the world government exercised monopolistic control over these weapons and also was sufficiently determined to use them should the occasion arise, then the occasion never would arise. No nation would ever dare become sufficiently recalcitrant to bring down upon itself these terrible weapons. In the opinion of world government skeptics, with this amount of power in its hands, the world government would soon engage in policies (such as a worldwide welfare state) that would make the lives of many of its citizens, especially those living in the rich nations, into a living hell. While I personally am very dubious that an omnipotent world state, if it ever came about in the real world, would do anything at all to make the lives of any appreciable number of its citizens into a "living hell," I concede that there is a sufficient probability of this very adverse outcome to make the omnipotent world state an impractical objective. Thus the proposal here is not for an omnipotent world state, but rather for a limited federal world government, the Federal Union of Democratic Nations.

Within the first several decades of the Federal Union's existence, it seems inescapable that several nations that currently possess nuclear weapons, will elect to keep them as part of their independent armed forces. This is virtually certain for the two nuclear superpowers, the United States and the Russian Federation. It is not part of this proposal that the world government concern itself, especially in the short run, with disarmament of any kind, nuclear or conventional. The leadership of the Federal Union should at most permit itself a modest amount of verbal approval toward nations that are voluntarily reducing their military expenditures and weapons stockpiles. The reasonable hope is, however, that the greater opportunities for amicable interaction and cooperation afforded by the existence of the Union, will gradually reduce mutual suspicion and mistrust among the member nations, so that they may gradually, and without apprehension, reduce their military commitments.

After nuclear disaster, the second biggest threat is environmental disaster. It is a distant second, however, simply because unlike nuclear disaster which can and probably will (if it occurs) be virtually instantaneous, environmental disaster will necessarily come about (if it does) very slowly and gradually. Owing to humanity's marvelous adaptability, oncoming environmental disaster might not even be noticed—until it is far too late to do anything about it. Among the more enthusiastic environmentalists, the basis of the problem is the extravagant living standards of the rich nations. Whether through voluntary choice or governmental fiat, the heavy footprint being impressed upon the natural environment by these absurdly high living standards needs to be lightened. While I myself believe that a clean, pure and uncrowded natural environment, populated by an abundance of wildlife, is very important to individual human happiness, at the same time I think it is unrealistic to try to pursue this objective by means of persuading the people of the rich nations to substantially reduce the living standards to which they have become accustomed. The Global Marshall Plan (GMP), the economic complement to the political proposal for a Federal Union of Democratic Nations, envisions living standards in all parts of the world being, on average, approximately as high as they are presently in the rich nations. To some environmentalists this prospect might seem completely "unsustainable." We can only hope that they are wrong about this, and that with efficient production, the Earth will be able to support a human population of at least 10 to 15 billion at a high standard of life comparable to that in the rich nations today. Declining living standards are a sure recipe for political instability, and so we cannot propose declining living standards in the rich nations. At the same time, extreme economic inequality, such as characterizes the contemporary world, is also a sure recipe for political instability at the international level. We would be well advised to try to greatly reduce, and hopefully close entirely, the economic gap. If it turns out to be impossible, because of natural resource constraints, to close the economic gap and at the same time keep living standards in the rich nations high, then quite frankly the prospects for humanity on this planet are bleak. But it is much too early to arrive at any such conclusion.

Given a certain human population of the Earth at a certain point in time, and given the available production technology at that time, the natural resource base (including both non-renewable and renewable resources) determines the average worldwide standard of living that can be attained. Anyone who is aware of the basic demographic realities of the contemporary world, and who is not suffering from the religious delusion that "God will provide," cannot help concluding that the Earth is not under-populated at the present time. It follows that the more we can slow down population growth, the better the chances will be that the Global Marshall Plan will be a success. High and relatively uniform living standards throughout the world would contribute to the long-term political stability under which the Federal Union of Democratic Nations would flourish, and along with it human civilization and culture.

During its early decades, the absolute top priority of the Federal Union of Democratic Nations should most definitely be the Global Marshall Plan. If the global economic development program is a failure, quite likely the global political initiative will also be a failure. The world today is beset by many problems other than economic poverty: epidemics of deadly diseases, the illegal drug industry, localized conflict situations, mistreatment of women, environmental degradation, threatened extinction of valued plant and animal species, and many, many others. Throughout this book, I have refrained from arguments and allegations that the establishment of a world government along the recommended lines would quickly lead to rapid and dramatic progress toward the amelioration of these kinds of problems. It cannot be predicted in advance just how much—or how little—progress could be made against these varied problems were there an active, functioning Federal Union of Democratic Nations in existence. The fact that no promises can be made that these problems would be successfully tackled in the short run might be taken by some as an argument against world government. But this would be an exceptionally shallow and unperceptive argument.

Many if not most of the "problems of the world" we know today are bound up integrally with economic poverty and economic inequality. For example, one reason illegal drugs are relatively inexpensive is that for many impoverished farmers around the world, they are a preferred cash crop. Localized conflict situations are often over economic resources—in oil-rich regions, for example, an important aspect of the problem is often contention over who is to get the major benefit from the petroleum resources of the area. It has been statistically verified, through findings from the World Values Survey, that the status of women is highest in the richest nations.[18] Much environmental degradation comes about owing to pressure from impoverished subsistence farmers in desperate quest for sustenance for their families. And more often than not, plant and animal species are endangered because their "natural habitats" are being invaded by humans.

Economic inequality aggravates the frustration and resentments generated by the condition of economic poverty. If everyone in the world had the same living standards as subsistence farmers in Botswana, the human population of the world would probably be relatively content, and international tensions would be far less than they are. The tribulations imposed by poverty on any given individual are far worse if that person is aware of other people, elsewhere in the world, who are enjoying a much higher standard of living. The emotion of envy easily transitions into resentment and hostility. It is an ineffable characteristic of humanity to want to blame other humans for any unsatisfactory event or condition. It is so much more satisfying to blame other people for various problems than it is to blame the uncaring natural universe, or "forces beyond anyone's control." The uncaring natural universe and "forces beyond anyone's control" can never be brought to account and punished. Individual human beings, on the other hand, can most definitely be brought to account and punished.

What is the significance of this psychological phenomenon, in terms of prospects for international stability and harmony? Consider this question: Would the United States of America be subjected to so much suspicion, distrust, resentment, hostility, and downright hatred throughout much of the world, if it were not one of the richest nations in the world? The answer is self-evidently negative. It would not be nearly as easy for the poorer people of the world to regard the United States so negatively if the average living standards of its people were equivalent to those of subsistence farmers in Botswana. The irony is, of course, that if average living standards in the United States were the same as in Botswana, and if at the same time the United States possessed the same armed forces, equipped with the same conventional and nuclear weaponry, that it does now, it would be a far more dangerous force in the world than it is now. Indeed, as far as the future prospects of humanity are concerned, it is very favorable that the single most militarily powerful nation in the world also happens to be one of the most prosperous. There are few nations in the world more content with the status quo than the United States, and given the military power of the United States, that is a very good thing.

According to the "demographic revolution," which has been going on in the economically advanced nations of the real world for the last two centuries, as living standards rise, the population growth rate ultimately declines. Economic progress initially leads to a decline in the death rate, and later on to a decline in the birth rate. During that time interval during which the death rate is declining but the birth rate remains high, the population growth rate becomes quite high, but this rate eventually declines as the birth rate declines. In much of the Third World, the birth rate remains quite high despite substantial decreases in the death rate. Thus the population growth rate is quite high, and the high population growth rate retards progress in per capita income. Slow growth in per capita income is responsible for the slow decline in the birth rate, which in turn keeps the population growth rate high. Back in the 1950s, the economist Harvey Leibenstein coined the term "low-level equilibrium trap" to describe the phenomenon.[19] This so-called "trap" is a classic "vicious circle." The Third World is making some progress toward breaking out of this particular vicious circle, but it is slow progress—and uncertain. The absolute gap in per capita income between the richest and the poorest nations has been getting bigger over the last several decades, and any expectation that this trend will change, in the absence of massive, coordinated intervention at the global level, is unduly optimistic. To make any such assumption would be seriously imprudent.

In order to reverse the widening economic gap, and to propel the Third World forcefully out of the "low-level equilibrium trap," we need a international development effort along the lines of the proposed Global Marshall Plan. The sheer magnitude of the economic problem we confront today is unprecedented in the history of humanity. It is unlikely that this problem can or will be overcome without a worldwide economic effort of equally unprecedented magnitude. Without question, there would be serious disadvantages involved in rapid economic development throughout the world: disruption of traditional ways of life, heavy pressure on the natural environment, aggravation of psycho-social problems associated with dislocation and rapid change. But these disadvantages are comparable to the inevitable adverse side-effects of potent medicines necessary to cure life-threatening diseases. Global human civilization may be likened to a person with a serious case of cancer. To this person, radical treatments like surgery and chemotherapy are hazardous as well as painful. But they may be the only alternative to death.

One popular bromide with which people in the wealthy nations endeavor to justify their relative indifference to Third World poverty is that the people of these nations don't really want economic progress—they are quite content with their simple, uncomplicated, stress-free lifestyles. If this proposition possessed any significant degree of validity, the First World nations would not be constantly besieged by hordes of determined Third World people desirous of escaping their "simple, uncomplicated, stress-free lifestyles." If a serious likelihood were to emerge of a real-world Global Marshall Plan, almost certainly the vast majority of people in the Third World would welcome it with open arms.

The benefits from raising the standard of life in the poorer nations, and closing the economic gap between these nations and the rich nations, are not confined to the higher personal welfare experienced by people who are eating better, housed more comfortably, better educated and informed, more secure against the adversities of age and disease, and so on and so forth. People in the rich nations, apprehensive about the higher taxes that will be required by a Global Marshall Plan, might ask why, on the "I am not my brother's keeper" principle, should they should be concerned with poverty in the Third World? I would hope that only the most hard-hearted individuals would be totally immune to the feelings of warm satisfaction associated with acts of concern and generosity. But aside from appeal to the higher qualities of humanity, there are very down-to-earth, practical reasons for assisting the poorer nations of the world in their efforts toward economic progress. The more poverty and economic inequality there is in the world, the more unstable the world will be for everybody, rich and poor. Poverty and inequality are breeding grounds for terrorists and terrorist supporters, for demagogues and dictators who are compelled by the resentments of their people to adopt uncooperative, confrontational attitudes toward the rich nations. A functioning Global Marshall Plan, supported by an active Federal Union of Democratic Nations, that was making clear progress toward its goal of a high level of economic prosperity in all nations throughout the world, would deliver a powerful message in support of global peace and harmony. Just as it is clear that the problem of global poverty cannot be cured quickly, it cannot be promised that the instability inherent in this poverty will be quickly eliminated. There will still be disruptive terrorists, demagogues and dictators. But we will have established *direction*—we will be engaged in an active program toward the diminishment and eventual elimination of the problem. We won't simply be drifting—hoping that the problem will somehow cure itself. This is rather like a person with cancer hoping that the problem will cure itself without incurring the risks of surgery or the discomfort of chemotherapy.

Recall those people in their boat, drifting down the river. If their boat had an engine and a rudder, they would not be at the mercy of the current, they could go where they wanted on the river. They could avoid being trapped in churning rapids or going over high waterfalls. Just as those people have a natural interest in equipping their boat with an engine and a rudder, so too humanity today has an interest in establishing a world government. We can't know in advance exactly where we will want our world government to take us. No doubt there will be considerable disagreement and debate over our direction. But at least if we are able to arrive at a reasonable consensus on direction, we will have the means to go in that direction.

# 8

# Prospects

## Summary of the Essay

The currently prevailing concept of world government, among both the large majority of world government skeptics and the small minority of world government advocates (the "world federalists"), is that of a very strong state entity that would stand in relation to its component member nations much as the federal government of the United States stands in relation to the fifty component states. Such a government would encompass all nations in the world without exception, would not tolerate the withdrawal of any nation from the federation under any circumstance, and would monopolize all heavy weaponry, including nuclear weapons. This concept of world government is descriptively referred to herein as the "omnipotent world state." According to advocates, such a government would virtually eliminate the possibility of nuclear holocaust, and would also enable effective global action to be taken against such long-term threats as economic inequality and environmental deterioration. According to skeptics, such a government would either quickly dissolve amid civil war, or it would stabilize itself by means of imposing a draconic totalitarian regime on the world.

Apart from the small minority of world federalists, it is almost universally assumed that there is no credible transition path, of a peaceful nature, from the current international status quo to the omnipotent world state. This essay does not challenge this consensus opinion. However, it does challenge the widespread view that no federal world government short of the omnipotent world state would be a worthwhile undertaking. The basis of the challenge is the proposition that there exist viable world government possibilities (exemplified by the proposed Federal Union of Democratic Nations) whose authority and effectiveness would lie somewhere between that of today's relatively ineffectual United Nations, and that of the omnipotent world state, and that these intermediate possibilitics would both significantly improve the processes of global governance in the proximate future, as well as laying a secure foundation for further gradual, evolutionary progress over the long term toward a highly authoritative and effective—yet democratic and benign—world government. In other words, a limited world government, as opposed to an unlimited world government, is both achievable and desirable. Or at least a more persuasive case can be made to this effect than can be made for the omnipotent world state. In fact, it is arguable that were the notion of limited world government to become sufficiently familiar to the international relations profession, the general public, and the political leadership, this might result in such a fundamental reappraisal of the general concept of world government that the establishment of an actual world government within the foreseeable future would become significantly more probable.

In support of this proposition, this essay explores the analogy between "evolutionary socialism" and "evolutionary world government." In the final years of the nineteenth century, Eduard Bernstein came forward with a proposal that the socialist movement of his day turn away from its dangerously counter-productive obsession with ideal socialism achieved instantaneously through bloody revolution, toward a more practical and promising vision of the essential goals of socialism achieved through gradual, peaceful reform efforts within the existing socio-political system. He proposed, in essence, that "revolutionary socialism" be replaced by "evolutionary socialism." In so doing, he laid the foundations for the social democratic movement that has done much toward the improvement of global human civilization throughout the twentieth century and into the twenty-first. By revising the orthodox Marxist concept of public-ownership socialism, and renouncing the orthodox Marxist doctrine of the necessity of violent revolution to achieve socialism, revisionists such as Bernstein made this new concept of socialism more attractive to a broad range of the population. With broader support, the socialist movement was significantly strengthened, and thereby became capable of achieving tangible, worthwhile, real-world reform objectives.

A close analogy exists between this historical redirection of the socialist movement and a potential future redirection of the world federalist movement away from its traditional focus on an omnipotent world state achieved instantaneously through some quasi-miraculous political enlightenment, toward a more practical and promising vision of the essential purposes of world government achieved through gradual, peaceful reform efforts within the existing international system. Contemporary world federalists, of course, do not preach violence of any sort, revolutionary or otherwise. Yet it is difficult to imagine how their ideal of an omnipotent world government—a government that would necessarily include all the nations of the world and would monopolize all significant military power—could come about in the absence of violence. To bring about such a world government by peaceful means would require a radical transformation of contemporary public attitudes toward world government. No such transformation seems imaginable within any reasonable period of time.

On the other hand, if the objective of "omnipotent world government" is replaced by the objective of "evolutionary world government," it is not at all implausible that dramatic progress might be achieved within the relatively near future. The proposed limited world government on which this book focuses, tentatively designated the Federal Union of Democratic Nations, provides a pragmatic avenue toward fundamental reform of the international system, Such a government would provide practical institutional support for strengthening the positive processes of global governance with which we are already familiar. It would not require any major short-run changes in the international system as it exists today. What it *would* do is to provide a firmer and more reliable institutional foundation for progress toward the more secure and prosperous future world we all desire.

Whereas the omnipotent world state would require all nations in the world to become members, and would deem any secessionist tendencies within member nations as treason to be forcibly suppressed, the Federal Union of Democratic Nations would allow nations to come and go as they please without restriction. Member nations could independently proclaim their independence at any time. Whereas the omnipotent world state would restrict the military forces of member nations to that minimum required for internal policing, and would exercise full and complete authority over all heavy armaments, including nuclear weapons, member nations of the Federal Union of Democratic Nations could maintain independent control over as much heavy weaponry, including nuclear weapons, as they deem necessary to the protection of their essential national interests.

Traditional world federalists, with their ideal of the omnipotent world state in mind, tend to scoff at the Federal Union proposal on grounds that it would represent no significant advance over the world as we know it today. That such a federation would represent no significant advance over the world as we know it today, cannot be known for certain, either by world government sympathizers or world government skeptics. This is simply because no such federation currently exists in the real world. The only way to establish for sure whether the Federal Union would be nothing more than a thoroughly useless and highly ephemeral will-of-the-wisp, or whether it would indeed represent the initial seedling of what will eventually grow into a mighty oak—is to establish the federation and observe its development. The obvious hope among advocates of this experiment is that its historical development—its "evolution," so to speak—will be favorable, so that at some future time, perhaps in 50 years or 100 years or perhaps longer, the reserved national rights of secession and independent armaments will be regarded as mere historical curiosities, and not as something of continued relevance to current political calculations and processes. At that point, the Federal Union of Democratic Nations would indeed have evolved into a reasonable facsimile of the omnipotent world state—although no violence would have been necessary to its creation, and its "omnipotence" (if that term is at all applicable to a government under the democratic control of its citizens), would be exercised intelligently and benevolently.

In addition to the reserved national rights of unilateral withdrawal and independent militaries, there is one more essential element of the Federal Union proposal: the dual voting system in the federation legislature. Although this feature does indeed represent a departure from "pure" democracy as defined by the one-person-one-vote principle, it is absolutely necessary to the long-term stability of the world federation. According to the dual voting system, each representative in the federation legislature would exercise two separate voting weights in two separate votes: the population vote and the material vote. In the population vote, each representative's voting weight would be equal to the population of his/her district, as a proportion of the total federation population. In the material vote, each representative's voting weight would be equal to the federation's revenues derived from his/her district, as a proportion of the total federation revenues. The population vote would be dominated by representatives from relatively poor but populous districts. The material vote would be dominated by representatives from the smaller number of relatively wealthy districts. For legislation to be approved, it must be supported by a significant majority in *both* the population vote and the material vote. By this means, the federation would not be able to approve, for example, an unduly egalitarian "global welfare state," since this would be opposed by the wealthy nations. At the same time, the federation would not be able to approve, for example, legislation that would tend toward the re-imposition of the exploitative trade and investment policies of the colonial era, since this would be opposed by the poorer nations. Both the rich nations and the poor nations would thus exercise a veto power against legislation that would unduly favor one category of nations over the other.

This departure from pure democracy is regarded as a short-term expedient to enable the establishment of a world federation in a world still characterized by a great deal of economic inequality among nations. It is not regarded as a viable long-term solution to the problem of global economic inequality. The long-term solution to this problem is a Global Marshall Plan (GMP), the complementary economic proposal to the political proposal for a Federal Union of Democratic Nations. The GMP would be modelled on the Marshall Plan of the post-World War II era, but as a "global" plan it would be on a far bigger scale both geographically and financially. It would be a global economic development effort on an unprecedentedly massive scale. Contributions by the wealthy nations into the effort would be much larger than their current foreign aid expenditures, ranging from about one percent of GNP up to around five percent. However, these contributions would not be so large as to have a significant downward effect on either the level, or the rate of growth, of per capita income in the wealthy nations. The global development fund would be allocated to the recipient nations on the basis of need, as measured by size of population and level of per capita income. More populous poorer nations would receive a larger share of the global development fund. All proceeds from the development fund must be invested in "generalized capital," an umbrella term comprising business enterprise capital (plant and equipment), social overhead capital (roads, hospitals, and so on), and human capital (education and training). The purpose of the program would be to raise the productive capabilities of the recipient countries, not to distribute direct welfare benefits to their populations.

Although there exists a significant amount of international development aid in today's real world, the Global Marshall Plan would mark a quantum jump in the scale of the aid. It is fully predictable that just as skeptics will disparage the Federal Union proposal as manifestly impractical in a political sense, so too these same skeptics will dismiss the Global Marshall Plan proposal as a colossal boondoggle in an economic sense. According to the skeptics, a GMP of the sort envisioned would have an immeasurably small improving effect on the intended beneficiaries, the general populations of the poorer countries. The only significant enrichment would be to a legion of dishonest businessmen and corrupt bureaucrats involved in the administration of the program. At the same time, the GMP would inevitably impose significant additional costs on the tax-paying citizens of the wealthy countries, through which they would be severely disadvantaged.

It cannot be predicted with any degree of certainty what the effect of a real-world Global Marshall Plan would actually be, simply because nothing of the kind has ever been attempted. I have briefly described some economic research of my own (in Chapter 2 above) that indicates that a very large increase in the growth rates of per capita income in the recipient nations could be achieved at the cost of a virtually imperceptible decrease in the rate of growth of per capita income in the contributor nations. To emphasize this critical point: the decrease would be in the *rate of growth* of per capita income in the wealthy contributor nations, not in the *level* of per capita income in the wealthy contributor nations. The described research utilizes a model of the global economy based on conventional economic principles, and incorporates empirical data from a reputable source (the World Bank). Nevertheless, the research hardly constitutes compelling evidence that a real-world Global Marshall Plan would be a success. To begin with, it is shown that if certain critical parameters in the model take on sufficiently adverse numerical values, the GMP would fail to bring about increased economic growth rates in the poor recipient nations (albeit the research also indicates that under the same adverse assumptions, this adverse outcome for the poor recipient nations would not measurably decrease economic growth rates in the rich contributor nations). Beyond that, there is no guarantee that results obtained from computer simulations of an economic model will have any bearing whatsoever on real-world outcomes. Economics, as a discipline, is not noted for forecasting accuracy.

It is because success of a Global Marshall Plan cannot be assured, that an essential element of the proposal is that the program be undertaken on a *tentative and provisional* basis, and that if favorable results are not observed within a reasonable trial period of, say, between 10 and 20 years, then the program will be gradually phased out and ultimately discontinued. In other words, a real-world Global Marshall Plan should be regarded as nothing more—and nothing less—than a *scientific experiment* to ascertain whether or not it is capable of achieving success.

In fact, the same thing is true of the Federal Union of Democratic Nations. Such a world federation has never been established in the real world, therefore we cannot know for sure what its fate will be if it is established. Just as the economic proposal for a Global Marshall Plan can and must be regarded as a scientific experiment, so too the political proposal for a Federal Union of Democratic Nations must be regarded in the same way. If the world federation were to develop poorly, its member nations, relying on their right to free secession, would gradually—or rapidly as the case may be—abandon it. But just as the *possibility* of failure is not a good argument for never trying a Global Marshall Plan, so too the *possibility* of failure is not a good argument for never trying a Federal Union of Democratic Nations. No momentous advance in human history, from the invention of the wheel on down, has ever been entirely free of the possibility of failure.

As a contribution to the literature on world government, this book contains three innovative elements that are virtually unprecedented. Or if there are precedents, they are obscure to the point of being invisible. The first innovative element is that the proposals are presented conservatively. No claim is made that these proposals, if adopted and put into effect, will definitely and necessarily be successful. The possibility of failure is openly, explicitly conceded, and the proposals are put forward clearly as *experiments* that may or may not be successful in the real world. It is part and parcel of these proposals that they incorporate viable, plausible "exit strategies," so to speak.

The second innovative element is the synergistic combination of political and economic components. While it is true that several prior world government proponents have proposed economic equalization as part of their programs for world betterment, none of them have done substantive research on the mechanisms of the economic development program required, and on its prospects for success, comparable to this author's work on a Global Marshall Plan. In many cases, past proponents of world government have virtually ignored the economic impediment to global political unification. To the extent that mainstream international relations authorities have incorporated an economic factor into their analyses (such as they are) of world government, this factor is implicitly assumed to be virtually impervious into the foreseeable future, and thus to constitute a permanent obstacle to any kind of stable world government into the foreseeable future.

The third innovative element is the specification of a precise blueprint for a *limited* world government (the Federal Union of Democratic Nations), in order to provide a firm basis for a comprehensive and thorough evaluation of the world government possibility. Although there have been a few hints, here and there, among authors with at least some degree of sympathy with the basic idea of world government, that it is possible to have a world government less powerful than the omnipotent world state ideal of conventional world federalist thinking, none of these hints have been very specific about the type of limitations that might be involved. Certainly no author prior to myself has proposed a world government that would allow member nations to depart from the federation at their own unilateral discretion, would permit member nations to maintain independent control over as much military power and armaments, including nuclear weapons, as they desire, and would incorporate a dual voting system (population and material) in the federation legislature, a system that would enable both the rich nations, as a group, and the poor nations, as a group, to veto legislation of which they do not approve.

Some examples follow of the customarily vague statements about possible limitations on the world state to be found in contributions by authors basically sympathetic to the idea of world government. In his somewhat notorious 2003 article entitled "Why a World State Is Inevitable," Alexander Wendt provides the following observation:[1]

> Lest I be accused of lacking imagination, however, it should be emphasized that the systemic changes needed for a world state could be fulfilled in various ways, and so a world state might look very different from states today. In particular, it could be much more decentralized, in three respects. First, it would not require its elements to give up local autonomy. Collectivizing organized violence does not mean that culture, economy or local politics must be collectivized; subsidiarity could be the operative principle. Second, it would not require a single UN army. As long as a structure exists that can command and enforce a collective response to threats, a world state could be compatible with the existence of national armies, to which enforcement operations might be sub-contracted (along the lines of NATO perhaps). Finally, it would not even require a world "government," if by this we mean a unitary body with one leader whose decisions are final (cf. Bull's [1977] "domestic analogy"). As long as binding choices can be made, decision-making in a world state could involve broad deliberation in a "strong" public sphere rather than command by one person.

With respect to Wendt's third point, virtually all world government proponents are adamant that any form of dictatorship or oligarchy must be strictly avoided, and are insistent that each and every citizen of the federation possess significant voting weight in electing high state officials. With respect to the first point, virtually all world government proponents also envision a federal structure in which the component nations would retain substantial autonomy (i.e. sovereignty) with respect to all domestic public choice matters that do not impinge heavily on the interests of other nations. It is the second point that is the most significant: the suggestion that a world state need not require the full disarmament of component nations, that member nations might still maintain "national armies." This is definitely *not* in line with the omnipotent world state concept. However, Wendt does not state explicitly that these potential "national armies" would be subject to *independent* control by the respective national governments. Also, he does not mention the possibility of free secession by member nations, nor does he address possible voting schemes (such as dual voting) in the world state legislature that address the difficult issue of global economic inequality.

Another author who has addressed the question of whether or not the world state should hold a monopoly on armed force is Luis Cabrera, who writes as follows:[2]

> Just as governing power need not be concentrated at the top, we should not presume that the highest-level governing bodies must have a monopoly on the legitimate use of force. Assuming again that something approaching a fully global governing system could eventually emerge, the application of subsidiarity to the question of armed forces, both police and military, likely would result in a dispersal of forces among the regions, where each supra-state region maintained forces capable of responding to armed violence in its region or as needed elsewhere. The global-level governing bodies also could maintain a military force to be deployed in crises, to augment regional forces in actions involving aggressive states or sub-state units, or to help oppose aggressive or expansive supra-state regions. In fact, what might be seen as an antecedent to such a global-level force has been proposed at various times in context of the UN's peacekeeping mandate.

In some ways, this suggestion parallels that of Wendt which raises the possibility of "national armies" within the overall military structure of the world federation. The difference is that Cabrera's suggestion envisions the world divided into several regions, each comprising a number of countries, with each region maintaining a military force of its own. Presumably each nation within a certain region would maintain its own "national army," which would be a component of its specific "regional army." While this organizational approach is certainly a possibility, Cabrera provides no explicit statement to the effect that the regional armies would be under the *independent control* of their specific regions. This is the critical issue—not how global military forces be subdivided and organized, but rather that there exist military forces separate from those of the supernational federation, and that these separate military forces be under the *independent control* of subsidiary political units, whether supra-national regions each consisting of several nations, or the nations themselves. It is not enough that this independent control be implied—it is necessary to state it explicitly.

On the control of nuclear weapons specifically, Daniel Deudney writes as follows:[3]

> The classical and modified remedies are even more divergent than their diagnoses. Classical nuclear one worlders proposed to solve the security crisis of the state system by creating an omnistate in which nuclear capability was to be *concentrated* and then *employed* to maintain peace between the disarmed or dismantled states. In contrast, the modified approach envisions an arrangement in which the territorial state system is not replaced, but rather is complemented with a nuclear containment

and restraint system. The classical remedies are essentially the application of prenuclear images of a world state to the nuclear problem, while the modified remedies are an extrapolation from the theory and practice of nuclear era arms control. The classical diagnosis saw states as perilously vulnerable in anarchy, and the classical remedy saw the states as obstacles and wanted to weaken them. In contrast the modified diagnosis identifies acute security problems as arising from the interplay of external anarchy and internal hierarchy, and the remedy aims to reconfigure states with mutual restraints, both internally and externally.

Translating this passage into the customary terminology utilized herein (at risk of over-simplification), the "classical remedy" to the nuclear problem resides in the omnipotent world state, while the "modified remedy" resides (presumably) in something between the world as we know it today, and the omnipotent world state. The "something between," as Deudney explains it, "aims to reconfigure states with mutual restraints, both internally and externally." The "reconfiguration" may, or may not, involve the foundation of a limited world government along the lines of the Federal Union of Democratic Nations under consideration herein. The problem with pronouncements such as that quoted of Daniel Deudney is that they are akin to the pronouncements of the fabled "Oracle of Delphi." The Oracle's pronouncements were notably ambiguous and obscure. Their true meaning was all a question of interpretation.

The quotations of Alexander Wendt, Luis Cabrera, and Daniel Deudney provided above are fairly representative of the genre. While these kinds of statements provide hints as to how the power of a potential world state might be subjected to limitations of various kinds, they lack both specificity and comprehensiveness. In contrast, an early example (1999) of this author's more straightforward exposition on these critical issues is the following:[4]

> Key restraints on the supernational state would include the following: (1) member nations would retain the right to raise and maintain military forces; (2) member nations would retain the right to withdraw (secede) from the supernational federation at their own unilateral discretion; (3) a dual voting principle would be employed in the legislative assembly; and (4) special budgetary provisions would be enacted to prevent legislative deadlocks from freezing the operations of the federation... The single most fundamental proposal which would militate against the world state becoming an instrument of oppression is the right of secession. This right would be reinforced by the right of member nations to maintain independent military forces. It is proposed that all military forces of the Union, whether maintained by the member nations or by

the Union itself, wear the same uniform, have similar weaponry, and be considered formally as components of the overall Union Security Force. But in the event of fundamental and irreconcilable conflict between the Union and a particular member nation, the nation would have both the formal authority and informal means (i.e. its own military) of resuming its independence from the Union.

This kind of statement leaves little doubt as to the operative meaning of "limited world government." Of course, it has the disadvantage of alienating adherents to the conventional world federalist ideal of the omnipotent world state. But it has the advantage of possibly enlightening world government skeptics that there are indeed serious alternatives to the omnipotent world state, and that perhaps the idea of world government is worthy of serious re-evaluation in light of these alternatives.

When Eduard Bernstein and other revisionists of the late nineteenth century showed that there was a plausible alternative to the hardline Marxist vision of public-ownership socialism achievable only through violent revolution, they alienated adherents to the hardline vision. But at the same time they enlightened skeptics of socialism (who at the time constituted the large majority of people) that there were serious alternatives to the hardline vision, and that perhaps the idea of socialism was worthy of serious re-evaluation in light of these alternatives. In due course, as we now know, Bernstein's vision of "evolutionary socialism" eventually won out in most countries over the hardline Marxist vision of "revolutionary socialism." In its social democratic form, the socialist movement went on to achieve notable successes toward the advancement of global human civilization.

Perhaps in the same way, the vision of "evolutionary world government" will eventually win out over the vision of the "omnipotent world state." If this happens, it might generate a rebirth of the world federalist movement. And perhaps, in the fullness of time, the creation of an actual world government. Such a government might eventually be recognized as a valuable tool in the cause of advancing global human civilization.

The concept of evolutionary world government envisions the gradual evolution of an initially very weak Federal Union into a highly authoritative, yet benign, world government. By "initially very weak" is meant primarily that the Federal Union would share military power with the member nations: that each member nation could—and likely many of them would—retain independent control over substantial military forces. But it is also envisioned that if and as the federation develops successfully, member nations with large military forces will gradually reduce these forces. A possible problem with this scenario is that if the nations are disarming while simultaneously the Federal Union continues to maintain large military forces, would this not eventually lead to the Federal Union becoming itself an "omnipotent world state," the possibility of which causes so much apprehension at the present moment in world history? While one cannot summarily dismiss the possibility of an adverse outcome of this kind, it does not seem overly likely for the simple reason that as time proceeds and the national governments are gradually disarming, the supernational government would most likely also be gradually disarming. For if the national governments were disarming but the supernational government continued to arm itself to the teeth, suspicions might be aroused in the national governments.

Much would depend on the degree of trust that develops between the national governments and the supernational government. The role of trust is paramount in human affairs, at both the individual and social level. For example, in the United States today, there is no tangible, physical barrier to prevent the armed forces of the nation from taking control and establishing a military dictatorship. What makes this unlikely is the long tradition of great respect for democratic governance within all sections of the U.S. population, including the military. This tradition would make it extremely difficult for high-level officers to organize a successful military coup. It is to be hoped that a similar tradition would develop within the global population that would prevent a potential future global government from becoming an oppressive agent in the long term.

But in the final analysis, this risk is similar to other unavoidable risks if world government is undertaken. These unavoidable risks have to be weighed against the unavoidable risks of continuing with national sovereignty as the reigning principle of international relations. We turn now to the question of relative risk.

## Weighing the Risks

Human existence, at the personal, organizational, and social levels, is filled with the need to make choices. For an individual person, a critical choice might be whether to take an attractive-looking new job or to remain with one's present job. For a business enterprise, a critical choice might be whether or not to introduce a new product line. For a democratically elected government, a critical choice might be whether to maintain taxation and spending at the current level, or to increase or decrease them. Whatever decision is taken, there are risks. If the person in question stays with his/her current job, and that job happens to be a unpleasant, low-paying, low-prestige, no-future type of a job, then that person will spend the better part of his/her life in a dissatisfied, unhappy state. But if the person takes the attractive-looking new job and shortly thereafter becomes unemployed for one reason or another (perhaps the company went bankrupt, or the individual encountered an incompatible supervisor), then that person is also likely to spend the better part of his/her life regretting the job change. If the business enterprise introduces a new product line and the line is unsuccessful, then it may be bankrupted. On the other hand, if the market for the firm's current product lines is declining and it does not introduce the new product line, then it may also be bankrupted. If the democratically elected government keeps taxation and spending at the current level, it might be swept out of office by a tide of public dissatisfaction. But if it increases (or decreases) taxation and spending, it might still be swept out of office by a tide of public dissatisfaction. Whatever choice is taken, whether it be the active choice (trying something new) or the passive choice (staying with the existing status quo), risk is inevitable. Whatever choice is taken, if "things go wrong," the outcome will be adverse—perhaps *very* adverse.

In the formal theory of "decision-making under uncertainty," there are three basic types of variable: the criterion variable, the control variable, and the state variable. The criterion variable is that which is to be maximized. For example, for a business enterprise considering whether or not to introduce a new product line, the criterion variable might be the expected value of profits. Control variables are those variables the decision-maker has control over: that the decision-maker sets to levels intended to maximize the criterion variable. For example, the business enterprise decides how much of its productive capacity will be devoted to existing product lines and how much to the new product line under consideration. The amounts of productive capacity devoted to each of the product lines are the control variables. State variables are random variables: these are variables whose values cannot be accurately predicted at the time the decision must be taken (i.e. the control variables must be set). For example, these would be the future market conditions for the various product lines of the firm. The actual, realized level of the criterion variable depends on both the control variables and the state variables. If the business enterprise of our example introduces the new product line and the market for it turns out to be limited, realized profits may become negative and the firm bankrupted. On the other hand, if the firm does not introduce the new product line and the market for its existing product lines declines, then realized profits may also become negative and the firm bankrupted.

Various decision-making rules have been proposed for dealing with this situation, which has many plausible real-world applications. According to the well-known "maximin" criterion, the decision-maker should set the control variables at the level that maximizes the criterion variable under the assumption that the state variables take on their worst possible values. That is, one first "minimizes" over the state variables, and then "maximizes" over the control variables: thus the "maximin" designation. This is a very conservative criterion and could easily lead to a highly adverse decision in terms of foregone opportunities. But it has the advantage that the decision-maker need make no judgments concerning the relative probabilities of various values of the state variables.

The decision-making rule favored in economics, and that economists suspect is the operative rule, implicitly if not explicitly, in most real-world cases of decision-making under uncertainty, is called "expected utility maximization." To make this rule operational, the decision-maker must attach probabilities ("subjective probabilities") to the various values the state variables might take on in the future, and the decision-maker must also specify a utility function which attaches a utility value to each possible value of the observable criterion (e.g., the profits of the firm). The decision-maker then sets the control variables at levels that maximize the expected value of utility, defined as the sum of the products of each possible utility value with its respective probability.

Economists assume that this is done in an unconscious and intuitive way similar to the way in which consumers determine their purchases of goods so as to maximize their utility subject to the relevant budget constraint. Consumers are no more consciously aware of this computational process than they are consciously aware of such physiological processes as respiration and the circulation of blood. But just as respiration and the circulation of blood are no less real for being unconscious, so too utility maximization is no less real for being unconscious. And similarly, expected utility maximization in decision-making under uncertainty is no less real for being unconscious. Or, at least, so most economists believe.

This book is concerned with one especially important choice out of the multitude of choices confronting humanity at the present juncture in our history: the choice between maintaining the status quo situation under which the United Nations remains the highest level of international organization in the world, or to proceed beyond the United Nations to establish a genuine and legitimate—albeit limited—world government along the lines of the proposed Federal Union of Democratic Nations. There is no escaping the fact that whatever we do, whether we establish a world government or do not establish a world government, we will confront serious risks. If we establish a world government, there is a risk that forcing the nations together into a single political organization will exacerbate the frictions and antagonisms among them, inciting civil disturbances, riotous mobs, and eventual civil war. Or there is the risk that this particular threat will be met and overcome by means of a totalitarian regime propped up by a draconian police apparatus—a bleak fate possibly even worse than warfare. On the other hand, if we do not establish a world government, it is possible that the future course of history will generate the same kind of hostile confrontations among competing blocs of nations with which all past history of humanity has been replete, and that some of these confrontations will escalate over into the same kind of fearful and devastating warfare that has plagued humanity since earliest recorded history. What divides the future from the past is the quantum jump in the potential destructiveness of warfare consequent upon the invention of nuclear weapons. Has this factor been taken into adequate account in weighing the relative risks of proceeding into the future without a world government in operation, versus with a world government in operation?

The argument of this book is that this entire question hinges on *what kind* of world government is intended. Among most of that tiny minority of the population that favors world government, the world government would be so powerful that no single nation, nor any group of nations, would be able to challenge its power. The world government would directly control all or most heavy weaponry in the world, including all nuclear weapons. This conception of world government is described as the "omnipotent world state." Personally, I concur with the majority that the omnipotent world state, established in the contemporary world, would be excessively risky: it would be far too likely to abuse its power. For this reason, such a world government cannot be peacefully formed, by social contract, among the nations of the contemporary world. This kind of a world government is indeed—if not impossible—at least so improbable as to justify its complete disregard. For most people at the present time, consideration of world government terminates at this point.

But to terminate consideration of world government on grounds that an extremely powerful world government, the omnipotent world state, would most likely be undesirable, is a profound error. Conceivably, in due course, this error might be fatal not only to global human civilization as we know it today, but to the human species itself. It is an error because there is *no need* for the world government to be "extremely powerful," so that its power would be comparable to the power currently exercised by the national governments over their component parts. There is nothing in the laws of nature, logic, or mankind preventing an appropriate *sharing* of power and authority between the national governments and the world government, so that there would be adequate guarantees for the legitimate rights of nations and adequate safeguards against the world government evolving into a monolithic tyranny buttressed by a suffocating bureaucracy. The Federal Union of Democratic Nations set forth in this book would definitely fit the definition of a "state" or a "government," while at the same time obviously being far short of an "omnipotent state" or an "all-powerful government."

In terms of the formal theory of decision-making under uncertainty, the *nature* of the world government represents the *value* of a decision variable. There is a wide range of values at which this variable might be set—reflecting the wide range of possible specific distributions of effective power between the world government and the national governments. It is a misconception that world government is an either-or, black-or-white, yes-or-no choice—that it is what, in analytical terminology, is referred to as a "dichotomous variable." Rather it is a "continuous variable" that may take on any of a wide range of different values.

True, the choice between "some world government" and "no world government" is a dichotomous choice, but once this particular choice has been made in the affirmative, the more interesting and challenging question emerges: what *type* of a world government do we want? As a matter of fact, if we were to broaden the definition of "world government" to signify merely "a large-scale political organization encompassing all or most nations of the world," the decision to have a world government was taken back in 1920 when the League of Nations was established. The United Nations of 1945 then slightly ratcheted up the power and authority of the existent world government. I am arguing here that the time has come to further ratchet up the power and authority of the existent world government by replacing the United Nations with the Federal Union of Democratic Nations.

Of course, to describe the League of Nations of the interwar period or the United Nations of today as a "world government" definitely would not be consistent with most people's understanding of "government." On the other hand, the proposed Federal Union of Democratic Nations is certainly consistent with the usual conception of a government. So there are actually two questions rather than one to be answered. The first question, whether we should have *any* sort of supernational government, should almost certainly be answered in the affirmative. The second question, given an affirmative answer to the first, is what *type* of a world government should we have? The proposed Federal Union of Democratic Nations described herein is, I believe, a very plausible candidate for the appropriate *type* of world government. If not this exact plan, then something close to it.

If we envision a relatively limited form of world government instead of a virtually omnipotent form of world government, the evaluation of the relative risk question is greatly altered. The risks of continuing with the sovereign nation-state system of the present day are not changed, but the risks of establishing a world government are greatly reduced. If we continue with the sovereign nation-state system of today, we continue to run the risk that this system will go on generating large-scale warfare in the future just as it has generated large-scale warfare in the past, despite the fact that the introduction of nuclear weapons has made warfare far more costly than ever before. Those who argue that nuclear weapons will "frighten" humanity into maintaining the peace indefinitely would seem to possess a deficient appreciation of history, which has demonstrated time and time again, in numerous diverse ways, that the storms of warfare can blow up very suddenly and unexpectedly out of what appeared to be calm, clear, blue skies.

As just one of numerous examples of this, consider the international condition as of 1900—shortly prior to the eruption of World War I. There was no conflict at that time between nations espousing capitalism and nations espousing socialism. There was some awareness of differences in economic status and culture, but much of the Third World was incorporated into the colonial empires of the major First World nations, and in any event the poorer regions represented no military threat to the advanced nations. Great advances had recently been made in terms of machine guns, long-range artillery, and high explosives, and there was an acute awareness of how destructive warfare would be if fought with these new weapons. The nations of Western Europe had achieved the highest living standards in history, and they were still advancing. Many of the royal heads of state of the European powers were related by marriage. What could possibly go wrong?

History showed what could go wrong. The German Kaiser, Wilhelm II, believed that his nation was greatly disadvantaged by not possessing an overseas colonial empire. Disgruntled by this situation, and also fond of military pomp and circumstance, Wilhelm gradually built up a huge military establishment so that other nations would be properly deferential toward German national interests—and this increased deference would somehow, someway, lead to German acquisition of a fine colonial empire. Therefore the other European nations found it necessary also to maintain huge military establishments for the usual "defensive purposes." The arms competition percolated along steadily.

Then, on June 28, 1914, the Archduke Francis Ferdinand, heir to the throne of the Austro-Hungarian empire, and his wife were assassinated in Sarajevo by a Serbian nationalist, one Gavrilo Princip. At first, few expected that the agitated negotiations that followed this outrage would lead to war. Nevertheless, as history duly recorded, they did lead to war. And not just to war, but to the most horrific war in the history of human civilization up to that point.

Can nothing analogous to this occur in the future? Are we so much superior to the people of 1900 that we can disregard the repeated lessons of history? Has the invention of nuclear weapons so much altered the calculus of warfare that never again will provocation and miscalculated brinkmanship generate a world-wide conflict? Clearly, these questions cannot be answered confidently in the affirmative. There is clearly some degree of risk. There are many people in the world today whose thought processes are very close to the thought processes of Kaiser Wilhelm II as of 1900. They certainly do not intend war, but they are quite bound and determined that the national interests of their respective nations be honored and respected by the rest of the world—or else.

Many powerful nations in the world today, although "peace-loving" in the sense that they are basically satisfied with the international status quo, find it necessary to maintain powerful military forces, in several cases armed with nuclear weapons. They are ready to disarm at any time—provided other nations do so first. Therefore a gigantic powder keg sits amid human civilization, with its fuse dangling down, just waiting to be lit. At the same time there are many other fanatic mentalities in the world today whose thought processes are very close to the thought processes of Gavrilo Princip, the Serbian nationalist responsible for the assassination of the Archduke and his wife in 1914. These people do not care that their activities might be regarded by others as intolerably provocative, so that these activities (such as assassinating national officials, exploding bombs in public places, etc.) might eventually light the fuse on the gigantic powder keg sitting amid human civilization. They are so warped and distorted with unreasoning hatred that they quite likely experience a warm, happy glow from the thought that their activities might set in motion a chain of events leading to catastrophic world war.

I do not assert that the foundation of a limited world government along the lines of a Federal Union of Democratic Nations would overnight eliminate this perilous situation. Owing to the reserved rights of member nations to free secession and independent military forces, the world with a Federal Union in existence might not look much different from the world as we know it today—in the short term. But with such a supernational federation in place, communication among the nations of the world would be improved, bargaining processes more streamlined, opportunities for cooperative action multiplied. With such a federation in place, the positive processes of global governance would be improved. Greater progress could be made toward reducing the risks attendant upon the international status quo situation with which we are familiar.

At the same time, the constitutional provisions underpinning the supernational federation would minimize the possibility that the federation would develop negatively—toward the global tyranny that is indissolubly linked, in the public imagination, with the concept of the omnipotent world state. The fact that a limited world government along the proposed lines would not immediately and fundamentally alter the world as we know it today might be considered a downside of the proposal. But at the same time, it can also be seen as an upside: the fact that the supernational federation would not immediately eliminate the hazards of the world situation as we know them today, also means that there would be minimal risk of adverse development in the direction of global tyranny. The bottom line is that implementing a limited world government would, on the whole, reduce the overall risks faced by the human race as we move forward into the unknown future.

## No Plausible Scenario?

Among world government skeptics, it is a tired cliché that there exists "no plausible scenario" by which world government could be peacefully inaugurated in the real world. The implicit challenge is that unless the proponents of world government can produce a detailed chronology of future events—a "plausible" chronology, no less—the case for world government can be disregarded. This challenge is quite absurd. Had anyone had an intuition in 1985 that the Soviet Union was in its final years, that person certainly could not have specified the exact course of events leading up to the USSR's dissolution in 1991. Quite clearly, therefore, it would be highly premature and most unwise to try to set forth any sort of a definite timetable for the achievement of world government, or to set forth precise details for the campaign of enlightenment necessary to establish the preconditions for this achievement.

Obviously a great many people must become aware of the blueprint for world government advanced herein (or something similar), and they must also consider this information sufficiently important to be worth sharing with others. Whether this process will commence this year, next year, or ten years from now, it is impossible to predict. Whether the process, once commenced, will proceed to the level necessary for success, is also impossible to predict. What may be argued strongly, however, is that for the greater good of humanity, this process *should* commence, and the sooner the better.

As a matter of fact, the "how can it possibly come to pass?" challenge to world government is merely a slightly more sophisticated variation on the more obviously faulty position that "world government has not happened in the past, ergo it cannot happen in the future." But this is quite obtuse—it is like asking "how could it come to pass" that a group of hungry, thirsty people wandering in a desert and suddenly finding an oasis containing a pond of clear, cold water surrounded by fruit trees, would thereupon eat and drink. Does any rational person actually need a detailed and scientifically accurate explanation to acknowledge that hungry and thirsty people, suddenly finding food and water, will proceed to eat and drink?

The real question is not "how will it happen?" but rather "should it happen?" That is to say, does the present proposal for a Federal Union of Democratic Nations represent an actual oasis (to continue with the metaphor) toward which our group of hungry, thirsty people in the desert should make haste to approach? Perhaps is it a mirage and so approaching it would represent only a waste of energy? Perhaps the water and/or the fruit is poisonous, so that partaking of either one would be fatal? The question of whether our metaphorical oasis is real and salubrious, or possibly otherwise, is analogous to the question of whether the Federal Union of Democratic Nations proposed here would or would not make a positive contribution to the future destiny of human civilization. *This* is the question which deserves careful thought and serious deliberation—not "*how could* it come to pass?" but "*should* it come to pass?"

Although it clearly impossible to specify a precise, detailed, and compellingly plausible schedule running from the here and now to the establishment of a world government according to the general specifications of the proposed Federal Union of Democratic Nations, I will conclude this chapter with some observations that provide the beginnings of a response to the challenge that there is "no plausible scenario" toward the foundation of a world government.

First and foremost, this proposal did not suddenly drop down, completely unheralded and unanticipated, out of the clear blue sky. The vast majority of sane, sensible, and informed people in the world today are fully aware of the serious global problems and the ongoing processes of globalization, are cosmopolitan in their outlook and favorably disposed toward increasing international cooperation. A wide and diverse assortment of authorities, experts, intellectuals, and politicians are continually preaching the cause of global understanding, and are constantly appealing for "fresh, new ideas" toward the furtherance of this cause.[5]

The basic idea of world government, of a universal political entity embracing—or at least open to—all of the peoples and nations of the world, has been under consideration and development literally for centuries. It is a concept that is fully accepted "in principle" by a very large proportion of those people who have ever thought seriously about it. The perceived obstacles are "practical" in nature: that is to say, world government would be good *in theory* but not, alas, *in practice*. But the proposed Federal Union of Democratic Nations is in fact a thoroughly pragmatic and sensible means of dealing with and overcoming the practical impediments to world government. In the light of this possibility, allegations that world government is impractical simply do not make sense. This plan is exactly the sort of "fresh, new idea" that so many people, everywhere in the world, are calling for. It gives the population of the world an attractive, secure avenue toward a better, safer, and more rewarding future.

There is nothing at all preposterous and unrealizable about the Federal Union blueprint for a functional, operational world government. It is not to be compared with lunatic fringe proposals toward world peace. The typical Christian televangelist, for example, has a very simple prescription for world peace: that everyone in the world "accept Christ into their heart." Should this vision be realized, it would no doubt greatly increase the financial revenues of these televangelists, but whether it would insure world peace is another question, After all, there was a profusion of bloodshed and warfare in medieval Europe, at a time when virtually everyone, ostensibly at least, had accepted Christ into their heart.

Another example of arrant nonsense is provided by assorted lunatic fringe anarchists and pacifists whose merry prescription for world peace is that "the people" take matters into their own hand, dissolve the governments, disband the armies, and live happily ever after in a myriad of self-sufficient little communes scattered over the face of the globe. Should this vision be realized, the little communes would waste no time accumulating stocks of weapons with which to do battle with one another. The battles might be on a smaller scale, but there would be many more of them, and the death toll might well be on the same order of magnitude as the death toll that could be realized by one single nuclear world war today.

The proposal for a Federal Union of Democratic Nations examined in this book has nothing in common with any and all schemes that envision drastic changes either in human nature or in the presently existing institutions of human civilization. It is a proposal for a careful, cautious, marginal, and evolutionary advance in the political institutions of humanity. No governments would be dissolved, no armies would be disbanded, and no one who had not already done so would be required to "accept Christ into his/her heart." The intent of the proposal is most accurately described as that of laying a more solid foundation for the future progress of human civilization. The Federal Union, in and of itself, is not expected to lead directly and immediately to this progress. Instead, it would provide a solid basis for *evolutionary* world government.

The world government skeptic might grant that *as individuals* a great many people might be favorably disposed toward world government if they were to become fully aware of such limited world government possibilities as the Federal Union of Democratic Nations, because they would see it as benefiting both their own personal interests and the interests of humanity as a whole. But the real problem lies not at the *individual* level but at the *organizational* level. According to the skeptic, organizations would naturally tend toward opposition to world government because they would see it as an organizational competitor to themselves, a competitor that would inevitably limit their own power and authority. However, it does not make sense to attribute to organizations a higher degree of paranoia than exists at the individual level. Any organization is built on the principle of cooperation toward a common goal, and thus it stands to reason that the leaders of organizations would be generally predisposed in favor of cooperation with other organizations.

This is not to deny that there are some organizations in the world today that would in all probability be opposed to world government: for example, the John Birch Society, America's Survival Inc., and the Ku Klux Klan. At the same time, there are numerous organizations that are definitely predisposed in favor of world government—assuming that a practical and effective scheme toward it could be devised. Citizens for Global Solutions is perhaps the foremost among several similar groups. In addition, there are a great many special interest organizations and think tanks which—although they have not yet gone on record in support of world government because they are not yet aware of a practical scheme toward it—are nevertheless in favor of progressive and outward-looking international policy. Some of the more important of these are the Carnegie Endowment for International Peace, the Council on Foreign Relations, the Institute for Policy Studies, and the Center for Strategic and International Studies. There are also many international organizations that might see in the Federal Union of Democratic Nations an effective instrument for the pursuit of their own goals: the many multinational corporations, the International Red Cross, the World Trade Organization, the International Monetary Fund, and the World Bank.

But then there are two other types of organizations of great importance in the contemporary world: the national governments, and the United Nations. Surely (according to the world government skeptic) both the national governments and the United Nations will perceive in a possible Federal Union of Democratic Nations a direct competitor against their own interests, power, and authority—as an organization that could and probably would encroach on their own "turf." Once again, I would respond to this position that it places far too much reliance on paranoiac tendencies. The human personnel of both the United Nations and the national governments, whether primarily politicians or administrators or rank-and-file employees, are not only (on the whole) sane, rational and intelligent people, but by virtue of the role of the organizations of which they are part, they are predisposed in favor of cooperation, authority, and governance. As a group, they are not predisposed toward paranoia. Therefore, many if not most of these people will recognize in the Federal Union of Democratic Nations a potentially very positive force in the world. The personnel of the national governments might look toward a potential world government much as do the personnel of the various state governments in the United States toward the federal government—as a helpful partner toward the pursuit of their own goals. And the personnel of the United Nations might look forward to a potential world government as a more effective means of pursuing their personal and professional goals.

Nor is it the case that the Federal Union of Democratic Nations would present a direct and immediate threat to the employment of the personnel of the national governments and the United Nations. What the long-term effect of the Federal Union on overall employment in governance organizations would be is difficult to predict. While world government skeptics invariably argue that world government would automatically increase the bureaucratic overload on human civilization, that is pure speculation. Certainly the overall objective would be to maintain aggregate administrative costs over all levels of government, including the supernational, the national, the regional and the local, at a reasonable level consistent with the central importance of good governance to human society.

The existence of a world government would enable certain administrative functions of national governments to be handled more efficiently and effectively at the supernational level. Thus the world government could well lead to reductions in the total number of employees involved with those specific functions. On the other hand, there might be an increase in the total number of personnel involved in other types of administrative functions. What will happen in the long run is therefore quite uncertain.

In the short run, however, over the first 10 to 20 years of the world government's operations, it is most likely that there will be a significant increase in the total number of personnel employed by governance organizations. To start with, the personnel of the Federal Union of Democratic Nations will likely be five to ten times more numerous than the personnel of the United Nations At the same time, there will likely be very little decrease in the personnel of the national governments. Thus the establishment of the world government would open up new employ-ment opportunities for all types of governance personnel: politicians, administrators, and rank-and-file employees. And some of these new op-portunities might seem very attractive indeed to those who would be qualified for them. Just as the governors of the states of the United States today may aspire to becoming the President of the United States, so too the national leaders of the future could aspire to becoming the Union Chief Executive of the Federal Union of Democratic Nations. It hardly seems unlikely that many of various national presidents and prime minis-ters would indeed, with considerable relish, imagine themselves rising to that honored and exalted position in human affairs.

It might be worth mentioning in this context that the United States of America, currently the single most powerful nation in the contemporary world, played an instrumental role in the foundation of both the League of Nations and the United Nations. Although the plan for a League of Nations originated in Europe, it was the determined advocacy of U.S. President Woodrow Wilson that ensured that the League would be incor-porated into the Treaty of Versailles that concluded World War I.[6] How-ever, Wilson was unable to overcome the resurgence of isolationism con-sequent upon the brief but costly U.S. participation in the war, and the United States did not join the League. This abstention may have been a factor that emboldened Nazi Germany to embark upon a course of "na-tional regeneration" that soon brought about a resumption of conflict. In historical perspective, the two decades between the end of World War I in November 1918 and the beginning of World War II in September 1939 are seen as merely an uneasy truce separating the two "German wars" of the first half of the twentieth century.

Remaining tendencies in the United States toward isolationism were virtually eliminated during the course of American involvement in World War II from December 1941 through August 1945. U.S. President Frank-lin D. Roosevelt was the prime mover in the genesis of the United Na-tions, intended as an improved and strengthened League of Nations.[7] If left to their own devices, neither Winston Churchill of the U.K. nor Jo-seph Stalin of the USSR would have been particularly interested in the U.N. Although institutionally very similar to the League of Nations it replaced, the United Nations was in principle much stronger than its pre-decessor, mainly because the two world superpowers at the end of the war, the United States and the Soviet Union, were both founding mem-bers. Unfortunately for the cause of world peace and progress, these same two superpowers were profoundly divided on ideological issues. The development and spread of nuclear weapons at this same time fur-ther complicated the extremely hazardous brew of postwar international relations.

To the handful of world federalists still remaining as of the early 1990s, the decline of Cold War tensions in the wake of the collapse and dissolution of the USSR presented humanity with another shining opportunity. Just as the end of World War I saw the establishment of the League of Nations, and the end of World War II saw the establishment of the United Nations, could not the end of the Cold War witness the establishment of a genuine world government of which the League and the U.N. were imperfect harbingers? More than a quarter of a century later, it is now apparent that this opportunity—if opportunity it was—was not exploited. But an opportunity might still be there, and it might still be exploited. So long as the objective is a limited world government along the lines of the Federal Union of Democratic Nations, and not the "omnipotent world state" envisioned by traditional world federalists, then the possibility exists. Therefore it is not improbable that in the future the United States of America will in fact champion world government. It is not improbable that some current or future U.S. president will follow in the footsteps of Woodrow Wilson and Franklin D. Roosevelt, and push for a new and higher form of international organization than ever before witnessed in the history of humanity. The likelihood of this happening, of course, depends critically on the specific form of world government that is envisioned.

The salient reality is that the case for world government is in fact far stronger than is commonly recognized at the present time. Of course, this does understand a limited world government with, at a minimum, the following key attributes: (1) member nations would retain the right to maintain military forces, armed with both conventional and nuclear weapons, under their direct control; (2) member nations would retain the right to withdraw peacefully from the supernational federation at their own unilateral discretion; (3) voting weight in the federation legislature would be determined in such a way (e.g., the dual voting system) that legislation must be acceptable both to the less populous rich nations of the world, and the more populous poor nations. These are precisely the central characteristics of limited world government as embodied in the blueprint for a Federal Union of Democratic Nations.

Despite these limitations, the proposed Federal Union would possess the essential attributes and trappings of state authority: it would have separate, democratically elective branches for legislative, executive, and judicial functions, it would have a capital city and a permanent administrative apparatus, it would possess significant military forces under its direct control, it would have an appreciable power of direct taxation, it would have the essential symbols of state authority: a flag, an anthem and emblems. It would take an active role in global governance from the moment of its inception. Very likely its early history would be devoted chiefly to the initiation, coordination, and successful prosecution of a very large-scale global economic development assistance effort, termed the Global Marshall Plan (GMP), designed to significantly reduce the economic gap between the rich and poor nations within a reasonable period of historical time. A political agency of this scale and significance would provide a powerful center around which to rally and invigorate the positive impulses in humanity toward global community and harmony.

The opportunities we possess today to make this age-old dream a reality are unprecedented in the history of humanity. The wonders of science and technology are continuing onward at a seemingly ever-increasing pace. The economic fruits of this advance are manifested in productivity levels that are astronomical in relation to all past historical eras. The economically advanced nations of the world, supported by sophisticated machinery and an equally sophisticated labor force, are providing their people with living standards that would have seemed veritably paradisiacal to the peoples of past ages. Thanks to automotive power and an immense road network, thanks to railroads and jet-powered airliners and cargo superships, the mobility of human beings and transportability of commodities are at levels never before achieved. The telephonic communications network enables people at opposite ends of the earth to converse together as if they were in the same room. Radio and television provide information and entertainment through the air in a manner that might seem magical if it were not so familiar. Over the last three decades, the development of the Internet has made available a vast profusion of detailed information to anyone with access to an inexpensive microcomputer. The practical problems of communications and transportation and coordination that would have confronted an effort at a universal world government in the past have been rendered virtually null and void. And with the production techniques we now have available—techniques that are likely capable of considerable further improvement—there seems to be no compelling reason why every living human being on Earth should not enjoy a reasonably high standard of living.

The major difficulties impeding the initiation of world government at this point in human history do not lie in the real world—rather they lie in the persistence of various preconceptions and misconceptions regarding the probable nature and characteristics of world government that are currently deeply embedded in the minds of so many people. Beliefs and attitudes that may have been perfectly sound and reasonable two hundred years ago, or even one hundred years ago, have been rendered perverse and dysfunctional by the march of time. What may have been plausible in the past is no longer plausible in the present. No doubt humanity has powerful tendencies toward inertial conservatism, toward clinging to a status quo policy well after it has become an obstacle to progress. But at the same time, humanity has demonstrated, time and time again throughout history, a very high level of intelligence, reason, and adaptability. It may take a long time for the truth to out—but eventually the truth does out, and humanity makes the appropriate adjustments and moves forward.

It is to be hoped that this will happen sooner rather than later with respect to the establishment of a world government. Mankind has climbed a long way up the mountain, but there always remains the danger of a fall. What is needed might be described as a "campaign of enlightenment"—a campaign to make the majority of humanity aware of the fact that whatever may have been the case in the past, at the present time there is a reasonable preponderance of evidence in support of the desirability of world government as a means of strengthening the probability that human civilization will avoid disaster and continue its long-term advance. What are the odds that a sufficient amount of enlightenment can be achieved within the near future to make world government a practical possibility? Obviously, no one can provide a precise answer to this question. But I would argue that the odds on this are much better than commonly believed.

Although it has been a consistent theme throughout this book that both professional opinion and popular opinion are at the present time strongly opposed to world government, I do not want to overstate this particular point for fear of inculcating in the reader hopeless despair regarding the prospects for world government within the fairly proximate future—or at least well within the lifetimes of many people now living. The basic premise is that opposition to world government mostly derives from misapprehension concerning the necessary characteristics of a world state—specifically, the belief that a world government must necessarily be militarily omnipotent and fully incapable of sharing significant power and authority with the component nation-states (i.e. the omnipotent world state). If this erroneous belief can be dispelled, then people can and will change their minds about world government. But the less distance there is between the prevalent conception of world government and the conception put forward in this book, the greater the likelihood that people will indeed change their minds on the subject.

All of the hope which this author continues to cherish—as I have throughout my entire adult life—of personally surviving long enough to see an operational world government, are bound up with the possibility that the vast majority of humanity has rejected, and continues to reject, the idea of world government because the vast majority of humanity has not yet awakened to the possibility of a limited world government along the lines of the Federal Union of Democratic Nations under consideration here. In and of itself, of course, the idea is not at all complicated—it does not take the proverbial "rocket scientist" to comprehend it and to appreciate its potential real-world significance. There is certainly no intellectual barrier here to impede the epiphany of any reasonably well-informed individual.

There are various sub-groups within the overall human race the majority of which needs to experience this epiphany if world government is to become a serious possibility. Specialists in international relations form one small component of what might be called the "intelligentsia": those involved in the production, preservation, and dissemination of knowledge. Another group, not completely exclusive of course, is the "political leadership," encompassing all those who are either themselves government officials, or who are actively involved in the selection of government officials. The "general public" might be defined as that large majority of the population who are not primarily members of either the intelligentsia or the political leadership. For world government to be inaugurated peacefully, clearly it is necessary that a substantial majority of all three groups, the intelligentsia, the political leadership, and the general public, be in favor of world government.

One could speculate at length on which of these groups is the natural leader of the other two, and on which might tend to lag behind the other two. For example, one speculation often voiced by disgruntled world federalists in the past is that the initial impetus to world government must come from "the people" as opposed to the national government officials. Presumably they mean by "the people" all those, whether of the intelligentsia or the general public, who do not qualify as members of the political leadership. I suspect that these disgruntled world federalists have greatly exaggerated the difference in opinion between the political leadership and the rest of the population, and that the real reason why national government officials have rejected world government is because the great majority of their respective citizen bodies are opposed to world government. But speculations on the relative importance of the various sub-groups in the campaign of enlightenment are likely to be inconclusive and unfruitful.

There are other matters on which we could speculate, with basically similar outcomes. For example, which nations would be more likely to join and which less likely to join—and how important is it that any particular nation join? The only general principle here, it would seem, is that the larger and more powerful a particular nation, the more valuable it would be as a charter member of the supernational federation. It is more important that nations such as the United States (the leading nation in terms of total economic output) and China (the leading nation in terms of population) join the federation, than that nations such as Monaco do so. An encouraging thought here is that the Federal Union need not claim universal membership by all nations of the world in order to be success-ful. The Union would aspire to universal membership as a long-term goal, of course, but it could be virtually as effective if it included a pre-ponderance of the nations of the world.

Another question concerns the role of existing world federalist or-ganizations, such as Citizens for Global Solutions, in the campaign for enlightenment. To date, their efforts have been quite dispersed and rela-tively ineffective. But conceivably, if they could mostly coalesce around a clear and definite plan of *limited* world government of increasing popu-larity, they could make an important contribution to the process. Still another question—looking farther down the road—concerns the role of the United Nations in the transition process. It would be most natural, of course, to have the United Nations dissolve itself as the Federal Union of Democratic Nations is inaugurated, just as earlier the League of Nations dissolved itself as the United Nations was initiated. Of course one would expect that a substantial number of U.N. Secretariat members could make an important contribution in the administrative apparatus support-ing the executive branch of the Federal Union. The possibility remains, however, that the basic U.N. organization could continue on as a focus for the minority of nations not taking charter membership in the Federal Union, somewhat in the same way that the European Free Trade Area (EFTA) was for a brief period of time a less ambitious alternative to the European Common Market (eventually the European Union).

In pondering prospects for the potential establishment of a Federal Union of Democratic Nations within the foreseeable future, it is also worth noting that there are already on the table a number of fairly well-known ideas toward the betterment of global human civilization. Exam-ples include Richard Falk's "humane governance," Daniele Archibugi and David Held's "cosmopolitan democracy," Thomas Pogge's "global justice," and Luis Cabrera's "global citizenship."[8] While there is no question of the commendable attitudes of the advocates of these kinds of ideas, their advocacies tend to be weakened by their ambivalence, eva-sion, or in some cases (for example, Richard Falk) outright rejection, of the possibility of world government as an instrumentality toward the pur-suit of these worthy objectives. Many well-intentioned individuals today urge that all humanity embrace a "new way of thinking" and develop a sense of global community, of brotherhood transcending national boundaries and embracing the entire human family. This is fine as far as it goes, but "global community" and similar terms denote merely abstract concepts. Many if not most individuals preaching these concepts today have not yet perceived that a properly designed federal world government, as a tangible symbol, could indeed make a major contribution to the attitudinal development they espouse—without incurring a significant risk of degenerating into a totalitarian nightmare. Proper safeguards are capable of reducing the probability of a totalitarian outcome to an acceptably low level. But with these safeguards in place, a functioning world government, by virtue merely of its existence, would provide potent assistance to the further development of the cosmopolitan attitudes advocated by the great majority of educated, enlightened people today. Given the realities of today's nationally oriented world, something along the lines of the Federal Union of Democratic Nations may be the only viable alternative for initiating and sustaining a gradual evolutionary trend toward an authoritative yet benign world government. Once this has been recognized and fully absorbed by advocates of humane governance, cosmopolitan democracy, and the like, these advocates might well become enthusiastic supporters of the Federal Union possibility.

The world government skeptic, of course, will likely proclaim the futility of speculating about either the overall strategy or the detailed tactics of the campaign of enlightenment. Such a campaign, the skeptic will say, will never have a chance of developing into anything noticeable—and this not for just one reason but for two. First, there is the tremendous conservative bias at all levels of society everywhere in the world. Given the present climate of both intellectual and popular opinion, world government is simply too big and bold an idea even to be given consideration, let alone ever to be actually implemented. Even if the possibility of world government were to gain a tiny foothold in human thinking and political activity, overwhelming forces would quickly be mustered in favor of maintaining the status quo on national sovereignty. The world government movement would very soon be stalled and checkmated.

The second reason why the campaign of enlightenment is doomed from the beginning, according to the skeptic, is the tremendous degree of apathy and disinterest among all segments of the population everywhere in the world. This is partly owing to the massive conservative bias against any hint of fundamental sociopolitical change—but it goes beyond that. People today are too busy with their personal careers, too preoccupied with their personal lives, and too overwhelmed by a tidal wave of information and entertainment emanating from the media, to have either the interest or the energy to undertake significant activity toward some higher goal and purpose.

In his time, Karl Marx railed against religion as the "opiate of the masses": as a deadening barrier against fundamental reform of the economic system. But now, the "masses" are rendered inert not merely by religion, but also by popular culture, spectator sports, television and movies. Not to mention that substantial subset of the population that is rendered inert by literal "opiates" in the form of marijuana, cocaine, heroin, and various other psychotropic drugs. Back in Marx's time, the leadership of the socialist movement did not come from the exploited "masses" but rather mostly from the middle and upper classes of society. Ironically, the leadership of the movement was not provided by those who stood to gain the most from a socialist transformation; it came rather from those with less to gain personally but better equipped with the knowledge and skills to effect social change. But today, the descendants of those socially responsible middle class and upper class people of the nineteenth century are far too concerned to protect their good names and reputations to even dream of becoming involved with anything so radical as a movement to establish a world government.

What response may be made to these arguments? Although the alleged "conservative bias" and "apathy and disinterest" are closely interrelated in a practical sense, they are conceptually distinct and may be addressed separately. With respect to the degree of conservatism in the population, it can hardly be disputed that it was appreciably higher during the second half of the twentieth century than it was during the second half of nineteenth century. In fact, people living during the second half of the twentieth century (i.e. people alive today) tend to positively envy those people who lived during the second half of the nineteenth century. What a positive and optimistic time that must have been (or so we think)—when people had no hint of the twentieth century disasters to come: of the world wars, the totalitarian regimes in Germany, Russia, China and elsewhere, the threat of nuclear holocaust, and the danger of environmental collapse brought on by the population explosion.

But there may be a tendency to exaggerate the impact of large social events upon the attitudes and emotions of individual human beings. Individual human beings are very adaptable, which means that they are not unduly upset by bad conditions nor unduly happy about good conditions. People today do not lie awake at night worrying about being killed in a nuclear holocaust, any more than they lie awake worrying about being killed in a car crash. By the same token, people in the nineteenth century did not happily congratulate themselves that they could not be killed in a nuclear holocaust—or in a car crash for that matter. Nor were people in the second half of the nineteenth century generally all that enthusiastic about the concept of social progress. No doubt some were enthusiastic, but certainly not all. There were plenty of political conservatives in those days, who were very conscious of such historical episodes as the Terror during the French Revolution, and who felt very much threatened by such things as the socialist movement codified by Karl Marx, and the general tendency toward extension of the voting franchise. Those conservatives could no doubt conjure up vivid images of civilization destroyed by the radical leveling policies of popularly elected demagogues. In retrospect, we look back to the latter half of the nineteenth century as an era of untroubled peace, plenty, security, and serenity. But it did not appear so to the people who were alive at that time.

In some ways, the people of today can look forward to the future with more confidence than could have the people of the nineteenth century. For one thing, the socialist menace is much reduced. Even though there are still a few important nations in the world that still subscribe to the communist form of socialism, none of the capitalist nations seems a likely candidate for any form of public-ownership socialism, communistic or otherwise. In the view of the large majority of humanity, public-ownership socialism has been thoroughly discredited both economically and politically—so much so that the people of the USSR, who vigorously championed the cause of socialism throughout most of the twentieth century, have themselves voluntarily renounced and repudiated it. In the light of what we now know, the principle of political democracy also does not seem to be such a hazard as it was once regarded. The demagogues so much feared by nineteenth century conservatives have not come to power and thereupon destroyed civilization by means of their radical leveling policies. Even nations with a tremendous amount of poverty and economic inequality, such as India, are politically stable despite their democratic institutions. In the one case in the twentieth century where a demagogue came close to destroying civilization, leveling policies were not involved. In the case of the German Third Reich spawned by the demonic charisma of Adolf Hitler, the instrumentality through which German civilization was very nearly destroyed was involvement in international warfare—not implementation of excessively egalitarian domestic policies. There is also the point that neither world civilization, nor German civilization, was actually destroyed by even such a cataclysmic conflict as World War II. Within fifty years after decimating itself in a horrific conflict, Europe emerged more prosperous than ever. This evidence of the recuperative powers of human civilization may indeed be fostering a certain amount of subliminal complacency that might be quite dangerous. To the extent that many people have the vague impression that human civilization could—if necessary—recover from a nuclear World War III, it makes that war more likely to occur.

Therefore, while there may have been slightly more optimism and willingness to experiment in the latter part of the nineteenth century than in the latter part of the twentieth century and beyond, the actual difference might not be all that great. In any event, there is obviously a happy medium on the attitude spectrum between conservatism and progressivism. All but the most ideologically rigid conservative will admit that under certain conditions, certain changes become desirable; while at the same time, all but the most ideologically rigid progressive will admit that under certain conditions, certain changes would in fact be undesirable. According to the oscillatory theory of history, social attitudes toward change and progress swing like a pendulum between extreme conservatism and extreme progressivism. But a swinging pendulum tends over time toward a static, perpendicular position. It is not all that implausible that we humans are learning from our mistakes, that we are less subject either to extremes of conservatism or extremes of progressivism, and that the political pendulum is tending toward a static position over the happy medium.

The proposal under consideration in this book for a limited world government in the form of the Federal Union of Democratic Nations might well embody that happy medium. It is progressive in the sense that it would advance the level of international cooperation and coordination substantially beyond what has been achieved by the United Nations. At the same time it is conservative because of the retained national rights to secession and independent military forces. These and other provisions of the plan would virtually eliminate the possibility that the world government would develop into either a crushing global tyranny or a crushing global bureaucracy. The Federal Union would be a step forward, clearly, but not a radical step forward. Once they adequately understand this proposal, most people might perceive it to be the careful, cautious, evolutionary advance that it is in reality.

But what about the skeptic's other allegation that the reigning apathy and disinterest of the human population stands as an impenetrable barrier against any significant part of the human race ever becoming aware of the inherent value and desirability of this form of limited world government? It cannot be denied that many people are very busy with their careers and their families, nor can it be denied that it is sometimes difficult to get the attention of very busy people. But it would be ridiculous to propose that people anywhere in the world—and particularly people in the wealthy, industrialized nations of the world—are so ground down and exhausted by work and family responsibilities that they are incapable of exerting themselves toward some great purpose. The skeptic points to the stultifying, deadening effect on human thinking and initiative of popular culture and spectator sports by conjuring up an image of inert couch potatoes watching television for hours at a time.

But the fact that this time is utilized for watching television rather than for sleeping demonstrates that most people possess untapped reserves of time and energy. Nor should the passive nature of some leisure time pursuits cause us to lose sight of the fact that other leisure time pursuits are quite active in nature. While some people spend a great deal of time watching spectator sports in stadiums and on television, many other people are out there participating in vigorous physical exercise by means of playing games, jogging, bicycling, swimming, and lifting weights. Many people also devote considerable amounts of leisure time to intellectual and cultural pursuits, as witnessed, for example, by the tremendous volume of book and magazine publishing. While it is true that people today experience a tremendous barrage of information from both print and electronic media, this does not necessarily mean that they have been battered by this barrage into a condition of indifferent passivity. They pick and choose from among this barrage what they will attend to. If something important happens, if some idea or movement comes along that is worthy of widespread attention and action, we have the communications media at our disposal to get the word out rapidly.

In short, I do not accept that apathy and indifference are the normal condition of humanity, nor do I accept that human beings are more prone to these attitudes in the contemporary age than they were in any prior age. In most ways, the individual person, as well as human society as a whole, is more flexible and adaptable today than at any time in the past. The human race as a whole is far better educated and informed than it has ever been in the past. We are far more aware of past history than we have ever been before. We recognize that humanity has made many mistakes in our past pursuit of progress—but we are also conscious of the fact that it is possible to learn from mistakes, that mistakes are necessary if any progress is to be made, and that the only truly final and fatal mistake would be to forsake progress for fear of making mistakes.

The foundation of a world state along the lines of the proposed Federal Union of Democratic Nations could well have a tremendously beneficial impact upon the future of human civilization. It could well be the instrumentality through which such potential disasters as nuclear Armageddon or environmental breakdown are avoided. It could be the instrumentality through which the misery of mass poverty throughout the Third World will be abolished. It could be the instrumentality through which individual human beings will achieve a higher level of moral existence than ever before—less vexed and distressed by resentment and hostility toward their fellow human beings, more receptive to attitudes of respect and friendship, and more disposed to actions of cooperation and support.

We cannot know whether a campaign to establish a world government will be crowned with success. We cannot know whether a world government, if and when established, would be a success. But we should not let the possibility of failure stay us from the effort. If our ancestors had refused to take risks, to venture beyond the familiar, to take positive action toward a better world, then we would still be living in caves and beating one another over the head with clubs. Now it is our turn—the future destiny of global human civilization, passed forward from generation to generation, has reached our hands. We should live up to the highest standards embodied in our humanity.

# Notes

## Chapter 1: Salvation or Damnation?

p. 2
1. Kenneth Waltz, *Man, the State and War: A Theoretical Analysis* (New York: Columbia University Press, 1959), p. 228.

p. 2
2. The famous "nasty, brutish and short" phrase is from Chapter 13 ("On the Natural Condition of Man as Concerning Their Felicity and Misery") of Thomas Hobbes's magnum opus *Leviathan* (1651). In historical context, *Leviathan* was a reaction to the disruption and bloodshed of the English Civil War of 1642 to 1651, during which King Charles I was executed (1649) by order of Parliament on the charge of treason.

p. 8
3. As one example, during the debate over Medicaid and Medicare in 1965, Senator Carl Curtis (R-Neb.)—originally elected in 1936 on an anti-New Deal platform—said of the proposed programs: "[I]t is not needed. It is socialism. It moves the country in a direction which is not good for anyone, whether they be young or old. It charts a course from which there will be no turning back... It is not only socialism – it is brazen socialism." He later added that Medicare "is not public welfare. It is not charity. It is not kindness. It is socialism. Socialism is not the answer to anything."

## Chapter 2: A Pragmatic Blueprint

p. 28
1. Richard Falk, "A New Paradigm for International Legal Studies: Prospects and Proposals," *Yale Law Journal* 84(5): 969-1021, April 1975.

p. 28
2. Grenville Clark and Louis B. Sohn, *World Peace through World Law: Two Alternative Plans*, third enlarged edition (Cambridge: Harvard University Press, 1966).

p. 29
3. Although this particular quote has been widely circulated, according to the Website "Lord Kelvin Quotations" there is no reliable source for it in books or newspapers published during Kelvin's lifetime. However, the same Website

reproduces an interview reported by *The Newark Advocate* (April 26, 1902) in which the following exchange occurs: Q: "Then it would appear that, in your opinion, we have no hope of solving the problem of aerial navigation in any way?" A: "No; I do not think there is any hope. Neither the balloon, nor the aeroplane, nor the gliding machine will be a practical success."

p. 30

4. Emery Reves, *The Anatomy of Peace*, second edition (New York: Harper and Brothers, 1945); Frederick L. Schuman, *The Commonwealth of Man: An Inquiry into Power Politics and World Government* (New York: Alfred A. Knopf, 1952).

p. 31

5. Brief overviews of the Federal Union proposal are contained in James A. Yunker, *The Idea of World Government: From Ancient Times to the Twenty-First Century* (New York: Routledge, 2011), and *The Grand Convergence: Economic and Political Aspects of Human Progress* (Palgrave Macmillan, 2010). A more comprehensive treatment is contained in Yunker, *Political Globalization: A New Vision of Federal World Government* (Lanham, Md.: University Press of America, 2007), Chapter 2.

p. 35

6. Professional literature is sparse on the relative advantages of a bicameral versus a unicameral legislature, probably because the issue rarely captures much attention. However, the National Democratic Institute for International Affairs has issued a concise but comprehensive paper entitled: "One Chamber or Two? Deciding between a Unicameral and a Bicameral Legislature" (Legislative Research Series Paper #3, available from its Website). See also Lawrence Longley and David Olson, eds., *Two into One: The Politics and Processes of National Legislative Cameral Change* (Boulder, Col.: Westview Press, 1991).

p. 35

7. Among virtually all of that small minority of contemporary people who subscribe to world federalism, it is assumed that any benign form of world government must necessarily be democratic. For example, Luis Cabrera, *Political Theory of Global Justice: A Cosmopolitan Case for the World State* (New York: Routledge, 2004), and Torbjörn Tännsjö, *Global Democracy: The Case for a World Government* (Edinburgh, U.K.: Edinburgh University Press, 2008).

p. 39

8. From the cases examined in *Separatism: Democracy and Disintegration* (Lanham, Md.: Rowman & Littlefield, 1998), edited by Metta Spencer, the most serious separatist movements in the recent past are those of Chechnya, Tatarstan, Sri Lanka, and Quebec. The book also examines historical cases of the disintegrations of the Austro-Hungarian Empire, the Ottoman Empire, and more recently, the USSR, Yugoslavia, and Czechoslovakia. See also Christopher Hewitt and Tom Cheetham, *Encyclopedia of Modern Separatist Movements* (Santa Barbara, Cal.: ABC-CLIO Inc., 2000), and Henry Hale, *Foundations of*

*Ethnic Politics: Separatism of States and Nations in Eurasia and the World* (New York: Cambridge University Press, 2008).

p. 39

9. For background on the Quebec secessionist movement, see, for example: Richard Simeon, ed., *Must Canada Fail?* (Montreal: McGill-Queen's University Press, 1977); Jane M. Jacobs, *The Question of Separatism: Quebec and the Struggle over Sovereignty* (New York: Random House, 1980); Mordecai Richler, *Oh Canada! Oh Quebec! Requiem for a Divided Country* (New York: Random House, 1992); Lansing Lamont, *Breakup: The Coming End of Canada and the Stakes for America* (New York: Norton, 1994).

p. 40

10. Illustrative references on the history, development, and current status of the European Union include: Michael Burgess, *Federalism and European Union. The Building of Europe, 1950-2000* (New York: Routledge, 2000); Anthony Pagden, ed., *The Idea of Europe: From Antiquity to the European Union* (Cambridge, U.K.: Cambridge University Press, 2000); John McCormick, *The European Union: Politics and Policies*, 4th edition (Boulder, Col.: Westview Press, 2007); Clive Archer, *Global Institutions: The European Union* (London: Taylor & Francis, 2008).

p. 42

11. The phrase "No taxation without representation" was directly inspired by the proclamation of Bostonian James Otis, Jr. (1725-1789) that "Taxation without representation is tyranny." This well-known phrase was coined in 1761 at the time of his legal challenge against the British-imposed "writs of assistance." During the 1760s, Otis proposed that voting representatives from the American colonies be installed in the British Parliament. Although the proposal received a certain amount of support on both sides of the Atlantic, and was endorsed by Adam Smith in his renowned *Wealth of Nations* (published in 1776), it never became a serious possibility. See the discussion of this question in Page Smith, *A New Age Now Begins: A People's History of the American Revolution* (New York: McGraw-Hill, 1976): pp. 186-187.

p. 44

12. The dominant role of slavery in bringing on the U.S. Civil War is clearly reflected in the large literature on the institution of American slavery and the origins of the Civil War. Illustrative contributions include Eugene D. Genovese, *The World the Slaveholders Made* (New York: Pantheon Books, 1969); David Brion Davis, *The Problem of Slavery in Western Culture* (Ithaca, N.Y.: Cornell University Press, 1966); Kenneth M. Stampp, *The Peculiar Institution: Slavery in the Ante-Bellum South* (New York: Alfred A. Knopf, 1956).

p. 48

13. Illustrative references on disarmament negotiations during the interwar period include: Philip Noel-Baker, *Disarmament*, 2nd edition (London: Hogarth Press, 1927); John Wheeler-Bennett, *The Pipe Dream of Peace: The Story of the*

*Collapse of Disarmament* (New York: W. Marrow, 1935); Philip Noel-Baker, *The First World Disarmament Conference, 1932-1933 and Why It Failed* (New York: Pergamon Press, 1979); Thomas Richard Davies, *The Possibilities of Transnational Activism: The Campaign for Disarmament between the Two World Wars* (Boston: Martinus Nijhoff, 2007).

p. 50

14. Illustrative references on arms control and reduction during the Cold War period include: Thomas C. Schelling and Morton H. Halperin, *Strategy and Arms Control* (New York: Twentieth Century Fund, 1961); John W. Spanier and Joseph L. Noge, *The Politics of Disarmament: A Study in Soviet-American Gamesmanship* (New York: Frederick A. Praeger, 1962); Gerald Smith, *Double-talk: The Story of the First Strategic Arms Limitation Talks* (Garden City, New York: Doubleday, 1980); Strobe Talbott, *Deadly Gambits: The Reagan Administration and the Stalemate in Nuclear Arms Control* (New York: Alfred A. Knopf, 1984).

p. 57

15. Illustrative accounts of some of the humanitarian disasters during the recent past include: Roy Gutman, *A Witness to Genocide* (London: Macmillan, 1993); Ed Vulliamy, *Seasons in Hell: Understanding Bosnia's War* (New York: St. Martin's Press, 1994); Fergal Keane, *Season of Blood: A Rwanda Journey* (New York: Viking, 1995); Ben Kiernan, *The Pol Pot Regime: Race, Power and Genocide in Cambodia under the Khmer Rouge, 1975-79* (New Haven, Ct.: Yale University Press, 1998); Scott Peterson, *Me against My Brother: At War in Somalia, Sudan and Rwanda* (New York: Routledge, 2000).

p. 59

16. Illustrative accounts of the long history of Christian-Muslim conflict include: Andrew Wheatcroft, *Infidels: A History of the Conflict between Christendom and Islam* (New York: Random House, 2005); A. G. Jamieson, *Faith and Sword: A Short History of Christian-Muslim Conflict* (Chicago: University of Chicago Press, 2006); Stephen O'Shea, *Sea of Faith: Islam and Christianity in the Medieval Mediterranean World* (New York: St. Martin's Press, 2007).

p. 60

17. According to *Ethnologue: Languages of the World*, 14th edition, edited by Barbara F. Grimes and Joseph E. Grimes (Dallas, Tex.: SIL International, 2000), English is spoken as a first language by 322 million persons, which is third on the list after Mandarin Chinese (885 million) and Spanish (332 million). Of the 107 languages on the *Ethnologue* list, only eight are spoken as a first language by more than 100 million people (somewhat under 2 percent of the total world population). Few doubt that English is the most popular among those speaking other than their mother language, but statistical estimates are imprecise. The British Council, based on work by David Crystal (*English as a Global Language*, Cambridge: Cambridge University Press, 1997), estimates roughly that about 350 million people use English as a second language to communicate with other persons within their own nation, and that another 750 million have studied

English as a second language to communicate with persons outside their own nation. The Council therefore estimates that approximately 1.5 billion persons are familiar with English either as a first language or a second language.

p. 61

18. The official consensus on the matter (rarely expressed in print because of its unbecoming overtones) was summarized some time ago by Edwin P. Reubens ("International Migration Models and Policies," *American Economic Review* 73(2): 178-182, May 1983, p. 179): "Internationalist doctrine envisages virtually unlimited, universal admission of all applicants, in whatever types and numbers. It rejects or ignores the national migration restrictions that everybody else takes for granted. In the real world, however, with vast economic disparities between the more and less developed nations (MDCs and LDCs), the intended unlimited flows would indeed make a drastic jump to worldwide equalization, it would probably be a zero sum, or even a negative sum transaction, as employment and consumption levels in the MDCs tumbled violently, to make a small individual accommodation for the millions of poor migrants from the LDCs. Long before this came about, the MDC citizens would react to slam shut that open door."

p. 62

19. Illustrative references in the general literature on world economic inequality, economic development, and related policy issues, are as follows: Gunnar Myrdal, *The Challenge of World Poverty: A World Anti-Poverty Program in Outline* (New York: Pantheon, 1970); Paul Alpert, *Partnership or Confrontation? Poor Lands and Rich* (New York: Free Press, 1973); Keith B. Griffin, *International Inequality and World Poverty* (New York: Holmes and Meier, 1978); Erik Dammann, *The Future in Our Hands* (Oxford: Pergamon Press, 1979); William Ryrie, *First World, Third World* (New York: St. Martin's Press, 1995); John Dixon and David MacArov, eds., *Poverty: A Persistent Global Reality* (New York: Routledge, 1998); David Held and Ayse Kaya, eds., *Global Inequality: Patterns and Explanations* (Cambridge, U.K.: Polity Press, 2006); K. S. Jomo and Jacques Baudot, eds., *Flat World: Big Gaps: Economic Liberalization, Globalization, Poverty and Inequality* (New York: Palgrave Macmillan, 2007).

p. 66

20. Most authorities on the world economy would agree that widespread poverty in the LDCs constitutes a "threat to stability and peace"—but the question remains, *how much* of a threat to stability and peace? The following statement from Paul Alpert (*Partnership or Confrontation? Poor Lands and Rich*, New York: Free Press, 1973, p. ix) is typical: "A conflict of far greater scope is emerging as the major threat to peace, continued progress, and the very survival of our civilization. This is the conflict between the rich minority and the vast, rapidly growing majority of the underdeveloped poor in Asia, Africa, and Latin America, the proletariat of humanity."

p. 70

21. Among the ancillary motivations for a Global Marshall Plan, aside from the

basic humanitarian objective of improving the economic conditions of life of billons of people and thereby improving overall global stability, one of the most important has to do with the future condition of the natural environment. When we consider the threat of ongoing environmental deterioration (an important component of which is "climate change," otherwise known as "global warming"), we need to understand that the odds that humanity will be able to deal successfully with this threat in the future will be augmented to the extent that there is greater global economic equality throughout the world—which translates into more comfortable living standards for people in what is commonly referred to as the "Third World." At the present time, the biggest threats to the natural environment are coming from poorer countries engaged in the process of economic development, the single most important example being the People's Republic of China. The rich countries are better able to "afford" a cleaner environment, even if there is some economic cost to pursuing this objective. But as the poorer countries of today become richer, they too will be able to afford more environmental cleanliness.

p. 70

22. The computations are described in James A. Yunker, *Common Progress: The Case for a World Economic Equalization Program* (Westport, Ct.: Praeger, 2000), pp. 50-59. The results obtained there are basically consistent with those of John B. Horowitz and Cecil E. Bohanon, "Income Redistribution: An International Perspective" (*Public Choice* 39(3-4): 305-323, December 1996).

p. 71

23. On the post-World War II Marshall Plan, see Harry Bayard Price, *The Marshall Plan and Its Meaning* (Ithaca, N.Y.: Cornell University Press, 1955); Immanuel Wexler, *The Marshall Plan Revisited: The European Recovery Program in Economic Perspective* (Westport, Ct.: Greenwood, 1983); Charles L. Mee, *The Marshall Plan: The Launching of the Pax Americana* (New York: Simon & Schuster, 1984); Greg Behrman, *The Most Noble Adventure: The Marshall Plan and How America Helped Rebuild Europe* (New York: Simon & Schuster, 2008).

p. 71

24. In chronological order, the books are *Common Progress: The Case for a World Economic Equalization Program* (Westport, Ct.: Praeger, 2000), and *Global Marshall Plan: Theory and Evidence* (Lanham, Md.: Lexington Books, 2014). In chronological order, the articles are: "A World Economic Equalization Program: Results of a Simulation," *Journal of Developing Areas* 10(2): 159-179, January 1976; "A World Economic Equalization Program: Refinements and Sensitivity Analysis," *World Development* 16(8): 921-933, August 1988; "Could A Global Marshall Plan Be Successful? An Investigation Using the WEEP Simulation Model," *World Development* 32(7): 1109-1137, July 2004; and "Swords into Plowshares: Financing a World Economic Equalization Program," *Journal of Policy Modeling* 28(3): 563-593, 2006. Although there are slight differences in data and model, all of these contributions utilize computer simulation of a

numerically specified model, using World Bank data, to indicate the possibility of dramatically increasing the rate of economic growth in the poor nations at the cost of a very minor reduction in the rate of economic growth in the rich nations.

p. 72
25. For typical expressions of negative evaluations of foreign aid, see William Easterly, *The White Man's Burden: Why the West's Efforts to Aid the Rest Have Done So Much Ill and So Little Good* (New York, Penguin Press, 2006) and Dambisa Moyo, *Dead Aid. Why Aid Is Not Working and How There Is Another Way for Africa* (New York: Farrar, Straus and Giroux, 2009). As may be noted from these examples, the best ammunition for the "aid doesn't work" school is provided by sub Saharan Africa. For a balanced commentary on *The White Man's Burden*, see Nicholas D. Kristof, "Aid. Can It Work?" (*New York Review of Books* 53(15), October 5, 2006).

# Chapter 3: Brief History of World Federalism

p. 80
1. Principal sources for this discussion of the early history of world federalism are Derek Heater, *World Citizenship and Government: Cosmopolitan Ideas in the History of Western Political Thought* (New York: St. Martin's Press, 1996), and Edith Wynner and Georgia Lloyd, *Searchlight on Peace Plans: Choose Your Road to World Government* (New York: Dutton, 1944). Two major historical documents from this early period are Émeric Crucé, *The New Cyneas*, originally published in French in 1623, and Emmanuel Kant, *Perpetual Peace: A Philosophic Essay*, originally published in German in 1795. Courtesy of the Google book preservation project, pdf files of the full texts of English translations of these two works are available online for free download.

p. 88
2. Another example of this is the substantial number of books on world government—in addition to Wynner and Lloyd's *Searchlight on Peace Plans*—that appeared while World War II was in progress: John S. Hoyland, *The World in Union* (London: Peace Books, 1940); Herbert Agar and the Committee of Fifteen, *The City of Man: A Declaration on World Democracy* (New York: Viking Press, 1941); Sylvester J. Hemleben, *Plans for World Peace through Six Centuries* (Chicago: University of Chicago Press, 1943); Wendell Wilkie, *One World* (New York: Simon & Schuster, 1943); Noble P. Bassett, *Constitution of the United Nations of the World* (Boston: Christopher, 1944); Hans Kelsen, *Peace through Law* (Chapel Hill: University of North Carolina Press, 1944); Lionel Curtis, *The Way to Peace* (London: Oxford University Press, 1944); Henrique Pinheiro de Vasconcellos, *The World State, or, The New Order of Common Sense* (Rio de Janeiro: Grafica Olimpia, 1944).

p. 89
3. John Rawls, *The Law of Peoples* (Cambridge: Harvard University Press, 1999), p. 36. For a brief but comprehensive summary of contributions by con-

temporary philosophers, as well as commentators from other disciplines, on the world government controversy, see the essay by Catherine Lu, "World Government," in *The Stanford Encyclopedia of Philosophy* (Edward N. Zolta, ed., 2016). From this essay it would appear that the spectrum of attitudes toward world government in the philosophy discipline reflects fairly accurately the spectrum of attitudes within the intellectual profession as a whole. That is to say, while many commentators are dissatisfied with the status quo and wish to see some sort of advance beyond the current international regime based on relatively unfettered national sovereignty, few go so far as to explicitly advocate world government. However, one notable example of the minority viewpoint is Torbjörn Tännsjö, a professor of practical philosophy at Stockholm University, who in his book *Global Democracy: The Case for a World Government* (Edinburgh University Press, 2008), argues that genuine global democracy can only be achieved through a powerful world government, even though there would be a risk that such a democratically controlled government might evolve into a tyranny of the majority over the minority. Tännsjö describes the necessary precondition to achieve this objective as follows (*Global Democracy*, p. 135): "The final step, I have conjectured, would be when the United States [as the world's sole superpower in the post-Cold War era] surrenders its military forces to the UN. The United States should be cajoled and shamed by the rest of the world to the point where surrender is irresistible." To most people, including this author, such thinking is, if not quite utopian, at least highly unrealistic. I would also comment that various contemporary analyses of world government by Rawls, Tännsjö, and numerous others, philosophers and otherwise, are almost invariably characterized by a failure to specify clearly the institutional characteristics of the world government under consideration. In most cases, the analyses are only fully sensible if the world government is assumed to be the traditional world federalist ideal of the omnipotent world state.

p. 91

4. On the history of the League of Nations, see, for example: Alfred Zimmern, *The League of Nations and the Rule of Law, 1918-1935*, second edition (Oxford: Oxford University Press, 1939); George Scott, *The Rise and Fall of the League of Nations* (New York: Macmillan, 1973); Elmer Bendiner, *A Time for Angels: The Tragicomic History of the League of Nations* (New York: Alfred A. Knopf, 1975); F. S. Northedge, *The League of Nations: Its Life and Times, 1920-1946* (New York: Holmes and Meier, 1986).

p. 96

5. Theodore Harris, *A Proposed Constitution for the United Nations of the World* (New York: C. F. Ruckstuhl, 1918).

p. 97

6. Illustrative references on the United Nations include the following: John Maclaurin, *The United Nations and Power Politics* (New York: Harper and Brothers, 1951); John G. Stoessinger, *The United Nations and the Superpowers* (New York: Random House, 1965); Alf Ross, *The United Nations: Peace and*

*Progress* (Totowa, N.J.: Bedminster Press, 1966); David A. Kay, ed., *The United Nations Political System* (New York: John Wiley and Sons, 1967); Geoffrey L. Simon, *UN Malaise: Power, Problems and Realpolitik* (New York: St. Martin's Press, 1995); Rosemary Righter, *Utopia Lost: The United Nations and World Order* (New York: Twentieth Century Fund Press, 1995); Ramesh Chandra Thakur, ed., *Past Imperfect, Future Uncertain: The United Nations at Fifty* (New York: St. Martin's Press, 1998); Ezra Stoller, *The United Nations* (Princeton, N.J.: Princeton University Press, 1999); Jane Boulden, *Peace Enforcement: The United Nations Experience in Congo, Somalia and Bosnia* (Greenwich, Ct.: Greenwood, 2001).

p. 105

7. A few representative examples from the large literature on the origins and course of the Cold War are the following: Harry and Bonaro Overstreet, *What We Must Know about Communism* (New York: W. W. Norton, 1958); Eliot R. Goodman, *The Soviet Design for a World State* (New York: Columbia University Press, 1960); Zbigniew K. Brzezinski, *Ideology and Power in Soviet Politics* (New York: Praeger, 1962); Daniel H. Yergin, *Shattered Peace: Origins of the Cold War and the National Security State* (New York: Houghton Mifflin, 1980); Bernard A. Weisberger, *Cold War, Cold Peace* (New York: Houghton Mifflin, 1985); Robert J. McMahon, *Cold War* (New York: Oxford University Press, 2003); John Lewis Gaddis, *The Cold War: A New History* (New York: Penguin, 2005).

p. 106

8. For the most comprehensive historical account of the post-World War II world government boom, see Joseph P. Baratta, *The Politics of World Federation*, Volume I: *United Nations, UN Reform, Atomic Control*, Volume II: *From World Federalism to Global Governance* (Westport, Ct.: Praeger, 2004). Shorter accounts of the period are contained in Derek Heater, op. cit., pp. 139-142; and Errol E. Harris, "Summary Outline History of World Federalism" (in Errol E. Harris and James A. Yunker, eds., *Toward Genuine Global Governance: Critical Reactions to "Our Global Neighborhood,"* Westport Ct.: Praeger, 1999), pp. 185-189. See also Frederick L. Schuman, *The Commonwealth of Man: An Inquiry into Power Politics and World Government* (New York: Alfred A. Knopf, 1952); Edith Wynner, *World Federal Government: Why? What? How?* (Afton, N.Y.: Fedonat Press, 1954).

p. 107

9. Emery Reves, *The Anatomy of Peace*, second edition (New York: Harper, 1945).

p. 108

10. Fremont Rider, *The Great Dilemma of World Organization* (New York: Reynal and Hitchcock, 1946).

p. 110

11. Giuseppe Antonio Borgese (1882-1952), previously a professor of Italian

literature at the universities of Rome and Milan, was a noted author, critic, poet, and anti-fascist who emigrated to the United States in 1931 and was naturalized in 1938. Once established in the U.S., he published two blistering assaults on fascism: *Goliath: The March of Fascism* (New York: Viking Press, 1937) and *Common Cause* (New York: Duell, Sloan and Pearce, 1943). He taught Italian literature at Smith College (1932-1935) and then at the University of Chicago (from 1936). He was a member of the "Committee of Fifteen" and collaborated on its manifesto published under the title *The City of Man: A Declaration on World Democracy* (New York: Viking Press, 1940). After World War II, as secretary of the Committee to Frame a World Constitution, Borgese was generally credited as the chief author of the Committee's draft constitution, "Preliminary Draft of a World Constitution," published by the University of Chicago Press in 1948 under the listed authorship of "Robert M. Hutchins and others." The "Preliminary Draft" is also available as an appendix to Borgese's *Foundations of the World Republic*, published by the University of Chicago Press in 1953.

p. 115

12. In chronological order, the principal books of Clarence K. Streit are as follows: *Union Now, A Proposal for a Federal Union of the Democracies of the North Atlantic* (New York: Harper, 1939); *Union Now with Britain* (New York: Harper, 1941); *Union Now: A Proposal for an Atlantic Federal Union of the Free* (New York: Harper, 1949); *Freedom against Itself* (New York: Harper, 1954); *Freedom's Frontier: Atlantic Union Now* (New York: Harper, 1961). In his time Clarence Streit was sufficiently well-known for *Time Magazine* to use his portrait on the cover of its March 27, 1950, edition.

p. 117

13. Gerald Mangone, *The Idea and Practice of World Government* (New York: Columbia University Press, 1951).

p. 121

14. The first edition of *World Peace through World Law* was published by Harvard University Press in 1958 under the sole authorship of Grenville Clark (1882-1967). Owing to Clark's advanced age at the time, he took on a co-author for the second and third editions (respectively published in 1960 and 1966 by Harvard University Press): Louis B. Sohn (1914-2006), at that time a Professor of International Law at Harvard University. Clark was independently wealthy but pursued an energetic career as a Wall Street lawyer and in appointive public service. He was a driving force behind the U.S. Selective Service System in both World War I and World War II. In addition to his work on *World Peace and World Law*, Clark was in later life a major supporter of the U.S. civil rights movement. In 1985, his memory was honored by the United States Postal Service through his inclusion in the "Great Americans" stamp series. Clark's edited memoirs were published under the title *Memoirs of a Man* (New York: Norton, 1975). Gerald T. Dunne authored the biography *Grenville Clark: Public Citizen* (New York: Farrar, Straus, Giroux, 1986).

p. 122
15. Many if not most of the larger public and university libraries have the world government proposals of Borgese and Clark-Sohn on their shelves. The interested reader in search of print material on the world government proposal of Philip Isely may have a more difficult time. However, much literature on the proposal is available directly from the World Constitution and Parliament Association Website. At this point, there is only a limited number of locations in the printed literature in which the WCPA's approach to world government may be examined. Two such locations are as follows: "A Constitution for the Federation of Earth" is included as the appendix to Errol E. Harris's book *One World or None: Prescription for Survival* (Atlantic Highlands, N.J.: Humanities Press, 1993), and two papers authored by Philip Isely ("A Critique of Our Global Neighborhood" and "A Bill of Particulars: Why the United Nations Must be Replaced") are included in Errol E. Harris and James A. Yunker, eds., *Toward Genuine Global Governance: Critical Reactions to "Our Global Neighborhood"* (Westport, Ct.: Praeger, 1999).

p. 123
16. For numerical computations demonstrating this, see James A. Yunker, *Political Globalization: A New Vision of Federal World Government* (Lanham, Md.: University Press of America, 2007), pp. 159-165.

p. 123
17. Fremont Rider (1885-1962), *The Great Dilemma of World Organization* (New York: Reynal and Hitchcock, 1946). Following many years as a travel writer of guidebooks to such disparate locations as New York City, Bermuda, and California, Rider gravitated into librarianship. Among historians of the subject, Rider is best known for his book *The Scholar and the Future of the Research Library: A Problem and Its Solution* (New York: Hadham Press, 1944).

p. 127
18. Strobe Talbott, "The Birth of the Global Nation," *Time*, July 20, 1992. In his most recent book *The Great Experiment: The Story of Ancient Empires, Modern States, and the Quest for a Global Nation* (New York: Simon and Schuster, 2008), Talbott has little to say about the "global nation" interpreted as a world government, and has only the following laconic comment to make regarding his 1992 *Time* essay: "The piece made me briefly popular with foreign policy liberals and, not so briefly, a target of brickbats from the right."

p. 128
19. Ronald J. Glossop, *World Federation? A Critical Analysis of Federal World Government* (Jefferson, N.C.: McFarland, 1993); Errol E. Harris, *One World or None: A Prescription for Survival* (Atlantic Highlands, N.J.: Humanities Press, 1993); James A. Yunker, *World Union on the Horizon: The Case for Supranational Federation* (Lanham, Md.: University Press of America, 1993).

p. 129
20. Anne-Marie Slaughter, *A New World Order* (Princeton, N.J.: Princeton Uni-

versity Press, 2004), p. 8.

p. 129
21. Campbell Craig, "The Resurgent Idea of World Government," *Ethics & International Affairs* 22(2): 133-142, Summer 2008.

p. 129
22. Jerry Tetalman and Byron Belitsos. *One World Democracy: A Progressive Vision for Enforceable World Law* (San Rafael, Cal.: Origin Press, 2005); Errol E. Harris, *Earth Federation Now: Tomorrow Is Too Late* (Radford, Va.: Institute for Economic Democracy, 2005); Glen T. Martin, *Ascent to Freedom: Practical and Philosophical Foundations of Democratic World Law* (Sun City, Ariz.: Institute for Economic Democracy Press, 2008); Jim Stark, *Rescue Plan for Planet Earth: Democratic World Government through a Global Referendum* (Toronto: Key Publishing House, 2008).

p. 129
23. Luis Cabrera, *Political Theory of Global Justice: A Cosmopolitan Case for the World State* (New York: Routledge, 2004); Louis P. Pojman, *Terrorism, Human Rights, and the Case for World Government* (Lanham, Md.: Rowman & Littlefield, 2006); James A. Yunker, *Political Globalization: A New Vision of Federal World Government* (Lanham, Md.: University Press of America, 2007); Torbjörn Tännsjö, *Global Democracy: The Case for a World Government* (Edinburgh: Edinburgh University Press, 2008).

p. 129
24. Andrew Wendt, "Why a World State Is Inevitable," *European Journal of International Relations* 9(4): 491-542, December 2003.

p. 130
25. Vaughn P. Shannon, "Wendt's Violation of the Constructivist Project: Agency and Why a World State Is Not Inevitable," *European Journal of International Relations* 11(4): 581-587, December 2005; Alexander Wendt, "Agency, Teleology and the World State: A Reply to Shannon," *European Journal of International Relations* 11(4): 589-598, December 2005.

p. 130
26. Eric A. Posner, "International Law: A Welfarist Approach," *University of Chicago Law Review* 73(2): 487-543, Spring 2006; Thomas G. Weiss, "What Happened to the Idea of World Government?" *International Studies Quarterly* 53(2): 243-271.

p. 131
27. Robert L. Carneiro, "The Political Unification of the World: Whether, When, and How—Some Speculations," *Cross-Cultural Research* 38(2): 162-177, May 2004.

p. 132
28. David Held and Mathias Koenig-Archibugi, eds., *American Power in the Twenty-First Century* (Malden, Mass.: Polity Press, 2004); Michael Mandel-

baum, *The Case for Goliath: How America Acts as the World's Government in the 21st Century* (New York: Public Affairs Press, 2005).

p. 132
29. See above note 25 (p. 130).

# Chapter 4: Brief History of Socialism

p. 134
1. There is an extensive popular, professional, and polemical literature which traces the complex real-world and intellectual history of socialism and Marxism. The range of style and treatment is very wide, from popular surveys such as Max Beer, *The General History of Socialism and Social Struggles* (London: Russel and Russel, 1957), and Edward Hyams, *The Millennium Postponed: Socialism from Sir Thomas More to Mao Tse-tung* (New York: Taplinger, 1974), through college textbooks such as Ben Aggar, ed., *Western Marxism: An Introduction* (Santa Monica, Cal.: Goodyear Pub. Co., 1979), to scholarly treatises such as George D. H. Cole, *A History of Socialist Thought,* five volumes (London: Macmillan, 1953-1960), and Carl Landauer, *European Socialism,* two volumes (Berkeley: University of California Press, 1960). Additional illustrative references include: R. N. Berki, *Socialism* (New York: St. Martin's Press, 1975); Alexander Gray, *The Socialist Tradition* (London: Longmans, 1963); E. K. Hunt, *Property and Prophets: The Evolution of Economic Institutions and Ideologies* (New York: Harper and Row, 1975); Joseph Martin, *A Guide to Marxism* (New York: St. Martin's Press, 1980); David McLellan, *Marxism after Marx: An Introduction* (New York: Harper and Row, 1979); Alfred G. Meyer, *Marxism: The Unity of Theory and Practice* (Cambridge, Mass.: Harvard University Press, 1970); Michael Newman, *Socialism* (New York: Sterling, 2005).

p. 136
2. The work of Karl Marx (1818-1883) provided a hard intellectual core for the socialist critique of capitalism, and thereby greatly strengthened the socialist movement in the nineteenth century. Representative examples of the numerous biographies of Marx include Franz Mehring, *Karl Marx* (London: George Allen and Unwin, 1948), David McLellan, *Karl Marx: His Life and Thought* (New York: Harper & Row, 1974), Fritz Raddatz, *Karl Marx: A Political Biography* (Boston: Little, Brown, 1979), and Francis Wheen, *Karl Marx: A Life* (New York: W. W. Norton, 2001). Marx's magnum opus *Das Kapital* (three volumes published between 1867 and 1894) is lengthy and notoriously unreadable—although it does contain numerous brilliantly written passages. Most modern readers prefer to get their Marx from edited compilations such as Robert Freedman, ed., *Marx on Economics* (New York: Penguin, 1962), and Robert C. Tucker, ed., *The Marx-Engels Reader* (New York: W. W. Norton & Company, 1978). Standard Western assessments of Marxist political economy are usually respectful but basically skeptical, as exemplified by Meghnad Desai, *Marxian Economics* (Totowa, N.J.: Rowman & Littlefield, 1979), Jacques Gouverneur, *Contemporary Capitalism and Marxist Economics* (Totowa, N.J.: Barnes and Noble,

1983), and Henry B. Mayo, *Introduction to Marxist Theory* (New York: Oxford University Press, 1960). However, a handful of twentieth-century Western scholars sympathetic to Marxism have endeavored to refine and update the original nineteenth-century Marxist critique of capitalism in light of twentieth-century theoretical and empirical developments: Paul Sweezy, *The Theory of Capitalist Development* (New York: Oxford University Press, 1942); Ronald L. Meek, *Studies in the Labour Theory of Value* (New York: Monthly Review Press, 1976). John E. Roemer, *Analytical Foundations of Marxian Economic Theory* (Cambridge: Cambridge University Press, 1981).

p. 142

3. Founded on the seminal contribution of Eduard Bernstein (see Chapter 5 for more detail), social democratic socialism (a.k.a. revisionist socialism, democratic socialism, social democracy, etc.) quickly developed a large literature which has continued down to the present day. The scornful attitude of hardline Marxists toward social democratic socialism is typified by the compilation of Lenin's polemical essays and articles issued by Progress Publishers (Moscow): Vladimir Ilich Lenin, *Against Revisionism*, second revised edition (Moscow: Progress Publishers, 1966). A later example in this same vein is P. N. Fedoseyev, ed., *What is "Democratic Socialism"?* (Moscow: Progress Publishers, 1980). Outside the Soviet Union, social democratic socialism tended to be viewed far more sympathetically—although it also attracted a considerable degree of scorn from right-wing conservatives. Examples from the tradition of British democratic socialism include the seminal contributions of Beatrice and Sidney Webb (*A Constitution for the Socialist Commonwealth of Great Britain,* New York: Longmans, Green and Co., 1920; *The Decay of Capitalist Civilization*, Westminster, U.K.: Fabian Society, 1923), as well as works by the famous literary luminaries affiliated with the Fabian Society: George Bernard Shaw, *The Intelligent Woman's Guide to Socialism and Capitalism* (New York: Brentano's, 1928), and H. G. Wells, *The Work, Wealth and Happiness of Mankind* (Garden City, N.Y.: Doubleday, Doran and Co., 1931). Later contributions in this tradition include E. F. M. Durbin, *The Politics of Democratic Socialism: An Essay on Social Policy* (London: D. Routledge and Sons, 1940), C. A. R. Crosland, *The Future of Socialism* (New York: Schocken, 1963), John Gyford and Stephen Haseler, *Social Democracy: Beyond Revisionism* (London: Fabian Society, 1971). During the first half of the twentieth century, social democratic socialism was pursued unsuccessfully in the United States by the perennial presidential candidate Norman Thomas (1884-1968), author of *America's Way Out: A Program for Democracy* (New York: Macmillan, 1931), and *Democratic Socialism: A New Appraisal* (New York: League for Industrial Democracy, 1953). Later adherents to the tradition of what is generally known as "American socialism" include the bestselling author Michael Harrington (*The Other America: Poverty in the United States*, New York: Macmillan, 1962; *The Twilight of Capitalism*, New York: Basic Books, 1980; *Socialism: Past and Future,* New York: Little, Brown and Co., 1989), and the "radical economists" Samuel Bowles (*Beyond the Waste Land: A Democratic Alternative to Economic Decline*, New York: Basic Books, 1983; *Democracy and Capitalism: Property, Community, and the*

*Contradictions of Modern Social Thought,* New York: Basic Books, 1986; *After the Waste Land: A Democratic Economics for the Year 2000,* Armonk, N.Y.: M. E. Sharpe, 1990), and Howard Sherman (*Radical Political Economy,* New York: Basic Books, 1972; *Foundations of Radical Political Economy,* Armonk, N.Y.: M. E. Sharpe, 1987).

p. 146

4. As befits what has been perhaps the most sweeping experiment in social engineering in all of human history, there is a very large literature on all aspects of the ex-Soviet Union and its erstwhile Eastern European satellites, of which the following represents a small illustrative subset. Concerning the general history and socio-political system of the Soviet Union, see: Louis Aragon, *A History of the USSR: From Lenin to Khrushchev* (London: Weldenfeld and Nicolson, 1964); Michel Heller and Aleksandr Nekrich, *Utopia In Power: A History of the USSR from 1917 to the Present* (London: Hutchinson, 1985); Peter Kenez, *A History of the Soviet Union from the Beginning to the End* (Cambridge: Cambridge University Press, 2006). On the decline and fall of the Soviet economic system see: Marshall I. Goldman, *U.S.S.R. in Crisis: The Failure of an Economic System* (New York: Norton, 1983); Padma Desai, *The Soviet Economy in Decline: Problems and Prospects* (New York: Basil Blackwell, 1987); Abram Bergson, "The USSR Before the Fall: How Poor and Why" (*Journal of Economic Perspectives* 5(4): 29-44, Fall 1991); Anders Aslund, *How Russia Became a Market Economy* (Washington: Brookings, 1995); Andrei Shleifer and Robert Vishny, *Privatizing Russia* (Cambridge, Mass.: MIT Press, 1995); Philip Hanson, *The Rise and Fall of the Soviet Economy: An Economic History of the USSR from 1945* (New York: Longman, 2003).

p. 161

5. For the "classical socialist period" in modern Chinese political and economic history (approximately 1950 to 1975), see: A. Doak Barnett, *Cadres, Bureaucracy and Political Power in Communist China* (New York: Columbia University Press, 1967); Nai-Ruenn Chen and Walter Galenson, *The Chinese Economy under Communism* (Chicago: Aldine, 1969); Gregory Chow, *The Chinese Economy* (New York: Harper and Row, 1985). On the extraordinary transition of the Chinese economy from planned socialism to market socialism, see William A. Byrd, *The Market Mechanism and Economic Reforms in China* (Armonk, N.Y.: Sharpe, 1991); David W. Chang, *China under Deng Xiaoping: Political and Economic Reform* (New York: St. Martin's Press, 1988); James A. Dorn and Xi Wang, eds., *Economic Reform in China: Problems and Prospects* (Chicago: University of Chicago Press, 1990); Dwight Perkins, "Reforming China's Economic System" (*Journal of Economic Literature* 26(2): 601-645, June 1988); Louis Putterman, *Continuity and Change in China's Rural Development: Collective and Reform Eras in Perspective* (New York: Oxford University Press, 1993).

# Chapter 5: Learning from the Past

p. 179
1. General overviews of the origins of social democracy, including detailed accounts of the life and times of Eduard Bernstein, are contained in Peter Gay, *The Dilemma of Democratic Socialism: Eduard Bernstein's Challenge to Marx* (New York: Columbia University Press, 1952), and Manfred B. Steger, *The Quest for Evolutionary Socialism: Eduard Bernstein and Social Democracy* (Cambridge: Cambridge University Press, 1997).

p. 183
2. Letter from Eduard Bernstein to August Bebel, October 20, 1898. In H. Tudor and J. M. Tudor, translators and eds., *Marxism and Social Democracy: The Revisionist Debate 1896-1898* (Cambridge: Cambridge University Press, 1988), pp. 323-328.

p. 184
3. For a collection of English translations of articles on revisionism by Bernstein and opponents such as Belfort Bax, Rosa Luxemburg, and Alexander Parvus, published shortly prior to the publication of *Voraussetzungen* (*Preconditions*), see H. Tudor and J. M. Tudor, translators and editors. *ibid.*

p. 185
4. Originally published in German as *Die Voraussetzungen des Sozialismus und die Aufgaben der Sozialdemokratie* (Stuttgart: J. H. W. Dietz, 1899), an English translation of the book, somewhat abridged, by Edith Harvey was published under the title *Evolutionary Socialism: A Criticism and Affirmation* (New York: B. W. Huebsch, 1911). A second English translation, without abridgements, by Henry Tudor was published under the title *The Preconditions of Socialism* (Cambridge: Cambridge University Press, 1993).

# Chapter 6: Could It Be Done?

p. 206
1. Kenneth Waltz, *Man, the State and War: A Theoretical Analysis* (New York: Columbia University Press, 1959), p. 228.

p. 209
2. Inis L. Claude, *Swords into Plowshares: The Problems and Progress of International Organization*, fourth edition (New York: Random House, 1971), p. 430; Stephen Goodspeed, *The Nature and Function of International Organization*, second edition (New York: Oxford University Press, 1967), p. 662-663.

p. 212
3. Mark Amstutz, *International Conflict and Cooperation: An Introduction to World Politics*, second edition (New York: McGraw-Hill College, 1999).

p. 213
4. For example, Eliot R. Goodman, in *The Soviet Design for a World State* (New

York: Columbia University Press, 1960), quotes the following from a postwar Soviet essay on international law by E. A. Korovin: "The dreams of Eden and Bevin [regarding the establishment of world government to reduce the peril of nuclear war] are quite removed from reality; they bring to mind the talk at the end of the First World War about 'superimperialism' and 'superstate,' about the gradual development of the League of Nations into a "world parliament" and so on—these were the arguments with which journalists and publicists, predominantly of the social reformist type, used to console both themselves and others. The chief fault of these theories lies in their authors' inability, either willingly or unwillingly, to understand the simple truth that the roots of aggressive nationalism which the 'world parliament' would supposedly check, lie in the very nature of capitalist society. It is scarcely possible that the contemporary gravediggers of sovereignty are so naive as to believe in earnest that peace and harmony on earth can be obtained by the creation of a world parliament... Is it not true that at the bottom of these political fantasies lies an extremely shrewd calculation—in the realm of political arithmetic and voting games? The eager troubadours of a world parliament are inspired by the thought of the voting majority in this new organ through which they can dictate their will to the rest of mankind."

p. 216
5. A few illustrative general references on nationalism are as follows: Hans Kohn, *The Idea of Nationalism* (New York: Macmillan, 1944); Barbara Ward, *Nationalism and Ideology* (New York: Norton, 1966); Karl Deutsch, *Nationalism and Its Alternatives* (New York: Alfred Knopf, 1969); Anthony D. Smith, *Theories of Nationalism* (New York: Harper and Row, 1971), Boyd Shafer, *Faces of Nationalism* (New York: Harcourt Brace Jovanovich, 1972); Ernest Gellner, *Nations and Nationalism* (Ithaca, N.Y.: Cornell University Press, 1983); T. V. Sathyamurthy, *Nationalism in the Contemporary World: Political and Sociological Perspectives* (Totowa, N.J.: Allenheld, Osmun, 1983); John Breuilly, *Nationalism and the State* (Chicago: University of Chicago Press, 1993); Eric J. Hobsbawm, *Nations and Nationalism since 1780: Programme, Myth, Reality*, second edition (Cambridge: Cambridge University Press, 1993); Michael Hechter, *Containing Nationalism* (Oxford: Oxford University Press, 2000); Benedict Anderson, *Imagined Communities: Reflections on the Origin and Spread of Nationalism* (New York: Norton, 2006); Richard Bosworth, *Nationalism* (New York: Routledge, 2007).

p. 219
8. A few illustrative references from the extensive political literature on the nature and attributes of state sovereignty are as follows: Bertrand de Jouvenal, *On Power: Its Nature and the History of Its Growth* (New York: Viking Press, 1949); Bertrand de Jouvenal, *Sovereignty: An Inquiry into the Political Good* (Chicago: University of Chicago Press, 1959); Francis H. Hinsley, *Sovereignty* (New York: Basic Books, 1966); William T. Bluhm, *Force or Freedom? The Paradox in Modern Political Thought* (New Haven, Connecticut: Yale University Press, 1984); Anthony de Jasay, *The State* (New York: Basil Blackwell, 1985); Hendrik Spruyt, *The Sovereign State and Its Competitors* (Princeton,

N.J.: Princeton University Press, 1994); Michael Ross Fowler and Julie Marie Bunck, *Law, Power, and the Sovereign State: The Evolution and Application of the Concept of Sovereignty* (University Park, Pa.: Pennsylvania State University Press, 1995); Saskia Sassen, *Losing Control? Sovereignty in an Age of Globalization* (New York: Columbia University Press, 1996); Dorothy Solinger, David A. Smith and Steven Topik, *State and Sovereignty in the Global Economy* (New York: Routledge, 1999).

p. 224

7. Illustrative references from the large literature on the European Union are as follows: David Weigall and Peter Stirk, eds., *The Origins and Development of the European Community* (New York: St. Martin's Press, 1992); Jeremy J. Richardson, ed., *European Union: Power and Policy-Making* (New York: Routledge, 1996); Richard McAllister, *From EC to EU: An Historical and Political Survey* (New York: Routledge, 1997); Clive Archer, *The European Union* (New York: Routledge, 2008).

# Chapter 7: Should It Be Done?

p. 243

1. The experimental approach has sustained the advance of human knowledge since time immemorial, but the enshrining of the concept as a cornerstone of Western scientific method is often credited to Roger Bacon (1214-1292), an English scholastic philosopher and Franciscan monk. By an odd coincidence, another founding father of scientific method shared the "Bacon" surname: Francis Bacon (1551-1626), an English jurist and philosopher who rose to the position of Lord Chancellor under James I. In his *Novum Organum* (1620), Francis Bacon argued that the combination of theoretical deduction and experimental testing would elevate human knowledge to lofty heights as yet undreamed. The contemporary consensus in science is that without experimentation, there would be no means of refuting erroneous theories and therefore the accumulation of knowledge would come grinding to a halt. A typical expression of this presumption is that of the physicist Michio Kaku (*Hyperspace*, New York: Oxford University Press, 1995, p. 263): "There are many examples of old, incorrect theories that stubbornly persisted, sustained only by the prestige of foolish but well-connected scientists. Many of these theories have been killed off only when some decisive experiment exposed their incorrectness. Thus the yeoman work in any science, and especially physics, is done by the experimentalist, who must keep the theoreticians honest."

p. 245

2. Some illustrative books on alcohol prohibition in the United States include the following: Henry Lee, *How Dry We Were: Prohibition Revisited* (Englewood Cliffs, N.J.: Prentice-Hall, 1963); John Kobler, *Ardent Spirits: The Rise and Fall of Prohibition* (New York: Putnam: 1973); Norman H. Clark, *Deliver Us From Evil: An Interpretation of American Prohibition* (New York: Norton, 1976); William J. Rorabaugh, *The Alcoholic Republic: An American Tradition* (New

York: Oxford University Press, 1979); David Kyvig, *Repealing National Prohibition* (Chicago: University of Chicago Press, 1979).

p. 248
3. Frederick L. Schuman, *The Commonwealth of Man: An Inquiry into Power Politics and World Government* (New York: Alfred A. Knopf, 1952), p. 468.

p. 249
4. James N. Rosenau and Ernst-Otto Czempiel, eds., *Governance without Government: Order and Change in World Politics* (Cambridge: Cambridge University Press, 1992).

p. 250
5. Some examples are as follows: Meghnad Desai and Paul Redfern, eds. (*Global Governance: Ethics and Economics of the World Order* (New York: Pinter, 1995); Thomas G. Weiss and Leon Gordenker, eds., *NGOs, the UN, and Global Governance* (Boulder, Col.: Lynne Rienner, 1996); Albert J. Paolini, Anthony P. Jarvis and Christian Reus-Smit, eds., *Between Sovereignty and Global Governance: The United Nations, the State and Civil Society* (New York: St. Martin's Press, 1998); Martin Hewson and Timothy J. Sinclair, eds., *Approaches to Global Governance Theory* (Albany, N.Y.: State University of New York Press, 1999); Majid Tehranian, ed., *Worlds Apart: Human Security and Global Governance* (New York: St. Martin's Press, 1999); Richard Falk, *Religion and Humane Global Governance* (New York: St. Martin's Press, 2000).

p. 250
6. Commission on Global Governance (Ingvar Carlsson and Shridath Ramphal, co-chairmen), *Our Global Neighborhood: The Report of the Commission on Global Governance* (New York: Oxford University Press, 1995), p. xvi.

p. 250
7. *Our Global Neighborhood*, p. 336.

p. 251
8. Errol E. Harris and James A. Yunker, eds., *Toward Genuine Global Governance: Critical Reactions to "Our Global Neighborhood"* (Westport, Ct.: Praeger Publishers, 1999.

p. 252
9. For a detailed critique of the global governance hypothesis, see James A. Yunker, "Effective Global Governance without Effective Global Governance: A Contemporary Myth," *World Futures* 67, no. 7 (2004): 503-553.

p. 255
10. The rogue state issue is a central component of the following representative analyses from the U.S. foreign policy literature on the post-Cold War national defense situation: Eric Herring, "Rogue Rage: Can We Prevent Mass Destruction?" (*Journal of Strategic Studies* 23(1): 188-212, March 2000); Stephen Blank, "Russia as Rogue Proliferator" (*Orbis* 44(1): 91-107, Winter 2000); Ashok Kapur, "Rogue States and the International Nuclear Order" (*International*

*Journal* 51(3): 420-439, Summer 1996).

p. 256
11. Kenneth Waltz and Scott Douglas Sagan, *The Spread of Nuclear Weapons* (New York: Norton, 1997).

p. 256
12. Gavrilo Princip (1894-1918) himself, understandably enough, did not assume responsibility for starting World War I, reportedly saying toward the end of his life, "Germany would have found some other excuse." Almost a hundred years later, historians are still debating the likelihood that, if the assassination had not occurred, some other incident would have precipitated the war. Some of the more recent contributions on the coming of World War I include: David Fromkin, *Europe's Last Summer: Who Started World War I?* (New York: Knopf, 2004); Richard Hamilton and Holger Herwig, *Decisions for War, 1914-1917* (New York: Cambridge University Press, 2004); David Stevenson, *Cataclysm: The First World War as Political Tragedy* (New York: Basic Books, 2005); James Joll and Gordon Martel, *The Origins of the First World War*, third edition (New York: Longman, 2006).

p. 257
13. Two of the most substantive historical accounts of the 9/11 attack thus far published are Richard A. Clarke, *Against All Enemies: Inside America's War on Terrorism* (New York: Simon & Schuster, 2004), and Lawrence Wright, *The Looming Tower: Al-Qaeda and the Road to 9/11* (New York: Random House, 2007). The official U.S. government account is the *9/11 Commission Report* of the National Commission on Terrorist Attacks on the United States (Washington D.C.: U.S. Government Printing Office, 2004), which contains a balanced appraisal of the various underlying factors responsible for the 9/11 attack (Chapter 2: "The Foundations of the New Terrorism").

p. 257
14. Since the 9/11 attack demonstrated beyond a reasonable doubt the existence of people determined to inflict the maximum amount of death and destruction on the First World nations generally and the United States in particular through terrorist attacks, regardless of the consequences, apprehensions about nuclear terrorism have become even more exacerbated. The possibility of nuclear terrorism is a major concern in such analyses of the current world situation as David E. Sanger, *The Inheritance: The World Obama Confronts and the Challenges to American Power* (New York: Harmony Books, 2009), and Ron Suskind, *The Way of the World: A Story of Truth and Hope in an Age of Extremism* (New York: HarperCollins, 2008). In Suskind's book, the winner of a Pulitzer Prize, several individuals are singled out for close attention as prime exemplars of the problems of the contemporary world. One of these is Rolf Mowatt-Larssen, a U.S. government official charged with devising methods of thwarting nuclear terrorists desirous of flattening New York and/or Washington. According to Suskind, Mr. Mowatt-Larssen is pessimistic about the matter, saying that a successful nuclear terrorist attack on the United States is not a question of *if*, but of

*when.*

p. 258

15. Michael A. Levi, *On Nuclear Terrorism* (Cambridge, Mass.: Harvard University Press, 2007); Graham Allison, *Nuclear Terrorism: The Ultimate Preventable Catastrophe* (New York: Henry Holt, 2004). See also Walter Laqueur, *The New Terrorism: Fanaticism and the Arms of Mass Destruction* (New York: Oxford University Press, 1999), Jeffrey Richelson, *Defusing Armageddon: Inside NEST, America's Secret Nuclear Bomb Squad* (New York: Norton, 2009); Magnus Ranstorp and Magnus Normark, eds., *Unconventional Weapons and International Terrorism: Challenges and New Approaches* (New York: Routledge, 2009), Jack Caravelli, *Nuclear Insecurity: Understanding the Threat from Rogue Nations and Terrorists* (Westport, Ct.: Praeger, 2008); Brian Michael Jenkins, *Will Terrorists Go Nuclear?* (Amherst, N.Y.: Prometheus Books, 2008); Jonathan Stevenson, *Thinking beyond the Unthinkable: Harnessing Doom from the Cold War to the War on Terror* (New York: Viking, 2008); Douglas Frantz and Catherine Collins, *The Nuclear Jihadist: The True Story of the Man Who Sold the World's Most Dangerous Secrets—And How We Could Have Stopped Him* (New York: Twelve Press, 2007); Ronald Kessler, *The Terrorist Watch: Inside the Desperate Race to Stop the Next Attack* (New York: Crown Forum, 2007).

p. 260

16. The European Union is the most prominent of the "counterweights" against United States power under current consideration: T. R. Reid, *The United States of Europe: The New Superpower and the End of American Supremacy* (New York: Penguin, 2005); Dingli Shen, "Why China Sees the EU as a Counterweight to America" (*Europe's World* online publication, Autumn 2006); Bruce A. Ritter, "The European Counterweight: A Leaderless Superpower" (*The Real Truth* online publication, January 6, 2006); Tony Judt, "The Nation: Fortunes of War; Europe Finds No Counterweight to U.S. Power" (*New York Times Week in Review*, April 20, 2003); Charles Kupchan, "Casting the EU as a Counterweight to the U.S. Would Only Divide Europe" (*Irish Times*, August 10, 2005).

p. 260

17. Barbara W. Tuchman, *The Proud Tower: A Portrait of the World before the War* (New York: Macmillan, 1966).

p. 274

18. Ronald Inglehart and Christian Welzel, *Modernization, Cultural Change and Democracy: The Human Development Sequence* (Cambridge: Cambridge University Press, 2005).

p. 275

19. The seminal contributions on this theory were Harvey Leibenstein, *A Theory of Economic Development* (Princeton, N.J.: Princeton University Press, 1954), and Richard Nelson, "The Theory of the Low-Level Equilibrium Trap in Underdeveloped Economies" (*American Economic Review* 46(5): 894-908, December

1956). Leibenstein's development of the concept was carried forward in his book *Economic Backwardness and Economic Growth: Studies in the Theory of Economic Development* (New York: Wiley, 1957), and in numerous papers later collected into the compendium *The Collected Essays of Harvey Leibenstein* (New York: New York University Press, 1989).

## Chapter 8: Prospects

p. 285
1. Andrew Wendt, "Why a World State Is Inevitable," *European Journal of International Relations* 9(4): 491-542, December 2003, p. 506.

p. 286
2. Luis Cabrera, *Political Theory of Global Justice: A Cosmopolitan Case for the World State* (New York: Routledge, 2004), p. 114.

p. 286
3. Daniel Deudney, *Bounding Power: Republican Security Theory from the Polis to the Global Village* (Princeton, N.J.: Princeton University Press, 2007), p. 259.

p. 287
4. James A. Yunker, "A Pragmatic Route toward Genuine Global Governance," p. 148. In Errol E. Harris and James A. Yunker, eds., *Toward Genuine Global Governance: Critical Reactions to "Our Global Neighborhood"* (Westport, Ct.: Praeger, 1999).

p. 297
5. Two representative examples of writing on the problems of the world and the need for "a new way of thinking" to cope with these problems are: Richard A. Falk, *Explorations at the Edge of Time: The Prospects for World Order* (Philadelphia: Temple University Press, 1992) and Kwame Anthony Appiah, *Cosmopolitanism: Ethics in a World of Strangers* (New York: Norton, 2006).

p. 301
6. Lloyd E. Ambrosius, *Woodrow Wilson and the American Diplomatic Tradition: The Treaty Fight in Perspective* (Cambridge: Cambridge University Press, 1990); John Milton Cooper, *Breaking the Heart of the World: Woodrow Wilson and the Fight for the League of Nations* (Cambridge: Cambridge University Press, 2010); J. Michael Hogan, *Woodrow Wilson's Western Tour: Rhetoric, Public Opinion, and the League of Nations* (College Station, Tex.: Texas A&M University Press, 2006).

p. 301
7. Townsend Hoopes and Douglas Brinkley, *FDR and the Creation of the U.N.* (New Haven, Ct.: Yale University Press, 2000); Stephen C. Schlesinger, *Act of Creation: The Founding of the United Nations* (New York: Basic Books, 2003); Justus D. Doenecke and Mark A. Stoler, *Debating Franklin D. Roosevelt's Foreign Policies, 1933-1945* (Lanham, Md.: Rowman & Littlefield, 2005).

p. 306

8. Richard Falk, *Humane Governance: Toward a New Global Politics* (Cambridge: Polity Press, 1995); Daniele Archibugi and David Held, eds., *Cosmopolitan Democracy: An Agenda for a New World Order* (Cambridge: Polity Press, 1995); Thomas Pogge, ed., *Global Justice* (Oxford: Blackwell, 2001); Luis Cabrera, *The Practice of Global Citizenship* (Cambridge: Cambridge University Press, 2010).

# Index

209-211
Syria, 57, 265

Talbott, Strobe, 127-128
Tarn, Sir William, 81
teleological reasoning, 130
Ten Hours' Bill, 192-193
tendentious terminology, 252
tentative and provisional, 72, 283
tentative step, 9
terrorism, nuclear, 237-259
theocracy, 233
"Theory of Collapse and Colonial
  Policy, The" (1898), 184
Thermidorean reaction, 86
Thirty Years' War, 85, 235
*Time* Magazine, 127
total factor productivity coeffi-
  cient, 72
trade, 12, 60-61
transfer fund, 72, 77-78
transportation, 30
treaties vs. contracts, 223-224
Treaty of Versailles, 94, 196, 222
Treaty of Vienna, 47
Treaty of Westphalia, 169
Treaty on Control of Arms on the
  Seabed (1971), 223
tripartite political system, 34
Truman, Harry, 14, 114, 116
Trump, Donald, 7, 265
Tuchman, Barbara, 260-265
Tutu, Desmond, 121
Twenty-First Amendment, 246

Ukraine, 254
undesirability vs. impossibility
  proposition, 248
unintended consequences, law of,
  1
Union Chamber of Representatives, 34-35
Union Districts, 37

*Union Now with Britain* (1941),
  113
*Union Now: A Proposal for a
  Federal Union of the Leading
  Democracies of the North At-
  lantic* (1939), 113
*Union Now: A Proposal for an
  Atlantic Federal Union of the
  Free* (1949), 114
Union Security Force, 53-58
United Nations Charter (1945),
  266
United Nations, 3, 13, 50, 96-104,
  300, 306
United States of Europe, 225, 227
United States, 64, 69, 74, 231,
  254, 271, 293
Universal Copyright Convention
  (1952, revised 1971), 223
unrestricted immigration, 61
Urban II, 235
Usborne, Henry, 111
utopia vs. dystopia, 1, 8
utopian delusion, 265-266

validation interval, 73
Versailles, Treaty of, 94
Vietnam War, 79, 126
violent revolution, 6
Volstead, Andrew, 245

Waltz, 2, 206-207, 256
War of Independence (U.S.), 41-
  43
war on alcohol, 246
war on drugs, 246
war to end wars, 90
wars of Islamic expansion, 236
Washington disarmament conference, 49
*Wealth of Nations, The* (1776),
  135
WEEP, see World Economic

# About the Author

James A. Yunker received his Ph.D. in Economics from Northwestern University in 1971, and is currently Professor of Economics at Western Illinois University in Macomb, Illinois. Author of ten books and approximately ninety journal articles, Yunker's contributions cover a wide spectrum from economic theory to contemporary policy issues. In addition to a large body of work appearing in economics journals, he has published in professional journals in education, library administration, criminology, political science, and international relations. Yunker is no stranger to controversy, and although his conclusions are sometimes directly contrary to prevailing conventional wisdom, his work is always characterized by careful and judicious appraisal of the existing evidence relevant to the issue under investigation. In his writing on controversial policy issues, Yunker's objective is to clarify and illuminate these issues in such a way that judgments on them may be based on informed reasoning rather than unconscious preconceptions.